Travels in the Reich, 1933–1945

TRAVELS IN THE REICH, 1933–1945

Foreign Authors Report from Germany

Edited by **OLIVER LUBRICH**

Translated by **Kenneth Northcott, Sonia Wichmann, and Dean Krouk**

The University of Chicago Press | Chicago and London

Originally published in German under the title *Reisen ins Reich, 1933 bis 1945: Ausländische Autoren berichten aus Deutschland.* Copyright © Eichborn AG, Frankfurt am Main 2004.

The University of Chicago Press, Chicago 60637
The University of Chicago Press, Ltd., London
© 2010 by The University of Chicago
All rights reserved. Published 2010.
Paperback edition 2012
Printed in the United States of America

21 20 19 18 17 16 15 14 13 12   2 3 4 5 6

ISBN-13: 978-0-226-49629-0 (cloth)
ISBN-10: 0-226-49629-5 (cloth)
ISBN-13: 978-0-226-00645-1 (paper)
ISBN-10: 0-226-00645-X (paper)

Library of Congress Cataloging-in-Publication Data

Reisen ins Reich, 1933–1945. English
  Travels in the Reich, 1933–1945 : foreign authors report from Germany / edited by Oliver Lubrich ; translated by Kenneth Northcott, Sonia Wichmann, and Dean Krouk.
    p. cm.
  In English; translated from German.
  Includes bibliographical references and index.
  ISBN-13: 978-0-226-49629-0 (cloth : alk. paper)
  ISBN-10: 0-226-49629-5 (cloth : alk. paper) 1. Germany—History—1933–1945. 2. Germany—Description and travel. 3. Germany—Foreign public opinion. I. Lubrich, Oliver, 1970– II. Title.
  DD253.A1R4513 2009
  943.086—dc22

                                                              2009043335

♾ This paper meets the requirements of ANSI/NISO Z39.48-1992 (Permanence of Paper).

CONTENTS

1939 to 1945

JOURNEYS TO THE END OF THE NIGHT

Oliver Lubrich

The idea of traveling to the Third Reich may today appear somewhat absurd. And perhaps it is for this reason that travel literature about Nazi Germany has been ignored as a theme. Yet between 1933 and 1945, many international authors went to Germany, and the texts in which they describe their experiences are as revealing as historical documents as they are diverse in their literary forms.

Foreign observers had various reasons to visit the Third Reich. Some of them already lived in Germany when Hitler was made chancellor—as language teachers (like Christopher Isherwood), for example, or as managers of a business (like René Juvet). They came to the country as students (like Shi Min), as recipients of academic scholarships (like Jean-Paul Sartre or W. E. B. DuBois), as visiting professors (like Denis de Rougemont), as tramps (like Jean Genet), or as participants in a regatta (like the later fighter pilot Richard Hillary). They were traveling as private persons (like Albert Camus, Annemarie Schwarzenbach, or Gunnar Ekelöf). They were passing through (like Virginia Woolf and her husband, Leonard). They were visiting the country to study art and learn the language (like Samuel Beckett). They worked as correspondents for foreign newspapers and radio programs (like Georges Simenon, William Shirer, Howard Smith, Harry Flannery, Jacob Kronika, or Theo Findahl). They moved around as clandestines (like Maria Leitner), so that they could evaluate the situation unnoticed. They came as guests of the German government (like Jacques Chardonne or József Nyírö) to take part in a tour or a writers' congress. They fought in the war as volunteers on the side of Germany (like the Swedish soldier in the SS Division *Nordland*, whose actions are narrated in the book *Twilight of the Gods*), or they arrived with the victorious Allied forces (like the reporter Virginia Irwin). There is a story behind every journey—a story that, in its own way, sheds light on different aspects of the daily life and history of the Third Reich.

The observers came from England and the U.S.A.; France, Belgium, and Switzerland; Sweden, Norway, and Denmark; Hungary, China, and many other countries. While in the prewar period prominent writers from all over the world visited Germany (both those who were well known at the time, like Sven Hedin or Thomas Wolfe, but also some who became famous later on, like Jean-Paul Sartre or Albert Camus), once the war had begun only citizens of Axis, neutral, or occupied countries could travel relatively freely in Germany. Professional observers increasingly outnumbered the tourists who came primarily for other reasons.

What did the authors who traveled to the Reich write about? What insights did they have? And how did they interpret what they saw?

DOCUMENTS

Various questions, reflecting different interests, may be asked of foreign authors' testimonies of their time in Nazi Germany. Their eyewitness accounts have a documentary value as historical sources. Strictly speaking, an author is never identical with a literary narrator or character. Every text is, to some extent, fictional, and, according to its genre, its artistic dimension emerges in different ways. Yet travel reports have a value not only as authentic representations but also as contemporary constructions. It is all the more surprising that some of the texts collected here had never been published in German (Block, Chardonne, Dodd, Flannery, Hauser, Irwin, Simenon, Wolfe, DuBois), and in two cases we are even dealing with an unpublished manuscript (Beckett, Kennedy).

Reports by foreign visitors open up new perspectives on European history. They contribute to the historiography of the Third Reich by focusing on everyday life from different angles and with different approaches. Because they register the reality of life in Nazi Germany through the eyes of an outsider, they report it in a different way than contemporary German witnesses have portrayed it. And, in a narrower sense, they reveal why, and in what circumstances, foreigners traveled in Germany and how they were able to experience the country.

What did the travelers consider noteworthy? The visitors describe the Germans' professional world and their leisure time, the public flying of flags, the new architecture and cultural activities, the effects of dictatorship, the system of terror and the persecution of the Jews, the political propaganda and the militarization of society, the psychology of conformism, blackouts and the economy of scarcity, air raids, forced labor, the war-wounded, the changing mood of the population—and finally the end of the war.

Many of the texts ask an important question: How did the Germans react? While most Germans submitted to the regime in many other respects, they showed only very qualified support for the war. While fanatics and hangers-on expressed their support widely, critical voices, which the Swiss author René Schindler classifies as a "secret Germany," were also heard from time to time.

The observers go beyond mere description—they analyze and develop models of interpretation for the Nazi regime. Thus Denis de Rougemont sees National Socialism as a sort of religion and its practice as a kind of cult. Howard Smith diagnoses a dynamic of totalitarianism, a dialectic of allegiance to Hitler, and fear of reprisals from the regime's enemies. According to this theory, the German people were only too well aware of Germany's crimes and therefore clung all the more desperately to their leaders, because they feared that, in the event of defeat, they would—justifiably—be punished by the victors.

PERCEPTIONS

What insight into the workings of the totalitarian system were travelers able to gain? What did they know? And at what point in time? What knowledge did they have of the persecution and massacre of the Jews, of war policy, and other crimes? What could anyone know? And how did they find out about it?

In his *Berlin Diary*, Christopher Isherwood captures the intensifying terror and the increasingly repressive atmosphere. He sees this development as a process that had begun long before 30 January 1933. His text passes over the date paying little attention to it; it is not presented as anything shocking. Nevertheless, Isherwood, who had already been living in Berlin for four years, held out for only a few weeks after Hitler came to power: he left the city in May 1933.

Georges Simenon's article, in which he describes his stay in February 1933, includes a truly polemical accusation that today could be called perceptive. A portrait of Kürten, the perverted serial killer of women, is given a title that suggests a resemblance to Hitler. At the beginning of April 1933, Annemarie Schwarzenbach took it as a matter of course that expressions of the Third Reich were "without exception repellent." At the end of the year, the Swedish poet Gunnar Ekelöf lamented the rupture of civilization that Nazism meant for Germany. And even Jean Genet experienced a "nation of thieves" that had placed itself collectively "outside the law."

Of all times, it was during the Olympic Games in 1936, when the regime was at pains to make the most harmless possible impression on foreign visitors, that Thomas Wolfe recognized Germany for the racist terror state it had become. Wolfe discusses the race laws and a friend's fear of the arbitrariness of those in power, the restrictive foreign travel regulations, and the anti-Semitic statements of a German woman traveling in the train with him. His protagonist is looking out of the train window at airfields and industrial plants that bear witness to the preparations for war. His assessment of the situation is crystallized by a concrete experience: meeting a Jew who fears for his life.

Meinrad Inglin describes an aggressive youth who, shortly after the outbreak of war, spits at a foreign car, and naive nurses who are delighted by Hitler. The correspondent Harry Flannery notes in 1941 that Jews are being deported to concentration camps. The Swedish journalist Gösta Block, who had worked for German radio for a time in 1942, is concerned about the daily harassment that people suffer. And the Swiss Konrad Warner writes about mass shootings and gassing (1943/44).

The American Martha Dodd, who at first—like Wolfe—was taken in by Germany and—like Genet—had sympathized with National Socialism, had already determined, before the outbreak of war and before Kristallnacht, that the persecution of the Jews would end in a "systematic policy of extermination." "All these years," she says, looking back over her stay from 1933 to 1937, "Hitler has been steadily and surely effecting the liquidation of German Jewry." National Socialism, she warns, "is bent on the extermination of their people," thus formulating a perfectly clear insight, the possibility of which most German witnesses denied after 1945.

Many other foreign observers recognized the crimes that were being prepared or carried out—even if we take into account the fact that Martha Dodd, as an ambassador's daughter, had access to privileged information; that a writer like Thomas Wolfe possessed the intellectual qualifications to examine his insights critically. Like most people living there at that time, René Juvet, who as a Swiss had grown up in Germany, had also witnessed the pogrom of November 1938. The house of his Jewish friends was devastated, the wife beaten, and the husband killed. Later on, in a quite ordinary compartment in a train, he met an SS man who was soothing his conscience with alcohol, and revealing the horrors of the camps.

All of this could be seen and heard and experienced if you were willing. But what limits were placed on what you were allowed to know? Most visitors felt an atmosphere of fear. Meinrad Inglin tells of a search as he entered the country. The professional journalists—Shirer, Smith, Flannery—describe censorship and the difficulties of obtaining information:

there was no free press, Germans were not allowed to listen to foreign radio broadcasts, the regime's announcements were propaganda. At the same
time, these correspondents prove that even under the conditions of disinformation it was possible to draw certain conclusions. William Shirer, for
example, established that the regime did not fully succeed in generating enthusiasm for war. Harry Flannery remarked that cinema audiences did not
totally accept the newsreel propaganda. Howard Smith developed a subtle
semiotics of the everyday. When Russian books vanished from bookstore
displays, it was clear to him that the invasion of the Soviet Union was
imminent. A few months later, the seemingly unambiguous propaganda
reports of the war, if read between the lines, indicated that the blitzkrieg
in the east had failed.

ATTITUDES

How did the travelers react to what they saw in Germany? How did people
from abroad respond to dictatorship and propaganda, to anti-Semitism
and terror? What sort of political assessments did the authors make—
explicitly or implicitly? What did they describe as positive? What might
they have found fascinating? What occurrences triggered a protest? What
factors did they experience as irritations that conflicted with their prior
understandings and prejudices? What, in any given case, would prompt
a final rejection? What episodes could perhaps be seen as turning points?

The visitors whose texts have been assembled in this volume represent
different attitudes that may be taken as representative, not, it is true, in
their relative numbers, but certainly in their range. They position themselves as Nazis (Jacques Chardonne, Wiking Jerk), they act inconsistently
(Heinrich Hauser, Shi Min), they change their minds (Thomas Wolfe,
Martha Dodd), or they are critical (Maria Leitner, Howard Smith). It is
possible to categorize their views: they can be sympathetic, neutral, aesthetic, analytic and distanced, or politically engaged.

What is noteworthy is that almost all the visitors undergo a change in
their attitudes. When they discuss the Third Reich, it is very clear that
travel narratives are flexible texts, rarely representing a consistent ideology but dealing with challenges, changes, and repositionings. Most of the
travel descriptions contain an inner dynamic. The reality of travel is too
complex to be represented by static models. (This observation has not
only political but also theoretical implications: the description of a journey can no longer be portrayed by a simplified, schematic discourse analysis, according to which a historical document always corresponds to a

contemporary mode of knowing and writing, unable ever to evade, exceed, or question it.)

Not only the narrators and the characters change, but sometimes even the writers. A certain dynamic can be observed at the level of narration *within* the texts (for example, by the end of his journey the traveler in Thomas Wolfe's story has become a different person from the man he was at the beginning). But there are also cases in which the author has been affected and repositioned *by* the text (for instance, the publication of Wolfe's novella had the very real result that he could not return to Germany, where he had, until then, been a very prominent figure). Writing has both a cathartic and a political function.

Only a few individual witnesses (Jacques Chardonne, Wiking Jerk) write outright apologias of the Third Reich. Many of the travelers (Jean Genet, Thomas Wolfe, Martha Dodd) did, it is true, come to Germany with romantic, Germanophile ideas, or even as more or less firm Nazi sympathizers; once there, however, they had experiences that questioned their original attitudes. They had moments of irritation, and they learned of the crimes committed by the Nazi regime. As a result, they took a critical look at the reasons for their fascination. And some even went so far as to describe the process of their disillusionment: frustration when their expectations were not met, disassociation from fascism—and even guilt feelings that they had spent time in Germany at all (Gösta Block, for example).

Other witnesses (Christopher Isherwood, Annemarie Schwarzenbach, Gunnar Ekelöf, Virginia Woolf) adopted a critical position from the outset. But even they saw themselves challenged on occasion. Thus, Christopher Isherwood's narrator has completely mixed feelings. On the one hand he feels more "uncomfortable" than ever before in his life under the terror of the dictatorship that is being established; on the other hand, he is as delighted as ever by the little everyday things—and so he feels ashamed: "[I] am horrified to see that I am smiling. You can't help smiling, in such beautiful weather." Virginia Woolf learned by experience that her confrontation with Nazism was a test of her character, which she hardly passed heroically. "We become obsequious," she found, even in face of the first dictatorial authorities, whose arbitrary actions she experienced at the border.

FOREIGN VIEWS

In what ways is it significant that the observers came from abroad?

International testimonies provide (at least) six advantages over those of German witnesses:

1. The foreign experience is *sudden*. While the locals witnessed National Socialism, the totalitarian regime, and the war as a gradual transition and escalation, for visitors, the change was abrupt and shocking. They were thus able to record it with a greater sense of immediacy and more accurately.

2. Travelers perceive *by contrast*. In comparison with what they were familiar with and what they expected, visitors to Germany found noteworthy or strange what many "natives" did not see—or want to see. Travel writing is a privileged medium of apprehension.

3. Ethnographic perceptions are *dynamic*. The impressions of the voyage change the understanding of the traveled reality and challenge the attitude of the observer. They can trigger or accelerate developments that the writers record immediately in diaries or letters and comprehensively in accounts or narratives.

4. Many travelogues are inherently *open*, self-reflexive, and self-critical. When they composed their texts about Nazi Germany, foreigners were less susceptible to censorship and self-censorship than their German contemporaries. They had fewer reasons to agree with Nazi leaders or identify with Germans as supposed victims of the war. Their writing is less invested—even in acknowledging their own mistakes and correcting their own misjudgments.

5. Travel literature can be linguistically, structurally, and generically *multifaceted*. International visitors had a much broader repertoire of techniques and styles at their disposal. They could draw on their countries' literary traditions and experiment with contemporary forms while the Germans were cut off from international developments.

6. Finally, foreigners in a totalitarian dictatorship are in an *ambivalent position*. They are simultaneously in the midst and at a distance. Ethnology might call this situation an extreme case of "participant-observation."

How was Germany viewed by foreigners? What stereotypical ideas were circulating? And what was the significance of Nazism in this context? Many travelers were not interested exclusively in politics, nor were they concerned necessarily with the present. They had ideas that were informed by history, by Germanic mythology and the Middle Ages, classical and Romantic literature, Goethe and Madame de Staël, the Grimms' fairytales and Friedrich Nietzsche, Ludwig van Beethoven and Richard Wagner, and in some cases by the First World War. For many, the German landscape was the source of an exoticizing fascination. Cultural patterns that had been shaped beforehand conditioned the understanding of the Third Reich and were related to what the travelers were observing in the present. The foreigners' views not only mirrored what was happening at the time but also represented the convergence of historical traditions.

Travelers can be likened to ethnologists. When a European country becomes the object of "foreign" views and ethnological observations, the traditional perspective of travel literature, the perception of the "other" is reversed. Karen Blixen, for example, is constantly summoning up associations with Africa and Arabia; she compares Nazi Germany with Tibet and fascism with an expansionist Islam. Her perception can be called "colonialist" to the extent that she is continuing to follow the patterns of classical travel accounts in which an enlightened European approaches a primitive society. Except that, in this case, the barbarism that is otherwise only assumed has in fact already revealed itself as such.

MAPS AND BORDERS

In Karen Blixen's text it becomes clear that other cultures and symbolically charged regions (Africa, Arabia) can play an important part in the construction of Nazi Germany. In what way are countries imagined that have a special significance with regard to Germany and, at the same time, a special significance for the attitude of travelers?

The perceptions of different dictatorships can be compared with one another on the basis of journeys to Italy and the Soviet Union. How were the authoritarian social orders evaluated? For example, was Mussolini's "classical" fascism seen as a positive alternative to German National Socialism, or was the Soviet Union seen as a counterweight to Hitler on the left? In Jean Genet's work—he had visited Italy several times on his journeys in Europe before going to Germany—there is no mention of Italian fascism; he seems only interested in National Socialism—as a total otherness and a radical provocation. Albert Camus and Virginia Woolf both stayed on in Italy after leaving Germany. Camus describes his arrival in Italy in *Light and Shade*—in clear contrast to his German experience—in euphoric terms: "I enter Italy, a land that fits my soul"; everything "is a pretext for my measureless love." Here, as elsewhere, Camus makes no expressly political connections. Also in Virginia Woolf's case, the contrast between the two countries is all the more remarkable because Mussolini had been in power for more than ten years longer than Hitler. Her diary entries on Germany (9 and 12 May 1935) are clearly political, and it is entirely because of Nazism that the country becomes intolerable to her. The notes from Italy that follow immediately (from 13 to 21 May) make no mention of the fascist regime in that country. In Perugia, where in 1908 she had stayed in the same hotel, she finds everything unchanged—"all the same."

Just as the accounts of travel in Hitler's Germany can be compared with those of travelers in Mussolini's Italy, they can also be related to reports of visitors to the Soviet Union under Stalin. For example, André Gide, who returned from his visit disappointed, wrote a famous book (*Le Retour de l'U.R.S.S.*, 1936). Martha Dodd, who flew from Berlin to the Soviet Union, saw it as the realization of a utopian dream—exotic, romantic—just as she had found the Nazi Reich *at the beginning* of her stay in Germany.

Travel literature creates symbolic topographies. For example, with regard to Italy and the Soviet Union, but also other countries that the foreigners visit or take as their subject, we might ask: On which symbolic maps do they situate Nazi Germany? And regarding the Third Reich itself: Which venues do they charge with political and artistic significance? For example, how do they compare the city and the provinces? And what is their vision of national frontiers?

The travelers' routes follow various patterns: Jean Genet crosses Germany from Poland via Breslau and Berlin toward Antwerp. Thomas Wolfe's protagonist goes home after a series of terrible experiences. Meinrad Inglin takes a tour. Martha Dodd stays in one place, Berlin, but makes excursions from there.

The ways in which the authors focused on the cities and, in contrast, the countrysides, shed light on their understanding of Germany and National Socialism. It is not the Berlin of classical modernism or the Bauhaus in Dessau which interested most travelers. The industrial regions only seldom play a role, though perhaps they do in Thomas Wolfe's work, where his protagonist travels by train through the Ruhr. Only Heinrich Hauser concerns himself more intensively with the growing imperial capital as an urban phenomenon.

Martha Dodd does not link nature and culture in Germany with modernity, but rather, in a romantic manner, with the past, and at times this is even a little eerie: rural Bavaria with its picturesque villages, Brandenburg, the North Sea coast, lakes and forests, castles. She activates the regions of Germany via symbolic locations—and, within them, German history—aesthetically, as a positive frame of reference. The metropolis, as the seat of crime, comes into conflict with the provinces, which appear idyllic. Dodd does not seem to have suspected that to oppose an urban (fascist) and a rural (intact) Germany was contrary—not only to the anti-urban self-image of the National Socialists but also to historical reality. (This

was evident, for example, in the distribution of votes for the National Socialist German Workers' Party [NSDAP] in the 1933 elections.) For her,
National Socialism does not seem to fit logically into the stratification of
Middle Ages, classicism, and romanticism but rather appears as a foreign
body. Located as it was in the city, the terror of the Nazi regime derives not
from the German heritage, but is a modernist phenomenon.

The descriptions of urban and rural landscapes always relate fascism, in
a certain way, to progress. While, in Martha Dodd's writings, National Socialism seems to be regarded critically as a product of modernity, other opponents of the regime—for example, Annemarie Schwarzenbach—take
the contrasting view that it is regressive and describe it as a return to the
Middle Ages. Sympathizers—like Jacques Chardonne—however, express
the dichotomy in diametrically opposed terms and contrast fascism positively with a modernity that they reject. The ambivalent, or changing, attitudes of many travelers—Heinrich Hauser, Max Frisch, and Karen Blixen
or Thomas Wolfe—are expressed in their respective descriptions of cities
and countryside.

The frontier and the crossing of it have a special function. Most travelers have their first contact with National Socialist Germany and its uniformed representatives at the border or at customs in the airport. Virginia
Woolf constructs her travel experience metaphorically (and literally) as a
crossing of a border. Howard Smith arrives in Switzerland just as Japanese
aircraft are attacking the U.S. fleet in Pearl Harbor. As a citizen of a nation with which Germany is now at war, he risks internment. Had he not
fled Germany at the last minute, he would not have been able to publish
his account, *Last Train from Berlin*. Crossing the border is for him and his
reportage a salvation. For the characters in Thomas Wolfe's story, the train
journey across the border (in this case to Belgium) is a relief, a liberation
from the pressure they had felt on German soil, which makes itself absolutely, and immediately, physically apparent.

DISEASES AND DESIRES

Meinrad Inglin combines two motifs: the crossing of the border and a
physical change. Inglin becomes ill as soon as he arrives on German territory; Germany triggers a reaction in him both bodily and allegorically. A
few travelers experience both the threat and the temptation, represented
by the foreign country under National Socialism, either as an illness or
as a seduction. How do the visitors react physically and emotionally to
the land which they are exploring? What was, if the occasion arose, the

erotic attraction of fascism? And what instinctive defensive reactions did it summon?

The metarational relationship of travelers to National Socialism, as expressed in the motifs of disease and desire, does not necessarily correlate with a political or moral attitude. However, the ethical and the physical often seem to enjoy a psychosomatic relationship. The first-person narrator in Thomas Wolfe's novella becomes actually nauseated when he learns that the Jew whom he has met has been arrested by the police. Howard Smith diagnoses in himself and his colleagues the "Berlin Blues," a sort of depression involved in living in the German capital.

An uncanny phenomenon that plays an explicit or subliminal role in many of the accounts is eroticism. In the twenties and early thirties, Berlin attracted gay travelers. Christopher Isherwood discovered that "Berlin meant boys." Did the rumor that was already circulating at the time about a relationship between fascism and homosexuality (the male bonding, the recognizable connection between repression and aggressive self-hatred, the conjectures about the homosexual SA leader Ernst Röhm) have a disturbing effect on politically conscious observers like Christopher Isherwood (and also W. H. Auden, Stephen Spender, and many others), and did it challenge them to analyze and express their opinions?

Did the sexual orientation of the visitors play a role in their perception of fascism? Christopher Isherwood and Jean Genet were both gay and reacted quite differently to the Nazis. The sexual orientation of some may have made them especially sensitive. Homosexual authors like Annemarie Schwarzenbach were critical from the outset. On the other hand, some authors, like the Frenchman Marcel Jouhandeau, who was traveling in Germany with Jacques Chardonne and other French collaborators (many of them homosexuals), found that it was precisely their homosexuality that led them to become involved with fascism or, at least, with fascists. In his *Diary of a Thief*, Jean Genet admits that he felt attracted by men in German uniforms. And he writes provocatively: "The French Gestapo contained two fascinating elements: treason and theft. With homosexuality added, it would be sparkling, unassailable." Fascism and eroticism merged at this point and were related to gay sadomasochism, as though the *fasces*, the bundle of twigs carried by the Roman lictors that gives fascism its name, was not only a sign of force but also of *fascinum*, a means of seduction. Susan Sontag has pointed to this connection: "Between sadomasochism and fascism there is a natural link." Sontag states that Nazism even exerts its erotic attraction on persons who were not themselves Nazis. As an example, she referred to Jean Genet.

Evidence of a certain excitement can, however, also be found in hetero-sexual men and women. Martha Dodd is impressed by the alleged physical beauty of many Nazis even when, politically, she is already developing a stronger and stronger distaste for them. Thomas Wolfe's disillusionment is completed in the face of an erotically coded—blonde, of course—fellow passenger (whose attributes change over the course of the text), a sexual-ized *Germania* who loses her powers of seduction.

In sum, it is possible to distinguish different variants of eroticization that can be found in all sexes and sexual orientations. While Leni Riefen-stahl used erotic motifs as a propagandist (for example, in her Olympic Games film), Jean Genet portrays as erotic the "deviant" side of fascism, a portrayal with a subversive function (and so does Luchino Visconti in his film *The Damned*). Thomas Wolfe configures his dissociation as a loss of physical attraction. In Martha Dodd, by contrast, seduction and distancing strangely coexist.

LEADERS AND FOLLOWERS

The traveler's eroticized eye is often directed toward the National Social-ist leaders. It is in them, as exemplary objects, that we can understand—as through cities, villages, and the countryside—how foreign observers viewed Germany, or rather the Third Reich.

Meetings with high-ranking Nazi officials are a repeated motif of many of the accounts. Georges Simenon ran into Hitler in an elevator and com-pares his physiognomy with that of a serial killer. Sven Hedin reports on several visits to the Führer, who was unable to carry on a conversation, and with Field Marshal Göring, who abandons himself to luxury in his estate of Karinhall (northeast of Berlin in the Schorfheide). Martha Dodd was introduced to the Führer by his chief press officer with the words, "Hitler needs a woman." She found the dictator, as she admits, curiously charm-ing. In her portrait she uses a few motifs that turn up again and again in descriptions of Adolf Hitler—for example, his soft face and especially the hypnotic effect of his eyes. William Shirer, who was able to see him give numerous speeches, attests to the fact that he had a surprising gift for rhetoric. Denis de Rougemont too describes the almost magic effect that he could exert on the Germans. And even the destruction of the Third Reich is allegorized in the mutilation of its political leadership. The Swedish SS fighter Wiking Jerk says that he saw the badly injured (and probably half-charred) corpse of the gauleiter of the capital, Joseph Goebbels, strung up "on a gallows" outside the Reich Chancellery.

By singling out the physiognomy (and psychology) of individual leaders, foreign observers put a face on the Third Reich. They accentuate the dictatorial power of a clique rather than the totalitarian participation of the masses. Accounts that describe prominent Nazis as "diabolical" seducers suggest a different interpretation of National Socialism from those that emphasize their banal mediocrity.

MASSES AND MEDIA

Alongside their discussion of the political leaders who embody the Germany of 1933 to 1945, various travelers describe their experiences with the anonymous Germans they encountered in everyday life and at special events. In the countries from which most of the reporters came, there were scarcely any official activities comparable to the mass spectacles mounted by the Nazis. For this reason, they foreground events like the Olympic Games, the Nazi party's political conferences, speeches by Adolf Hitler, marches of the SA [*Sturmabteilung*], or military parades. They observe the growing fanaticism of audiences listening to the Führer's addresses, but also the unsuccessful attempt, at the beginning of the war, to instill enthusiasm among the population (both of these are mentioned, for example, in the work of William Shirer). Denis de Rougemont tells how he attended a rally at which he was surrounded by thousands of people who were moved to ecstasy, and where he began to understand the cultic nature of the regime. Mass psychology has no effect upon the foreigner who does not feel as if he belongs to the collective whole. "I am alone," says de Rougemont of himself as an unmoved, sober observer in the midst of the ecstatic crowd, "and they are a community." By reflecting upon these mass demonstrations, the individual traveler can set himself apart from the anonymous collective mass of Germans, and assert his own identity in the foreign country.

One of the most impressive techniques used by the Nazis to constitute the nation as one body was the organized deployment of mass media. If the impression of public rallies challenged an individual traveler—especially one speaking a foreign language and one who was not accustomed to a comparably organized propaganda in his own country—to ponder the connections between the masses, technology, and modernity, so did the use of mass media. How did travelers experience and evaluate the exposure to the "people's radio," newsreels, the *Stürmer* (an especially anti-Semitic weekly Nazi newspaper published by Julius Streicher), and the *Völkischer Beobachter* (the daily newspaper of the Nazi party from April 1923 to April 1945)? Their reports of the broadcasts of special communiqués from the

military or of the installation of loudspeakers in public places, betray a
certain respect for the manipulative techniques of the propaganda machine,
and they use this to explain the early successes of the regime (Denis de
Rougemont, Harry Flannery). On the other hand, they also report that
the audience in the cinema does not always react in the way they were
expected to, when, for example, Winston Churchill or their Japanese allies
appeared on the screen (which surprises Flannery), or that the propaganda
reduces itself ad absurdum (Howard Smith). Occasionally the limits of the
machine's influence and, with it, of National Socialist power are revealed.

FORMS AND GENRES

Some of the texts through which foreign observers reacted to the Nazis
and their propaganda contain provocative elements. The respective contents, political positions, and linguistic forms are connected. The travelers who visited Germany between 1933 and 1945 used numerous literary
genres as the means of communicating their experiences: diaries, letters,
narrative, novella, novel, memoir, reportage, or pamphlet, as well as several
mixed forms. What is the significance of their choice of genre? What messages does the style convey? What semantics are involved in the literary
form? And what role does the observer's language play?

Reality and fiction are inseparably linked. Factual content cannot be
completely separated from poetic texture. No text can reproduce reality
purely and fully. It is always limited by the point of view of an individual,
shaped by age, sex, origin, prior knowledge, reading, and language, and conditioned by the circumstances of the journey and the historico-political
situation. It is always the result of decisions. And not only in the sense of
the selection of what is described, but also in the choice of medium and
mode. Every text, no matter how much its author strives for objectivity and
impartiality, rests on metaphors that mean more than the writer is aware
of, and he employs rhetorical strategies, each of which proclaims its own
message. Howard Smith, for example, writes his observations in pregnant
images and concentrates them into theses: the Third Reich is like a rotten
apple with a thick skin. The Germans follow their leaders as though they
were clinging to the tail of a mad lion.

The authors use many different modes of apprehension: Denis de
Rougemont interviews people he considers representative. Several travelers
devote themselves to reading German authors for information about the
country's development and its situation. Thus, Meinrad Inglin reads sev-

eral works of Ernst Jünger, who had been close to the National Socialists before they developed into a mass movement. His writings seemed to offer his Swiss readers a key to the ideology. Martha Dodd visits Hans Fallada (the author of *Little Man—What Now*), who resigned himself to "inner emigration" and from whom she gets the impression that "he was not and could not be a Nazi—what artist is?"

Many travelers are interested in art. Samuel Beckett is concerned with the works of banned Jewish painters and avant-garde movements. Karen Blixen illuminates the state of German cultural life: theater, film, architecture. She remarks that, in the first full year of the war, the theatrical repertoire included French and English plays. She visits shoots for the anti-Semitic propaganda film *Jew Süss*, and she describes the new monumental, neoclassical buildings. Max Frisch also reconsiders his relationship to the German tradition and the Third Reich in terms of architecture.

The form in which a journey is described is by no means a matter of indifference. The language, style, genre, and literary techniques all contain subtle statements about their object. From this point of view, it may not be a coincidence that Thomas Wolfe reflects on his farewell to German culture in, of all things, a novella with the help of an "unheard-of event"—the famous definition of the genre coined by Goethe (in a conversation with Eckermann), whose *Faust* he quotes at the end of his text. When Meinrad Inglin uses the artistic device of projecting the feverish illness that he may have contracted during his journey in the form of Gothic episodes and surrealist images (his wanderings through the labyrinth of the empty halls of the police headquarters; the bluish taxis on the nocturnal streets from which officers stare at him like "strange creatures out of an aquarium"; his vision of the North Sea breaking on the ice-covered coast in a snowstorm; the trenches in the cityscape; the voice of the Führer, which the feverish man hears from his sickbed in the hospital), this mad distortion can be read as a political allegory of Germany's situation in the spring of 1940.

Martha Dodd dramatizes her own growing awareness as a complex bildungsroman. Annemarie Schwarzenbach and Gunnar Ekelöf seek a dialog and write letters. Theo Findahl and Jacob Kronika choose the intimate form of the diary, to which they can confide their horror in secret. The medium itself already contains a message. The literary form has its own far-reaching implications.

The type and place of publication are also significant. Are we dealing with texts meant as private records or ones written for publication? Did the account appear in Germany or abroad? In what medium was it published?

We must bear in mind that the epistolary genre became less and less an option because the increasing consolidation of the power of the National Socialist regime meant a greater fear of censorship by the secret police. Radio reports that were broadcast "live" were censored beforehand, and foreign correspondents who cabled or telephoned their reports back home to the print media had to fear reprisals; documents sent from Germany were liable to inspection; books that appeared in Switzerland before 1945 were subject to war censorship in that country; and all texts that were published in Germany had been censored under the conditions of total "Gleichschaltung" (alignment).

A reflection also takes place on the level of language(s). German expressions turn up in many foreign reports. How such terms are selected and whether or not they are spelled correctly are signs of how well the travelers understand, speak, and write German, and, accordingly, indicate the limits of their perception. Beyond this, the German linguistic elements cause an ironic break in the non-German text. This is true especially in the case of Samuel Beckett, who intersperses his diary entries with numerous German words, some of which, though written unconventionally, give evidence of an astonishingly differentiated acquaintance with the German language. For example, on 9 October 1936 in Hamburg, Beckett notes that he had dinner with a "Herr Hoppe as Tischgenosse (not mitesser = skin maggot!)" and then had a conversation with "Herr Martion, der Kaufmann lernt u. genau so auss[i]eht" and finally went to bed "under kolossal Pferdedecke that [. . .] explains German for nightmare being *Alp*." (Beckett's actual notes translate as follows: "Herr Hoppe as my table partner (not fellow-eater, which = skin maggot)," then talked to "Herr Martion, who is training to be a business man and looks like it," and he finally goes to bed "under a colossal horse blanket.")

Besides this, German quotations bear witness to a linguistic reflection of fascism. In different texts they function as corpora delicti, marking topoi and mechanisms of the ideology ("buzzword" [Schlagwort] or "stew" [Eintopfgericht] in Denis de Rougemont; "Jew money" [Judgeld] in Thomas Wolfe; "air-raid shelter" [Luftschutzraum], "porters" [Dienstmänner], and "Deutschland über Alles" in Harry Flannery). Inasmuch as concepts that had come into everyday usage are isolated in the foreign texts, the travelers reveal the influence of Nazism on the German language and thus the level of its penetration into German society. The travelers collected material that could be used for elaborating a theory of language in the Third Reich in the way that Victor Klemperer developed it in his study *LTI Lingua Tertii Imperii* (*LTI Language of the Third Reich* [1947]).

DESTRUCTION

Ultimately, the way its destruction is described permits a final interpretation of Nazi Germany as seen through the eyes of foreign observers. The air war plays an ever more important part in the accounts written between the years 1940 and 1945.

In his much-discussed intervention on *Air War and Literature*, W. G. Sebald advanced the thesis that the devastation of German cities by Allied air raids has been tabooed by postwar German writers, and the few that have attempted it have proven unequal to the task. For foreign writers there is neither taboo nor failure. Their reports contain ample and forceful accounts of destruction.

The Norwegian author Theo Findahl strings together nature metaphors and similes that concretize the monstrosity: "the whole street is like a lake" / "the Tiergarten is now a jungle" / "the business quarter a sea of fire!" / "a red-hot wind is whipping through the street." The air raids revert the modern metropolis to a state of nature. In addition, Findahl invents scenarios that border on the uncanny and tend toward surrealism: burning trains full of corpses that careen madly over the railroad tracks circling the city; pumas that escape from the zoo; crocodiles that are "boiled" in the aquarium. Taking it a step further, this foreign witness opens up historical and mythological spaces, for example, when he compares the bombing of Berlin with the fall of Pompeii. As a counterpart to Jerusalem, the power center of the Third Reich is an *unholy* city. Its destruction appears as a punishment for anti-Semitism, persecution of the Jews, and the Holocaust. As the city of Ninus, the son of Semiramis who assumed his identity and is described in Calderon's drama *The Daughter of the Air* as a fascinating "monster," so Berlin-Nineveh appears as the capital of a criminal power. And while Babel, as the biblical locus of profane megalomania, is not invoked, its role is assumed by the nearby and symbolically equivalent residence of the diabolical queen whose illegitimate rule must also be atoned for. Findahl fades the skeletons of the houses of "Germania" into the ruins of the capitals of other failed empires: Nineveh, Carthage, Rome. He narrates the history of the Third Reich as the tale of a city that meets its end in ruins. Berlin's destruction thus repeats historical patterns and renews moral laws.

The narratives of journalists like Konrad Warner and Jacob Kronika increase in linguistic intensity in moments of terror. In their representations of burning cities, the asphalt—one of the central motifs of discourse on modern life in the 1920s—undergoes a terrible metamorphosis; from being a symbol of urbanity and progress it becomes a symbol of disaster. Fleeing from the houses that are collapsing around them, the inhabitants sink into the burning and melting streets, as in an infernal fantasy.

Numerous passages in testimonies of air raids can be understood as magical realism. Behind the description of the incomprehensible we can see what is only an apparently unreal dimension. The foreign authors who spent time in Germany discovered a special literary form for the destruction of German cities and the killing of the civil population. This form allowed them to combine what was real and what was unbelievable, and neither to deny nor to render harmless the terrible reality, neither to repress nor to transfigure it.

While hoping that the bombs would bring the war to an end, many reporters feared that their neighbors would be killed—or that the shelter in which they themselves had taken refuge would receive a direct hit.

The accounts that follow offer us perceptions of Hitler's Reich from within, yet with an alien gaze, at a distance, and yet contemporary.

Translated by **KENNETH NORTHCOTT**

ABOUT THIS ANTHOLOGY

The present anthology is, of course, far from complete. Further articles—by, for example, Knut Hamsun, Michel Tournier, Lörinc Szabó, Kurt Vonnegut, Louis-Ferdinand Céline, and many others—might be taken into account.

The texts that are included meet the following criteria:

1. The accounts are based on actual experiences. Pure fictions are left out.

2. The writers look at Germany through foreign eyes. Most of the texts are written by foreigners. René Juvet, a Swiss who grew up in Germany, is a special case. True, Heinrich Hauser is German by descent; however, he visited the country from exile—and wrote his account in English.

3. The writing and, where applicable, the publication of the account took place within a short space of time. We are not dealing with retrospective memoirs that record—after a great lapse of time and with subsequent historical knowledge—events that took place long before. In individual cases, the contemporary accounts can be compared with later memories. Christopher Isherwood, for example, writes of his experiences in Berlin in 1933, first in his autobiographical novel *Goodbye to Berlin* (1939), and then again, almost four decades later, in his autobiography *Christopher and his Kind* (1977). Virginia Woolf's diary entry from the year 1935 can be compared with an account of the same events that her husband, Leonard Woolf, gives in his memoirs, *Downhill All the Way* (1968). In both cases, the original testimonies reveal far more differentiated and contradictory concerns and discomforts about the authors' own roles, which are rescinded in the later variants.

4. The selections are confined—in the broadest sense of the term—to literary texts. The criterion is a linguistic working-up of the events described that reveals a creative aspiration and thus a certain level of reflection. Primarily technical texts—in a more narrow sense, journalistic news

articles or pragmatic travel guides—were not considered for inclusion. Since it is difficult to define the field of what is literary, the transitions of genre between travel writing and neighboring forms are hard to determine with accuracy.

5. The thematic interest rests in what can be learned about Germany from 1933 to 1945. No account is taken of works whose content trails off largely into the private sphere or exhausts itself in political ideology without actual observations.

6. The extreme case of testimonies are texts written by survivors of concentration camps. The Shoah literature constitutes its own genre. In *Le grand voyage* (1963), Jorge Semprún dissolves the situation of the deportees in the freight car, from the window of which they can see the passing countryside (and, among other things, the valley of the Moselle), into thoughts and retrospections. Semprún recalls his days-long transport to the Buchenwald concentration camp in, of all things, the form of a travel story.

EDITORIAL POINTERS

The ordering of the extracts is oriented to the chronology of the events they describe. The chronology section in the backmatter gives an overview of important historical dates. The prewar period and the World War II period are separated into two halves. In order to make the texts more accessible, titles have been added to the individual sections. Short introductions to the contexts of author, journey, and work are included before each extract to help with a better understanding of the texts. A bibliography provides information about the writer, literature, and scholarship. In each case, as far as possible, the first editions served as a basis.

Idiosyncrasies of the originals in orthography and punctuation have been retained. Obvious and unremarkable mistakes have been quietly corrected. Immaterial changes, such as the italicization of titles, tweaks to indentation, and the standardization of quotation marks, have been made silently. Elaborations and explanations are set in square brackets. Omissions within the selections are noted: [...]. Extracts from the same text that do not immediately follow one another in the original are separated by the symbol: ===. Line ornaments that appeared in the original extracts have been retained, although standardized; line spaces have also been retained. All emphases in the original text have been italicized.

ACKNOWLEDGMENTS

I would like to thank Hans Christoph Buch, Hans Magnus Enzensberger, Gert Mattenklott, Yahya Elsaghe, Hinrich Seeba, and Alberto Manguel; Marko Martin, Geoff Wilkes, Tobias Döring, and Viktor Otto; Julian Garforth, Mark Nixon, and James Knowlson; Naomi Lubrich, Heidi Lubrich, and Robin Ostow; Nina Peter, Rina Schmeller, and Michael Strobl; Alan Thomas, Katherine Frentzel, and Margaret Mahan; Marita Keilson, Georg Schoeck, László-Attila Burger, Heiner Frühauf, and Niclas Sennerteg for support, suggestions, and information.

1933 to 1939

Goodbye to Berlin

Christopher Isherwood was twenty-five years old when he went to Berlin in 1929. The German capital had attracted him as it had his compatriots, W. H. Auden, Stephen Spender, and James Stern. Isherwood worked as a teacher of English, enjoyed the nightlife, and witnessed the collapse of the Weimar Republic. In the sixth and final part of his autobiographical and documentary novel *Goodbye to Berlin* (1939), "A Berlin Diary. Winter 1932–3," Isherwood describes his final days in Germany after the National Socialists came into power. After the last, halfway-democratic elections of 5 March 1933, in which the Nazis obtained almost 44 percent of the votes, Isherwood went to London in April for four weeks before returning again to Berlin for a few days to organize things for his final departure. John van Druten developed *I Am a Camera* (1951) as the stage version of Isherwood's stories about the cabaret singer Sally Bowles (the eponymous story had first appeared independently in 1937). Joe Masteroff, John Kander, and Fred Ebb created the musical *Cabaret* (1966) out of this play, and Bob Fosse made a film out of the musical with the same name (1972). Isherwood had published a further novel about his experiences in Germany, *Mr. Norris Changes Trains* (1935). He gives a renewed account of his time in Berlin in his memoirs—narrated in the third person—*Christopher and his Kind* (1977).

Schleicher has resigned. The monocles did their stuff. Hitler has formed a cabinet with Hugenberg. Nobody thinks it can last till the spring.

: : :

The newspapers are becoming more and more like copies of a school magazine. There is nothing in them but new rules, new punishments, and lists of people who have been "kept in." This morning, Göring has invented three fresh varieties of high treason.

Every evening, I sit in the big half-empty artists' café by the Memorial Church, where the Jews and left-wing intellectuals bend their heads together over the marble tables, speaking in low, scared voices. Many of them know that they will certainly be arrested—if not to-day, then to-morrow or next week. So they are polite and mild with each other, and raise their hats and enquire after their colleagues' families. Notorious literary tiffs of several years' standing are forgotten.

Almost every evening, the S.A. men come into the café. Sometimes they are only collecting money: everybody is compelled to give something. Sometimes they have come to make an arrest. One evening a Jewish writer, who was present, ran into the telephone-box to ring up the Police. The Nazis dragged him out, and he was taken away. Nobody moved a finger. You could have heard a pin drop, till they were gone.

The foreign newspaper correspondents dine every night at the same little Italian restaurant, at a big round table, in the corner. Everybody else in the restaurant is watching them and trying to overhear what they are saying. If you have a piece of news to bring them—the details of an arrest, or the address of a victim whose relatives might be interviewed—then one of the journalists leaves the table and walks up and down with you outside, in the street.

A young communist I know was arrested by the S.A. men, taken to a Nazi barracks, and badly knocked about. After three or four days, he was released and went home. Next morning there was a knock at the door. The communist hobbled over to open it, his arm in a sling—and there stood a Nazi with a collecting-box. At the sight of him the communist completely lost his temper. "Isn't it enough," he yelled, "that you beat me up? And you dare to come and ask me for money?"

But the Nazi only grinned. "Now, now, comrade! No political squabbling! Remember, we're living in the Third Reich! We're all brothers! You must try and drive that silly political hatred from your heart!"

: : :

This evening I went into the Russian tea-shop in the Kleistrasse, and there was D. For a moment I really thought I must be dreaming. He greeted me quite as usual, beaming all over his face.

"Good God!" I whispered. "What on earth are you doing here?"

D. beamed. "You thought I might have gone abroad?"

"Well, naturally. . . ."

"But the situation nowadays is so interesting. . . ."

I laughed. "That's one way of looking at it, certainly. . . . But isn't it awfully dangerous for you?"

D. merely smiled. Then he turned to the girl he was sitting with and said, "This is Mr. Isherwood. . . . You can speak quite openly to him. He hates the Nazis as much as we do. Oh, yes! Mr. Isherwood is a confirmed anti-fascist!"

He laughed very heartily and slapped me on the back. Several people who were sitting near us overheard him. Their reactions were curious. Either they simply couldn't believe their ears, or they were so scared that they pretended to hear nothing, and went on sipping their tea in a state of deaf horror. I have seldom felt so uncomfortable in my whole life.

(D.'s technique appears to have had its points, all the same. He was never arrested. Two months later, he successfully crossed the frontier into Holland.)

: : :

This morning, as I was walking down the Bülowstrasse, the Nazis were raiding the house of a small liberal pacifist publisher. They had brought a lorry and were piling it with the publisher's books. The driver of the lorry mockingly read out the titles of the books to the crowd:

"*Nie Wieder Krieg!*" he shouted, holding up one of them by the corner of the cover, disgustedly, as though it were a nasty kind of reptile. Everybody roared with laughter.

"'No More War!'" echoed a fat, well-dressed woman, with a scornful, savage laugh. "What an idea!"

: : :

At present, one of my regular pupils is Herr N., a police chief under the Weimar régime. He comes to me every day. He wants to brush up his English, for he is leaving very soon to take up a job in the United States. The curious thing about these lessons is that they are all given while we are driving about the streets in Herr N.'s enormous closed car. Herr N. himself never comes into our house: he sends up his chauffeur to fetch me, and the car moves off at once. Sometimes we stop for a few minutes at the edge of the Tiergarten, and stroll up and down the paths—the chauffeur always following us at a respectful distance.

Herr N. talks to me chiefly about his family. He is worried about his son, who is very delicate, and whom he is obliged to leave behind, to undergo an operation. His wife is delicate, too. He hopes the journey won't tire her. He describes her symptoms, and the kind of medicine she is taking. He tells me stories about his son as a little boy. In a tactful, impersonal way we have become quite intimate. Herr N. is always charmingly polite, and listens gravely and carefully to my explanations of grammatical points. Behind everything he says I am aware of an immense sadness.

We never discuss politics; but I know that Herr N. must be an enemy of the Nazis, and, perhaps, even in hourly danger of arrest. One morning, when we were driving along the Unter den Linden, we passed a group of self-important S.A. men, chatting to each other and blocking the whole pavement. Passers-by were obliged to walk in the gutter. Herr N. smiled faintly and sadly: "One sees some queer sights in the streets nowadays." That was his only comment.

Sometimes he will bend forward to the window and regard a building or a square with a mournful fixity, as if to impress its image upon his memory and to bid it good-bye.

: : :

To-morrow I am going to England. In a few weeks I shall return, but only to pick up my things, before leaving Berlin altogether.

Poor Frl. Schroeder is inconsolable: "I shall never find another gentleman like you, Herr Issyvoo—always so punctual with the rent. . . . I'm sure I don't know what makes you want to leave Berlin, all of a sudden, like this. . . ."

It's no use trying to explain to her, or talking politics. Already she is adapting herself, as she will adapt herself to every new régime. This morning I even heard her talking reverently about "Der Führer" to the porter's wife. If anybody were to remind her that, at the elections last November, she voted communist, she would probably deny it hotly, and in perfect good faith. She is merely acclimatizing herself, in accordance with a natural law, like an animal which changes its coat for the winter. Thousands of people like Frl. Schroeder are acclimatizing themselves. After all, whatever government is in power, they are doomed to live in this town.

: : :

To-day the sun is brilliantly shining; it is quite mild and warm. I go out for my last morning walk, without an overcoat or hat. The sun shines, and Hitler is master of this city. The sun shines, and dozens of my friends—

my pupils at the Workers' School, the men and women I met at the I.A.H.[Internationale Arbeiter-Hilfe]—are in prison, possibly dead. But it isn't of them that I am thinking—the clear-headed ones, the purposeful, the heroic; they recognized and accepted the risks. I am thinking of poor Rudi, in his absurd Russian blouse. Rudi's make-believe, story-book game has become earnest; the Nazis will play it with him. The Nazis won't laugh at him; they'll take him on trust for what he pretended to be. Perhaps at this very moment Rudi is being tortured to death.

I catch sight of my face in the mirror of a shop, and am horrified to see that I am smiling. You can't help smiling, in such beautiful weather. The trams are going up and down the Kleiststrasse, just as usual. They, and the people on the pavement, and the teacosy dome of the Nollendorfplatz station have an air of curious familiarity, of striking resemblance to something one remembers as normal and pleasant in the past—like a very good photograph.

No. Even now I can't altogether believe that any of this has really happened. . . .

Hitler in the Elevator

Between the years 1928 and 1946, the Belgian journalist and writer Georges Simenon undertook numerous journeys in France, throughout Europe, and around the world. He wrote about thirty reports of his travels—for example, on Africa, Tahiti, and Panama. In 1933, Simenon traveled through Belgium, Poland, the Baltic States, Austria, Czechoslovakia, Hungary, Romania, and the Soviet Union. The outcome of his journey was a seven-part series on "Europe 33," part six of which deals with Germany: "La génération du désordre" ("The Generation of Disorder"). It appeared on 22 April 1933 in the journal *Voilà*.

While Simenon and his wife were staying in Berlin, Nazi propaganda in the run up to the Reichstag elections of 5 March 1933 was in full swing. The two travelers were staying in the hotel where Adolf Hitler was also in residence, and Simenon promptly met him in the elevator. Communist activists told him that the Nazis, whose office they had bugged, were planning a violent coup. This information, which the reporter passed on to *Paris-Soir*, went unheeded. Two days later (on 27 February 1933), the Reichstag was set on fire, an act that was used by the Nazis as a pretext for the promulgation of emergency laws. Simenon's article on Germany is illustrated with photographs. One of them shows a man with a moustache. The caption reads: "This is not Hitler, though it looks like him. It is Kürten, the Düsseldorf vampire." The psychopathic serial killer Peter Kürten (1883–1931) had stabbed or beaten women to death and supposedly even drunk their blood.

At the conclusion of his European journey, Simenon managed to secure an interview with Leon Trotsky (1879–1940) in Turkey. Besides his journalistic writings, this tremendously productive author published over one thousand short stories and nearly four hundred novels. After 1929 he developed the character of Chief Inspector Maigret, whom he featured in numerous books.

I saw him, the Messiah, ten days before the elections, as he was coming back to his apartment in the Kaiserhof. I was staying in the same hotel, a hundred meters from where Hindenburg was living. It was snowing. The sky was leaden. All the foreign newspapers had articles with headlines such as "Poverty in Germany!"

And, in fact, every hundred meters, a well-dressed man, very polite, would ask you for a mark, or more or less, while raising his hat.

Somewhere, I came across a funeral cortège followed by thousands of men in brown shirts. And, here and there, there was a police car with machine guns at the ready.

It was the funeral of a Hitler supporter killed by the communists.

The day after, I read, in the most serious of the Paris newspapers, "*Terror in Germany*."

Because, here and there, there were a few more deaths!

Special correspondents wrote, in all seriousness, "*It is impossible for the party of violence to win*."

They shouldn't be blamed. It was the first time they had set foot in Germany, and these thousands of brown shirts, these cars with machine guns, really made an impression on them.

Not the Germans! They walked past without even a glance at the cortège. And if they read that five communists and three Nazis had been killed the night before, they were no more surprised than when you learn every day that twenty people have been killed in automobile accidents.

The "Führer" was calm too, surrounded by his general staff in the Kaiserhof. I met him in the elevator, just as [I had met] Emil Jannings, who was staying on the floor above. The Kaiser's wife came to pay Hitler a visit and even hosted a tea at the hotel, where, on the next day, there was a masked ball.

And the foreign journalists cabled: "*Return of the Monarchy . . .*"

Hitler went on a short trip to Munich and the papers said: "*Negotiations with the Wittelsbachs . . . Things are heating up. Bavaria is against the Führer . . .*"

I read things like this in the foreign newspapers, but no one in the Kaiserhof in Berlin was excited, anxious, or surprised.

One evening a grand council was summoned, and it was decided that, before the elections, some excuse had to be found to muzzle the communists. Hitler proposed organizing a fake assassination attempt on himself to galvanize his troops. Goebbels, more calm, dissuaded him, saying that a fake assassination might give some people the idea of staging a real one.

So they fell back on the Reichstag. It was one week before the elections, a Saturday. I wired the news to the Paris evening newspaper. No one dared publish it. Wednesday evening, the Reichstag burned and not a single German showed the least surprise!

Good Lord! Can you imagine the naiveté of the foreign correspondents who write columns seeking the "truth"?

Hitler triumphed and the same correspondents were flabbergasted.

"He is Papen's man!"
"He is the Crown Prince's man!"
"He is Hugenburg's man!"
"He is a puppet!"
"He is the new Siegfried . . ."

What did I just tell you? Ah, yes! "Orgies," nudism, the exchange-rate premium, Freudianism, small boys and small girls, imbalance and fever, sport, heroin, cocaine, and how many other things, etc.

Well, there you are! There are some tens of millions of Germans who are under the impression that this is all over, that they have recovered their equilibrium, that they have finally been given a goal in life.

And it is Hitler who has done this!

People were running around aimlessly and enjoying themselves as best they could, without conviction, each to his own taste, and this all ended up in a universal boredom.

Hitler licked them back into shape. He is going to clean them up, have them hold their heads high, renew them from top to bottom, just as I saw them surge along the roads in 1914, sure of themselves, with confidence in their destiny and in their enlisted men.

No more need of individual worries, of books on theosophy, the esoteric, the erotic. All that needs to be done to feel a great shiver of delight is to march to the strains of a band, shouting "Hoch! Hoch! Hoch!"*

And to recover the pride and the joy of being born a citizen of Greater Germany!

Translated by **KENNETH NORTHCOTT**

Why Could the Nazis Come?

After receiving her Ph.D. (on the history of the Upper Engadine) in Zürich in 1931, Annemarie Schwarzenbach published fictional and travel books. She went on several expeditions, among others to Beirut, Baghdad, Persia, Afghanistan, and the Belgian Congo. Schwarzenbach wrote a series of letters (eighty-eight altogether, mainly between the years 1930 and 1933) to Erika Mann (1905–69), with whom she was unhappily in love; and fifty-two more (from 1933 to 1942) to Erika's brother, Klaus Mann (1906–49), with whom she felt a kind of spiritual kinship. She stayed in Germany on various occasions: in 1931 she moved to Berlin; in 1937 she visited the Free City of Danzig; and in 1938—after the Anschluss—Austria. From the capital she sent her impressions of Germany, before and after the Nazis' assumption of power, to Erika Mann (19 January and 3 February 1933) and Klaus Mann (8 April 1933).

Berlin, 8 April 1933

My dear Klaus,
It has been such a long time since we talked, and in the present circumstances this first letter is a difficult undertaking. I have only been here eight days, but long enough for countless observations, conversations, and discussions. Of course, conditions are frightful in every respect; expressions of the Third Reich are, without exception, repellent and, in the light of the humanistic feeling that

we all take for granted, degrading and deeply opposed to every concept of culture. Of course, the "discipline" is, at the very least, bogus, for in spite of all Hitler's appeals and admonitions, individual actions of the worst sort take place every day. Of course, the exclusion of the Jews is having catastrophic results not only for the Jews themselves but also for the institutions that are affected, for businesses and presumably for the whole German economy. Of course, Germany is once again isolating itself, making itself hated and breeding that hatred at home for generations to come. But we don't need to talk about that—I'm sure you hear more than enough of it. Discussions about it seem quite fruitless to me, because any halfway intellectually oriented person, if European at least, naturally belongs to the opposition. I only ask myself—and it becomes daily more urgent— whether the people fully realize the significance of what is happening: in other words, can they see that it is not only an abhorrent tendency that is temporarily gaining the upper hand here, but that a whole people—and, in spite of everything, a highly gifted one that cannot be eliminated from the history of European culture—is declaring its adherence to this path for years to come by virtue of what, in spite of everything, constitutes a powerful revolution? The theoretical thinker does not have to acknowledge such processes; the historically oriented thinker and, especially, those involved must try to understand them and come to terms with them. We are all involved. To turn aside is really as good as giving oneself up and committing suicide. After all, we have to live and we are part of the German cultural sphere. Declaring oneself a member of the opposition—and what else can we do?—can only be done in full awareness of the fact that we cannot escape from these processes, simply because they affect us in the very core of our being. The opposition too has a task. I mean, you cannot turn away from Germany; that would be to overrate the freedom of the individual. Opposition would then be not flight or renunciation or even pharisaical scorn but nurture of those intellectual values in which we believe until a better time comes.

So much for the oppositional stance. But further: those who today belong to the opposition—and, at the moment, that means the remnants of the "thinkers and poets"—have until now held the same ideas; that is, in general terms: what is good and reasonable, international understanding and tolerance, in short, human and cultural progress. The Social Democratic program had no other goal. Many people in Germany were of this mind. Many had the best intentions, many tried to act in this spirit. It failed; fourteen years and, in the end, the state collapsed like a house of cards. How can that be? Only someone who has no idea of the laws of history, especially of cause and effect, can insist that the wicked Nazis came and struck a line through the Social Democrats' plans. According to Marx, the proletariat had to have strangled capitalism in the class struggle—that did not happen. Why not? Were things not bad enough for the proletariat? Why could the Nazis come? "The National Socialist movement is unstoppable"—how can it be if Social Democracy offers a form of government so much more humane and reasonable?

A few reasons are clear—the severity of the peace terms, French policy, the wild rearmament taking place all over Europe (Poland spends *half* of its budget on rearmament; England has had a standing army only since the war; France, Russia, fascist Italy are rearming constantly and inexorably), rising unemployment, and the demoralization of the masses. In short, repercussion had to come. Again: to the purely theoretical thinker we say: the writer, among others, is equally disgusted by the repercussion, even though it was unavoidable, but the person involved has to perceive its inevitability and understand the movement it gives birth to, even if finding it repellent. Finally, these uniformed bandits and mercenaries with their barbaric savagery are actually the same people who, a few years ago, were going off for the weekend with their girlfriends, with collapsible boats and rubber balls, and were not amenable to the seductive words of popular speakers without good reason—

In short—it is the old tragedy of the conflict between thought and action—what is the point of thirty, a hundred, five hundred sophisticated people who can agree about what is the progressive, the humane, and the only desirable, when the "people" in their millions follow the dictates of necessity and despair?

It is dawning on me that Plato was not a statesman after all, and that the powerful movements of which history is made simply bypass the insights that are reached by thought, they contradict them—and we are suddenly embroiled in them, whether as underdogs or happy fellow travelers. I'm not sure if that isn't fatalism.

Meanwhile a lot of clever people realize that the high-toned movement for "national" discipline and order is already displaying the darkest symptoms of degeneracy that lead to bolshevism—perhaps the citizens will then see that class terror from the right, despite the military flags, is no more palatable than it is from the left—Capitalist enterprises, supervised by commissars, suspect something similar.

Klaus—it is *so* late—I'm going to break off, and I think that you will notice, as soon as you read this, why I am telling you all this in such a naive and schematic way (you will already have considered it all). In any case, we shall be unable to breed any feelings of revenge in the face of such tragic events from which there is no escape and almost no "guilt"—for what we want to, and should, reproach the new leaders with is paltry compared with the torrent of fate we have been tossed into. Write soon, Klaus, dear, and tell me how you are. Beware of the devil-worshiper, whom I don't like at all. You, on the other hand, a lot—

Your Miro

Translated by **KENNETH NORTHCOTT**

Hitler Needs a Woman

Martha Dodd had studied at the University of Chicago, had already worked for the *Chicago Tribune*, and had married for the first time when, in 1933, her father, the historian William Edward Dodd (1869–1940), was appointed United States ambassador in Berlin. She decided to accompany him to Germany. As a twenty-four-year-old, she arrived in Europe in the summer of 1933 with her parents and her brother. In 1939, after her return, and still before the beginning of World War II, she published her book on the four and a half years that she spent there. In Britain the book was entitled *My Years in Germany*, and in the United States, *Through Embassy Eyes*. After her father's death, Dodd, with her brother Edward Dodd Jr. (1905–52), published *Ambassador Dodd's Diary* (1941). Besides her political works, Dodd wrote some fiction, including a roman à clef entitled *Sowing the Wind* (1944/45) about the fighter pilot and armaments organizer Ernst Udet (1896–1941).

The following extracts from *My Years in Germany* narrate the arrival of the Dodd family in July 1933 (they travel to Berlin via Hamburg), a tour in August 1933 (to Southern Germany, Austria, and the Rhineland), and a meeting with Adolf Hitler. The young American was invited by Hitler's foreign press chief, Ernst (known as "Putzi") Hanfstaengl (1887–1975), with the words, "Hitler needs a woman." (Hanfstaengl, who had grown up in the United States, fled to England in 1937; during the war he was an adviser to the U.S. government.)

We had a slow sail up the Elbe and finally docked at Hamburg. Germany was here at last, with all of its profound meaning, the new future only guessed at and begun, to which my father gave all the idealism of his deeply emotional and disciplined life, with which he expected to co-operate and [from] which he hoped to benefit. I was moved by the eagerness, which he unconsciously expressed in returning in one of the highest positions our country can offer to its citizens, to the country he had so well loved, understood, and defended. For us, his children, here was a new adventure breaking into our middle youth, not sought after, not really fully appreciated; it was not an end or a beginning for us—or so we thought—but an episode occurring in the security of circumstance and love. It was not recklessness for us; it was our parents' gift of an experience which could open or close or mean nothing in our lives. We greeted Germany with excited hearts, taking the future in our stride with the uncapturable nonchalance of youth, ready for anything or for nothing.

We must have presented one of the most amazing spectacles in the history of diplomatic arrivals, though, of course, we were completely unconscious of it at the time. My father had misread a telegram sent by the counsellor of the Embassy. He thought that the tickets to Berlin, the private car, etc., had all been arranged, so we didn't bother about arranging for them on board, and in the confusion of disembarking forgot to get our necessary cards. Until the last moment he was busy with interviewers and newspapermen. One of the journalists was a correspondent of a Jewish newspaper in Hamburg. He wrote an article saying that my father had been sent over to solve the Jewish problem. Later we heard about it, and realized how badly garbled the account was. The German papers were very polite to us, but took the occasion to point out that this was the way of Jews.

My brother had planned to drive our Chevrolet to Berlin, but had done nothing about the red tape of getting it off the ship, with the permits and licences, and so on, that it involved.

The Counsellor, the adviser to the Ambassador and next in rank to him, a gentleman of the most extreme Protocol (we hadn't yet heard this word) school, with grey-white hair and moustache which looked curled, elegant dress, gloves, stick and proper hat, a complexion of flaming hue, clipped, polite, and definitely condescending accent, was so horrified at our informality that his rage almost—not quite—transcended the bounds allowed by his rigid code of behaviour. We had no pretentious car, we had no chauffeur; valets, secretaries, and personal maids were ominously missing—in fact, we looked like simple ordinary human beings the like of which he had not permitted himself to mingle with for perhaps most of his adult life.

Finally, everything was put in order, my brother driving the modest car and the rest of us going by a regular train to Berlin (we should have at least taken the "Flying Hamburger," the fastest and most expensive special). My father sat in one compartment talking over the political developments of Germany with the Counsellor, who was attempting in the most polished manner he could summon, to hint that my father was no longer a simple professor, but a great diplomat, and his habits and ways of life should be altered accordingly. But the honest and subtle, gentle and slightly nervous scholar was to remain as firm in his integrity of character as if there had been no change in his environment or position. I didn't realize how futile all admonitions were, and I am sure my father was as supremely indifferent to them then as he was to be later when great pressure from all sources was applied to effect the desired transformation.

My mother and I were in another compartment, she uneasy and heavy of heart at the thought of the duties and change in life-patterns confronting her; and I sound asleep on her shoulder, both of us shrouded in expensive flowers.

The train stopped suddenly and I had just time enough to rub my eyes, jam on my hat and step onto the platform, a little dazed and very embarrassed. Before me was a large gathering of excited people; newspapermen crowding around us, and the ever-watchful Counsellor attempting to keep them away; Foreign Office representatives, other diplomats, and many Americans, come to look over the strange Ambassador and his family. The flashlights were a steady stream of blinding light and somehow or other I found myself grinning stupidly into the camera with bunches of orchids and other flowers up to my ears. My father took the newspapermen aside and gave them a prepared statement of greeting and we were hustled away.

I was put into a car with a young man who, I soon learned, was our Protocol secretary. I finally got the definition. He was pointing out the sights of Berlin to me. We drove around the Reichstag building, which he duly named. I exclaimed: "Oh, I thought it was burned down! It looks all right to me. Tell me what happened." He leaned over to me, after several such natural but indiscreet questions, and said, "S-ssh! Young lady, you must learn to be seen and not heard. You mustn't say so much and ask so many questions. This isn't America and you can't say all the things you think." I was astonished, but subdued for the time being. This was my first contact with the reality of Germany under a dictatorship and it took me a long time to take his advice seriously. Long habits of life are hard to change overnight.

We arrived at the Esplanade Hotel and were ushered into the Imperial suite. We gasped at its magnificence and also at what we thought the bill would be. Again the rooms were so filled with flowers that there was scarcely space to move in—orchids and rare scented lilies, flowers of all colours and descriptions. We had two huge high-ceilinged reception rooms lined with satin brocades, decorated with gilt and tapestried furniture and marble tables. Our welcoming friends finally left us to our own devices and my father went to bed with a book. Mother and I sat around, small and awed by the glamour of being the Ambassador's family, receiving cards that began coming in and more baskets of flowers, wondering desperately how all this was to be paid for without mortgaging our souls. We did not know then that the hotel has special rates for visiting "potentates," and had been even more considerate in our case. The Adlon hotel manager had wired us to accept a suite in his hotel free of charge, or at such a low rate that it seemed free, but Ambassadors had had the habit of residing at the Esplanade and we were not allowed to break the precedent.

My father was in magnificent humour at dinner-time. We all went down to the hotel dining-room to order the meal. My father was pouring out his German, teasing the waiters, and asking them questions—most undignified behaviour for an Ambassador. I never heard so many "*Dankeschoens*" and "*Bitteschoens*" in my life in one single evening, and it was my first introduction to the almost obsequious courtesy of German waiters. We had a good but heavy German dinner and I tasted my first German beer.

After we had finished, we decided to walk around a bit near the hotel before going to bed. We walked the length of the Sieges Allee lined on each side with rather ugly and pretentious statues of former rulers of Germany. My father would stop before each one and give us a short historical sketch of his time and character. He was in his element here as he knew German history almost by heart and if he missed out on something, he made a mental note for future study. I am sure this was one of the happiest evenings we spent in Germany. All of us were full of joy and peace. We liked Germany, and I was enchanted by the kindness and simplicity of the people, as far as I had seen them. The streets were dully lit, almost like a small American town late at night; there were no soldiers on the streets; everything was peaceful, romantic, strange, nostalgic. I felt the press had badly maligned the country and I wanted to proclaim the warmth and friendliness of the people, the soft summer night with its fragrance of trees and flowers, the serenity of the streets.

I was laid up in bed for the next few days with a bad cold. Sigrid Schultz came to see me. She is the correspondent for the Chicago *Tribune* and has been in Germany for over ten years. Small, a little pudgy, with blue eyes and an abundance of golden hair, she was very friendly and intelligent, with a mind alert if not always accurate, and a great news-hound. She had known the Germany of the past and she was sick at heart now. She told me many stories about the Nazis and their brutalities, the Secret Police before whom she was regularly summoned for the critical reports she wrote. I didn't believe all her stories. I thought she was exaggerating and a bit hysterical, but I liked her personally and was interested to get a line on some of the people I was going to be associated with—diplomats and journalists.

I had a letter to the already quite famous American newspaperman H. R. Knickerbocker from Alexander Woollcott which I soon sent by post. He called up and asked me for a tea date. He was a small, slender man with red hair and warm, bright brown eyes, and a mobile mouth. We danced—which he does beautifully—and he asked me if I knew German or Germany, or anything about the Nazis. After revealing to him what must have seemed like appalling ignorance, he talked a bit about the Nazi leaders and soon shifted to other things. I wasn't interested in politics or economics and was mainly concerned in getting the "feel" of the people. I was delighted by them and still remember my joy that afternoon at the Eden Hotel, watching their funny stiff dancing, listening to their incomprehensible and guttural tongue, and watching their simple gestures, natural behaviour and childlike eagerness for life.

During this first month we were receiving calls from Germans and Americans, listening to all sorts of points of view to which I did not respond very deeply, being so utterly absorbed in understanding the temper and heart of a foreign people. Unconsciously, I began to compare them, as we went around to reasonable or cheap restaurants—not at all in the accepted fashion of diplomats—to the French. The Germans seemed much more genuine and honest, even in the merchant class. I was pleased that they did not try to cheat us when it was so clear that we were foreigners, that they were very solemn and sympathetic when we first started to speak our pathetic German. They weren't thieves, they weren't selfish, they weren't impatient or cold and hard; qualities I began to find stood out in my mind as characteristic of the French. We joked a lot, and I think only my father took seriously the warnings that the servants were apt to be spies and that dictaphones and eavesdroppers were encircling us.

Among the various newspapermen I met at this time was Quentin Reynolds, the Hearst correspondent. He was a big hulk of a man, with curly hair, humorous eyes and a broad beaming face. Sharp and tough and unsentimental, I thought him an excellent newspaperman. He had been in Germany a few months and was picking up the language rapidly. He knew intimately such legendary figures as Ernst ("Putzi") Hanfstaengl, and arranged for us to meet at a party given by an English journalist. It was a lavish and fairly drunken affair with an interesting mixture of Germans and foreigners. Putzi came in late in a sensational manner, a huge man in height and build, towering over everyone present. His face was heavy and dark, rather underslung and concave in shape. He had a soft, ingratiating manner, a beautiful voice which he used with conscious artistry, sometimes whispering low and soft, the next minute bellowing and shattering the room. He was supposed to be the artist among the Nazis, erratic and interesting, the personal clown and musician to Hitler himself. He usually dominated every group he was in by the commanding quality of his powerful physical presence, or by the tirelessness of his indomitable energy and never-ending talk. He could exhaust anyone and, from sheer perseverance, out-shout or out-whisper the strongest man in Berlin. I was fascinated and intrigued by my first contact with a Nazi high up in official circles, so blatantly proclaiming his charm and talent. Bavarian and American blood produced this strange phenomenon. He could never have been a Prussian and he was proud of it.

===

FIRST IMPRESSIONS OF GERMANY

Quentin Reynolds suggested to my brother and me that we take our Chevrolet and make a trip with him through Southern Germany and Austria. With a little persuasion my parents thought it would be a good way for us to study Germany.

So the three of us set out in August, a little over a month after our arrival, and made for the south. It was an exciting trip and the lack of German gave us some amusing moments in asking directions and ordering food. We stopped off at Wittenberg and saw the ninety-seven theses of Luther nailed, in bronze, on the church door, and went on to Leipzig, my father's old university town. There, of course, we drank many steins of beer in the old Auerbach Keller in honour of the meeting of Faust and Mephistopheles. All along the roads and in the towns we saw the Nazi banner, with the red background, the white circle in the centre emblazoned with the mystic crooked cross. Driving in and out of towns we saw large banners strung across the road on which I recognized the word "Jude." We realized this was anti-Semitic propaganda, but we didn't—at least I didn't—take it too seriously. Furthermore, I couldn't read the German well enough to have a full understanding of the words, and I must confess the Nazi spirit of intolerance had not yet dawned on me in its complete significance.

Enthusiasm was wild—or so it seemed on the surface. When people looked at our car and saw the low number, they "Heiled" energetically, probably thinking we were an official family from the great capital. We saw a lot of marching men, in brown uniforms, singing and shouting and waving their flags. These were the now-famous Brown-Shirt Storm Troopers, through whose loyalty and terroristic methods Hitler seized power. The excitement of the people was contagious, and I "Heiled" as vigorously as any Nazi. Quentin and my brother frowned on me and made sarcastic remarks about my adolescence, but I was enjoying everything fully and it was difficult for me to restrain my natural sympathy for the Germans. I felt like a child, ebullient and careless, the intoxication of the new regime working like wine in me.

We stopped in Nürnberg for the night and, after having reserved attractive and cheap rooms, went out to roam over the town and get a bite to eat. As we were coming out of the hotel we saw a crowd gathering and gesticulating in the middle of the street. We stopped to find out what it was all about. There was a street-car in the centre of the road from which a young girl was being brutally pushed and shoved. We moved closer and saw the tragic and tortured face, the colour of diluted absinthe. She looked ghastly. Her head had been shaved clean of hair and she was wearing a placard across her breast. We followed her for a moment, watching the crowd insult and jibe and drive her. Quentin and my brother asked several people around us, what was the matter. We understood from their German that she was a Gentile who had been consorting with a Jew. The placard said: "I have Offered Myself to a Jew." I wanted to follow but my two companions were so repelled that they pulled me away. Quentin, I remember, unfeeling and hard-boiled as I thought he was, was so shaken by the whole scene that he said the only thing he could do was to get drunk, to forget it—which we all did on red champagne.

I felt nervous and cold, the mood of exhilaration vanished completely. I tried in a self-conscious way to justify the action of the Nazis, to insist that we should not condemn without knowing the whole story. But here was something that darkened my picture of a happy, carefree Germany. The ugly, bared brutality I thought would make only a superficial impression on me, but as time went on I thought more and more of the pitiful, broken creature, a victim of mass-insanity.

I urged Quentin not to write up the story. It would make a sensation because of our presence—the new Ambassador's children. It was an isolated case. It was not really important, would create a bad impression, did not reveal actually what was going on in Germany, overshadowed the constructive work they were doing. I presented many foolish and contradictory arguments. He decided not to cable the story, but only because he said there had been so many atrocity stories lately that people were no longer interested in them; he would write it as a news-story when he returned. But when we got back to Berlin we discovered that another journalist had been in the town and had cabled the story immediately and that all the press everywhere had headlined it, and also commented on our being witnesses.

The next morning we headed south. My brother was trying to make Innsbruck to see a girl of his, so we sped through the country, stopping only long enough to get food and gasoline and have a drink or two. We drove to Bayreuth but we were too late for the opera so we only visited the opera-house for a moment and in the dark, and hurried on. Quentin took the wheel and we sped over mountains and hills and curves at a mad rate. Little south-German villages, beautiful solid white houses, flying by us on each side, looking ancient and ghostly and lonely as our headlights flashed over them for a second.

We finally got to Innsbruck, tired but miraculously alive, and soon went to bed. The next morning we looked around the town, one of the most beautiful spots in Europe. The scenery was magnificent and the people even more helpful and friendly than in other places—but, of course, it was not a Nazi town. [...]

We finally left Austria, with its grace and charm, softened careless speech, and went back to Germany, having only once received a Nazi salute as we were nearing the border. It was strange returning to Germany, the music and poetry we had been so full of seemed ominously absent. Again as we travelled north along the Rhine, we saw the flags and the marching men, the brown uniforms, the martial character of the nation beginning to impress itself. It didn't seem as spontaneous in the Rhine country as in other parts and we were wondering as we drove along and tried to talk with the people, what reservations they were making. The Nazi emblems and symbolism seemed grafted on to this dark and vivacious people.

We stared, in the usual fashion of tourists, at the famous Lorelei Rock, dark and mysterious above the murky, slow-moving Rhine, stared in wonder at the ancient ruins, evocative and beautiful, isolated and majestic on the tops of wild mountains. We drank more than the usual portion of golden wine, like liquid sun caught in a glass. Finally, the time was up and we drove quickly towards Berlin, passing through the dark and deeply-wooded Harz, memories of the myths, legends, and fairy stories in our minds.

Back in Berlin again, feeling already as if it were home, and rested and fresh from the exhilaration of travel, we began to open our eyes to things about us, to contrast the Germany we had been travelling through with the Prussia we resided in.

Quentin called to say that his home office was annoyed that he had missed the story in Nürnberg. The Foreign Office called at our home, seemingly very much perturbed; regretted and apologized for the incident of isolated brutality which they assured me was rare and would be punished.

===

Hanfstaengl had been calling up and wanting to arrange for me to meet Hitler. Hanfstaengl spluttered and ranted grandiosely: "Hitler needs a woman. Hitler should have an American woman—a lovely woman could change the whole destiny of Europe. Martha, you are the woman!"

As a matter of fact, though this sounded like inflated horse play as did most of Putzi's schemes, I am convinced he knew the violence and danger of Hitler's personality and ambitions, and deceived himself, at least partially, and wished frantically that something could be done about it.

So, for some months, when he was not telling assembled guests that he would like to throw a hand-grenade into the house of the little doctor which was below his apartment, he was trying to find a woman for Hitler. However, I was quite satisfied by the role so generously passed on to me and rather excited by the opportunity that presented itself, to meet this strange leader of men. In fact, I was still at this time, though growing critical of the men around Hitler, their methods and perhaps the system itself, convinced that Hitler was a glamorous and brilliant personality, who must have great power and charm. I looked forward to the meeting Putzi told me he had arranged.

Since I was appointed to change the history of Europe, I decided to dress in my most demure and intriguing best—which always appeals to the Germans: they want their women to be seen and not heard, and then seen only as appendages of the splendid male they accompany—with a veil and a flower and a pair of very cold hands. We went to the Kaiserhof and met the young Polish singer, Jan Kiepura. The three of us sat talking and drinking tea for a time. Hitler came in with several men, bodyguards and his well-loved chauffeur (who was given almost a State funeral when he died recently). He sat down unostentatiously at the table next to us. After a few minutes Jan Kiepura was taken over to Hitler to talk music to him, and then Putzi left me for a moment, leaned over the Leader's ear, and returned in a great state of nervous agitation. He had consented to be introduced to me. I went over and remained standing as he stood up and took my hand. He kissed it very politely and murmured a few words. I knew very little German, as I have indicated, at the time, so I didn't linger long. I shook hands again and he kissed my hand again, and I went back to the adjoining table with Putzi and stayed for some time listening to the conversation of the two music-lovers and receiving curious, embarrassed stares from time to time from the leader.

This first glance left me with a picture of a weak, soft face with pouches under the eyes, full lips and very little bony facial structure. The moustache didn't seem as ridiculous as it appeared in pictures—in fact, I scarcely noticed it; but I imagine that is because I was pretty well conditioned to such things by that time. As has often been said, Hitler's eyes were startling and unforgettable—they seemed pale blue in colour, were intense, unwavering, hypnotic.

Certainly the eyes were his only distinctive feature. They could contain fury and fanaticism and cruelty; they could be mystic and tearful and challenging. This particular afternoon he was excessively gentle and modest in his manners. Unobtrusive, communicative, informal, he had a certain quiet charm, almost a tenderness of speech and glance. He talked soberly to Kiepura and seemed very interested and absorbed in meeting both of us. The curious embarrassment he showed in meeting me, his somewhat apologetic, nervous manner, my father tells me—and other diplomats as well—are always present when he meets the diplomatic corps *en masse*. This self-consciousness has created in him a shyness and distaste for meeting people above him in station or wealth. As time went on, Hitler's face and bearing changed noticeably—he began to look and walk more and more like Mussolini. But this peculiar shy strain of character has to this day remained.

When I left the Kaiserhof with the ecstatic and towering jitterbug Putzi, I could lend only half an ear to his extravagant, senseless talk. I was thinking of the meeting with Hitler. It was hard to believe that this man was one of the most powerful men in Europe—even at this time, other nations were afraid of him and his growing "New Germany." He seemed modest, middle class, rather dull and self-conscious—yet with this strange tenderness and appealing helplessness. Only in the mad burning eyes could one see the terrible future of Germany.

When I came home to dinner I described my impression of the "great leader" to my father. He, of course, was greatly amused at my impressionableness, but admitted with indifference that Hitler was not an unattractive man personally. He teased me and urged me not to wash my hands for weeks thereafter—I would certainly want to retain as long as was hygienically possible, the benediction of Hitler's kiss. He said I should remember the exact spot and perhaps, if I *must* wash, could wash carefully round it.

I was a little angry and peeved at his irony, but tried to be a good sport about it.

That night I had a small party at my house. Young Stresemann, whom I had met shortly after I arrived in Germany, the musically talented eldest son of the famous statesman, came, as did the Frenchman of whom I was very fond despite my conflict with his political views, and a man named Hans Thomsen, who was in the Kanzlei of the Fuehrer and supposed to be very close to him. Of Danish descent, and with the suavest and gentlest manner I had met among Germans, he was both charming and interesting to me. As time went on he frequented our house with his friend, Miss Rangabe, with clock-like regularity—and never missed a party of mine or my parents for a year to two. He seemed to be an ardent Nazi, approaching the whole problem, I thought, from a reserved and intellectual point of view. There was very little hysteria about him; I thought, as many did who met him, that he might have private and personal reservations, but that on the whole he was one of the best representatives they could have. He was extremely popular with the diplomatic corps as a whole, and his soft, restrained manner made more friends for his party than almost any man in our circle. Diplomats, including my father, would take him aside and consult fairly confidentially with him, describing what they considered were terrible mistakes in policy, internal and foreign; and would make friends with the blond-haired, soft-spoken, subtle and mature diplomat, so that Thomsen enjoyed an "inside" track with the corps, freely and frankly offered, and perhaps as freely made use of by the Germans.

Hanfstaengl came late, as usual, that night and when he arrived was in jubilant spirits. He carried on an animated conversation with young Stresemann about music, and both agreed that Schubert's *Unfinished* was one of the most glorious bits of music ever written. Judge a German by his musical tastes and you have a pretty definite clue to his intellectual position in general. I went to the victrola and put on the Horst Wessel Lied which someone had given me. It is fairly good marching music and when sung by large throngs can be quite stirring—and is the double National Anthem of the Germans. Hanfstaengl was enjoying it, not entirely without humour. Thomsen suddenly got up, went to the victrola, and turned it off abruptly. There was a strange tenseness on his face. I asked innocently why he didn't like it. He answered, very sternly: "That is not the sort of music to be played for mixed gatherings and in a flippant manner. I won't have you play our anthem, with its significance, at a social party." I was startled and annoyed.

Hanfstaengl gave Thomsen a vivid look of amusement tinged with contempt and shrugged his shoulders. He said later: "Yes, there are some people like that among us. People who have blind spots and are humourless—one must be careful not to offend their sensitive souls."

Somehow the evening was spoiled. The guests kept up their lively conversation and discussion, but most of them, not being fanatic Nazis and some definitely anti-Nazi, now knew that Thomsen was not a gay, intelligent, lighthearted, or reasonable friend, but a passionate partisan. They reacted to this in their individual ways and they were all a little self-conscious in his presence.

Unconsciously this may have been the turning-point of my reactions of a simple and more social nature to Nazi dictatorship. Accustomed all my life to the free exchange of views, the atmosphere of this evening shocked me and struck me as a sort of violation of the decencies of human relationship.

The Sick Man of Europe

The Swedish poet Gunnar Ekelöf was living in Berlin in the fall of 1933. At Christmas—because of a lack of money—he returned home to Sweden. From here he wrote letters reporting on his German experience. Ekelöf realized that the assumption of power by Adolf Hitler and the changes it brought with it represented a dramatic rupture in civilization. In the following letter to fellow author Agnes von Krusenstjerna (1894–1940) he diagnoses the collapse of bourgeois morality in Germany. At Christmas, Ekelöf wrote to the author Elmer Diktonius (1896–1961) with the same clarity: "Germany is a moral hell, I have never liked Germany and now I hate it as Europe's sickest man, source of infection, great fog. And that's that." Impressions from Germany, where he had stayed on previous occasions, also featured in Ekelöf's prose texts: "Zoologische Gärten" ("Zoos"), "Reiseeindrücke: Mitropa-Schlafwagen" ("Travel Impressions: Mitropa Sleeping Car").

Malmö, 16 December, 1933

Dear Agnes,

[...] It is perhaps unnecessary to send you greetings from Germany, which I am very happy to have left behind. I cannot imagine anything more depressing than being stationed in Berlin. As a francophile I am a German-hater; but not only because of that—for many other reasons as well. Germany has in a depressing way assumed the role of "the sick man of Europe." It is a rotten, sinking bourgeoisie that does not shrink from the worst infamies as soon as a power struggle is involved. The rod and switch have appeared again. I am somewhat apprehensive about repercussions in Sweden but don't believe they will be so bad. Germany is sick at its innermost core, an unsatisfied and broken-down sadist who strikes out at everyone around him and uses self-glorification to silence his doubts. We are still, for the time being, fairly healthy.

Well, I don't have much more to write about. [. . .]

Your devoted
Gunnar

Translated by **SONIA WICHMANN**

A Sort of Simultaneity

From September 1933 to June 1934, Jean-Paul Sartre was the holder of a scholarship—for which his predecessor, the sociologist Raymond Aron (1905–83), had encouraged him to apply—at the French Academic House in Berlin-Wilmersdorf. In Berlin, the young intellectual devoted himself primarily to the philosophy of Edmund Husserl (1859–1938). His diaries from this period are lost, as is his correspondence with Simone de Beauvoir (1908–86), who visited him twice in Berlin. However, there are individual reminiscences of his German experience in Sartre's *Carnets de la drôle de guerre* (*Notebooks from a Phony War*) from spring 1940, before France's defeat by Germany. The following entry is dated 28 February 1940. In further notes from his diary, Sartre reflects upon his engagement with the writings of Husserl and Martin Heidegger (1889–1976), his limited knowledge of German, and how difficult it was to get to know German women.

I think there's a quite special pleasure in feeling oneself stand out against the background formed by a group; in feeling a kind of solidarity round one, which one escapes at the very moment one yields to it. I think what entranced me above all was felt simultaneity. Normally, while I write, my neighbour's leafing through a review and, not far away from me, two fellows are playing chess: that too is simultaneity. But in a sense it's abstract—scattered in a thousand little local, isolated acts. I only think it, and scarcely feel it. Whereas, because of the solidarity that united us, each of my gestures in the unity of our set would give itself as simultaneous with some other gesture of one of my comrades: that used to confer upon it a kind of necessity. I was horrified, in Berlin, to see how much the Germans enjoyed that kind of simultaneity. At the Neue Welt, an immense hangar where thousands of Germans come to drink beer, they used to present teams of Bavarians on the stage, who could do nothing except sharply indicate that simultaneity: one would throw his hat into the air, while another danced and the third sounded a hunting-horn, etc. The charm of the display was very obviously the "while"—which has nothing in common with the multiplicity in unity of a corps de ballet, since it's real diversity in a merely affective unity.

So it was something we used to feel quite strongly, and which de-lighted me.

"Are You Still Alive?"—30 June 1934

In *My Years in Germany*, Martha Dodd explains how her initial sympathy, growing enthusiasm, and defiant partisanship for the Nazi regime gradually, but by no means without complications, developed into a clear-sighted rejection of it. In order to be able to convey and reflect upon her complex experience, she uses specific literary forms that succeed each other in her account. The book begins like a classic travelogue, recording first impressions from an ethnographic point of view. It develops into a bildungsroman that tells how the young woman underwent a fundamental change. This model is then contrasted with a series of portraits of politicians, journalists, and diplomats. These are followed by a systematic analysis of the National Socialist regime and its aims, ending in a political manifesto: the call to the Western democracies resolutely to oppose Hitler before he is in a position to implement his dual program: waging a war of aggression and exterminating the Jews. A French edition of the book appeared only a few weeks before the German victory in France; it was entitled *L'ambassade regarde* (*The Embassy Watches*, 1940). The following passage describes the day of the so-called Röhm-putsch. On 30 June 1934, Hitler liquidated internal rivals, most notoriously his old friend and chief of SA (the Nazi Party's paramilitary force), Ernst Röhm (1887–1934).

Saturday, June 30th, was as beautiful and warm a day as we had yet had in Germany. I determined to spend the day on the beach, imitating the German habit of acquiring a sunburn as early as possible in the season. I had a date with a friend of mine, a young secretary in a foreign embassy. In less than a week, I planned to go to Russia and, since I had heard the heat was unbearable, I was getting in training as well.

We took down the top of the Ford roadster and drove to Gross Glienicke, a lovely and fairly private lake near Wannsee. I baked in the sun the whole day, retiring to the shade only for cooling drinks and sandwiches. It was a beautiful serene blue day, the lake shimmering and glittering in front of us, and the sun spreading its fire over us. It was a silent and soft day—we didn't even have the energy or desire to talk politics or discuss the new tension in the atmosphere. At six o'clock we decided we had had enough sun and we drove slowly and quietly back to Berlin, our heads giddy and our bodies burning from the sun.

We passed through lanes of acacia trees, their beautiful white clustered blossoms, like bunches of rich ivory-tinted grapes, falling heavily forward and down, their scent like ripe grapes in the sun-laden air. Then there would be lanes of green coolness as we sped by luxuriant dark trees, then a stretch of sun-warmed sharp pine odour, almost like dry pungent dust in the nostrils.

We were not thinking of yesterday or to-morrow, of the Nazis or of politics. Men and women were speeding by us both ways on bicycles, with small children in little wagons on the side, or in baskets on the front; a swift throb of a motorcycle mounted with strange goggled figures from another world, women carrying flowers, sturdy men walking with knapsacks by their sides. It was a homely, hot, and friendly day—I had my skirts pulled up to the edge of my bathing suit underneath, to get the last touch of the sun and the sudden cooling breezes which came when we had a long road of swiftness before us. I was happy, pleased with my day and my companion, full of sympathy for the earnest, simple kindly German people, so obviously taking a hard-earned walk or rest, enjoying themselves and their countryside so intensely.

It was six o'clock when we drove into Berlin. I pulled down my skirt and sat up straight and proper as befits a diplomat's daughter. The atmosphere had changed, fewer people were on the streets, many of them in curious static groups. Soon we noticed there was an unusual number of police standing around. As we drove nearer and nearer to the heart of the city, we saw heavy army trucks, machine guns, many soldiers, S.S. men, and especially large numbers of the green uniformed Goering police—and no S.A. men. The familiar Brown Shirt was significantly absent. As we came closer to home, we realized something very serious was happening. More truckloads of arms and soldiers on the edges of the streets and in the parks, some streets blocked off, guards and police everywhere. Hardly a person dressed in civilian clothes could be seen as we neared Tiergarten Strasse, and traffic seemed to have stopped. We had a diplomatic number so were allowed free passage. Across from our house entrance was another sinister lining of trucks, soldiers, and the paraphernalia of war. Standarten Strasse, only a few blocks from our entrance, was roped off, and a cordon of police thrown around it. This was the street whose name had been changed to honour the distinguished Roehm, favourite of Hitler.

My companion was alarmed by this time. He let me off at the head of the lane that led to our Embassy and sped away to his own. I flew towards the house in the broiling sun. Breaking suddenly into our darkened house, the cool air striking me in the face, I turned a little dizzy, my eyes blinded for a moment from the lack of light. I stumbled up the first flight of stairs. When I got halfway up I saw the shadowy figure of my brother at the head of the steps. He called out nervously, "Martha, is that you? Where have you been? We were worried about you. Von Schleicher has been shot. We don't know what is happening. There is martial law in Berlin." [...]

My mother came downstairs, and we all sat in the green reception room talking apprehensively, trying to piece out the picture. My brother continued with his story of the events of the day and the night before, which he had heard from newspapermen and some of our young diplomatic friends who had been phoning us frantically all day. My father was in the office preparing telegrams for the State Department. We closed all the doors as we noticed the servants loitering around the hall, softly entering the room on every pretext. They looked white and scared. Of course, we couldn't, and didn't, trust them for an instant.

Roehm had been caught in the night or early Saturday morning, after Hitler and Goebbels had flown from Bonn, Hitler having been with the Krupps a day or two before. Supposedly there was to be an uprising Saturday morning—to be led by Roehm—and Hitler found Roehm suddenly asleep, in bed with one of his young S.A. friends, after a riotous evening! He awakened and arrested him, made him dress and tore the insignia from his uniform and dragged him to prison along with his friends. Some people say he was shot that night in bed, others that he was shot early Saturday morning in prison. But the accepted story is, strangely enough, the one the Nazis themselves have told. Roehm was held in prison for two days and a night and offered but one alternative—suicide—which he resolutely refused. He denied to his last moment that he had been engaged in any treasonable act against his leader and proclaimed his loyalty to Hitler until they shot him.

One of Hitler's charges against him, in fact one of the first charges, was homosexuality. It seemed strange, even to the gullible German people, that

Hitler would suddenly, for this reason, murder an old friend, a comrade of "du" intimacy, whom he had known to be a homosexual ever since they joined forces some ten years before this event. Roehm was accused of corrupting the moral of his army, of living extravagantly and licentiously on the people's money. But Hitler had been aware of this for many years, and furthermore Roehm lived no more extravagantly than his cohorts, Goering and others, and not much more licentiously.

In fact, it was such an open secret that Hitler and Roehm had been the dearest of friends through long years of trials and tribulations, that the rumours, when I first arrived, did not exclude slurs on Hitler's personal morality, though no proof could be presented against him.

By the middle afternoon of the 30th June Roehm was arrested and von Schleicher shot. Berlin was being governed by Goering, while Hitler and his little dark clubfooted friend were cleaning up Bavaria in their inimitable way. It was continually repeated during these days that Goering had planned to liquidate Goebbels as well as less important figures—and that the only reason Goebbels escaped being murdered was his anticipation of Goering's intentions and his consequent absence from Berlin and shadowing of Hitler himself. Goering's police were in charge. A heavy hand, dark with vengeance, was striking here and there, everywhere, sometimes according to plan, sometimes by whim, even carelessly, because a little more blood could not deepen or change the stain already there. Hundreds were killed that week in Berlin, over a thousand in Germany. Would there be disorder, would there be rioting, would there be a revolution, would the German people take this occasion to rise up and overthrow the masters of their misery? Those were the questions foremost in our minds and in the minds of most people.

We sat around whispering over the possibilities. I decided to postpone—perhaps even cancel—my trip to Russia. Telephone calls came in regularly, and Fritz, the short, blond, obsequious, efficient, Slavic-faced butler, was at our heels every time we moved. I think he was afraid to learn what his Fuehrer had done. I am sure he was afraid of the consequences; and the dread of going home alone that night through the Berlin streets was clear on his face.

During the next two days newspapermen called to give us further reports; two friends, each from a foreign democratic Embassy, asked if they could come over Monday night. A Nazi leader was going to speak, was to put the people's minds at rest and explain the lightning-like fury of their dictator. [...]

Our family had a silent meal, interrupted occasionally by indignant outbursts from one or another member of the family—my mother, for

instance, unable to recover from the horror of the von Schleichers' igno-
minious murder. None of us anticipated with any calm the outbreak of a
revolution. Yet this was to be considered—and seriously. The situation was
foreboding. Our only consolation during this day and the uneasy days that
preceded and followed—until it became clear that Hitler had liquidated all
chances of protest or revolt—was that we were together. [...]

We all moved from the green room into the ballroom where we formed
a circle waiting to hear Goebbels. The voice finally broke from the radio
onto our listening ears. As I remember, it was not a long speech but was
delivered with all the mastery of oratory and demagogy Goebbels is noted
for. An incomparable speaker, he manipulates his voice and tones, crescen-
dos and diminuendos, rhythm and timing, as if he were handling a musical
instrument. His voice can be honeyed with softness and persuasion, brittle
with sarcasm, deep with wrath—he hisses like a snake and coos like a dove.

I have heard the Doctor speak on many occasions, and each time the
words are clear and formed, controlled and inhuman. He doesn't get the
fuzzy, furry tones of Hitler and Goering, he never allows his voice to go
into a screaming hysteria or break into the sharp and hideous staccatos
of his Leader. On the other hand, one senses there is not a sincere note in
anything he utters. He is conscious of the mastery of his art; he uses his
brain, he twists his logic, but there is never a sign of a heartbeat, real or af-
fectedly real, in a syllable he emits so cautiously from his thin, cruel, subtle
mind and mouth. To me, Goebbels as a personality is symbolized by his
voice. Inhuman and opportunistic, he is the type of supremely malevolent
hypocrite that National Socialism can produce. He is the most hated man
in Germany. Among his own party groups and among the people, there is
always the fear of his power with Hitler, his mental savagery, his instability,
and of that product of his cunning brain, the Bureau of Propaganda and
Enlightenment.

There were many sarcastic smiles that passed between our family and
our friends that night as we listened to Goebbels trying to explain the swift
and devastating wrath of his master in striking death to the heart of all
opposition. He admitted a small number of dead, viciously attacked habits
of vice and sexual aberration and extravagance, and pretended that Roehm
had planned an insurrection against Hitler, in collaboration with a foreign
power, by implication with Schleicher and others. [...]

Reiner, the adjutant of Roehm, was arrested and held prisoner for many
months. I had been at a party at Roehm's house only a week before the
Purge. Roehm did not appear but Reiner was the host. It was a very lavish
affair in an elaborate home. A bar downstairs supplied all that could be

desired by the jaded palates. Beautiful decorations, a fine dance orchestra, lovely and magnificently gowned women, men from all classes of society—coarse and refined, rich and poor, degenerates and innocents alike. It was one of the strangest parties I had been to in Berlin and one of the motliest. I didn't like, for the most part, the type of women there, and I didn't like the loose, drunken atmosphere. It seemed strained and ugly to me. So I left at about ten-thirty. I heard later that it turned out to be a rather disgusting affair.

This same Reiner, after months in prison, came out pale, with his hair shorn, having missed execution by the skin of his teeth, permanently disgraced in the S.A. And as I have said, unsavoury rumours circulated as to how he bought his freedom.

The slogan of these days, when you met a friend on the street, was, as we learned, by Saturday night, "*Lebst du noch*"—which means, translated freely, "Are you still among the living?" I told Thomsen that this was the rumour going around and he frowned angrily. A true story was of a certain Schmitt who was a marked man, an S.A. fellow, in Munich. The Hitler fanatics went after him and shot him. Later they discovered that they had got the wrong Schmitt, so they summarily returned the ashes to his wife, with an apology presented in person by a Nazi. Many wives and families were notified of the decease of their husbands and fathers in this manner. [...]

My brother's friend had positively hair-raising stories to tell about what was happening at Lichterfelde, a prison in a suburb outside Berlin which had been transformed into a shooting gallery, with human bodies as targets. The S.S. guards were on twenty-four hour duty, indicating that the Nazis thought there would be revolution and that their picked troops had better be on the job.

This one young man was reporting regularly to Lichterfelde. He told us that a court-martial was set up in which a few Nazis, including Goering, were the judges. The charges were made and the sentence passed—without the defendant having a chance to say a word—and the victim led before a firing squad, the whole procedure taking place in a few minutes. Different groups of S.S. men did the shooting—they were told that there was a blank cartridge somewhere among the ten or twelve guns used, and each man could think that his shot was not the one that hit the human target. There was a huge hole dug outside the camp where supposedly the bodies were thrown in. They were to be burned later and returned to their families in packages through the mails, or kept in small boxes to be called for at post offices.

At this time, and also later, we learned that several young foreign office attachés, with S.S. or other affiliations, were forced to be present at the execution, to witness the entire scene—no doubt, the Nazis' conception of self-discipline; the steeling of character put into practice. I know, however, that they were young, sensitive boys whose souls were shocked and sickened by this enforced and unwilled participation in the horrible drama.

An eyewitness of Ernst's murder said that Ernst had died very bravely, without a shadow of fear on his face, proclaiming loudly to the last that he was completely innocent of the charges made against him and that he had always remained loyal to the Leader—his dying words "Long live the Leader. Heil Hitler."

Some of the stories we heard that night were so ghastly and cruel—and incidentally made such good news—that [Victor] Bodker rushed to his office and sent a special story—which, if anyone cares to look it up (Reuter News Service, June 30, and days following, 1934), I can guarantee will make informative and reliable background.

That night was a nerve-racking one for all of us. Walter Duranty [*New York Times* Correspondent in Moscow] was engaged in rapid fire dialogue with Thomsen and my two friends in the foreign embassies. The latter, of course, had to maintain a certain discretion and caution in what they said, but Duranty felt no such restriction. With his stick striking the floor in emphasis, sitting precariously on the edge of the sofa whenever he was excited, he answered Thomsen's pointed and sarcastic questions about Russia and asked equally pointed and sarcastic questions of Thomsen on Germany, and especially on events of the past two days. Elmina [Rangabe, the Greek Minister's daughter], watching the trend of the conversation, heatedly defended Germany and the action of the Nazis. She really hero-worshipped Hitler and told me often that she thought he was one of the greatest men who ever lived.

After the other guests had left, my brother went out with the newspapermen to dig up some more news, and I went to bed.

It was a sleepless night I spent—I suppose, all of us spent. I heard, as I had also on Saturday and Sunday, the faint sound of shooting as a sort of counterpoint to fitful and disturbed dreams. My personal experience of that night did not vary from that of my friends. Many people told me that the shots from Lichterfelde could be heard most of the night, and a friend of mine who lived near this suburb reported that intermittently throughout the night and during that awful week he was awakened by the deadly staccato metal sound.

The Miracle of Life

After he had broken off his study of German language and literature, Max Frisch took up journalism. In 1933, he was working as a reporter in middle, eastern, and southern Europe. In April 1935, he went to Germany to write a three-article piece for the *Neue Zürcher Zeitung* (30 April to 13 June 1935). Frisch apparently traveled from Berlin with his Jewish girlfriend, Käte Rubensohn, with whom he visited the country on different occasions. (He recalls this relationship and their stays in Berlin and Nuremberg in his autobiographical narrative, *Montauk*, published in 1975.) Frisch's first novel, *Jürg Reinhart*, had been published in Germany in 1934, the year before his visit as a reporter. In his account, Frisch takes pains to distinguish German culture—which, as a German-speaking Swiss, he could claim as his own—from German society, which had been infected by Nazism. The precariousness of undertaking such a division is revealed when the author—who began to study architecture in Zürich in the following year (1936)—tries to draw a line between the traditional and the Nazi Germanies with regard to individual buildings, overlooking aesthetic and ideological continuities. Thus in the main railroad station in Stuttgart (completed in 1928), the "best railroad station in Germany," he enthusiastically sees "the most beautiful and the most exalted creativity of our age." While Frisch was staying in Germany, the station's architect, Paul Bonatz (1877–1956), was already acting as a consultant to Fritz Todt (1891–1942) in Hitler's Reichsautobahn project.

I

I have just crossed the frontier, and when one of us, whose homeland is the language itself, steps upon German soil for the first time, he senses a strange tension, right now a kind of anxiety. We cannot, and will not, deny that since the years of our first and great life-shaping impressions, we feel a grateful love for the German land, which has, among other things, given us a Riemenschneider and a Dürer, a Goethe and a Bach, in short, which has become our formative experience. Nor can we forget that the most genuine and prominent Swiss, who did not allow our relationship to German culture to be a subservient one, but molded it into a fruitful give and take, would be forever unthinkable without the spirit of German culture. So, when we cross this national boundary we are already coming from a Germany of the spirit: Will our love now be disappointed when we see the real Germany, or even be misused, misunderstood, and mutilated as a "longing for the Reich," so that our feeling changes to outrage? And if in the here and now we couldn't rediscover the spiritual Germany whose classical language serves as an artistic model for us, would we then have to consider that everything spiritual, everything we have loved, is passé, and renounce the present situation, or can we trust the silent ones who are still in the country, a Carossa, for example, or whatever their names are? That is the question: whom do we finally find the more credible, the popular speaker or the poet, and what is more authentic for us, the screaming crowd or the individual who is, admittedly, powerless but nevertheless makes history, at least the history of ideas? It is not curiosity that prompts us to undertake this journey, we are concerned with a belief, a mental terra firma that we used to take for granted and that has now become questionable, but without which we cannot perhaps thrive, for no serious Swiss German, whether he is a poet or some other sort of artist, may lightly give up his neighboring Germany, lose it spiritually, and terminate our cultural unity. All I mean to say is that for this reason a trip to Germany is perhaps less of a test for the Germans, as all too many arrogant people who set themselves up as examining and punitive angels say it is, but rather a test of our own intellectual attitude, our inner breadth, and confidence that can make us wary of any overestimation of the present.

I am spending my first evening in the Schloßpark in Stuttgart: the innumerable plane trees rise like giants over me, ancient crowns reaching heavenwards, still without leaves, surrounded by spacious lawns on which, in some places, we are surprised to see a crocus in bloom. Rilke said of such individual flowers, which give a shy and childlike impression, that they stood up and said: blue. And in the background we can see the outlines of the handsome old castle that has not yet been rebuilt after the fire that damaged it, now gilded by the evening sun, behind a network of budding branches. There is a dark green pond in front of my bench, in which the swans are swimming and their necks are reflected in the calm water like long, erect white candles. And above it all a slender tower rises and stands there, rusty red, in the stillness of the evening: When the revolution of the Second Empire was taking place, the city cleansing department was housed up there; but it is not a church, the most beautiful and the most exalted creation of our age belongs to the main railroad station, incidentally to the best railroad station in Germany.

Today, in one of the party's bookstores, I saw depicted all the heads whose names I knew from hearsay: Hitler and Frederick the Great, Hindenburg and the sainted Horst Wessel, and lying there among all sorts of books on combat, and narrative works, were three unsheathed daggers. To help render the spirit of these works persuasive? In the morning, I had a conversation with the head of a large German publishing house and learned, among other things, that the sale of German books in Switzerland had fallen sharply, they are up against a dogged mistrust, amounting almost to a boycott, even of purely poetic works, certainly if the author is not already well known and well thought of; the novel that wallows in blood and dirt—especially the creations of those nimble gentlemen who moved their peasant hearts into the right place after the upheaval and cannot now have enough of the stench of manure—are not even bought in Germany any longer. For man does not live by soil alone.

In the afternoon, I looked round this attractive city that, like Zürich, rises up out of its valley on tree-covered hills, and as soon as I noticed that every townhouse here has two or three flagpoles sticking out of it, I was seized with a silly, but powerful, urge to count those long poles; in the first street alone I quickly counted over a hundred and had tired myself out with walking before encountering a single house without that piece of equipment, upon which, upon command, popular enthusiasm can at all times be hoisted. [...]

II

The Miracle of Life: that is the name of the largest exhibition of the year in Berlin, it is undeniably a magnificent achievement. In the vestibule, by way of spectacle, there is a glass human being whose individual organs are shown by a system of internal lighting, a work of leading-edge German technology; the exhibition is also German in its pedagogical attitude, something you come across everywhere in this country. The whole thing is topical because it illustrates one of the main pillars of National Socialist ideas, namely, natural science.

In the first of the main halls, a triumph of decorative art, the whole process of life in the human body is portrayed; in flawless models we see the circulatory system and the workings of the heart, a cube that contains the amount of blood that passes daily through our hearts, and we are constantly astonished at the way the gifted exhibitors manage to render almost unimaginable concepts visible. [...]

The healthy human being is wonderful!—that is what this first hall could be called; but the next rooms already attempt to exploit our enthusiasm, because everything that follows means, more or less: only the Nordic being is healthy and wonderful!

First there is the bell of life that chimes every five minutes, because every five minutes seven Germans die and five are born. Right, two too few. For this reason the room is called "The family as the support of life," and everything now builds up to having children. (A woman had the nerve to write to a magazine: As a woman it enrages me to hear what is said nowadays about the "woman who has not given birth"; according to this, are all females who risk their health and their life to help children, the sick and old people, to appear dishonorable?) And again the bell of life rings out over there: seven dead, five born, again two too few. For this reason the Führer says in large letters: The mother is the most valuable female citizen in my state. And before you find time to size up the state's official blessing on having children and ask yourself a few questions as to how this makes sense in view of unemployment and the problem of People without Space ("Volk ohne Raum") that itself creates a need that can only be filled in an eastward direction, before you can gather your thoughts, you once more hear the children propaganda bell—already six Germans too few!

In the next room into which I escape, I am greeted by well-painted pictures of blond young men with spades, and girls with long hair, pure, brave, and faithful. The slogans on the walls are by different authors, by Schiller and Hitler, Darré and Goethe, by Fichte and by lesser-known gauleiters. The housing developments can honestly and joyfully convince us, especially as we have already seen and admired them; tasteful, and yet extremely inexpensive little houses, which, at a distance from the city, in the green countryside, make it possible to lead a healthy and contented life and which are, as much as we know, very much sought after whereas in the exclusive residential neighborhood of Wannsee, and elsewhere, "For Sale" notices are displayed on every second big house. Side by side with the achievements that are on exhibit here and which we must acclaim—as long as we do not, for our part, approach them with a rigid prejudice—we repeatedly, sad to say, come upon the repellent and basic error of German propaganda:

From time immemorial, German nature has vacillated, both in the individual and in the nation as a whole, between the fear of inferiority and an exaggerated self-assurance; Germany's central position between eastern and western culture—which can be both fertilizing and endangering—may contribute to this. And indeed, it is the fundamental problem that every German person faces: neither to lose himself in submission to what is foreign nor, on the other hand, to ossify within a timorous suit of self-armor, but to find that creative balance between receptivity and self-abandonment, between inner contemplation and egotism that alone made a Goethe possible. The German nation is still a young nation, almost a juvenile one, and is therefore in a ferment and has never seen itself realized unlike France, for example, which is inwardly older; and perhaps this explains why it cannot yet have a balanced serenity and security, any more than a young and developing person can. This overreaching self-esteem is an extreme swing of an inner pendulum; and we know, too, about German self-doubt that can reach the point of self-laceration and knows no equal. In short, we are certainly not looking at the German soul naively, but the self-praise that exalts its own race by throwing all else into the gutter is revolting. What this exhibition has to say about the Jews, whom it mocks as the chosen people, makes it extremely hard for us not to forget the eternal Germany that lies beyond the Third Reich; and we might well wish that today's Reich, after the necessary damming up of the stream, should not continue to carry the question of race to extremes.

A gallery of Asiatic heads of the wildest sort is on display, Polish and Russian Jews selected for their repulsiveness, to the point where one is tempted to think of a counterdisplay of SA faces from which it would be easy to achieve an equally repellent impression. A line of verse by the Jew Harry Chaim—also known as Heinrich Heine—serves as a sarcastic slogan; and this is followed by the dregs of postwar painting, a selection of lubricious pictures that are supposed to stand for non-Aryan art in toto; it is of course essential for the sake of simplicity that Liebermann and others are missing. The essay that follows teaches us about racial styles: a picture was shown to a number of different young people and they were asked to express their feelings about it. The Nordic young man writes a few words, sober and disciplined. The western European lets his extravagant imagination run riot, comes across as ingenious, and lacks the depth of the Nordic youth; in short, it is posing and attitudinizing. The Jew writes the longest contribution: the picture—which shows a church that has been blown to pieces, with a soldier standing before the smoldering ruins—means nothing to him; apparently, the soldier wants to plunder what treasures are left in the church, but is afraid of the heat of the flames; besides this, the writer declares that he is opposed to war, which he regards as sheer nonsense and the nations should come to an understanding; nevertheless he thinks it is better that churches rather than houses should be destroyed, since houses have a material value. So we see: the Jew, without any relationship to what is happening nationally, greedy and cowardly, pacifistic, internationalist, and materialistic. And when, after this, the next section shows logically arranged themes—above all, children of epileptics, drunkards, and syphilitics—the misery appears to stem from a non-Aryan race; even if this relationship is not explicitly stated. So the willing visitor who is strolling through the otherwise well-ordered and sequential exhibition must notice the connection for himself; and when what follows is a presentation of German eugenics, where human beings are bred like racehorses, which has no repellent component, quite the contrary, in fact—thanks to this more than skilful method of Nazi popular enlightenment— after what we have seen before, we have to breathe a sigh of relief and believe it.

The most impressive thing, however, was watching the visitors' faces. They looked blankly at what was presented to them without exchanging a single word with their companions. (The Berliner is otherwise not so given to silence; if you get in the way of a cyclist he immediately shouts, You'd be better off sleeping at home, missy!) Here everything is silence, and then the doctor who is leading the group draws attention to a chart of famous German men who all came from families with large numbers of children— Goethe and Schiller and a few others were forgotten—and pointing to [Carl] Loewe, who was the twelfth child to be born in his family, says: "You see, ladies and gentlemen, we would never have had these geniuses if families in those days had not had a lot of children." And not one of these adults dares to smile. We admire discipline of this sort, which they use to stifle their opinions, or is it that they have nothing more to stifle already?

III

[. . .] I ask a friendly and clever bookseller—with whom I was able to have almost an hour's conversation—among other things, what did the German reading public buy? He answered without hesitation: the silent book. And Wiechert's great success in the previous winter confirms this remarkable, readily understandable, and comforting information; History could provide enough examples of the idyllic writers often being the most admired in wartime. The shrill, aggressive book, on the other hand, does not always owe its sometimes large editions to its popularity with readers; if it is easy for an authoritarian state to secure the desired sale of such books, it is all the more difficult to gain real friends for what is forced upon people. My bookseller, who quickly recognized by my uninhibited question that I was a Swiss, expressed himself as follows: We are experiencing here a quite remarkable difference between what has to be bought and what is read. He then went on to talk of a time when intellect was not exactly at the forefront, and he thought he could discern a deep desire for thoughtfulness— for books, that is, in which you do not simply read again what can already be heard, day in day out, on the street, in the cinema, and at home on the radio, but, even once, the thoughts of a more inclusive, a higher, and a more eternal spirit. He was certainly right in his assertion that today's reader is definitely demanding a lot more of books, which should, in any case, be more than mere pastimes: in the first place, most Germans have little free time to spend privately and as they like; also the energy they devote to reading belongs for the most part to the state, which wants its expensive propaganda to be seen and read and furnishes, as is well known, Strength through Joy [an organization aimed at strengthening community bonds by providing recreational opportunities for German workers], so much so that my friends' maid is in despair because she has no time to darn the stockings; and in the second place, people nowadays can more rarely afford to buy a book. The new Emil Strauß, for example, is doing poorly because it costs nine marks. Empty purse, sick at heart—the latter above all: there is a deep desire for something uplifting that will bring relief and redemption, something that the reader has every right to expect from a writer. *Das Herz ist wach* [*The Heart Is Awake*] was the literary hit of the year, an exchange of love letters, which, in my view, is pallid and utterly worthless, illuminating only because of its success with the reading public: it leads us into the realm of the belletristic, the fanciful, certainly not a relief and, at best, an escape, but apparently there are many who confuse the two. [. . .]

CORRECTION

The scholarly director of the great "Miracle of Life" exhibition in Berlin has kindly drawn my attention to what is certainly not a trivial error of objectivity—which I regret all the more, since any evil intention of presenting a false picture was far from my thoughts—and that I herewith take back. My excuse is that I did not consider it advisable to take notes on the spot and was, therefore, forced to rely on my uncensorable memory. The bell of life that I wrongly characterized as a "children propaganda bell" is, rather, a children triumph bell because it is not true that every five minutes two fewer Germans are born than die, but vice versa; thus what I had spoken of as a goal to be reached had, to a large extent, already been achieved.

Translated by **KENNETH NORTHCOTT**

On the Rhine with Mitzi

In May 1935, Virginia Woolf, her Jewish husband, Leonard Woolf, and their tame marmoset, "Mitzi," took a trip to southern Europe. From Holland, the Woolfs traveled by car right across Germany en route to Austria and Italy. Their stay is recorded in Virginia Woolf's diary. Leonard Woolf (1880–1969) remembers the journey in his memoirs, *Downhill All the Way* (1967). He finds it amusing that the illustrious group of travelers in their motorcar was received by a crowd of cheering people who had actually been waiting for Hermann Göring. It was the marmoset, of all things, that seemed to save the Woolfs from attacks by the "native savages": "no one who had on his shoulder such a 'dear little thing' could be a Jew," Leonard Woolf wrote sarcastically.

Thursday 9 May

Sitting in the sun outside the German Customs. A car with the swastika on the back window has just passed through the barrier into Germany. L. [Leonard Woolf] is in the customs. I am nibbling at *Aaron's Rod* [by D. H. Lawrence, 1922]. Ought I to go in & see what is happening? A fine dry windy morning. The Dutch Customs took 10 seconds. This has taken 10 minutes already. The windows are barred. Here they came out & the grim man laughed at Mitz. But L. said that when a peasant came in & stood with his hat on, the man said This office is like a Church & made him move it. Heil

Hitler said the little thin boy opening his bag, perhaps with an apple in it, at the barrier. We become obsequious—delighted that is when the officers smile at Mitzi—the first stoop in our back.

That a work of art means that one part gets strength from another part.

At Ulken [Unkel]: home reached late after being turned aside to make way for the Minister President. [The Woolfs stayed at the Rheinhotel Schultz at Unkel, having unwittingly driven through a reception organized for Hermann Göring in Bonn.]

By the Rhine, sitting at the window, looking out on the river. The waiter has been talking. He has been in America: democratic; talks as if he were host. Like a little supple monkey. "Let me see now, you like good coffee. What have we nice?" & so on. Also the manager—was in the City Road—wanted to go back & keep a German hostel in Bedford Place. We were chased across the river by Hitler (or Goering) had to pass through ranks of children with red flags. They cheered Mitzi. I raised my hand. People gathering in the sunshine—rather forced like school sports. Banners stretched across the street "The Jew is our enemy" "There is no place for Jews in—." So we whizzed along until we got out of range of the docile hysterical crowd. Our obsequiousness gradually turning to anger. Nerves rather frayed. A sense of stupid mass feeling masked by good temper. So we came here, Unkel, an old country house, with curved bannister, shallow steps, a black grated stair door, & courtyard. A number of little eyes in the roof, rabbits & doves in outhouses. The innkeeper is playing cards with his wife. They all want to go away—back to Islington, back to Washington—Oh so lovely, said the waiter, who wants to go on talking.

Sunday 12 May

Innsbruck

L. says I may now tell the truth, but I have forgotten 2 days of truth, & my pen is weeping ink. Let me see. We went on from the old country house Inn, which ran their charges up high, & drove down the Rhine, & tried to see it as an engaged couple in 1840—no good. An ugly pretentious country—operatic scenery. High, but insignificant hills, bristling with black & green fir trees, with correct towers & ruins—a river that runs with coal barges like Oxford Street; traffic on the cobbled roads: & then a wall had fallen, & we were made to cross over to the right side again. And so to—to where? I begin to forget. The dullest day of them all. But we got to [...] Heidelberg, which is—yes—a very distinguished University town, on the Neckar. The dons & their daughters were having a musical evening.

I saw them tripping out to each others houses with pale blue Beethoven quartets under their arms. Something like the Verralls & the Darwins in old Cambridge—the same dress, & nice intelligent faces. Great rhododendrons blooming. Still hot & blue. And the river like sliding plate glass. And next day to Augsburg—a dull town, but with a bath. A room with a bath. The country steadily improves—becomes shaped & spaced. From Augsburg to Innsbruck where I sit in the empty room—the hotels quite empty, & the town quiet as the grave, & very stately. What did we see today? Great snow hills, with black rifts in them. Torrents. Lakes; one copper green. And it rained for the first time & was cold in the mountains. Fancy living with dirty snow at the door in May! Lovely, but utilitarian, pine woods. Black troops herded together. The Hitler feeling relaxed, though every village had a painted sign "Die Juden sind hier unwunscht" [*sic*]. But this seemed to be put up by authority. Changed into Austria at last; & we are now almost out of earshot.

Harvest Festival, 1935

Konrad Warner was a correspondent for a number of Swiss periodi-
cals and newspapers. His book *Schicksalswende Europas? Ich sprach
mit dem deutschen Volk...* (*Europe's Fatal Turning Point? I Talked with
the German People...* , 1944) is largely a description of his stay in Berlin from the middle of November 1943 until the end of March 1944.
Warner then returned to Switzerland and published his *Tatsachenbericht* (*Factual Report*) in the same year (the introduction is dated "Early
Summer 1944"). In individual episodes, he reports on earlier journeys,
for example, in 1938 in the Nuremberg area. The following passage, in
which Warner recalls an experience in the year 1935, is a look back from
the perspective of the year 1944. (The book, which appeared under a
pseudonym, was subject to Swiss wartime censorship and in the stacks
of the Swiss National Library even today bears the mark "Cens.")

I saw Hitler at the harvest festival 1935 on the Bückeburg near
Hameln, the old Pied Piper city. An immense crowd of people
surged around the side of the hill—at the foot and the top of which
rostrums had been erected—stood, squatted on chairs that they
had brought with them, lay on blankets, just as tightly packed and
uncomfortable as they are today in the bombed-out cities after a
major air raid. Huge flagpoles surrounded the area and the emblems of the Third Reich waved in the October sky.

The crowd waiting for the arrival of Hitler and his retinue was enormously tense and expectant. As—in the distance on the plain down below—the motorcade came closer, the uninterrupted "Heil!" of thousands and thousands of voices rolled like a hurricane from the hillside down towards the man who had managed to cast his spell on the German people.

Then, from the lower rostrum, he made a speech that culminated in the intoxicated enthusiasm of the crowd. Together with his immediate retinue, he walked up the central aisle that had been kept clear for him. But his progress was slow. Peasant women from Bückeburg, from Weserbergland, from Westphalia, clad in their attractive traditional costumes, stood on both sides, and they all thrust themselves forward so as to see him, to give him their hands and to look into his blue eyes. His face was wreathed in smiles, and suddenly he stood in front of me, not a yard away, and looked into my eyes for a few seconds. There is no doubt that he achieved a great effect. The enthusiasm of the thousands with their incessant cries of "Heil" intoxicated everyone and still further increased the effect that this man's personality exerted. He reached out everywhere to touch hands—which people, in their hundreds, were thrusting out at him from all sides—stroke cheeks, and ruffled hair. Close behind him came Göring, with a broad grin, Goebbels, Hess, and the others, all in the best of spirits and greeting people on all sides.

Down below, at the foot of the hill, an artificial village had been built. A small military maneuver was to take place. Infantry were leading the way, supported by tanks. A universal, surprised, and appreciative Aaah! accompanied the breakneck speed of the tanks. Shots rang out, machine-gun fire chattered its way into the peaceful beauty of the autumn Sunday, fires flared up in the dummy houses, tanks drove through them and left nothing standing. The Aaah magnified into loud applause, and suddenly, from behind the wooded hill, war planes appeared flying low over the "captured" village and destroyed what was left of it with bombs and by strafing. The drone of the engines blended with the cheers of the crowd, which had no idea that one day other engines would roar over their heads, and that one day the destruction would not be visited upon sham stage-set houses, but would destroy their own cities.

Translated by **KENNETH NORTHCOTT**

The Dream of Sixty Million People

The francophone Swiss intellectual Denis de Rougemont arrived in Germany in November 1935 to take up a post for a year as lecturer at the Johann Wolfgang Goethe University in Frankfurt am Main. Otto Abetz (1903–58), who was later to become German ambassador to occupied France, had arranged the appointment. De Rougemont had come through a difficult time, which he describes in his *Journal of an Unemployed Intellectual* (1937), and had managed to keep his head above water by doing translations from the German. His *Journal d'Allemagne* (*German Journal*, 1938) contains observations of everyday life in Nazi Germany and reproduces conversations with people who represent differing views of the regime ("A minor industrialist," "A Communist," "An Israelite," "The students," and many others). De Rougemont develops the central insight of his stay—the religious nature of Nazi power—around his experience of one of Hitler's appearances. His best-known work is probably his cultural critique of love and love-death, *L'amour et l'occident* (*Love in the Western World*, 1939).

End of October 1935

Friends were surprised that I accepted the post that I was offered quite by chance, as the result of a meeting in the Deux-Magots one fine evening in July. My response is that the proposition was

not made in ignorance of my beliefs, and that is what ensures my freedom here. My first book says enough about my love of Central Europe;
and my second, enough about my ideas on totalitarian regimes. I do not
know whether they hope to convert me by the offer to let me see one at
closer quarters. If that should be the case, why should I shrink from it?
If they are right, it is important to say so and retract what I said before.
If they are wrong, then I shall know all the better why. In any case, to live
in Hitler's time and not go to see and hear him, when one night on the
train is all that is required, is to deprive oneself of certain rudiments of a
complete understanding of our age. But still it would mean little just to
see *him* through one's own eyes. He has to be seen as though through the
eyes of his people, through the eyes of his followers, and through the eyes
of his victims; as he is built up and as he is suffered . . . So I have accepted
for a year.

    And now here I am after almost a month in this Western city, not far
from the Rhine. An old imperial city, old culture, modern wealth, at a
bad time. I knew it a little, from some brief periods as I passed through
it, and from a two-day stay "before the regime." But I arrived, convinced
that everything that I had loved about this country had changed after
January 1933. Perhaps this idea did throw me off the track during my
first days here. A modern variant of the traveler's classic illusion. You cross
the border of one of these new countries: you imagine that everything,
human beings as well as things, will show us signs of the revolution. In
fact, in that early morning in the train station in Saarbrücken, it was the
purely mechanical "Heil'ler" (*Heil Hitler* already eroded) of the workmen entering the buffet that struck me (scarcely eight months after they
had become Germans of the Third Reich!). Then two or three incidents,
which I will relate, and those briefly seen interiors while I was looking for
an apartment. But in the course of the following weeks, it seemed to me
that the revolution became almost invisible again. In any case, it is a well-
known phenomenon: the first contacts make you aware of the strangeness of a strange land; immediately afterwards, the opposite happens
and you become aware of the resemblances. In this way I rediscovered my
old Germania in the cafés, in the medieval city, in the sweet smell of the
tobacconists, in the sadness of the leaden skies lowering over the grey and
overscrubbed streets.

    Method: *Take care not to attribute to National Socialism all the charac-
teristic traits of present-day German life.* It is the mistake that is constantly
made by reporters who had only a superficial acquaintance, or none at all,
with the old Germany.

5 November

Opening session of our department's winter semester. Dr. N., full professor, receives me in his office before the short ceremony.

"How many students will I have?"

"Probably about forty. Before '33 (*always this threshold!*)—there were nearly three hundred, but that was far too many in view of the number of jobs that were available. Measures have been taken to curb unemployment among intellectuals. There are enrollment quotas now. And, of course, non-Aryans . . ." (making a gesture to show that they were excluded).

We enter the great hall. There are, in fact, at most forty, three or four in brown or black uniforms. The new "lector" is presented, after which Dr. N. gives his short speech, he raises his arm in a timid gesture—"and in honor of our Romance studies, *Sieg Heil!*" A short silence and then he continues—"And also in honor of Germany! . . ." Embarrassment. Everyone has noticed his hesitation.

It is only by very small hints of this sort that I have, up until now, been able to distinguish the true thoughts of the people I am going to be living with. Like all repressed people, they scarcely betray themselves except by some "revealing lapses." Still it would be an exaggeration to deduce from Dr. N.'s hesitation that he is ill disposed towards the regime. Perhaps, quite simply, he has not yet acquired the habit of making the gesture which has, regularly, to mark the end of every official speech.

6 November

At first we used to run to the window every time the street echoed to the sound of singing. It was either a black or brown group marching along three in a row, or else a formation of the *Hitlerjugend* [Hitler Youth], the *Jungvolk* [Youth (boys)] or the *BDM* [League of German Girls]. Plump young girls, or very young boys.

But we were already familiar with the rhythm of the songs—a phrase, then silence for four paces. The processions are as much a part of the German atmosphere as traffic jams are of the Parisian. You simply take no notice any more.

9 November

The city is decked out for the anniversary of the 1923 Munich putsch. Few flags in the wealthier districts, only one or two per villa, but the buildings in the commercial streets and in the working-class districts are red from top to bottom. Only the Palais Rothschild is bare, scandalously bare, behind its immaculate lawn.

At the corner of the Opernplatz, a half-dozen booted S.S. men barred my way, thrusting their collection boxes under my nose. "For the W.H.W." [*Winterhilfswerk*, "winter charity campaign"]. My "No, thank you" left them speechless.

I have heard that this effort is both praised and disparaged. According to some people, the proceeds of the weekly collection are used only to provide the poor with clothes, coal, and bread. According to others, the money extorted from the timid passersby "goes for armaments," which means that no one knows where it goes. Whatever the case may be, I have already noticed that the state retains 7 percent of my salary as a "voluntary contribution" to the W.H.W. I have therefore done my duty, if duty there be. And beyond that, I think it essential that one passerby in a thousand — me, for example — refuses, on principle, to respond to these noisy solicitations. The spectacle of poor people being assailed by these insolent groups, and donating their pfennigs because they are afraid of being blacklisted, engenders a feeling of general shame. Let us at least try to remain honorable. (It is true that my gesture loses much of its impact because I am a foreigner.)

Brick-red colored banners have been suspended over the main roads bearing this slogan, or "Schlagwort" [catchphrase], *The Fight against Hunger and Cold Is Our War.*" Is that a pacifist declaration, or is it only possible to enthuse the Germans by talking of "war", even if it is against the cold?

Last Sunday was the day of the *Eintopfgericht* [the stew]. On that day, every household is restricted to one dish, a concoction of bacon, cabbage, and potatoes, so that the difference between the cost of that and a normal meal can be donated to the W.H.W. In order to set a good example, and as propaganda, the city's notables eat their meal in public, at tables set up in front of the opera house. The whole thing is done without any sense of fun, but with a sense of taking pains. Apprenticeship to the new sense of civic responsibility with a suspicious look at one's neighbor, who is a member of the party. The imposition of middle-class morality on Spartan morals.

End of December

Christmas. Once again the regime fades out of the picture. Every home sees a revival of the old Germany, the land of piety and forests, and once more it is the life of these homes that spreads out into the shopping streets, to the shop windows lit up at midday and smelling of fresh pine trees. "O Heil'ge Nacht!" oh holy night of intimacy, when once again I hear the heartbeat of my "beloved Germania" . . .

2 January 1936

My landlord's son is a thin and pallid person, wounded in the war, who can do no more than take care of the house and the rents. Every time someone goes out, he is in the habit of walking downstairs whistling a martial air, in order to see whether the door has been locked after them. Last evening, he presented me with my bill for December. Besides the expected 70 marks there were an additional 45 marks for gas and electricity for the previous three months. Thinking that he had made a mistake, I called him in this morning.

"There is no mistake," he says, "that is exactly what I have had to pay out for you according to the meter!"

"But the lease said that light and heat were *included?*"

"Maybe, but that's what you've cost me."

"I am sorry, my dear sir, but you should have anticipated this from the outset. I am standing by our agreement." (I have taken up Poincaré's pose.)

"I can no longer rent the apartment to you under those conditions."

"And I can no longer pay for it."

And that's the way these Germans are! In order to make themselves liked, they start off, out of generosity or maladroitness, by making too advantageous an offer without calculating the risks that they are running. When experience shows them that they are losing by it, instead of proposing a new agreement, they lose their heads, try to bluff, and war is declared.

It's the story of the treaty of Versailles *in nuce.*

25 January

Walking along the main streets of the city and looking at the people, I say to myself: basically, there has been no revolution. Everything is almost like it was before, except that people no longer kill *in the streets* (I think this is what the good people call "order"). They have done nothing but reestablish the capitalist situation and delay the inevitable; by that I mean settling accounts with the economic mistakes of the nineteenth century. But we have to recognize that their social revolution has more reality about it than the economic one does. The point is that the former depends, on the whole, on skillful propaganda—it is first of all moral, egalitarian, and corrective;

the latter would require a creative spirit. But, they have more orators than thinkers, more masons than architects.

And yet all that scarcely satisfies me, there must be a key to it somewhere. Something underneath. Something invisible that, as far as they are concerned, tops all else . . .

7 March

As I was crossing the Opernplatz last night, about midnight, the peddlers were touting a special edition of the local party newspaper. "Special meeting of the Reichstag summoned for tomorrow!"

Eleven o'clock in the morning. I hear the radio from the floor above without understanding what is being said. It must be the Führer's speech. No one in the building is answering the bell and all the doors have been double-locked.

One o'clock. The speech has just ended. A song, *Deutschland über alles*. Doors are banged on my floor. Hurried footsteps on the staircase. The landlord's son comes out of the cellar gesticulating, a bottle in his hand, and comes up the stairs two at a time, whistling the *Horst Wessel Lied*. Neighbors are talking animatedly. I catch the word "Frankreich" shouted out on a number of occasions. Flags are already appearing on the balconies. What did *he* say?

Afternoon. Special editions of the newspapers announce the "liberation of the Rhineland." Liberation means rearmament in this country. Here we are, transported back to the days of the Franks and the Visigoths, when a free man's dignity was confirmed by his right to carry a weapon in war and keep it at home in times of peace.

The whole city is beflagged. Brown processions parade, singing. I have not seen the troops; they marched by at dawn in the direction of the Rhine.

"Is it war?" the man at the newsstand asked me. War, good God! Just because you are putting a few soldiers on your borders. The French aren't that crazy.

He seemed completely bewildered.

9 March

French newspapers. "We shall oppose force from the right with the right to use force!" That means: we shall oppose guns with rhetoric. That was a sure thing.

Nevertheless, people here were a bit afraid. A woman telephones me, still anxious. "As soon as the speech was over, I rushed to the window to see whether there weren't some French planes overhead!"

Extraordinary how people in this country are affected by arms, by warlike concerns. I cannot help feeling that the stimulation of these "liberated" populations is vaguely obscene. It occurs to me that "freien" ("liberate") also means "marry." The reoccupation of the Rhineland is a kind of sexual act, just as much as a political one. How else is the bizarre euphoria that is in the air, in the movements of the crowds, in the glances exchanged, and the comments tossed around to be explained?

Enormous red placards are being posted on the billboards: "The Führer speaks!" The day after tomorrow in the Festhalle. Tall white flagstaffs have already been erected in the squares, teams of workers are installing loudspeakers at hundred-meter intervals between the linden trees along the avenues.

Passersby are walking more quickly. The endocrine glands are secreting. It would be interesting to measure the increase in intercourse in a city awaiting its master.

Night of 10–11 March

The S.S. drum, two slow beats then three close together, didn't stop in the whole city all day long yesterday. It's three o'clock in the morning. I was awakened by the drum rolls close by and I can still hear them in the distance. Now it's our turn. The powwow is on. Even sleep itself must be brought into line, and the unconscious subjected to the rhythm of gloom.

11 March

A sacred ceremony.—Three o'clock in the afternoon, in a café near the opera house. I say to my companion, the Swiss-German dramaturge L.:

"Do you believe in the collective soul? Is it not a grandiloquent formula designed to designate the *lack* of a personal soul in individuals who are stirred up by the mechanical movements of a crowd?"

L. both nods and shakes his head:

"Go and listen to the Führer, we'll talk about this again tomorrow. But go at once because the doors open at five o'clock."

"But it's not scheduled till nine, and I have a ticket."

"Come and see!"

The whole of the Opernplatz can be seen from the door of the café. Thousands of S.A. and S.S. men are already lined up, motionless. The

Führer will appear on the balcony at eleven o'clock. From now until then, these men will not stir.

I lose myself in the labyrinth of barriers until I reach the area around the Festhalle—a whole crowd of people have been camping out there since morning—and I cannot get through the doors until ten past five. How can thirty-five thousand people be seated in ten minutes? I slip into the crowded ranks behind the seats. From there, I shall have a good view of the platform erected in the center of the oval like a square tower, draped in red and harshly lit by converging floodlights. Brown uniformed masses rise up in rows as far as the third balcony, their faces indistinct. A tremendous roll on the drums, occasionally interrupted by a fanfare on the fifes. We wait, we squeeze more and more tightly together, formations of the Workers' Front come to occupy the corridors, their shovels shouldered. Notices have announced a general and simultaneous call of the Party in all forty-five halls in the city. Including everyone that the special trains and buses have poured into this city of seven hundred thousand since last evening, not to mention the influx of people who have walked in from the countryside, there will be a million people on hand.

I have come with the idea of also listening to the crowd. I am standing in the midst of working men, young militiamen on fatigue duty, young girls and poorly dressed women: they say almost nothing. They hand each other opera glasses, or a sausage. They ask what time it is. From time to time we hear the sound of the swelling crowd through the open windows, a hundred thousand people press against the walls of the hall.

A few women faint, they are carried out, and this makes a little breathing space. Seven o'clock. No one is getting impatient, *nor do they joke*. Eight o'clock. The dignitaries of the Reich appear, preceded by shouts from outside. Göring, Blomberg, the generals all greeted with joyful shouts of *Heil*. The gauleiter utters a few nasalized commonplaces, barely listened to. I have been standing, squashed and supported by the crowd, for four hours. Is it worth it?

But then a murmur runs through the surging crowd, trumpets can be heard outside, the arc-lights in the hall are turned out as illuminated arrows are lit up on the vaulted ceiling, pointing to a door on the level of the first balcony. A spotlight picks out a small man dressed in brown, bareheaded, smiling ecstatically, standing on the threshold. Forty thousand people, forty thousand arms have been raised in a single movement. The man comes forward very slowly, saluting with a slow gesture, like a bishop, to a deafening thunder of rhythmic *Heils*. (I soon hear nothing but my neighbors' raucous cries against a tempestuous background and muffled blows.) He advances, step by step, receiving tributes along the whole length of the aisle leading to the platform. It takes six minutes, a very long time. No one can notice that I have my hands in my pockets; they are all standing rigidly to attention, motionless and shouting in time, their eyes glued to the illuminated spot, to that face with its ecstatic smile, and tears run down their faces in the darkness.

Then suddenly, everything calms down. (But there is a renewed surge of the crowd outside.) He has raised his arm energetically—his eyes raised heavenwards—and the *Horst Wessel Lied* rises hollowly from the parterre. "*Comrades, shot by reds and reactionaries, are marching, in spirit, with us in our ranks.*"

I have understood.

It is not possible to understand something like this without a special sort of shiver and heartbeat—but the mind still remains lucid. What I now experience is what one has to call the *sacred horror*.

I thought I was going to a mass meeting, some sort of political demonstration. *But it is worship that they are engaged in!* And it is a liturgy that is unfolding, the great sacral ceremony of a religion of which I am not a part and which crushes and repels me with much more force—*even physical force*—than all these horribly tense bodies.

I am alone and they are a community.

13–21 March

After the event, I am astonished at my blindness—like the initiate who remembers his unnecessary fright, his naive questions, while undergoing his first tests—but now everything becomes clear and it all ties in. I was collecting observations of detail and theoretical interpretations, true and believable, one by one, but in their totality they left me in a state of some confusion. Capitalism and socialism, bellicosity and passivity, Spartan spirit and a taste for comfort, cynical youth and old hackneyed reactionaries, uneasy bourgeoisie and involved members of the opposition. And only my Jewish friends interpreted the regime in a way astonishingly similar to the prejudices of the average Frenchman. It was as if they felt nothing of what was living around them, as if they did not sense something strange in the atmosphere that made all the "objective" descriptions of our journalists, seen from here, seem to describe an unreal world where no German could recognize either his hidden pain or his hope. "There must be a key to it," I wrote at that moment. I have found it, the key, but how can I make the French feel what I have felt, what I have *miterlebt* (the word cannot even be translated) at this present time? The epoch's most powerful realities are emotional and religious and yet the only things anyone talks to me about are the economy, political technique, and law. Whenever I try to evoke, no matter how unimpassionedly, the speech that revealed "their" secret to me, I am thought to be pro-Hitler! The fact is that the people of this age don't believe in rational judgment but only in gut reaction. Do not describe to them the massacre of a crowd by machine guns; far from being indignant, they will ask you to repeat it. Thus, in judging me from their standpoint, they do not for one moment imagine that, having experienced so intensely what I have related, I do not enjoy it as much as they do already.

[. . .]I listened to him for an hour and a half, and I saw him, when he had left the crowd of worshipers, standing in his car, which was driving very slowly down a narrow ill-lit street. A single line of S.S. men separated him from the crowd. I was in the front row, two meters away from him. A good marksman could easily have felled him. But on a hundred similar occasions this good marksman never materialized. This is the main thing I know about Hitler. You can reflect on it. Reflect on, or even rave about it.

You do not shoot at a man who is nothing and everything. You do not shoot at a petit bourgeois who is the dream of sixty million people.

21 June, night

Festival of the Summer Solstice.—In the dark night, on uneven ground, we are stumbling along following the silent, hurrying crowds to a square of light surrounded by flags. Three thousand "Youth Leaders" and party bosses are lined up on all four sides, waiting for midnight, when the fire in the center will be lit. The flaming torches held by those in the front row form a flashing and reddish fence above the black or brown shirts and the white blouses. Above this, in the depth of the night, waves a wall of flags, a wall of banners under the light of floodlights, whose beams melt away in the heights.

We are sitting on the grass, beside the standard-bearers of the party's old guard, four shame-faced civilians who only come up to their boots. Behind us there is empty space, across which, from time to time, a car passes.

A harsh, nasal voice speaks from a platform that we cannot see. (I have heard the speech already and give my neighbors Emmanuel Mounier and his wife a digest of it in advance.) It is the classic speech of a *local gauleiter*, an anthology of the Führer's "sayings." But now, a broadcast event is announced.

Spoken chorus: "We were lying in the mud, oppressed and humiliated..." A few mournful and muffled drum beats. "The nation was divided, misled..." We hear the sounds of civil war, shouts, the rattle of machine guns, fragments of disordered choirs filled with hatred. A dreary silence. Then a clearer voice is raised: "But the old Germanic legend tells us that the Liberator will come down from the snowy mountains..." Popular music, followed by fanfares: "The old legend has become reality! *He* has come to awaken his people!" And now the military voices describe the splendors of the new Reich, the recreated community, the factories in full production, the motorized army, liberty reconquered...

This whole drama is visibly inspired by the Protestant liturgy; it copies its overall plan: the Decalogue, confession of sins, promise of grace, creed. But in place of a holy law, the demands of which lead to penitence and humility, we are told of an odious treaty, the genesis of spite, of humiliation. In place of grace, the hero who came "from on high" brings pride to his people. And the articles of the creed are replaced by the very orthodox enumeration of the successes of the regime. In this country, as in Russia, it is the here-on-Earth that is right, that finally shows what it is capable of!

What a sad song the *Horst Wessel Lied* is, when it is not echoing in the streets under the hammering jackboots like a challenge, or like a sacred hymn to the Führer under the vaulted roof of a sonorous hall, but when it rises and is lost in the empty sky of a beautiful summer night! Midnight. The flame shoots out of the enormous pyre, lighting up the motionless red faces. Where is the joy of the Midsummer's Eve bonfire that you leap over, screaming? (This fire is much too big, and in any case no one breaks ranks.)

Later on, the songs of the squads of young girls, leaving with the crowd for the city, will remind us of the happy nostalgia of the Wandervögel of other times. Poor Germany, awkward and rigidified in an arrogance that it has been taught and that it believes manly (like those great boots, which are encumbering if you are not sitting on a horse). It flogs everything that was likable about it with shameful, somber rage. To frighten us? No, to reassure itself by the fear that it instills in itself.

Has Hitler hypnotized his nation, now prey to the nightmare of force, with the cry *Germany awake!*? Or is it that the truth of this nation has become apparent only today and that we were the ones dreaming when we thought it had charms...?

Translated by **KENNETH NORTHCOTT**

A Party for Tom

In the following excerpt from her book on Germany, Martha Dodd reports on her meetings with the U.S. writer Thomas Wolfe in the summers of 1935 and 1936. Wolfe's German publisher, Heinrich Maria Ledig-Rowohlt (1908–92), the son of the founder of the publishing house Ernst Rowohlt (1887–1960), remembers the American woman who became a familiar figure among the foreigners in the social life of Berlin, "seductive as an angel of wrath." In Berlin the diplomat's daughter seemed to have affairs not only with various Nazis, but also with a Russian diplomat who was apparently assigned to her. (In the book he is discreetly referred to as a "young secretary of another embassy.") From Germany, she toured the Soviet Union. The young woman began to be politically active and to pass on information to the Russians. At least, the files of the Soviet secret service show that she continued her private espionage activity (codename: "Lisa" and later also "Juliet 2") for several years, and after the war, she and her husband, Alfred Stern (1897–1986), supported communists in the United States. Dodd and her husband were accused of espionage and were watched by the FBI. Their case was investigated by the House Committee on Un-American Activities, under Joseph McCarthy (1909–57), and brought to court. They moved to Mexico in 1953. When the U.S. authorities sought her extradition, the couple emigrated to Prague in 1957. In 1962 they went to Cuba, but in 1968 returned to Europe and settled in Czechoslovakia, where Dodd died in 1990. The espionage case against her in the United States was dropped in 1979.

Thomas Wolfe came to Germany two years after we arrived. National Socialism had already settled down into its pattern of oppression and exploitation. There were no more illusions about the revolution to come, or about Hitler's promises both to the outside world and to his followers. It was, after two years, a cynical, cruel, ruthless rape of the German people, made fact by regular procedure.

But Wolfe came, strangely enough, with high enthusiasm about Germany—many American writers are naive politically until they have some personal experience with Fascism and oppression. He had studied and loved the great German writers and artists and felt more closely akin to the Germanic spirit than to any other. It took him some time to learn what was happening, as it does most people who have not been passionately interested in the political and economic developments in Europe. What really finished his illusions about Germany were his observation and experience with men and women whose lives and spirit had been crushed by the terror. He came back again the following year, attended the Olympics, and learned his final lesson.

I had a party for Tom almost the day he arrived. Again, we tried to get together some interesting writers and critics. But this time it was hopeless. His German publisher, Rowohlt, came, of course, and a few others; but I filled in with American friends and the Embassy staff, who had heard vaguely that Tom was a distinguished writer and flocked to take a look at a freak. Part of the trouble was that the American Embassy was known to be extremely critical of Nazi Germany and we dreaded to ask intellectuals or free-thinking people, for fear the German officials would take this opportunity to observe them, follow them, or in other ways intimidate them. In fact, in the last year and a half, not more than half a dozen antagonists of the National Socialist regime came to our house. If I wanted to see these friends, I would arrange for it in a way to ensure their safety.

The Germans, even the Nazis, loved Thomas Wolfe. He had long articles written about him, comparing him to a much-loved Bavarian poet of the people. His book *Look Homeward Angel* had been acclaimed by pre-Hitler Germany, and his personality and later works by post-Hitler critics. He wrote several articles about Germany and his impressions, some of which appeared in newspapers and others in magazines. The fanatic Hitler-followers accepted and praised him, the enemies of Hitler were devoted to his personality, respected the power and lyricism of his prose. In fact, there actually seemed to be something Germanic about him which they all could claim. If he were alive now, I doubt if he could return to the country; certainly the official Nazi attitude is one of hostility.

He had written things since then on Germany, after the impact of study and observation had touched his mind and heart, which could never be published there. It would not surprise me if his books, past and future, were confiscated.

In his short month or two there the first time, he became a legend around Berlin. For the first time since Hitler's coming to power, the famous Romanisches Café, formerly the centre of literary lights, artists and intellectuals, took on life. He seemed to give a sort of animation to the streets and café. People began shyly to enter the almost deserted café. Tom, a huge man of six feet six, with the face of a great poet, strode the streets, oblivious of the sensation he created, with his long powerful strides, his head high, his posture free and full of a lumbering rhythm.

To the desolateness of the intellectual life of Germany, Thomas Wolfe was like a symbol of the past when great writers were great men. Something of the angel and the demon in him, as his best friend once told me, he gave back to the intellectual and creative people of Berlin a sense of their past, of the dignity and power and freedom of a mind not under stress. Certainly he was the most vital experience literary Berlin had had in the Hitler years, and, for months after, people would gather to talk of him. But when he had left, the famous café, no longer animated by his booming voice and reckless gestures, with his circle of friends and admirers around him, again was deserted and silent. I have heard that he attracted men to the café who had not been in such public places since Hitler; and that the Secret Police, aware of this, planted spies for weeks after in the café, to try to ferret out some free opinion that might have been less cautiously expressed after the sense of security and oblivion of terror that Wolfe's presence had given them.

Part of Tom's uncritical attitude toward Nazism can be explained by his own state of delirium. He had just published his book, *Of Time and the River*, after five years of writing, during which time most of the critics said he was through, that he had written himself out in his first book and would never be able to repeat his success. He had escaped from America before publication-time and fled to Paris. His book had been an overwhelming success immediately and was on the best-seller list in a few days, with the critics proclaiming him one of the greatest writers of his time. He was in a state of high nervous tension, wherein everything took on the proportions of a gigantic and infinitely beautiful dream. He loved everything and everyone, his high spirits flooded everything he did, thought, saw, or felt. And his moods of despair were equally terrifying in their intensity. He was mad with the music of his own personality and power, almost beside himself, and no one could come near him without feeling the charged atmosphere of his tremendous excitement.

Several of us took a trip with Tom to Weimar, the home of Goethe in his adult and later years, and to the Wartburg. We tried futilely to show him that all was not unconditionally superb in Germany. He was to learn for himself; in the meantime, he was in a ferment, taking all of it in and waiting for the passion of the moment to become quieter.

He was fascinated by the little garden house of Goethe and measured his height against that of the great poet, to find that he, Tom, was taller; and stood almost hypnotized by the famous saddle chair upon which Goethe composed. The little house somehow pleased us all more than the pretentious city house, which we saw later. We walked around the grounds, enjoyed the smooth green lawns and magnificent trees. A storm was rising and we stopped for a moment to listen to the wind in the trees, wild and full, like music from an organ, like a great poem. The sky was darkening and the trees twisting and raging in the weird and beautiful symphony of sound. We thought of Walpurgis Nacht.

We visited the town house where Goethe lived pompously after he had become a citizen of great stature and a public servant. The atmosphere here was stuffy; one felt within the walls of this place that Goethe's soul had atrophied. There was no longer the sympathy for the youthful Goethe, the dreamer, the seeker, the troubled genius, passionate and baffled in his attempt to find meaning in the destiny of the human race. He had become the burgher, self-satisfied, smug, quite conscious of his role in the world and in literature, shutting himself off from people, including the faithful Christiana who could not trespass into his section of the house, and the struggle of the human heart. In the garden were one or two "blut büchen," red beech trees, flaming against the blue sky.

We went finally to his tomb and that of Schiller. There were very few flowers on Goethe's, but Schiller's tomb was heavy and almost concealed with floral tributes from admirers, among whom were National Socialist societies. Outside was another blood beech, with magnificent rich crimson foliage, as if it had sprung, burning, from the heart of the poet.

We drove on through the soft early-summer air and scenery, through luxuriant fields, some covered with the German mustard plant, like a huge golden wave falling and undulating over the earth. At Eisenach we found the spirit of Luther, if not around us at least in ourselves. We took pleasure in refreshing our memory of one of the greatest and simplest of Germans. In an hotel on the top of the mountain, *Die Wartburg*, about which many legends have arisen and which is the scene of the Venusberg drama, we drank cold Moselle wine and then walked around the castle. It was dark outside, but one could distinguish, among the churning, stormy clouds the rugged outline of the mountain. Below were the small, yellow lights of Eisenach. Here the scene was morbid and romantic, with some of the strange barbarism of Wagner, peopled with the dark heroes and legends of the new Nazi religion. Though the scene appealed to me in some ways, I could not help a feeling of revulsion, remembering what a revival of Wagner's grandiose magic and a perversion of heroic Germanic legend had become, in Nazi symbolism and ideology.

Next morning, misty and cold, we visited the castle where Luther had stayed in retirement to write his Bible. The ink-spot on the wall is amusingly preserved, to remind visitors that Luther had a very human reaction to the devil.

On the way back to Berlin we passed again through the Harz mountains, covered with black forests, which inspired the Brothers Grimm and many an ancient German to pass along a lore of beauty and imagination to succeeding generations.

The trip was a joy and a revelation. We were made conscious again of the Germany of the past; great, deep, courageous chapters in the history of literature and progress were unfolded. I think I learned at this time, once and for all, not to confuse the real German character and people with their present oppressors. Hitler will undoubtedly have a role in history, but it will be an unsavoury one, one which the inheritors of the great literary, artistic, philosophic traditions of giant men will detest remembering.

Tom left soon after, with many of his illusions intact, though some were wavering. The following year he returned, a much soberer person, this time eager to learn what lay beneath the surface of Nazi success and effectiveness. He met even more Germans than in the first year, learned what made the wheels go around, in the partisans as well as the non-partisans of the regime. He still drank convivially with Rowohlt during long evenings of violence—since both men were very emotional—and discussion. What he concluded about the effects of National Socialism on human society and freedom, he had already written, and though he carried with him always—as most of us do who know anything about Germany and its people, past and present—the warm affection and reverence they have so marvellously deserved, his feeling for their tragic frustration left him no alternative but to stay away from present-day Germany.

"I Have a Thing to Tell You"

Thomas Wolfe had a special relationship with Germany, which he regarded as his spiritual homeland. He stayed in the country six times—
for two weeks in 1926, two weeks in 1927, three months in 1928, a month
in 1930, two months in 1935, and a month in the summer of 1936 (Au-
gust/September), when the Olympic Games were held in Berlin. Wolfe
deals with his final sojourn in that city, which was also his farewell visit
to Germany, in a chapter of his posthumous work *You Can't Go Home
Again* (1940) that deals with a series of displacements and disillusion-
ments. The material was also condensed into a novella, *I Have a Thing
to Tell You* (1937). In this novella, Wolfe describes his personal goodbye
to Berlin, his departure by train, and his final understanding of what was
happening in Germany, revealed to him by an outrageous and significant episode that took place at the Belgian frontier. (It may not have
been coincidental that, for his literary farewell to Germany, Wolfe chose
the form that had been so brilliantly defined by Goethe, who described
the novella as the treatment of "an unheard-of event that has occurred,"
"eine sich ereignete unerhörte Begebenheit.")

Thomas Wolfe's notebooks contain statements about his fervent
love for Germany ("one of the most beautiful and enchanting countries in the world"), confessions of the fascination that power held for
him ("A dictatorship at full strength has an impressive aura of glittering success"), and evidence of his own anti-Semitism ("I do not like
Jews"). Finally, however, Wolfe decides to do what he can, as a writer,

to combat fascism ("if we are really going to combat the evil of Fascism, we must first begin by understanding its good"), even if he, who was well liked in Germany, should be harmed by it. "I am going to tell you a little story and it is a little story that may hurt me too," Wolfe noted. "I'm taking a chance when I tell it." While *You Can't Go Home Again* has been available in a German translation since the 1950s (*Es führt kein Weg zurück*), and Thomas Wolfe's stories have appeared in a number of collections, the novella of 1937, of all things, remained undiscovered in Germany. Heinrich Maria Ledig-Rowohlt recognized himself as a model for the character of Franz Heilig in the novel (who in the novella is given the name Franz Hartmann). Wolfe had worked up his utterances and linguistic idiosyncrasies "with phonographic accuracy." Rolf Hädrich made a semidocumentary film of this chapter of the novel for German television, *Erinnerungen an einen Sommer in Berlin* (*Memories of a Summer in Berlin*, 1972).

I

At seven o'clock the phone beside my bed rang quietly. I stirred, then roused sharply, from that fitful and uneasy sleep which a man experiences when he has gone to bed late knowing he has got to get up early. It was the porter.

"It is seven o'clock," he said.

I answered: "All right. Thank you. I'm awake."

Then I got up, still fighting dismally with a stale fatigue which begged for sleep and with a gnawing tension of anxiety which called for action. One look about the room assured me. My old leather trunk lay packed and ready on the baggage rest. Now there was very little more to do except to shave and dress and drive to the station. The train was not due until half-past eight, and the station was not three minutes distant. I thrust my feet into my slippers, walked over to the windows, tugged the cord and pulled up the heavy blinds.

It was a gray morning. Below me, save for an occasional taxicab or motor car, the quiet thrum of a bicycle, or some one walking briskly to his work, with a lean, spare clack of early morning, the Kurfürstendamm was bare and silent. In the center of the street, above the tram tracks, the fine trees had already lost their summer freshness—that deep intensity of German green which is the greenest green on earth and which gives to all their foliage a kind of forest darkness, a legendary sense of magic and of time. The leaves looked faded now and dusty. They were already touched here and there by the yellowing tinge of autumn. A tram, cream-yellow, spotless, shining as a perfect toy, slid past, with a kind of hissing sound upon the rails and at the contacts of the trolley. Except for this the tram made no noise. Like everything they made, the tram was perfect in its function.

Even the little cobblestones that paved the tramway were spotless as if each of them had just been gone over thoroughly with a whisk broom, and the strips of grass on either side were as green and velvety as Oxford sward.

On both sides of the street the great restaurants, cafes and terraces of the Kurfürstendamm were also bare and empty. Chairs were racked upon the tables, and everything was clean and still. Three blocks away, at the head of the street, the clock on the Gedächtnis-Kirche struck seven times. I could see the great bleak masses of the church, and in the trees a few birds sang.

Some one knocked upon the door. I turned and crossed and opened it. The waiter stood there with his breakfast tray. He was a boy of fifteen years, a blond-haired solemn child with [a] fresh pink face. He wore a boiled shirt and a waiter's uniform that was spotless-clean, but that, I think, had been sawed off and shortened down a little from the costume of some more mature inhabitant to fit its present owner. He marched in solemnly, stolidly uttering, in a gutteral and toneless voice, his three phrases of English, which were: "Good morning, sir," as I opened the door; "If you bleeze, sir," as he set the tray down upon the table; and "Sank you very much, sir," as he marched out, turned and closed the door behind him.

For six weeks the formula had not varied by an atom, and now as he marched out again I felt a feeling of affection and regret. I told him to wait a moment, got my trousers, took some money and gave it to him. His pink face reddened into happiness. I shook hands with him, and then the boy said: "Sank you very much, sir." And then, very quietly and earnestly: "*Gute Reise.*" He clicked his heels together and bowed formally; and then closed the door. And I stood there for a moment, with that nameless feeling of affection and regret, knowing that I should never see him again.

Then I went back to the table and poured out a cup of the hot rich chocolate, broke a crusty roll, buttered it, spread it with strawberry jam and ate it. The pot was still half full of chocolate, the dish still piled with little scrolls of creamy butter. There was enough of the delicious jam, the crusty rolls and flaky croissants to make a half-dozen breakfasts, but I had eaten all I wanted. I brushed my teeth and shaved myself, put shaving brush and toothbrush, all the other things, together in a little leather case, and put it away in the old trunk. Then I dressed. By seven-twenty I was ready.

Hartmann came in as I was ringing for the porter. He began to laugh as he saw me, closing his eyes, contorting his features and snuffling with laughter through his sourly puckered lips as if he had just eaten a half-ripe persimmon. Then he looked anxiously at me and said: "You are ready, then? You are going?"

I nodded. "Yes. Everything's all ready. How do you feel, Franz?"

He laughed suddenly, took off his spectacles and began to polish them. Without his glasses, his small face had a tired and worn look, and his weak eyes were bloodshot and weary from the night before. "Oh, Gott!" he cried with a kind of gleeful desperation. "I feel perfectly *dret-ful!* I have not efen been to bett! May I tell you something?" he said, and peered at me with the serious intensity with which he always uttered these words, "I feel like hell—I really do."

He spoke good English. He had lived and worked in London for a year or two and since then his knowledge of the language had made his services extremely useful to the exporting firm that employed him. He rarely made an actual mistake in accent or pronunciation, yet one was instantly aware that he was speaking in a foreign tongue. It is not easy to describe—it was, more than anything else, perhaps, a certain intonation of the voice—a voice that spoke familiar words with the latent rhythm of another speech. He spoke without difficulty—there was occasionally a certain awkwardness in tense, an unsure exercise of idiom, a Germanic transposition of the English words—but his speech was always fluent, and his meaning clear. Yet, even when he spoke such simple words as "You are ready, then?" one was aware of a certain carefulness with "then," as of one who had been schooled to say the word correctly. Or again, when he used such phrases as "Now, I may tell you something"—an expression that he used habitually, one felt a sense of strangeness not so much from the way he spoke the words (he spoke them very well, with a slight tendency toward the lisp, almost as if he were saying "thumthing") as from the rather curious use he put them to. Thus, if one asked a casual question—where to buy a shirt, or where to get a bus, or whether there had been a call upon the telephone—Hartmann would turn with an air of almost startled earnestness and say: "Now I may tell you something—someone *did* call, yes."

I looked at him a moment as he put his spectacles back on.

"Then you've had no sleep at all?" I said.

"Oh, yes," he said wearily. "I have slept an hour. I came back home. My girl was asleep—I did not want to wake her up. So I laid down upon the couch. I did not efen take off my clothes. I was afraid I would be coming too late to see you at the station. And that," he said peering at me most earnestly again, "would be *too* dret-ful!"

"Why don't you go back home and sleep today after the train goes? I don't think you'll be able to do much at the office, feeling as you do. Wouldn't it be better if you took the day off and caught up on your sleep?"

"Well, then," said Hartmann abruptly, yet rather indifferently, "I will tell you something. It does not matter. It really does not matter. I will take something—some coffee or something"—he shrugged his shoulders—"it will not be too bad. But, Gott!" again the desperately gleeful laugh, "how I shall sleep tonight! After that I shall try to know my girl again."

"I hope so, Franz. I'm afraid she hasn't seen much of you the last month or so."

"Well, then," said Hartmann, as before, "I will tell you something—it does not matter. It really does not matter. She is a good girl—she knows about these things—you like her, yes?—you think she is nice?"

"Yes, I think she's very nice."

"Well, then," said Hartmann, "I may tell you: she *is* very nice. We get along together very well. I hope they will let me keep her," he said quietly.

"They? Who do you mean by 'they,' Franz?"

"Oh," he said, wearily, "these people—these stupid people—that you know about."

"But, good Lord, Franz! Surely they have not yet forbidden *that*, have they? Why you can step right out on the Kurfürstendamm and get a dozen girls before you've walked a block."

"Oh," said Hartmann, "you mean the little whores. Yes, you may still go to the little whores. That is quite all right. You see, my dear shap"—here Hartmann's small face puckered in a look of impish malice and he began to speak in that tone of exaggerated and mincing refinement that characterized some of his more vicious utterances—"I will now tell you something. Under the Dritte Reich we are all so happy, everything is so fine and healthy that it is perfectly God damn dret-ful," he sneered. "You may go to the little whores in the Kurfürstendamm. But you cannot have a girl. If you have a girl you must marry her and—may I tell you?" he said frankly—"I cannot marry. I do not make enough money. It would be *quite* impossible!" he said decisively. "And may I tell you this?" he continued, pacing nervously up and down the room, taking rapid puffs at his cigarette. "If you have a girl, then you must have two rooms. And that also is quite impossible! I have not efen money enough to afford two rooms."

"You mean, if you are living with a girl you are compelled by law to have two rooms?"

"It is the law, yes," said Hartmann, nodding with the air of finality with which a German states established custom. "You must. If you are living with a girl, she must have a room. Then you can say," he went on seriously "you are not living with each other. You may sleep together every night. But then, you see, you will be good. You will not do some things against the Party. . . . Gott!" he cried, and lifting his impish face, he laughed again. "It is all quite dret-ful."

"But if they find, Franz, that you're living with her in a single room?"

"Well, then," he said quietly, "I may tell you she will have to go." And then, wearily, with the tone of bitter indifference that had become so marked in one short year: "It does not matter. I do not care. I pay no attention to these stupid people. I have my work. I have my girl. If they let me keep them that is all that matters."

But now the porter had come in and was busy adjusting the straps of the leather trunk. I packed my briefcase with the letters, books and manuscript that had accumulated and gave it to the man. He dragged the baggage out into the hall and told us he would wait for us below.

I looked at my watch, found that it still lacked three-quarters of an hour until train time, and then asked Hartmann if we should go immediately to the station or wait at the hotel.

"Well, then," he said, "I may tell you that we can be waiting here. If you wait here another half an hour I should imagine there would still be time."

He offered me a cigarette. I struck a match for him. Then we sat down, myself at the table, Hartmann upon the couch against the wall. And for a moment more we smoked in silence.

"Well, then," said Hartmann, "this time, it really is to be good-bye.... This time you really will be going," he said, peering at me sharply with his earnest, anxious look.

"Yes, Franz. I've got to go this time. I've missed two boats already. I can't miss another one."

We smoked in silence for a moment, and then suddenly, earnestly, as before, "Well, then, may I tell you something? I am sorry."

"And I, too, Franz."

"We will all be terribly missing you," he said.

And again we smoked in troubled silence.

"You will come back, of course," said Hartmann presently. And then, most emphatically, "You must, of course. We like you here"—and in a moment, very simply, quietly, "you know, we do so love you."

I did not say anything, but something tightened in my throat. And he, peering at me anxiously again, continued: "And you like it here? You like us? Yes!" he cried, in answer to his own question. "Of course you do!"

"Of course, Franz."

"Then you must come back," he said quietly. "It would be quite dret-ful if you did not."

I did not speak, but again I noticed, as I had so often done before, the deep and tragic resonance of his quiet voice, a voice touched somehow, for an American, with unfathomed depths of living, with a resignation that had long since passed despair, a fortitude that had gone far past both pride and hope. He looked at me searchingly again, but I said nothing. In a moment Hartmann said: "And I—I too shall hope that we shall meet again."

"I hope so, Franz. I believe we shall, some day." And then, trying to throw off the sadness that had fallen on us, I said strongly: "Of course we shall! I will come back, and we shall sit together talking just the same as we are now."

He did not answer, but for a moment his face was contorted by the look of bitter humor I had seen so often.

"You think so," he said and smiled his wry and bitter smile.

"I'm sure of it!" I said more positively than ever. "We'll sit together drinking, we'll have parties, we'll stay up all night and dance around the trees and go to Aenna Maentz at three o'clock for chicken soup. All of it will be the same."

"Well, then," he said quietly, "I hope that you are right. I am not too sure," said Hartmann, "I may not be here."

"You!" I said, and laughed derisively. "Franz, you know you will be here as long as Karl is here. You couldn't get along without each other. You'll always be together. Besides, the firm has got to have you for the English trade."

"I am not so sure," he said. He was silent a moment longer, puffing at his cigarette, and then he continued, rather hesitantly: "You see—there are these fools—these stupid people!" He ground his cigarette out viciously in the ashtray and, his face contorted in a wry smile of defiant, lacerated pride, he cried angrily: "Myself—I do not care. I do not worry for myself. I have my little life!" cried Hartmann—"my little chob—my little girl—my little room. These people—these fools!" he cried—"I do not notice them. I do not see them! It does not bother me!" he cried. And now indeed his face was bitter as a grotesque mask. "I shall always get along," said Hartmann. "If they run me out—well, then, I may tell you that I do not care! There are other places!" he cried bitterly. "I have lived in England and Vienna. If they take my chob, my girl"—he cried scornfully and waved his hand impatiently—"may I tell you that it does not matter? And if these fools— these stupid people—if they take this little life of mine, I do not think that is so terrible. You think so? Yes?"

"Yes, I think so, Franz. I should not like to die."

"Well, then," said Hartmann quietly, "with you it is a different matter. You are American. With us, it cannot be the same. I have seen men shot, in Munich, in Vienna—I do not think it is too bad"—he turned and looked searchingly at me again, "no, I should imagine it is not too bad," he said.

"Oh, hell, you're talking like an idiot now! No one's going to shoot you. No one's going to take your job or girl away."

Hartmann did not answer for a moment. Presently he said, abruptly: "Now I think that I may tell you something. In the last year here these

fools—these stupid people—have become quite dret-ful. All the Chews
have been taken from their work, they have nothing to do any more. These
people come around—some stupid people in their uniforms," he said contemptuously—"and they say that everyone must be an Aryan man—this
wonderful plue-eyed person eight feet tall who is being Aryan in his family
since 1820. If there is a little Chew back there—then I should imagine it
will be a pity." Hartmann jeered. "This man can no more work—he is no
more in the Cherman spirit. It is all quite stupid." He smoked in silence for
a moment, then continued. "This last year these big fools are coming round
to Karl and me. They demand to know who I am, where I am from—
whether I am porn or not. They say I must be proving to them that I am
an Aryan man. Otherwise I can no longer hold my chob."

"But, my God, Franz!" I cried, and stared at him in stupefaction. "You
don't mean to tell me that—why *you're* not a Jew! *Are* you?"

"Oh, *Gott*, no! Hartmann cried, with a sudden shout of gleeful desperation. "My dear shap, I am so God-damn Cherman it is simply dret-ful."

"Well, then," I demanded, puzzled, "why should they bother you? Why
do they worry about your being Aryan if you're German?"

Hartmann was silent a moment longer before he answered, and the look
of wounded humor in his face had deepened perceptibly before he spoke
again. "My dear Paul," he said, "now I may tell you something. I am completely Cherman, it is true. Only, my poor dear mother—I do love her so,
of course—but, Gott!" He laughed again through a closed mouth, with a
kind of bitter merriment in his face, as if he were laughing with an unripe
persimmon in his mouth. "Gott! She is such a fool. This poor lady," he said,
a trifle contemptuously, "was loving my father very much, so much, in fact,
that she did not go to the trouble to marry him. So these people come and
ask me all these questions and say 'Where is your father?'—and of course
I cannot tell them. Because, alas, my dear old shap, I am this bastard. Gott!"
he cried again, seeing the look of stupefaction on my face, and, with eyes
narrowed into slits, laughed through the corners of his mouth. "It is all so
dret-ful—so stupid—and so horribly funny!" Hartmann cried.

"But Franz! Surely you must know who your father is—you must have
heard his name?"

"My *Gott*, yes!" he cried, and laughed through his closed lips again.
"That is what makes it all so funny."

"You mean you know him, then? He is living?"

"But of course!" said Hartmann. "He is living in Berlin."

"But do you ever see him?"

"But of course!" he said again. "I see him every week. We are *quite* good friends."

"But—then I don't see what the trouble is—unless they can take your job from you because you are a bastard. It's embarrassing, of course, but can't you explain it to them? Won't your father help you out?"

"I am sure he would," said Hartmann, "if I told this thing to him. Only, I cannot tell him. You see," he went on quietly, after a moment's pause, "my father and I are quite good friends. We never speak about this thing together—the way he was knowing my mother. And now, I would not ask him to help me—because it might be seeming I was taking an advantage. It might spoil everything."

"But your father—is he known here? Would these people know his name?"

"Oh, *Gott*, yes!" Hartmann cried out gleefully. "That is what makes it all so horrible—and so dret-fully amusing. They would know his name at once—perhaps they say I am this little Chew and throw me out because I am no Aryan man—and my father," Hartmann choked, bent half over in his bitter merriment—"my father is this big Nazi—this most important person in the Party!"

For a moment I looked at him and could not speak. As he sat there, smiling his embittered and disdainful smile, the whole legend of his life became plain. He had been life's tender child, so sensitive, so affectionate, so amazingly intelligent. He had been the fleeceling lamb thrust out into the cold to bear the blast and to endure the bitter strife of want and loneliness. He had been wounded cruelly. He had been warped and twisted and yet he had maintained a kind of bitter hard integrity.

"I'm so damned sorry, Franz! I never knew of this."

"Well, then," said Hartmann indifferently, "I may tell you that it does not matter. It really does not matter." He snuffled a little through his lips, flicked the ash off his cigarette and shifted his position. "I shall do something about it—I have engaged one of these little men—what do you call them?—lawyers—oh, Gott! but they are dret-ful!" Hartmann shouted gleefully—"to make some lies for me. This little man with his papers—he will feel around until he discovers fathers, mothers, sisters, brothers—everything I need. If he cannot, if they will not believe—well, then," said Hartmann, "I must lose my chob. It does not matter."

"But these fools," he said again with an expression of disgust—"these dret-ful people! Some day, my dear Paul, you must write a bitter book. You must tell all these people just how horrible they are. Myself—I am a

little man. I have no talent. I am only a little clerk. I cannot write a book.
I can do nothing but admire what others do and know if it is good. But
you must tell these dret-ful people what they are. I have a little fantasie,"
he went on with a look of impish glee—"when I feel bad—when I see all
these dret-ful people sitting at the tables putting food into their mouths,
walking up and down in the Kurfürstendamm, then I imagine that I have a
little ma-shine gun. So I take this little ma-shine gun and go up and down
and when I see one of these dret-ful people I take the little ma-shine gun
and I go—ping-ping-ping-ping-ping!" As he uttered these words he took
aim and hooked his finger rapidly, saying "ping-ping-ping" in a rapid, childish key. "Oh, Gott!" he cried esctatically, "I should so enchoy it if I could go
around with this little ma-shine gun and use it on all these stupid fools. But
I cannot. My ma-shine gun is only in imagination. With you it is different.
You have a ma-shine gun you can really use. And you must use it," he said
earnestly. "Some day you must write this bitter book in which you tell these
fools where they belong. Only," and he turned anxiously toward me, "you
must not do it yet. Or if you do, you must not say some things in your next
book that will make these people angry with you here."

"What kind of things do you mean, Franz?"

"These things about"—he lowered his voice and glanced quickly toward
the door—"about politics—about the Party. Things that would bring
them down on you. It would be quite dret-ful if you did."

"Why would it?"

"Because," he said, "you have a name here. I don't mean with these fools,
but with the people left who still read books. If you should spoil it now—if
you should write some things now that they would not like—the Reichs-
schriftenkammer would forbid your books. And that would be a pity. We
do so like you here—I mean the people who do understand. They cannot
believe that they are reading a translation. They say that it must sound as
if it had been written in Cherman in the beginning and—Oh, Gott!" he
shouted gleefully again—"they call you this very great writer."

"That's a good deal more than they do at home, Franz."

"I know. But then, I notice, in America they love everyone a year—and
then they spit upon him. Here, with many people you must have it—this
name of yours," he said earnestly. "And it would be too dret-ful if you spoil
it now. You will not?" he said, and again looked anxiously at me.

I did not answer for a moment, and then I said: "A man must write what
he must write. A man must do what he must do."

"Then you mean if you felt you had to say some things—about
politics—about these stupid fools—about—"

"What about life?" I said. "What about people?"

"You would say it?"

"Yes, I would."

"Efen if it did you harm? Efen if it spoiled you here?" And, peering anxiously at me, he waited for my answer.

"Yes, Franz, even if that happened."

He was silent a moment more and then, with apparent hesitancy, said: "Efen if you write something—if they say to you that you cannot come back?"

I too was silent now. There was much to think of. But at last I said: "Yes, even if they told me that."

He straightened sharply, with a swift intake of anger and impatience. "Then I may tell you something," he said harshly. "You are one big fool." He rose, flung his cigarette away and began to pace nervously up and down the room. "Why should you go and spoil yourself," he cried. "You are at home here. Everybody understands you. And for a little politics"—he said bitterly—"because there are these stupid fools, you would now go and spoil it all."

I made no answer. In a moment, still walking feverishly up and down he said: "Why should you do it? You are no politician. You are no propaganda Party man. You are not one of these Goddamn little New York *Salon-Kommunisten*." He spat the word out viciously, his pale eyes narrowed into slits. "May I now tell you something?" He paused abruptly, looking at me. "I hate these bloody little people—they are everywhere the same. You find them everywhere—in London, Paris and Vienna. They are bad enough in Europe, but in America!" Hartmann shouted, his face lighting up with impish glee—"Oh, *Gott!* If I may tell you, they are simply dret-ful! Where do you get them from? Even the European esthete says, 'My Gott! these bloody men, these awful people, these damned esthetes from the Oo Ess Ah—are dret-ful!'"

"Are you talking now of Communists?"

"Well, now, I may tell you something"—curtly and coldly, with a kind of arrogant dismissal that was becoming more and more characteristic of him—"it does not matter what they call themselves. They are all the same. They are these little *expressionissmus, surrealissmus, kommunissmus* people—but really they are all the same. I am so tired of all these belated little people," he said, and turned away with an expression of weariness and disgust. "It simply does not matter what they say. For they know nothing."

"You think then, Franz, that all of communism is like that—that all communists are just a crowd of parlor fakes?"

"Oh, *die Kommunisten*," said Hartmann wearily. "No, I do not think they are all fakes. And *Kommunissmus!*" he looked at me, shrugged his shoulders with an air of protesting agreement, and said: "Well, then, I think that it is very good. I think that some day we may live like that. Only, I do not think that you and I will see it. It is too great a dream. It is more than to expect. And these things are not for you. You are not one of these little propaganda Party people—you are a writer. It is your duty to look about you and to write about the world and people as you see them. It is not your duty to write propaganda speeches and call them books. You could not do that. It is quite impossible."

"But if by writing about the world and people as you see them you come in conflict with these propaganda Party people—what then?"

"Then," he said roughly, "you will be a great big fool. You can write about the world and people without these Party people coming down on you. You do not need to mention them. And if you do, and do not say nice things, then you cannot come back. And for what? If you were some little propaganda person in New York, you could say these things and then it would not matter. Because they can say anything they like—but they know nothing of us, and it costs them nothing. You have so much to lose. You have a name. The people admire you here!" Anxiously, earnestly, searchingly again, he looked at me and said: "And you? You do so like the people, too?"

"Enormously."

"You must, of course," he quietly replied, then added gently: "They are really a good lot. They are big fools, of course, but they are not too bad."

He was silent a moment, ground out his cigarette in the ashtray and then said, a little sadly, "Well then, you must do what you must do. But you are one big fool. Come on, old shap," he said. He looked at his watch and put his hand upon my arm. "Now it is time to go."

We paused a moment, looking at each other, then we clasped each other by the hand.

"Good-bye, Franz," I said.

"Good-bye, dear Paul," said Hartmann quietly. "We shall miss you very much."

"And I you," I answered.

Then we went out.

II

The hour had come: along the station platform there was a flurry of excitement in the crowd, a light flashed, the porters moved along the quay. I turned and looked up the tracks. The train was sweeping down on us. It bore down swiftly, sweeping in around the edges of the Zoölogic Gardens, the huge snout of the locomotive looming bluntly, the fenders touched with trimmings of bright green. The great machine steamed hotly past and halted. The dull line of the coaches was broken vividly in the middle with the glittering red of the Mitropa dining car.

We swung to action. My porter, heaving up my heavy leather case, clambered quickly up the steps and found a seat for me. There was a blur of voices all around, an excited tumult of farewell. Hartmann shook hands hard and fast, his small and bitter face was contorted as if he were weeping, as indeed he was. With a sudden shock of recognition I saw how close together were his laughter and his grief. I heard his curiously vibrant, deep and tragic voice saying, "Good-bye, good-bye, dear Paul, *auf wiedersehen.*"

Then I climbed up into the train. The guard slammed the door. Even as I made my way down the narrow corridor toward my compartment the train started, was in motion. These forms, these faces and these lives all slid away.

Hartmann kept walking forward, waving his hat, his face still contorted with that strange grimace that was half bitter mirth, half sorrow. Then the train swept out around the curve. And he was lost.

We gathered speed. The streets and buildings of the West slipped past me—those solid ugly streets, those great solid ugly buildings of Victorian German style, that yet, with all the pleasant green of trees, the window-boxes bright with red geraniums, the air of order, substance and comfort, had always been as familiar and as pleasant to me as the quiet streets and houses of a little town. Already we were sweeping through Charlottenburg. We passed the station without halting and on the platforms, with the old and poignant feeling of loss and of regret, I saw the people waiting for the Stadtbahn trains. Upon its elevated track the great train swept on smoothly toward the West, gathering in momentum slowly. We passed the Funkturm. Almost before I knew it we were running through the western outskirts of the city, toward the open country. We passed an aviation field. I saw the hangars and a flock of shining planes. Even as I looked a great silver-bodied plane moved out, taxied along and gathered speed, lifted its tail and, as we vanished, broke slowly from the earth.

And now the city was behind us. Those familiar faces, forms and voices of just six minutes past were now remote from me as dreams, imprisoned there as in another world, a world hived of four million lives, of hope and fear and hatred, anguish and despair, of love, of cruelty and devotion, that was called Berlin.

And now the land was stroking past, the level land of Brandenburg, the lonely flatland of the north that I had always heard to be so ugly and that I had found so strange, so haunting and so beautiful. The dark solitude of the forest was around us now, the loneliness of the *kiefern* trees, tall, slender, towering and straight as sailing masts, bearing upon their tops the burden of their needled and eternal green. Their naked poles shone with that lovely gold-bronze color that is itself like the material distillation of a magic light. And all between was magic too. The forest dusk was gold-brown, also, with this magic light, the earth gold-brown and barren, the trees themselves alone and separate, a pole-like forest filled with haunting light.

And then, the light would open and the wood be gone. And we were sweeping through the level cultivated earth, tilled thriftily to the very edges of the track. And I could see the clusters of farm buildings, the red-tiled roofs, the cross-quarterings of barns and houses. Then we would find the magic of the woods again.

I opened the door of my compartment and went in and took a seat beside the door. On the other side, in a corner by the window, a young man sat and read a book. He was an elegant young man dressed most fashionably. There was a kind of foppish elegance about his costume that one felt somehow was Continental, even though one did not know from what place upon the Continent he came.

What struck me therefore with a sense of shock was the American book he was reading. Even as I pondered on this puzzling combination the door was opened and a woman and a man came in.

They were Germans. The woman was no longer young, but plump, warm, seductive-looking, with hair so blonde it was the color of bleached straw, and eyes as blue as sapphires. She spoke rapidly to the man who accompanied her, then turned to me and asked me if the other places were unoccupied. I replied that I thought so, and looked inquiringly at the young man in the corner. And he too replied, in somewhat broken German, that he believed so. The woman nodded her head in satisfaction, spoke with quick authority to her companion and he went out and presently returned with their baggage—two valises, which he arranged upon the baggage rack above their heads.

He was a tall, blond, fresh-complexioned German, who conveyed indefinably an impression of bewildered innocence. The woman, although most attractive, was obviously much the older of the two. One knew for a certainty she was in her thirties, and she might even already have attained her fortieth year. There were traces of fine wrinkles at the corners of her eyes, a kind of physical maturity and warmth which had in it the wisdom of experience, but from which some of the freshness of youth had gone.

The young fellow obviously was in his early twenties. One felt instantly, without knowing why, that there was no family relation between these two: it was completely evident that the young man could not have been a brother, but it was also evident that they were not man and wife. Again, the woman, with the seductive warmth of her appeal, had an almost shameless physical attraction, a kind of naked allure such as one often sees in people of the theatre—in a chorus girl or in the strip woman of a burlesque show. Beside her assurance, her air of practice and authority, her sharply vivid stamp, the young man was almost countrified. And he certainly did look nervous and uneasy in the art of travel: I noticed that he kept his head down most of the time, and did not speak unless she spoke to him. And when she did, he would flush crimson with embarrassment, two wedge-shaped flags of color deepening in his fresh pink face to beetlike red.

It was hard not to fall back upon an ancient parable—to assume that the boy was the village hayseed in the toils of the city siren, that she had duped him into taking her to Paris, that the fool and his money would soon be parted. And yet, there was certainly nothing repulsive about the blonde-haired woman. She was decidedly a most attractive and engaging creature. She even seemed to be completely unaware of that astonishing quality of sexual magnetism which she undoubtedly did possess, and to express herself sensually and naturally with the innocent warmth of a child.

While I was busy with these speculations the door of the compartment opened again and a stuffy-looking little man with a long nose looked in, peered about truculently and rather suspiciously, and then demanded to know if the remaining seats in the compartment were free. We all told him that we thought so. Upon receiving this information, he too, without another word, disappeared down the corridor, to reappear again with a large valise. I helped him stow it away upon the rack above his head; although I do not think he could have done it for himself, he accepted my service without a word of thanks, hung up his overcoat, fidgeted and worried about, took a newspaper from his pocket, sat down and opened it, banged the compartment door rather viciously, and, after peering around sourly and mistrustfully at the rest of us, rattled his paper and began to read.

While he read his paper I had a chance to observe this sour-looking customer from time to time. In a well known phrase of modern parlance, he was "nothing to write home about." Not that there was anything sinister-looking about the man—decidedly there was not. It was just that he was a drab, stuffy, irascible-looking little fellow of the type that one is always afraid one is going to encounter on a trip but that one hopes fervently he won't meet. He looked like the kind of fellow who would always be banging down the window of the compartment without asking anyone else about it, always fidgeting and fuming about — always, in short, trying by every cranky, crusty and ill tempered means to make his traveling companions as uncomfortable as possible.

Yes, he was certainly a well known type, but aside from these unpleasant aspects he was wholly unremarkable. It was only when he had intruded himself into the intimacy of a long journey and began immediately to buzz and worry around like a troublesome hornet that he became memorable. At this moment, in fact, the elegant young gentleman in the corner by the window almost ran afoul of him. The young fellow took out an expensive-looking cigarette case, and, smiling amiably, asked the lady if she objected to his smoking. She immediately answered, with great friendliness, that she minded not at all. I myself received this welcome information with considerable relief, took a package of cigarettes from my pocket and was on the point of joining my unknown young companion in the luxury of smoke when old Fuss-And-Fidget opposite me rattled his paper viciously, glared sourly at us and then, pointing at a sign upon the wall of the compartment, croaked dismally, "*Nicht Raucher.*"

Well, all of us had known that at the beginning, but we had not known that Fuss-And-Fidget was going to make an issue of it. The young fellow and I glanced at each other with a slightly startled look, grinned a little, caught the lady's eye, which was also twinkling with the comedy of the occasion, and were obediently about to put our cigarettes away unsmoked when Fuss-And-Fidget looked sourly around at us a second time and then said bleakly that as far as he was concerned it was all right. He'd just wanted to point out to us that we were in a nonsmoking compartment. The implication plainly was that from this time on the crime was on our heads, that he had done what he could as a good citizen to warn us, but that if we proceeded with our guilty plot against the laws of the land it was no further concern of his. Being thus reassured, we produced our cigarettes again and lighted up.

Time passed in silence now, and presently I fell into a dozing sleep, from which I would start up from time to time to look about me, then to doze again. Again and again I started up to find old Fuss-And-Fidget's eyes fixed on me in a look of such suspicion and ill tempered sourness that the expression barely escaped malevolence. Moreover, he was so fidgety and nervous that it was almost impossible to sleep longer than for a few minutes at a time. He was always crossing and uncrossing his legs, always rattling his newspaper, always fooling with the handle of the door, half opening the door and banging it to again, as if he were afraid it was not securely closed. He was always jumping up and going out into the corridor, where he would pace up and down, look out the windows at the speeding landscape, and fidget up and down the corridor again, holding his hands behind him, twiddling his fingers nervously as he walked.

Meanwhile, the train was advancing across the country at terrific speed. Forest and land, village and farm, tilled land and pasture rushed past us with the deliberate but devouring movement of the high velocity. We slackened a moment as we crossed the Elbe but there was no halt. Two hours after our departure from Berlin we were sweeping in beneath the arched, enormous roof of the Hannover station. There was a halt of ten or fifteen minutes here. I had fallen into a doze but as the train slackened and began to come into the outskirts of the old city I awoke. But fatigue still held me. I did not get up.

The others in the compartment—everyone except myself and the elegant young gentleman in the corner—got up and went out upon the platform to get as much fresh air and exercise as our short stay allowed. Meanwhile, my companion in the corner had put down his book and, after peering out the window for a moment, turned to me and said in English, marked by a slight accent, "Where are we now?"

I told him we were at Hannover.

He sighed a little and said, "I am tired of traveling. I shall be glad when I get home."

"And where is home for you?"

"New York," he said, and seeing a look of surprise upon my face he added quickly: "Of course I am not American by birth as you can see. But I am a naturalized American and my home is in New York."

I told him that I lived there too, and he asked me if I had been long in Germany.

"No, not recently. I came over about two months ago."

"At first, when you came in this morning, I thought you were German. But then I saw you could not be German from your accent. When I saw you reading The Paris Herald I decided that you were English or American."

"I am American, of course."

"Yes, I can see that now. I," he said, "am Polish by birth. I went to America fifteen years ago to live, but my family still live in Poland."

"And you have been to see them, naturally?"

"Yes. I have two brothers living in the country. I am coming from there now," he said. He was silent for a moment and then added with some emphasis, "But not again. Not for a long time will I visit them. I am sick of Europe," he went on. "I am tired of all this foolish business, these politics, this hate, these armies and this talk of war—the whole damn stuffy atmosphere—here"—he cried indignantly and, thrusting his hand into his breast pocket, he pulled out a paper, "Will you look at this?"

"What is it?"

"A paper—a permit—which allows me to take twenty-three marks out of Germany. Twenty-three marks!" he repeated scornfully, "—as if I want their God-damn money."

"I know. You've got to get a paper every time you turn around. Look here!" I cried, and reaching in my own breast pocket I pulled out a mass of papers big enough to choke a horse. "I got all of these in two months' time."

The ice was broken now. Upon a mutual grievance we began to warm up to each other. It quickly became evident that my new acquaintance, with the patriotic fervor of his race, was almost passionately American.

"Oh," he said, "it will be good after all this to be back there where all is Peace—where all is Friendship—where all is Love."

I had myself some reservations on this score, but I did not utter them. His fervor was so genuine and warm that it would have been unkind to try to qualify it. And besides, I too was homesick now and his words, generous and wholehearted as they were, warmed me with their pleasant glow.

For I, as he, was weary and oppressed, exhausted with these pressures, worn out with these tensions of the nerves and spirit, sickened by the cancer of these cureless hates which had not only poisoned the life of nations but had eaten in one way or another into the lives of all my frends, of almost everyone that I had known here. And so, like my new-found fellow countryman, I too felt, beneath the extravagance and intemperance of his language, a certain justice in comparison. And I felt further that it would be very good to be back home again, out of the poisonous constrictions of this atmosphere, where, whatever we might lack, we still had air to breathe in, winds to clear that air.

My new friend now told me that he was a member of a brokerage concern in Wall Street. This seemed to call for some similar identification on my part and I gave him the most truthful answer I could make, which was that I worked for a publishing house. He remarked then that he knew the family of a New York publisher. And when I asked him who these people were he answered, "The Edwards family."

I said: "I know the Edwardses. They are friends of mine and Mr. Edwards is my publisher. And you," I said, "your name is Johnnie, isn't it? I have forgotten your last name, but I have heard it—"

He nodded quickly, smiling. "Yes, Johnnie Stefanowski," he said. "And you?—what is your name?"

I told him.

He said, "Of course. I know of you."

And instantly we were shaking hands, with that kind of stunned but exuberant surprise which reduces people to the banal conclusion that "it's a small world after all."

And now indeed we had established contact at a thousand points and found we knew in common scores of people. We discussed them enthusiastically, almost joyfully. By the time the other people returned to the compartment and the train began to move again we were engaged in rapid conversation.

Our three companions looked somewhat startled to hear this rapid-fire of conversation, this evidence of acquaintanceship between two people who had apparently been strangers just ten minutes since. Our little blonde lady smiled at us and took her seat; the young man also. Old Fuss-And-Fidget, all ears now, glancing quickly, sharply, from one to the other of us, listened attentively to all we said.

The cross-fire of our talk went back and forth, from my corner of the compartment to my friend's. I felt myself a sense of embarrassment at the sudden intrusion of this intimacy in a foreign language among fellow travelers, with whom we had heretofore maintained a restrained formality. But Johnnie Stefanowski evidently was troubled not at all and smiled in a friendly fashion at our companions as if they too were parties to our conversation and could understand every word we said.

Under this engaging influence, everyone began to thaw out visibly. The little blonde lady now began to talk in an animated way to her young companion. In a few moments Fuss-And-Fidget chimed in too. In a very short time the whole compartment was humming with this rapid interplay of English and of German.

Johnnie Stefanowski now proposed that we seek out the *Speisewagen* and procure refreshment. "I am not hungry," he said indifferently. "In Poland I have had to eat too much. I am sick of food—but would you like some Polish fruits?" he said, indicating a large paper-covered package at his side. "I believe they have prepared some things for me—some fruits from my brother's estate, some chickens and some partridges. I have no appetite myself, but wouldn't you take something?"

I told him that I was not hungry yet.

He suggested thereupon that we get a drink. "I still have these marks," he said, "seventeen or eighteen of them. I no longer have any need of them. But now that I have met you I think it would be nice if we could spend them. Shall we go and see what we can find?"

To this I agreed. We arose, excused ourselves to our companions and as Stefanowski left his seat, old Fuss-And-Fidget asked him if he was willing to change seats. Indifferently the young man answered, "Yes, take my seat, of course. It does not matter to me where I sit."

We went out into the narrow corridor and, moving forward through several coaches of the hurtling train, we finally reached the *Speisewagen*, skirted the hot breath of the kitchens and seated ourselves at one of the tables in one of the beautiful, bright clean coaches of the Mitropa service. Stefanowski seemed to have a Polish gentleman's liberal capacity for drink. He tossed his brandy off at a single gulp, remarking rather plaintively: "It is very small. But it is good and does no harm. We shall have more."

Pleasantly warmed by brandy, and talking together with the ease of people who had known each other for many years, we now began to discuss our companions in our own compartment.

"The little woman—she is rather nice," said Stefanowski—"I think she is not very young, and yet, she is quite charming, isn't she? A personality."

"And the young man with her?" I inquired. "You do not think he is her husband?"

"No, of course not," replied my companion instantly. "It is most curious," he went on in a puzzled tone, "he is much younger, obviously, and not the same—he is much simpler than the lady."

"Yes. It's almost as if he were some young fellow from the country, and she—"

"Is like someone in the theatre," Stefanowski nodded. "An actress. Or perhaps some music-hall performer."

"And the other man?" I said. "The little one? The fidgety little fellow who keeps staring at us. Who is he?"

"Oh, that one," said my friend impatiently. "I do not know. I do not care. He is some stuffy little man—you always meet them on a trip—it does not matter. But shall we go back now?" he said, "and talk to them? We shall never see them after this: and it would be interesting to find out who they are."

I agreed. Accordingly, my Polish friend now called the waiter, got our bill and paid it—and still had ten or twelve marks left from what remained of the waning twenty-three. Then we got up and went back through the speeding train to our compartment.

The lady smiled at us as we came in. And our three fellow passengers all regarded us with a kind of sharpened curiosity. It was evident that during our absence we had been the subject of their speculation. Stefanowski smiled and spoke to them at once. His German was somewhat broken but coherent, and he was a man of such natural warmth and social assurance that his deficiencies did not bother him at all. Our companions responded quickly, even eagerly, to our greeting, and immediately gave free expression to their curiosity, to the speculations which our meeting, our apparent recognition of each other, had aroused.

The lady asked Stefanowski where he came from—*"Was sind sie für ein Landsmann?"* And he replied that he was an American.

"Ach so?"—for a moment she looked surprised, then added quickly, "but not by birth?"

"No," said Stefanowski, "I am Polish by birth. But I live in New York now. And my friend here"—he indicated me, and they all turned to stare curiously at me—"is an American by birth."

They nodded in satisfaction and, smiling with eager curiosity, the lady said—"And your friend here—he is an artist, isn't he?"

Stefanowski said I was.

"A painter?"—the lady almost gleefully pursued the confirmation of her own predictions.

"He is not a painter. He is a writer." My young Polish friend said *"Dichter,"* which means poet, which I amended quickly to *"ein schriftsteller."*

All three of them thereupon looked at one another with nods of satisfaction, saying ah, they thought so, it was evident, etc. Old Fuss-And-Fidget even now chimed in with a sage observation that it was apparent "from the head." The others nodded in agreement, and the lady, now turning again to Stefanowski, said, "But you—you are not an artist, are you? You do something else?"

He replied that he was a business man—a *"Geschäftsmann"*—that his business was in Wall Street, a name which apparently had imposing connotations for them, for they all nodded in an impressed manner and said "ah" again.

We went on then and told them how we had never seen each other before that morning, but how each of us had known of the other through many mutual friends whom we had known for years. This news delighted everyone. Our little blonde lady nodded triumphantly, burst out in excited conversation with her companion and with Fuss-And-Fidget, the effect of which was, "What did I tell you? I said the same thing, didn't I? It's a small world after all, isn't it?" etc.

Now we were all really wonderfully at ease with one another, all talking eagerly and naturally, as if we had known one another for years. The little lady began to tell us all about herself. She and her husband were, she said, proprietors of a business near the Alexanderplatz. No—smiling—the young man was not her husband. He was a young artist and employed by her. In what sort of business? She laughed—one would never guess. She and her husband manufactured mannikins for window-shop display. Their business, I inferred, was quite a large one. She told us that they employed over fifty workers, and occasionally they had had almost a hundred. For this reason, she had to go to Paris once or twice a year. For, she explained, Paris set the fashion in these figures as it did in clothes.

Of course, they did not buy the Paris models. *Mein Gott!* that was impossible with the present money situation as it was. Nevertheless, hard as it was, she had to get to Paris somehow once or twice a year, just in order to keep up with "what was going on." She took this young man with her on these trips. He made designs, drew models of the late show-window modes in Paris, and duplicated them for her when he returned.

Stefanowski now remarked that he did not see how it was even possible, under present circumstances, for a German citizen to travel anywhere. It had become difficult enough for a foreigner now to travel in and out of Germany. The money complications were so confusing and so wearisome. I added to this an account of my own experiences of the summer in my brief travels—the difficulties that had attended even a short journey to the Austrian Tirol. Ruefully I displayed the pocket full of papers, permits, visas and official stamps I had accumulated in two months. Upon this common ground we all again were vociferously agreed. The lady affirmed that it was stupid, exhausting and, for a German with business out of his own country, almost impossible. She added quickly, loyally, that of course it was also necessary, but then began to give an account of her own difficulties, which went swiftly into a bewildering maze of checks and balances, and which finally ended by her waving her hand charmingly, saying, "*Ach Gott!* it is all too complicated, too confusing, to explain."

Old Fuss-And-Fidget put in here, with confirmations of his own. He was, he said, an attorney in Berlin—a "*Rechtsanwalt*"—who had formerly had extensive professional connections in France and in other portions of the Continent. He had visited America as well, he added. He had been there, in fact, as recently as 1930, when he had attended an international congress of lawyers in New York. He even spoke a little English, which he now unveiled for us, and he was going now, he told us, to another international congress of lawyers which was to open in Paris within the next day or so and which would last a week. But it was hard for a German to make a trip even of this short duration. And as for his former professional activities in other countries, they were now, alas, impossible.

He asked me if any of my books had been translated and published in Germany and I told him they had. They were all warmly curious, wanted to know the title and my name. Accordingly, I wrote out for them the German titles of the books, the name of the German publisher, my own name. The little lady put the paper away in her pocketbook and announced enthusiastically that she would buy the books on her return to Germany. And Fuss-And-Fidget, after carefully reading the paper, folded it and put it away in his wallet, remarking that he too would buy the books when he returned.

Stefanowski now picked up his bulky paper package, opened it and demanded that everyone partake. There were some splendid pears and peaches, a plump broiled chicken, some fat squabs and various other delicacies. Our companions protested that they could not deprive him of his lunch, but the young man insisted with a vigorous warmth that was obviously a characteristic of his goodhearted nature that he and I were going to the dining car for luncheon anyway, and that if they did not eat the contents of the package it would go to waste. Whereupon, they all helped themselves to fruit, which they pronounced delicious, and the lady promised she would later on investigate the chicken. Upon these assurances, with friendly greetings all around, my Polish friend and I departed for a second time.

III

It is astonishing how short a time it takes to get acquainted on a journey. As we made our way a second time along the corridors of the speeding train I reflected that already Stefanowski and I were as accustomed to each other as if we had been friends for many years. As to the new-found friends in our compartment, we were delighted with them all. In the most extraordinary way, and in the space of fifteen minutes' time, we seemed to have entered into the lives of all these people and they in ours. Now we were not only immensely interested in the information they had given us about themselves: we were as warmly, eagerly concerned with the problems that confronted them as if their troubles were our own.

During a long and sumptuous meal—a meal that began with brandy, proceeded over a fine bottle of Bernkasteler and wound up over coffee and more brandy and a good cigar, a meal on which we were both exuberantly determined to spend the remainder of our German money, we discussed our companions again. The little woman, we agreed, was charming. And the young man, although diffident and shy, was very nice. We even had a word of praise for Fuss-And-Fidget now. After we had cracked his crusty shell the old codger was not bad. He really was quite friendly underneath.

"And it does show," said Stefanowski quietly, "how good people really are, how easy it is to get along with one another in this world, how people really like each other—if only—"

"—if only—" I said, and nodded.

"These damned politicians," Stefanowski said.

At length we called for our bill and paid it. Stefanowski dumped his marks upon the table, counted them: "You'll have to help me out," he said. "How many have you got?"

I dumped mine out. We had enough to pay the bill, to give the waiter something extra. And there was enough left over for a double jolt of brandy and a good cigar.

So, grinning with satisfaction, in which our waiter joined amiably as he read our purpose, we paid the bill, ordered the brandy and cigars, and, full of food, of drink, and of the pleasant knowledge of a job well done, we puffed contentedly on our cigars.

We were now running through the great industrial region of western Germany. The pleasant landscape had been darkened by the grime and smoke of enormous works. Now it was grim with the skeletons of enormous smelting and refining plants, disfigured with great heaps of slag, with mountainous dumps. It was a new portion of the land, one of the few I had not seen before. It was brutal, smoky, dense with life, the grimy warrens of industrial towns. But it had the brutal fascination of these places too, the thrilling power of raw, enormous works.

Stefanowski informed me that we were already almost at the border and that, since our own coach went directly through to Paris, we should have no additional need of money for porter's fees.

This made us remember the difficulties of our fellow travelers, who were Germans. We agreed that the existing law which permitted native citizens to take only ten marks from the country was, for people in the business circumstances of our little blonde companion and old Fuss-And-Fidget, a very trying one.

At this moment Stefanowski had a brilliant inspiration, the result of his own generous impulse. "But why," he said, "why can't we help them?"

"How? In what way can we help them?"

"Why," he said, "I have here a permit that allows me to take twenty-three marks out of the country. You have no permit, but everyone is allowed—"

"To take ten marks," I said and nodded. "So you mean then," I concluded, "that since each of us has spent his German money—"

"But can still take as much as is allowed out of the country—yes," he said. "So we could suggest it to them—" he went on.

"—that they give us some of their marks to keep, you mean?"

He nodded. "Yes. It is not much, of course. But it might help."

No sooner said than seized upon. We were almost jubilantly elated at this opportunity of doing some slight service for these people to whom we had taken such a liking. At this moment, even while we were smiling confirmation at each other, a man in uniform came through the car, paused at our table—which was the only one that was now occupied—and quietly but authoritatively informed us that the Pass-Control had come upon the train and that we must return at once to our compartment to await examination. We rose, knowing now we had no time to lose, hastened back along the coaches of the swaying train, entered our compartment again and immediately told our fellows that the inspection would soon begin and that the officials were on the train.

There was a flurry of excitement. Everyone began to get ready. The blonde lady took out her purse and passport and with a worried look began to count her money. Stefanowski watched her quietly for a moment and then, taking out his own certificate and showing it, remarked that he was officially allowed possession of the sum of twenty-three marks, that he had had the sum in his possession, but now had spent it. I took this as my cue and remarked that I too had spent the ten marks that the law allowed me.

Our little blonde companion looked eagerly at both of us and read the friendship of our meaning.

"Then you mean?" she said, and gleefully—"but it would be wonderful, of course, if you would!"

"Have you as much as twenty-three marks?" said Stefanowski.

"Yes," she nodded quickly, with a worried look, "I have more than that. But if you would take the twenty-three and keep them until we are past the frontier—"

He stretched out his hand. "Give them to me," he said quietly. The transfer was completed, the money in his pocket, in the wink of an eye.

In another moment Fuss-And-Fidget had taken ten marks from his pocket and without a word passed them across to me. I thrust the money in my pocket, and we all sat back, a little flushed, excited but triumphant, trying to look composed.

A few minutes later an official opened the compartment door, saluted and asked for our passports. He inspected Stefanowski's first, found everything in order, took his certificate, saw his twenty-three marks, stamped the passport and returned it to him.

Then he turned to me. I gave him my passport and the various papers certifying my possession of American currency. He thumbed through the pages of the passport, which were now almost completely covered with stamps and entries, and finally smiled quite kindly, and returned my passport to me. Then he inspected the passports of the little blonde lady, her companion and Fuss-And-Fidget. Everything, apparently, was in order, save that the lady had confessed to the possession of more than twenty marks, and the official regretfully informed her that he must take from her anything in excess of ten. It would be held at the frontier and restored to her, of course, when she returned. She smiled ruefully, shrugged her shoulders, and gave the man twelve marks. All other matters were evidently now in order, for the man saluted and withdrew.

So it was over then! We all drew a deep breath of relief, and commiserated our charming lady friend upon her loss. But I think we were all quietly jubilant, too, to know her loss had been no greater, that we had been able in some degree to lessen it. I asked Fuss-And-Fidget if I should return his money now or later on. He told me to wait until we had crossed the frontier into Belgium. At the same time, he made some casual explanation, to which none of us paid any serious attention at the time, to the effect that his ticket was good only to the frontier, and that he would utilize the fifteen minutes of our wait at Aachen, the frontier town, to buy a ticket for the remainder of the trip to Paris.

We were now, in fact, approaching Aachen. The train was slackening speed. We were going through a pleasant countryside, a smiling landscape of green fields and gentle hills, unobtrusively, mildly, somehow unmistakably European. The seared and blasted districts of the mines and factories were behind us. We were entering the outskirts of a pleasant town.

This was Aachen. In another moment the train was slowing to a halt before the station. We had reached the frontier. There was to be a wait of fifteen minutes and a change of engines. All of us got out—Fuss-And-Fidget to get a ticket, the others to stretch their legs and get a breath of air.

My Polish friend and I got out and walked forward along the platform to inspect the locomotive. The German locomotive which would here be supplanted by its Belgian successor was a magnificent machine, almost as big as one of the great American engines. The evidence of high velocity was legible in every line of it. What was most remarkable was the tender, a wonderful affair, the whole of which seemed to be a honeycomb of jetting pipes. One looked in through some slanting bars and saw a fountain-like display, composed of thousands of tiny little jets of steaming water. It was a marvelous machine, which bore in every line the evidence of the tremendous engineering talent that had created it.

Knowing how vivid, swift and fugitive are those poignant first impressions that come at the moment when we change from one country to another, I waited with an almost feverish interest for the approach of the Belgian locomotive. I knew in advance it would not be so good as the German one because the energy, the intelligence, the strength and the integrity which produced it were inferior, but I was eagerly sensitized to observe the exact degree and quality of these differences between the powerful, solid and indomitable race that I was leaving and the little people I would now encounter.

Presently we walked back along the platform, found our little blonde-haired lady and, flanking her on either side, began to stroll up and down beside the train. At length, observing the station clock and seeing that the moment scheduled for departure had already come, we moved quickly back towards our own coach and our own compartment.

As we approached it was evident that something had happened. There were no signs of departure. The conductor and the station guard stood together on the platform. No warning signal had been given. And, moreover, there was now evident a kind of subdued tension, a sense of crisis that made my pulse beat quicker as I approached.

I have often observed this phenomenon in life, its manifestations under certain conditions are nearly always identical. A man has leaped or fallen, for example, from a high building to the pavement of a city street. Or a man has been shot, or beaten. He has been struck by a motor car; or again, a man is dying quietly on the street before the eyes of other men. But always, the manifestation of the crowd is just the same. Even before you see the faces of the people, when you see their backs, their posture, the position of the head and shoulders, you know what has happened.

You do not know, of course, the precise circumstance, but what you sense immediately is the final stage of tragedy. You know that someone has just died or is dying, and in the terrible eloquence of backs and shoulders, the *feeding* silence of the watching men, you sense a tragedy that is even deeper. It is the tragedy of man's cruelty and his lust for pain, the tragic weakness that corrupts him, that he loathes but that he cannot cure.

And always, the manifestation of this tragedy is just the same. Even before one arrives one knows from this silent eloquence of shoulders, backs and heads that something ruinous and horrible has happened. I knew the signs too well. And now, as I hastened along beside the train and saw the people gathered in the corridor in that same feeding posture, waiting, watching, in that deadly fascinated silence, I was sure that once again in life I was about to witness death.

That was the first thing that came to me—and I believe to all of us—that someone had died. And what stunned us, what stopped us short, appalled, was that death had come to our compartment. The shades were tightly drawn, the door closed, the whole place sealed impenetrably. We had started to get on the train when this thing burst upon us. And now we saw our lady's young companion standing at the window in the corridor. He motioned quickly to us, a gesture warning us to remain where we were. And as he did it flashed over all of us that the subject of this tragic visitation was the nervous little man who had been the companion of our voyage since morning.

The stillness of the scene, the shuttered blankness of that closed compartment, were horrible. Even as we stared, appalled and horror-stricken, at that fatal curtained closet, which had so short a time ago housed the lives of all of us, and which had now become the tenement of death, the curtained door of the compartment was opened and closed quickly, and a man came out.

He was an official, a burly-looking fellow, with a visored cap, a jacket of olive green. He was a man of forty-five or more, a Germanic type with high blunt cheekbones, a florid face and tawny mustaches, combed out sprouting, in the Kaiser Wilhelm way. His head was shaven, and there were thick creases at the base of the skull and across his fleshy neck. He came out, climbed down clumsily to the platform, signaled excitedly to another officer and climbed back into the train again.

It was a familiar type, one that I had seen and smiled at often, but one that now became, under these ominous circumstances, sinisterly unpleasant. Even the man's physical weight and clumsiness, the awkward way he got down from the train, the awkward way he climbed up again, the thickness of his waist, the unpleasant width and coarseness of his clumsy buttocks, the way his sprouting mustaches seemed to quiver with passion and authority, the sound of his guttural voice, raised coarsely, somewhat phlegmily, as he shouted to his fellow officer, the sense that he was fairly panting with an inflamed authority—all these symptoms had now become, under the ominous prescience of the moment, loathsome, sinister, repellent.

All of a sudden, without knowing why, I felt myself trembling with a murderous and incomprehensible anger. I wanted to smash that fat neck with the creases in it. I wanted to pound that inflamed and blunted face into a jelly. I wanted to kick square and hard, bury my foot, dead center in the obscene fleshiness of those clumsy buttocks. And I knew that I was helpless, that all of us were. Like all Americans, I had never liked the police or the kind of personal authority that it sanctifies. But this feeling, this intensity, with its murderously helpless rage, was different. I felt impotent, shackled, unable to stir against the walls of an obscene but unshakable authority.

The official with the sprouting mustaches, accompanied now by his colleagues, opened the curtained doors of the compartment again, and now I saw that they were not alone. Two other officials were in the compartment and our nervous little companion—no, he was not dead!—he sat there *huddled*, facing them. He sat looking up at them as they bent over him. His face was white and pasty. It looked greasy, as if it were covered with a salve of cold fat sweat. Under his long nose his mouth was trembling in a horrible attempt at a smile. In the very posture of the men as they bent over him there was something revolting and unclean.

But the official with the thick creased neck had now filled the door and blotted out the picture. He went in followed by a smaller colleague, the door was closed again behind him, and again there was that vicious and ill omened secrecy.

All of this had happened in a moment while we had looked on with stupefied surprise. Now the people gathered in the corridor began to whisper to one another. In a moment our little blonde lady went over, whispered to the young man at the window and then came back, took Stefanowski and myself by the arm and led us away, out of hearing.

Then, as both of us whispered, "What is it?" she looked around cautiously again and said with lowered voice: "That man—the one in our compartment—was trying to get out of the country and they've caught him."

"But why?—What for?—What has he done?" we asked, bewildered.

Again she glanced back cautiously and then, drawing us toward her till our three heads were almost touching, she said, in an awed and almost frightened tone, "They say he is a Jew. They searched his baggage—he was taking money out."

"How much?" said Stefanowski.

"I don't know," she whispered. "A great deal, I think. Several thousand marks. They found it."

"But how—" I began. "I thought everything was finished. I thought they were done with all of us when they went through the train."

"Yes," she said, "but don't you remember he said something about not having a ticket the whole way. He got off the train to get one. And I think that's when they caught him," she whispered. "I think they had their eye on him. That's why they did not question him when they came through the train"—as indeed, I now remembered, "they" had not—"And they caught him here," she went on. "They asked him where he was going and he said to Paris. They asked him how much money he was taking out; he said ten marks. Then they asked him how long he was going to remain in Paris, and for what purpose, and he said he was going to be there for a week and that he was attending this congress of lawyers that he spoke about. They asked him then how he proposed to stay in Paris for a week and attend this congress if all he had was ten marks. And I think," she whispered, "he got frightened then. He began to lose his head. He said he had forgotten, that he had twenty marks besides, which he had put into another pocket. And then, of course, they had him. They searched him. They searched his baggage, and they found more," she whispered in an awed tone. "Much, much more."

For a moment we all stared at one another, too stunned to say a word. Then the little woman laughed in a low, almost frightened, sort of way, a little uncertain "o-hoh-hoh-hoh-hoh" ending on a note of incredulity.

"This man," she whispered again, "this little Jew—"

"I didn't know he was a Jew," I said, "I should not have thought so."

"But he is," she whispered, and looked stealthily around again to see if we were being overheard. "And he was doing what so many of the others have done—he was trying to get out with his money." And again she laughed, the uncertain little hoh-hoh-hoh that mounted on a note of incredulous amazement. And yet, I saw, her eyes were troubled, too.

All of a sudden I felt sick, empty, nauseated. That money, those accursed ten marks, were beginning to burn a hole in my pocket. I put my hand into my vest pocket and the coins felt greasy, as if they were covered with sweat. I took them out and closed them in my fist and started to cross the platform toward the train.

The woman seized me by the arm. "Where are you going?" she gasped. "What are you going to do?"

"I'm going to give that man his money. I can't keep it now."

Her face went white. "Are you mad?" she whispered. "Don't you know that that will do no good? You'll only get yourself arrested and, as for him—he's in trouble enough already. You'll only make it so much worse for him. And besides," she faltered, as the full consequences came to her, "God knows what he has done, what he has said already. If he has told that we have transferred money to one another—we may all be in for it!"

We had not thought of this. But now we did. And as we saw the possible consequence of our act we just stood there and stared helplessly at one another. We just stood there, three abreast, feeling dazed and weak and hollow. We just stood there and prayed.

And now they were coming out of the compartment. The fellow with the sprouting mustache came out first, carrying the little man's valise. He looked around. It seemed to me he glared at us. We just stood still and prayed. We expected now to see all of our baggage come out. We thought that we were in for it.

But in a moment the other three officials came out of the compartment, with the little man between them. They marched him right along the platform, white as a sheet, greasy looking, protesting volubly, in a voice that had a kind of anguished lilt. He came right by us. I made a movement with my arms. The greasy money sweated in my hand and I did not know what to do. I started to speak to him. And at the same time I was praying that he would not speak. I tried to look away from him, but I could not look away. He came toward us, still protesting volubly that everything could be explained, that all of it was an absurd mistake. And just for a moment as he passed us, he stopped talking, glanced at us, white-faced, smiling pitiably, his eyes rested on us for a moment, and then, without a sign of further recognition, he went on by.

I heard the little blonde woman at my side sigh faintly and I felt her body slump against me. We all felt pretty weak and hollow. In a moment we went on across the platform and got up into the train. The evil tension had been snapped. People were now talking feverishly, still in a low tone but with obvious released excitement. Our little blonde companion leaned from the window of the corridor and spoke to the fellow with the sprouting mustache who was still standing there. "Are—are you going to keep him here?" she said in a low tone. "You're not going to let him go?"

He looked at her stolidly for a moment. Then an intolerable smile broke deliberately across his brutal features. He nodded his head, slowly, with the finality of a gluttonous satisfaction: *"Nein,"* he said, *"Er bleibt."* And, shaking his heavy head ever so slightly from side to side, *"Geht nicht!"*

They had him. Far down the platform we heard the sudden fifing shrill of the engine whistle. The guard cried warning; all up and down the platform doors were slammed. Slowly the train moved from the station. We rolled right past him, very slowly. They had him. They surrounded him. He stood among them, protesting volubly, talking with his hands now, insisting all could be explained. And they said nothing. They had him. They just stood and watched him, each with the faint suggestion of that intolerable slow smile upon his face. They raised their eyes, unspeaking, looked at us as we rolled past, with the obscene communication of their glance and of their smile.

And he—he too paused once from his voluble and feverish discourse as we passed him. He lifted his eyes to us, his pasty face, and he was silent for a moment. And we looked at him for the last time, and he at us—this time, more direct and steadfastly. And in that glance there was all the silence of man's mortal anguish. And we were all somehow naked and ashamed, and somehow guilty. We all felt somehow that we were saying farewell, not to a man but to humanity; not to some nameless little cipher out of life, but to the fading image of a brother's face. We lost him then. The train swept out and gathered speed—and so farewell.

I turned and looked at Stefanowski. He, too, was silent for a moment. Then he spoke.

"Well, then," he said, "I think that this is a sad ending to our trip."

And we? We went back in and took our former seats in our compartment. But it seemed strange and empty now. The ghost of absence sat there ruinously. He had left his coat and hat; in his anguish he had forgotten them. Stefanowski rose and took them, and would have given them to the conductor. But the woman said: "You'd better look into the pockets first. Perhaps there's something in them. Perhaps"—quickly, eagerly, as the idea took her—"perhaps he has left money there."

Stefanowski searched the pockets. There was nothing there. He shook his head. The woman began to search the cushions of the seats, thrusting her hands down around the sides. "It might just be, you know," she said, "that he hid money here." She laughed excitedly, almost gleefully. "Perhaps we'll all be rich."

The young Pole shook his head. "I think they would have found it if he had," he said—and here he paused suddenly, peered out the window, and thrust his hand into his pocket, "I suppose we're in Belgium now. Here's your money." And he returned to her the money she had given him.

She took it and put it in her purse. I still had the ten marks in my hand and was looking at them. The woman looked up, saw my face, then said quickly, warmly, "But you're upset about this thing! You look so troubled."

I put the money back and in a moment said: "*Ich fühle gerade als ob ich Blutgeld in meiner Tasche hätte.*"

She leaned over, smiling, and put her hand reassuringly upon my arm: "*Nein. Nicht Blutgeld—Judgeld!*" she whispered. "Don't worry about it. He had plenty more!"

My eyes met those of Stefanowski for a moment and his too were grave. "This is a sad ending to our trip," he said again.

And she—our little blonde companion—she tried to laugh and joke, but her eyes were also full of trouble. She tried to talk us out of it, to talk herself into forgetfulness.

"These Jews!" she cried. "These things would never happen if it were not for them! They make all the trouble. Germany has had to protect herself. The Jews were taking all the money from the country—thousands of them escaped, taking millions of marks with them. And now, when it is too late, we wake up to it! It is too bad that foreigners must see these things, that they've got to go through these painful experiences—it makes a bad impression. They do not understand the reason. But it is the Jews!" she whispered.

We said nothing and the woman went on talking, eagerly, excitedly, earnestly, persuasively, but really as if she were trying to convince herself, as if every instinct of race and loyalty was now being used in an effort to justify something that had filled her with a sense of shame and sorrow. But even as she talked her clear blue eyes were full of trouble. And at length she stopped. There was silence for a moment. Then gravely, quietly, the woman said: "He must have wanted very badly to escape."

We remembered then all he had said and done throughout the journey. And now every act and gesture, every word became invested with a new and terrible meaning. We recalled how nervous he had been, how he kept opening and shutting the door, kept getting up to pace up and down along the corridor. We recalled how he kept peering around at us suspiciously, how eagerly he had asked Stefanowski if he would change places with him when the Pole had got up to go into the dining-car with me. We recalled his explanations about having to buy passage from the frontier to Paris, the explanations he had given to the conductor. And all these things, which at the time we had dismissed as irascible ill temper or trivial explanation, now were revealed in a sequence of terrible significance.

"But the ten marks!" the woman cried at length. "In God's name, since he had all this other money, why did he give ten marks to you? It is so stupid!"

And we could find no reason, except that he had done it because he thought it might alleviate any suspicion in our minds about his true intent; or, what was even likelier, I thought, that he was in such an inner state of nervous frenzy that he had acted blindly, wildly, on the impulse of the moment.

We did not know. We never would find out the answer now. We discussed the money he had given me. The young Pole remarked that I had given the man my name and my address and that if he was later on allowed to complete his journey, he could write to me. But we all knew I would never hear from him again.

Late afternoon had come. The country had closed in, the train was winding through a pleasant, romantic landscape of hills and woods. There was a sense of forest dusk, cool darkling waters, the slant of evening and the wane of light. We knew somehow that we had entered another land. Our little blonde companion peered anxiously out the window and then asked if we were really now in Belgium. The conductor assured us that we were. We gave the man our late companion's hat and coat and explained the reason for them. He nodded, took them, and departed.

The woman had her hand upon her breast, and now when the man had gone I heard her sigh slowly with relief.

In a moment she said quietly and simply: "Do not misunderstand. I am a German and I love my country. But—I feel as if a weight has lifted from me *here*"—she put her hand upon her breast again. "You cannot understand perhaps just how it feels to us but—" and for a moment she was silent as if painfully meditating what she wished to say. Then quickly, quietly: "We are so happy to be—*out!*"

Out? I too was "out." And suddenly I knew just how she felt. I too was "out," who was a stranger to her land, who never yet had been a stranger in it. I too was "out" of that great land whose image had been engraved upon my spirit in my childhood and my youth, before I had ever seen it. I too was "out" from that land which had been so much more to me than land, which had been for me so much more than place. It was a geography of heart's desire. It was a soul's dark wonder, the haunting beauty of the magic land. It had been burning there forever, like the dark Helen burning in man's blood. And now, like the dark Helen, it was lost to me. I had spoken the language of its spirit before I ever came to it. I had spoken the accents of its speech most brokenly from the hour when I first entered it, yet never with a moment's strangeness. I had been at home in it and it in me. It seemed I had been born in it and it in me. I had known wonder in it, truth and magic in it, sorrow, loneliness and pain in it. I had known love in it, and for the first time in my life I had tasted there the bright delusive sacraments of fame.

Therefore, it was no foreign land to me. It was the other half of my heart's home. It was the dark lost Helen I had found, it was the dark found Helen I had lost—and now I knew, as I had never known before, the countless measure of my loss—the countless measure of my gain—the way that now would be forever closed to me—the way of exile and of no return—and another way that I had found. For I knew that I was "out." And that I had now found my way.

To that old master, now, to wizard Faust, old father of the ancient and swarm-haunted mind of man, to that old German land with all the measure of its truth, its glory, beauty, magic and its ruin—to that dark land, to that old ancient earth that I had loved so long—I said farewell.

I have a thing to tell you:

Something has spoken to me in the night, burning the tapers of the waning year; something has spoken in the night; and told me I shall die, I know not where. Losing the earth we know for greater knowing, losing the life we have for greater life, and leaving friends we loved for greater loving, men find a land more kind than home, more large than earth.

Whereon the pillars of this earth are founded, toward which the spirits of the nations draw, toward which the conscience of the world is tending—a wind is rising, and the rivers flow.

Into the Bottomless Pit

In July 1936, Albert Camus, along with his wife Simone Hié and his friend Yves Bourgeois, left Algeria for a trip to Europe. In its course, the three of them undertook extended kayak tours, which was a special challenge for Camus, who was suffering from tuberculosis. Via Marseilles, Lyons, and Switzerland they reached Austria—from where they made a detour to Berchtesgaden. In Salzburg, when Camus reads a letter from an Algerian doctor who supplied Simone with drugs and who was also her lover, he decides to leave his wife. He spends a few days alone in Prague. In spite of all the personal problems, the three continue their journey together. They travel to Germany, to Dresden, Bautzen, Görlitz, and Breslau. (It is the middle of August and the Olympic Games are just finishing in Berlin.) Finally they return to Algeria via Czechoslovakia, Vienna, Venice, and Marseilles. Camus treats this short visit to Germany in various ways: in short sketches in his diary (1936, eight lines), in a passage in "Death in the Heart" (half a page), which is a chapter of his autobiographical essay "L'Envers et l'Endroit" ("The Wrong Side and the Right Side," 1937), and in an episode in his unfinished novel *La Mort heureuse* (*A Happy Death*, 1938, five pages). Whereas in the essay Camus indicates only what he eventually *might* report, the account in the novel fragment about the escaped murderer Mersault—who, as the protagonist of the famous novel *L'Étranger* (*The Stranger*), has almost the same name, Meursault—grows more elaborate and concrete without being any the less desperate. Should the pessimistic undertones of the travel experience be attributed to biographical circumstances? Should they be ascribed to the philosophical outlook of the later theorist of the absurd? Or should they be understood as a reaction to Nazi Germany and thus as a subtle political statement?

I left Prague not long after. And I certainly took an interest in what I saw later. I could note down such and such an hour in the little Gothic cemetery of Bautzen, the brilliant red of its geraniums and the blue morning sky. I could talk about the long, relentless, barren plains of Silesia. I crossed them at daybreak. A heavy flight of birds was passing in the thick, misty morning, above the sticky earth. I also liked Moravia, tender and grave, with its distant, pure horizons, its roads bordered with sour plum trees. But inside I still felt the dizziness of those who have gazed too long into a bottomless pit. I arrived in Vienna, left a week later. Still the numbness held me captive.

What of the Color-Line?

W. E. B. DuBois spent two years studying in Wilhelminian Berlin (1892–94). In 1928, during the Weimar Republic, he once again visited the city on his way to the Soviet Union. In July 1936, the African American sociologist and historian finally returned to Germany for a five-month research trip. He had received a fellowship from the Oberlander Trust, "For the promotion of cultural relations between the United States and Germany." DuBois was interested in the industrial working world, especially vocational training. But he also confronts the question, as he put it in one of his articles: "What of the color-line?" He describes his experiences in the African American weekly *Pittsburgh Courier* for which he wrote a column, "Forum of Fact and Opinion." Because of his journey to National Socialist Germany and an interview that appeared in a German-language newspaper in New York, DuBois had some criticism to deal with after his return to the U.S.A.

I have been to Europe, in all, nine different times, remaining periods varying from two months to two years. I have seen briefly and indistinctly, but personally, some of the main changes and results of modern history. I saw in 1892–4 the triumphant Europe of the 19th century; with England mistress of the seas and lands beyond; with France the undisputed center of Art and Taste; and Germany the new and mighty focus of Science, Education, and military organization.

Eight years later I saw the great exposition in Paris, which opened the new and fateful century. In 1906 I saw Scotland and England from Land's End to Sky, with the Lake and Shakespeare country. In 1911 I witnessed and was a part of what promised to be, and indeed might have been the greatest movement for the unification of mankind ever planned: the First Races Congress, at the University of London, with distinguished representatives of every major group of peoples in the world. It was an amazing meeting, and yet even as we met and talked and planned, a little war vessel visited the almost unheard of harbor of Agadir and the World War was foreshadowed.

Just after the unending tragedy of that war I saw Europe again. I sat beside the Congress of Versailles and walked over endless fields of the dead, and heard and saw the beginnings of the struggle to re-establish civilization. In '21 and '23 I returned to Europe in the vain attempt to help in some little way in the reconstruction of a world free for democracy and a democracy free for Black Folk. I visited the assembly of the League of Nations at Geneva; I saw Paris, Brussels and London; I traveled in Spain and Portugal, and finally, for the first [time], I saw Africa.

In 1928 I saw Germany again for the first time since my student days, and then went on to view the astonishing experiment in Russia; then I looked at the Black Sea, Constantinople, the greatest city of men; I saw the Parthenon at Athens and again the Bay of Naples.

Finally, I return in 1936 to London and Berlin, to Paris and Vienna, and perhaps to other parts of the world which I have never seen. And of the education I have ever had, these journeys among men and things have formed the major part.

Most men have singular reasons in mind for the seeing of Europe. Perhaps to most Americans it is a matter of curiosity: to see the old, the funny, the unusual; to convince themselves that there are people who do not speak English, and that French and German and Italian are actually used by some queer folk to express their thoughts and not as exercises in schools. Other folk want actually to see and touch things a thousand years old instead of a hundred, and to look on landmarks of human history. To some folk Europe is a storehouse of Beauty — of the Alps, the Venus of Milo, the Sistine Madonna, the Lorelei and the Kremlin. And then, to not a few others, it is a Holiday where one goes to spend money, buy champagne cheap and do things they wouldn't dream of doing at home.

The real reason of Europe which most men are not prepared to see is that here lies the center of modern human culture. Civilization does not center in the United States or in Australia. And I mean by Civilization those thoughts and actions and records and co-operative actions of men which give the chief meaning to modern life. There is not a problem which we face today which Europe is not facing also, and with few exceptions doing more, systematically, to solve than we are. For that reason, despite all our boasting and national pride, we turn continually and repeatedly toward Europe to know and understand the last word of human culture in matters of vital and everyday interest to us.

[...] It is impossible to understand and appreciate modern culture without knowing Europe. [...]

Because Europe is as civilized as it is, there is a possibility there of human contacts, especially for colored people, that America cannot afford. I have not especially sought such contacts, but they have been all the more welcome and valuable because they have come naturally. Even on this trip it was a great source of knowledge and understanding to dine with Malinowsk[i], the great English anthropologist [sic]; to have a visit from De Cleene, the colonial expert, in Belgium; to meet in Germany, Westermark, who knows more of African tongues than any man; and to lunch with H. G. Wells in London. It is safe to say that more is being done today in the scientific study of races and race relations in Europe than elsewhere in the world. And this is the primary reason why I am here.

===

It is difficult at once to estimate the impression of Germany and in Europe which the Olympic Games and colored competitors has made. It is, however, wide and deep. In two countries of the modern world colored citizens are appearing as citizens with equal rights at least on certain occasions. In France there are colored teachers and artists and professional men. On this visit, particularly, I was struck by a colored bus conductor on the Boulevard Raspail and a colored soldier crossing the square by the Comidie Française and a black man, possibly a student, sitting in a café on the Boulevard St. Michel. It is fairly common then in France to see black men as Frenchmen. It is not so common in England. One sees colored folk, but they figure as colonials. Now and then there is a physician with a city or provincial practice; or a lawyer; but such things are still rather exceptional.

Here now in sports, which Europe is discovering and spelling with a large "S," particularly in Germany, Russia, and Italy, and for a longer time in

France, and of course for a very long time in England—here comes, among the Americans, black men and women. In the first place, the Europeans are rather astonished. The man in the street has assumed that the chief industry of black men in America is being lynched. He hears that there is no meeting or commerce between black and white in America, and yet the American Olympic teams arrive at Berlin with thirteen black competitors. The German papers pick them out for comment: usually they mention the fact that such and such American competitors are Negroes. The French papers pick them out and print their colored faces. That would be astonishing enough; but these black athletes are extraordinary performers. Jesse Owens ran before the astonished eyes of the world. He was lauded and pictured and interviewed. He can scarcely take a step without being begged for his "autogramme." He is without doubt the most popular single athlete in the Olympic Games of 1936. There was the 100-meter race with two black men ahead. There was the high jump and Johnson with no competitors. All this is going to be big with promise for the future, but it must be followed by other things. We must be represented, not only in sports, but in science, in literature, and in art.

===

Berlin is settling down to normalcy after the Olympian Games. The decorations had mostly disappeared from the streets by September 1. The crowds on the streets seemed ordinary, and the cafés on Unter den Linden half empty. Probably the number of foreigners who visited the games was large, but scarcely as many as were expected. On the other hand, Germany poured into Berlin in overwhelming numbers. As a specimen of organization the games were superbly done; as a gesture toward international peace and good will, their value cannot be over-estimated in a world which sees a Spanish civil war of terrible cruelty, the steady re-arming of the leading nations, and a world atmosphere of suspicion and distrust.

===

Men need places where they can renew their strength; where they can catch again faith in themselves and in their fellow men. The more simple-minded folk find this in wayside places of prayer, such as one sees in Italy and Southern France and Germany. The more sophisticated of men are not in less need of renewal of faith—rather more. But it must be something more than a sign; it must be a revelation.

Thus Westminster Abbey and Chartres and R[]eims are shrines where the faithful visit, but also centers of renewed striving. Such another shrine I am visiting now. I am at Bayreuth, a little city of less than 40,000 souls, in the hills of Northern Bavaria. It is a town built around the name and memory of one man, Richard Wagner. Musicians come to hear music in technical perfection; but others, like myself who know little of music, come from an interest in the development of the human soul and for the spirit of Beauty, which this shrine commemorates and makes eternal.

I pass twice or thrice daily in my walks a walled garden and home, where, as Wagner said, "My fancies found Peace." Behind the home he lies today in a broad and peaceful grave. On the corner of Lis[zt] street, where I live, is the house where Franz Lis[zt], the master, died. At the corner of Wahnfried street, where I daily turn toward town, I pass the former home of H. S. Chamberlain, the American, who, writing in German, did more perhaps than any one to establish in Germany the theory of Nordic superiority.

===

I can see a certain type of not unthoughtful American Negro saying to himself: "Now just what has Bayreuth and opera got to do with starving Negro farm tenants in Arkansas or black college graduates searching New York for a job? It may be all right for the fortunate to rest and play, but is it necessary to pretend that this has any real vital connection with our pressing social problems?"

I think it has. I have long thought so. The whole meaning and end of my earlier teaching was to stress just this point. The message of Richard Wagner stressed this point. He lived. He had a hard time earning a living. Nearly always he was in debt. He had a hard time getting an education and at last had to give it up. He was not appreciated. Today, long dead, he is. I have stood beside the great and wordless mound that is his tomb—I can almost see it as I write. I walked today in the city museum of his mementoes just as some day some humble and unknown reader of this will have a world worshiping his dead genius. But the world did not always worship or even tolerate Wagner. Of the 40 years of his grown life, he passed over 26 as an exile from his own fatherland, where he was long neither tolerated nor appreciated. His first wife neither understood him nor cared much for him. His second wife came to him while her husband was yet living, and in the face of a bitter punishment which the world of that day knew how to administer even better than we, stuck by him, eventually married him, and by her sense, her learning and her utter sacrifice, made him the great master that he became. The musical dramas of Wagner tell of human life as he lived it, and no human being, white or black, can afford not to know them, if he would know life.

Nuremburg is one of those ancient tales in stone, which loses the air of reality. You can today see parts of its three walls, still standing gray and grim as Martin Luther saw them. You can walk in a castle that was old when Shakespeare wrote "Hamlet," and thread narrow streets which heard the earliest echoes of the far-off African slave trade. The drama in music which Wagner wrote of this town was a tale of the old labor guilds, and how they organized in those days not only handworkers but artists. It tells of the effort of a natural untaught singer to triumph over the jealous and petty rules of a labor union, and of the great competition when Walter's Prize Song carried off the honors and the bride.

I saw the opera in Munich. The splendid settings and the marvelous beauty of the music made an unforgettable memory. [. . .]

Faring further in his restless quest for the adequate expression of human experience and emotion, Wagner wrote in the pain and doubt and hesitation of 40 years, the great Trilogy called "The Ring of the Nibelungs." It is as though someone of us chose out of the wealth of African folklore a body of poetic material and, with music, scene and action, re-told for mankind the suffering and triumphs and defeats of a people.

===

I am bathing myself in music. It is cheap—the best orchestra seats for one and two dollars, and the gallery for 50 cents. I have heard since Bayreuth, Bizet's "Carmen," Rossini's "Barber of Seville," Mozart's "Marriage of Figaro," and "Magic Flute," Wagner's "Flying Dutchman" and—unforgettable night—"Tristan and Isolde," Verdi's "Rigoletto" and "Traviata," Massenet's "Manon," with the beautiful dream sung well, but not so divinely as Hayes sings it. And last, last night, the Ninth Symphony—there where the hoarse horns and dead strings suddenly become human voices, in the noblest hymn to Joy man ever wrote for God. These classics of popular music, without knowing which one cannot talk to civilized folk, are practically unhearable for most Americans. They should be part of the education of every man of culture. They are costly luxuries for the most part in America, and unappreciated at that. Some day no school curriculum will be complete without such compulsory courses in the world of music and drama.

As usual I made a discovery even here "along the color line." It was in Hanover in September. There was a Verdi opera on at the local city opera. For no German city of any size is without a theater and opera house, where from October to May citizens may hear the best in music and drama for the cost of a woman's spring hat the season. I went, although the title of the opera was quite new to me: "The Power of Fate" ("La Forza del Destino"). Singular I thought that I should not even have heard the title before of this work of the master. As I read the libretto, however, I began to understand why. It was a music drama of the color line. Leonore de Vargas loved Alvaro, a brown mulatto. The father surprising them in elopement, is accidentally killed by Alvaro's pistol. Leonore flees to a hermit's retreat, while her brother pursues Alvaro. Both enlist under assumed names and, unknown to each other, in the Italian-French war, win high honors and become close friends, when the brother discovers Alvaro's identity. Alvaro refuses to fight him and flees to a monastery. The brother tracks him and after years finds and taunts him as a cowardly mulatto and bastard. Alvaro kills him and then calls for help at a hermit's hut, only to discover Leonore. She dies in his arms, crying "All parting is but a dream." As I read this story I rather wondered how the Nordic audience would take the presence in the orchestra of a very brown listener, to a race play. But all difficulty was surmounted just as we arrange the black Othello for Atlanta: Alvaro was blonde and actually lighter than the brother! Race was eliminated neatly, unless one listened too closely to the words. Am I quite alone? Who ever heard of this colored hero of Verdi?

===

One of the most difficult things in this world is to distribute honestly the reward for thought and action which has benefited mankind. In the German Museum of Science and Technique there is a room which seeks to distribute such honors. In the entrance stands a great monument to Goethe with a portrait of Alexander von Humboldt, and Frederick the Great. And then in another circular room with a beautiful parquet floor, are the pictures and statues of men who studied mathematics, germs, electricity and optics; who speculated on the universe and named the stars and dissected light; and flew in the air and cured men. It is a splendid collection, but, of course, it is predominantly German. A few foreigners have found a place there like Copernicus and Bunsen but for the most part this Hall of Fame tells what Germans have done. It would be a finer and bigger thing if, ignoring nation and language, this hall could have brought together the great contributors of science and technique the world over but perhaps that was too much to expect. But, on the whole, in all the exhibits here, commercialism and nationality have been restricted. The restriction is sometimes poor. For instance, Faraday's apparatus is exhibited; but a German invention which came years after is given the place of honor. The German inventors of telegraphy are emphasized, while Morse's telegraph is simply there.

===

The contrast between North and South Germany is broad. Munich isn't a world city. It has retained its individuality. It is a city of the theater, of music, of marvelous old buildings, and of beer. Americans who have tasted strong beer made for long keeping, wide distribution, and exportation have no idea of the delicacy and satisfying quality of the best German beer. It is always astonishing, especially in South Germany, to see how much time is spent in the beer hall; and yet one is still tempted now, as in other days, to say that it is hard to see how ordinary, educated human beings could spend their time better. Certainly in America the movies, the cabarets, and the card parties would not provide an enticing substitute. The beer halls are large and well aired. The music, when there is music, is good. The proportion of alcohol in the best beer is very small, and the social intercourse of friends with friends and of strangers with each other gives a public courtesy which one cannot find in the American attempt to be at once exclusive and public.

===

I have written already a word here and there about minor aspects of the German scene. I am sure my friends have understood my hesitations and reticence; it simply wasn't safe to attempt anything further. Even my mail, when Mrs. DuBois sent me a minor receipt to sign, was opened to see if money was being smuggled in.

But now I have ended my sojourn—or at least shall have long before this is published; and to insure its reaching The Courier on time I am taking it to a foreign land to mail.

This does not mean that I have not enjoyed my five and more months in Germany. I have. I have been treated with uniform courtesy and consideration. It would have been impossible for me to have spent a similarly long time in any part of the United States, without some, if not frequent cases of personal insult or discrimination. I cannot record a single instance here.

It is always difficult to characterize a whole nation. One cannot really know 67 million people, much less indict them. I have simply looked on. I have used my eyes and, to a lesser extent, my ears. I have talked with some people, but not widely, nor inquisitively.

Chiefly I have traveled. I have been in all parts of Germany: in Prussia, including Meckl[e]nburg, Brandenburg, Hanover and Schlesien; I have seen the Hansa cities of the northwest and East Prussia; I have looked on the North Sea and the Alps, and traveled through Saxony, Thuringia, Westphalia, Wurtemburg and Bavaria. I have seen the waters of the Rhine, Elbe, Weser, Oder and Danube. I have seen all the great German cities: Berlin, Hamburg, Luebeck, Bremen, both Frankf[u]rts, Cologne, Mayence, Stuttgart, Breslau, and Munich, not to mention Vienna and Strassburg. I have seen Germany; and not in the mists of a tourist's rush, but in slow and thoughtful leisure. I have read German newspapers of all sorts and places; I have read books, listened to lectures, gone to operas, plays and movies, and watched a nation at work and play. I have talked with a half dozen officials.

Germany in overwhelming majority stands back of Adolf Hitler to-day. Germany has food and housing, and is, on the whole, contented and prosperous. Unemployment in four years has been reduced from seven to two millions or less. The whole nation is dotted with new homes for the common people, new roads, new public buildings and new public works of all kinds. Food is good, pure and cheap. Public order is perfect, and there is almost no visible crime. And yet, in direct and contradictory paradox to all this, Germany is silent, nervous, suppressed; it speaks in whispers; there is no public opinion, no opposition, no discussion of anything; there are waves of enthusiasm, but never any protest of the slightest degree. Last winter 12 million were in want of food and clothes, and this winter not less than 9 million, perhaps 10. There is a campaign of race prejudice carried on openly, continuously and deter-minedly against all non-Nordic races, but specifically against the Jews, which surpasses in vindictive cruelty and public insult anything I have ever seen; and I have seen much. Here is the paradox and contradic-tion. It is so complicated that one cannot express it without seeming to convict one's self of deliberate misstatement. And the testimony of the casual, non-German-speaking visitor to the Olympic Games is worse than valueless in any direction.

When a group or a nation acts incomprehensively, the answer lies in a background of fact, unknown or imperfectly comprehended by the onlooker. So it is in this case. Germany has lived through four horrors in living history that no people can experience and remain entirely normal. These are: War; the Treaty of Versailles; Inflation; Depression, and Revolution. Save the few who were actually in the trenches of the A. E. F., our generation in America has no adequate notion of war. There is a war monument in Hamburg which is the most eloquent and ghastly memory I have ever seen. It is a square, straight shaft of gray granite, and it says simply: "40,000 sons of this city gave their lives for you in 1914–18." Forty thousand dead youth from a single German city! Then came a treaty of peace which was no less than devilish in its concealed ingenuity. One might agree in blaming Germany for the war—although this is by no means as clear today as it seemed then to us—but who of the laymen knew or dreamed that what the peace treaty did was so to hamstring German industry as to make the earning of a living in Germany so difficult that bankruptcy followed on a scale that was revolutionary? The treaty deprived Germany not simply of one-eighth of her territory, population and arable land, but what was far more important, of a fifth of her coke, three-fourths of her iron, one-fourth of her blast furnaces, two-thirds of her zinc foundries, one-fifth of her livestock, all of her merchant marine, and most of her railway equipment. And then saddled her with a debt based on unheard-of principles, which no land could or did pay. In other words, in order to establish peace, the capitalists of England, France and America made the orderly return of Germany to work and self-support impossible without internal revolution. This revolution meant a redistribution of wealth and income in Germany comparable only to the French and Russian revolutions. And the people who paid in Germany were the thrifty, the workers, the civil employees—the very classes who had opposed war in the first place. And the persons who bore the brunt of criticism in Germany for the treaty were the labor unions, the teachers, the middle class who hated war and wanted to build a new state, above the power of capital and the army. Adolf Hitler rode into power eventually by calling the government of Germany, which negotiated the treaty of Versailles, traitors who stabbed Germany in the back when she was down.

Germany not only had the flower of her youth murdered in a senseless war, but had her bread and butter taken away in an equally senseless peace. The accumulated savings of the nation disappeared; pensions, in a land of pensioned civil servants, were stopped; loans were paid in worthless money; property values dropped to nothing; industry was in bankruptcy and labor out of work. She struggled up and partially out of the morass, but when depression settled on the world, Germany was worse off than others, because she was hopelessly in debt, and by the unanimous decision of the world not allowed to pay her debt in the only possible way: by the export of her manufactures. Adolf Hitler rode into power by accusing the world of a conspiracy to ruin Germany by economic starvation. He promised to remedy this by making Germany self-sufficient and giving her an army capable of defending her rights. Revolution was staring Germany in the face, and a Marxian revolution which would make a dictatorship of the proletariat and made a socialistic state. Industry was frightened; the Junkers (landed nobility) were frightened; the managers, engineers and small shopkeepers were frightened; they all submitted to a man who had at first been a joke, then a pest, and who suddenly loomed as a dictator. Union labor, with its 8,000,000 members, holding the wide balance of power in the state, proceeded to squabble as to whether to usher in the millennium immediately or gradually, and through this squabble Adolf Hitler and Big Industry drove a carriage and four. He made a state without a single trade union and where the discussion of change is a crime.

===

Hitler set up a tyranny; a state with a mighty police force, a growing army, a host of spies and informers; a secret espionage, backed by swift and cruel punishment, which might vary from loss of job to imprisonment incommunicado, and without trial, to cold murder. None used to the freedom and discussion of a modern state can endure Germany, save as a dire necessity or an ideal toward something better.

But this was not all that Hitler did. Had it been, he and his state would have disappeared long ere this. He showed Germany a way out when most Germans saw nothing but impenetrable mist, and he made the vast majority of Germans believe that his way was the only way and that it was actually leading to the promised land. Nine out of every ten Germans believe this today, and as long as they are convinced of this, they are going to uphold Hitler at any cost. They know the cost which they pay and they hate it. They hate war, they hate spying, they hate the loss of their liberties. But in return for this immense sacrifice, they have domestic peace after a generation of wars and rumors of wars; they have a nation at work, after a nightmare of unemployment; and the results of this work are shown not simply by private profits, but by houses for the poor; new roads; an end of strikes and labor troubles; widespread industrial and unemployment insurance; the guarding of public and private health; great celebrations, organizations for old and young, new songs, new ideals, a new state, a new race. Have they paid, are they paying too much for all this? Would other and less dangerous roads [have] led to this same end? Germany is not asking this. She is simply saying, "HEIL HITLER!"

===

When an American Negro says, "I have met no discrimination on account of race," it is well for those of us who know to apply considerable doses of salt. For our people, in self-defense, have adopted a well-known protective mechanism: under given circumstances, we carefully ascertain where we are wanted or endured, and where we are insulted or debarred. Then we go only where we can, and of course suffer no discrimination. When, therefore, I say I have not suffered from race prejudice in Germany, this calls for explanation.

There is race prejudice in Germany, and a regular planned propaganda to increase it and make it characteristic of the Third Reich. But it is not instinctive prejudice, except in the case of the Jews, and not altogether there. I mean that German prejudice is not the result of long belief, backed by child teaching and outward insignia like color or hair. It is a reasoned prejudice, or an economic fear. Consequently, in the case of Negroes, it does not show itself readily. My friend used to say that she liked Paris because she could start out without wondering where she would get lunch. So in Berlin or elsewhere in Germany: I can go to any hotel which I can afford; I can dine where I please and have the headwaiter bow me welcome; I can go to any theater and find the strange lady next to me bow pleasantly or pass a conventional word if necessary; I can join a sightseeing tour without comment, etc. In fine, I have complete civic freedom and public courtesy. Of course, if my appearance is pronounced, I shall be an object of curiosity and even excited attention: a black man in a small German city would be a matter of crowds and staring that might be very annoying, but he would not be insulted nor guyed; nor, least of all, would he be refused such accommodation or courtesy as he demanded.

On the other hand, in social lines, there are limits: I have been invited to dinner in German homes and eaten with German women and men in good restaurants. On the other hand, no German woman of good standing would marry a Negro under ordinary circumstances, nor could she do so legally. It is a question if she could legally marry a Japanese. In public dance halls and in the half-world Negroes must be welcomed with care and secretly; police spies would quickly suppress any open commerce.

In the case of Jews, one meets something different, which an American Negro does not readily understand. Prejudice against Jews in Germany comes nearer being instinctive than color prejudice. For many centuries Germans have disliked Jews. But the reasons have varied, and are not at all analogous to white dislike of blacks in America. [...]

There has been no tragedy in modern times equal in its awful effects to the fight on the Jew in Germany. It is an attack on civilization, comparable only to such horrors as the Spanish Inquisition and the African slave trade. It has set civilization back a hundred years, and in particular has made the settlement and understanding of race problems more difficult and more doubtful. It is widely believed by many that the Jewish problem in Germany was episodic, and is already passing. Visitors to the Olympic Games are apt to have gotten that impression. They saw none who wish oppression. Just as Northern visitors to Mississippi see no Negro oppression. [...]

Adolf Hitler hardly ever makes a speech today—and his speeches reach every corner of Germany, by radio, newspaper, placard, movie and public announcement—without belittling, blaming or cursing Jews. [...] Every misfortune of the world is in whole or in part blamed on Jews—the Spanish rebellion, the obstruction to world trade, etc. One finds cases in the papers: Jews jailed for sex relations with German women; a marriage disallowed because a Jewish justice of the peace witnessed it; Masons excluded from office in the National Socialistic Party, because Jews are Masons; advertisements excluding Jews; the total disfranchisement of all Jews; deprivation of civil rights and inability to remain or become German citizens; limited rights of education, and narrowly limited right to work in trades, professions and the civil service; the threat of boycott, loss of work and even mob violence, for any German who trades with a Jew; and, above all, the continued circulation of Julius Streicher's St[]uermer, the most shameless, lying advocate of race hate in the world, not excluding Florida.

===

On the night I was leaving Berlin, I invited to my room a German friend whom I had met several times and who seemed to me peculiarly to represent a type of German thought and feeling for which I had deep respect.

He was not the German of fiction or the stage. He was slim, almost delicately made, with a fine, spiritual face, a mass of light hair, and perhaps 40 years of age. He was a university man, had fought in the World war, and was now an important government official, not high in rank, but efficient and trusted. He had the eyes and deep earnestness of the German idealist—the sort of leidenschaft and empfindlichkeit that in the past has made Germany great.

I wanted to talk to him frankly and openly and see how far my conclusions agreed with his. He was late. He always is. He is married only to his work and takes no account of time. To him midnight is early and 7:30 finds him at his desk. I had a bottle of old port from Borchardt's, cakes and fruit, and a box of Reemstma, erste Sorte, the best cigaret I ever tasted.

He came at half-past nine and began telling me about the difficulties of keeping labor on the farm, at the very time that Hess, Hitler's chief deputy, was appealing frantically for more meat and food to feed Germany; factories in the suburbs were attracting the young men and even girls. "And you know," he said, "the restrictions on coming into Berlin for work have recently been raised to admit more servants." So that was the reason Berlin was so busy, with no idlers nor criminals, during the Olympian Games. The city was barred against all but those at jobs.

Starting here, I took the conversation boldly into questionable ground: Speaking of these factories and of industrial enterprise in general in Germany, I asked frankly, "How far is private profit the object of Germany['s] industry under the Third Reich?" "It is not the main object," he answered; "the main object is the well-being of the people. Profit is now taxed heavily and will be taxed more heavily. It will soon be regarded as dishonest to make a large profit. German industry is already under such strict state control and guidance that private profit is destined to disappear." I lighted a cigaret, and said: "In that case, what is the difference between Germany and Russia?" I reminded him of the numberless likenesses in method that made Hitlerism and Stalinism alike. He readily admitted the similarity of aim, but thought the two lands differed chiefly in their foreign propaganda. I reminded him of the propaganda of Germany in South America and Spain.

Then I said: "Granted that Germany and Russia are the two greatest Socialistic states of the Modern World, and are pursuing their attack on private business along essentially the same lines, why is there that bitter and continuous attack of Germany on Russia and things Russian?" "I have wondered," I continued, "if all this talk is a smokescreen to hide the reason for re-arming of Germany. The ostensible reason being Bolshevism, the real reason, colonies." This, my friend did not answer directly. He emphasized the fact that Germany could not remain unarmed in an arming world, and that German youth, having had so little discipline for so many years, needed the discipline of military service. In fact, he hoped, from the new army, a slow but sure movement which would change the present government for the better. I could not gather just how this would happen, "but," he added, "2,000,000 persons cannot permanently rule 60,000,000." I was thus surprised to learn that the party, the N.S.D.A.P. (National So[z]ialistische Deutsche Arbeiter Partei), which rules Germany today and is the German state, has only two million members. He does not expect the coming change to be in the nature of revolution, but a gradual broadening of the basis of the state. In my own mind I still clung to the idea of the new army being for colonies. And this was strengthened when I saw the colonial exposition at Breslau: It was to accompany a national colonial congress, but that was suddenly and mysteriously postponed.

I turned then to an analogous question: could Germany really expect to be a self-sufficient economic unity, independent of foreign raw materials? "Oh, no," he said. "At present we must attempt to be as independent as possible, but no four or eight years' plan can furnish artificial raw materials as cheaply as they can be grown in colonies. The present agitation is only a threat, and the only measure of self-defense."

"But," I said, "is it possible to regiment and propagandize the minds of a people; can the young be educated to the goose-step and develop that ability and leadership, that independence of action and expression which is indispensable to a nation and a great people?" "There is the danger," he frankly admitted. "The free German spirit will seek freedom and find it. Even today there are stems of change. The Hitler youth are becoming less military and physical and more humanistic and educational. Hitler must, like Mussolini, change his councillors more often if his regime will survive."

Rust, the present minister of education, is no friend of higher education. He wants technical training. Recently at Bamberg he said that artisans, not college students, built the great cathedral there. Under his administration German university students have fallen from 42,000 to 28,000. "But the tide is turning," said my friend, "already the lack of trained students is being felt."

Then I took the bull by the horns, and asked: "How can Germans support race prejudice?" He said earnestly, "Much has been done to the Jews that we are sorry for. Streicher is a fanatic and his paper should not be allowed publication. But, remember this: the Jews, forming but 5 or 6 percent of our population, form 75 percent of the membership of our stock exchanges; a majority or very large percent of our lawyers, physicians, teachers and professional men: in some German states they were in majority in the ruling councils of the state; they presided in our courts; they came in in increasing numbers as immigrants from the East, and brought in a new, more greedy and less scrupulous element than the older German Jewry. The German people in the depths of their post-war misery felt a bitter jealousy and fear of this foreign element that was usurping power in their own state. It needed only a demagogue to capitalize this feeling. Much has been done of which we are ashamed. But the worst is over. Betterment will slowly follow in time."

===

When this is published I shall be in Hawaii, in that marvelous experiment in race mingling that lies in the midst of the Pacific. It will be Christmas and the sound of singing will ring the earth, calling for peace and good will in a world where there is no peace, and less good will.

But, as I write, it is not Christmas, it is October; and I am still in that Germany whose inner meaning I am trying, with the clumsy tool of the written word, to picture to my far-off readers.

===

I crossed the Tyrolean Alps in the gathering darkness: past Berchtesgaden, where Hitler lives, looking down on Munich, and waiting to talk with Mussolini's daughter (or is it his son-in-law) on things that may be big with the fate of Africa and Europe. Now I am turning again north and east—to Russia, to Manchoukuo, to China, to Japan. I shall see again the Towers of the Kremlin and the black waters of the Volga, the plains of Genghis Khan, the great Wall of China and all of dream and fairyland of youth done into the prose of the twentieth century. But before I go, one thought:

I cannot get over the continual surprise of being treated like a human being. I know my white American friends will name it, and rightly, the W. K. Inferiority Complex. It is, and thus a fact. I wrote this professor, whose fame is world-wide, and told him I was passing through his German city; might I call on him? He was at my hotel to meet me; he begged me, after I had rested, to have a simple supper with him and his wife; he came later in his car and we went to his home. He showed me his workroom, his library, the unfinished manuscript of his book. Then we went to the dining room, where his wife made me welcome. We ate, with wine and cigarets.

Above all, we talked, frankly and intimately. So frankly that he said, hesitatingly, at last: "Of course, you won't quote us." To this has science come in the Land of Free Thought and Teaching!

But the point I am pressing is not Science—it is human fellowship: where in America could this have happened? At Chicago? At Columbia? At Harvard?

HH Without Ceasing

Samuel Beckett had just completed his novel *Murphy* when he left on 28 September 1936 for a long trip to Germany, from which he did not return to Dublin (via London) until six months later, on 1 April 1937. Beckett's route took him through numerous places: Cuxhaven, Hamburg, Hanover, Brunswick, Wolfenbüttel, Berlin, Potsdam, Halle, Weimar, Erfurt, Naumburg, Leipzig, Dresden, Pillnitz, Meissen, Freiberg, Bamberg, Würzburg, Nuremberg, Regensburg, and Munich. In the course of this six-month sojourn abroad, Samuel Beckett kept a wide-ranging notebook—his mysterious *German Diary*, which remained unknown for a long time and even today may only be published in quotations and individual excerpts. The work is characterized by a concentration on details, for example in the precise routes he took or in his intensive discussion of paintings, especially of forbidden art, that the young author saw in the backrooms of museums and galleries or in private collections. In Munich, Beckett attended a performance by the comedian Karl Valentin (1882–1948). In what follows, selected entries from Samuel Beckett's *German Diary* are published for the first time.

A word of explanation: Gretchen Wohlwill (1878–1962), Eduard Bargheer (1901–79), and Willem Grimm (1904–86) are painters. *Grieben* was a widely used guidebook. In the last section, Beckett is first of all talking about the north portal of the Jakobskirche zu Regensburg (ca. 1180–90). Beckett discovered the words "Heil Hitler" on the north portal of the Church of the Dominicans. German words that structure Beckett's account appear in italics.

 What follows is a brief glossary of German words and phrases from Beckett's diary.

> *Vierjahresplan*: Four-year plan
> *sehr volkstümlich*: very folksy
> *Kolonien*: colonies
> *Rohstoffe*: raw materials
> *F[e]ttwaren*: fats
> *Bierstube*: pub
> WHW (*Winterhilfswerk*): a Nazi organization to provide clothes, etc., for
>   needy families
> *Schererei*: hassle
> *Glaspalast*: crystal palace
> *Haus der deutschen Kunst*: Gallery of German art (in Munich)
> *Brücke*: the bridge—a German avant-garde art movement of the early
>   twentieth century
> *überwunden*: vanquished
> *Grüss Gott*: may God bless you—a common greeting in southern, Catholic
>   areas of Germany

28 October 1936 [Hamburg]

Interminable harangue by Goering on *Vierjahresplan* relayed from Berlin. *Sehr volkstümlich. Kolonien, Rohstoffe, Futtwaren* [*sic*]. He has lost X kilos, + A. H. [Adolf Hitler] eats neither flesh nor butter.

24 November 1936 [Hamburg]

Gretchen Wohlwill, Flemmingstr. 3. Intelligent (Jewess). Some pleasant watercolours of Lisbon, the boat in which she cruised, etc. Formerly mistress of Eduard Bargheer. Drawings + watercolours by Bargheer + Grimm. Feel interested in Grimm, perhaps because of all the abuse I have heard applied to him. Wohlwill naturally excluded from all professional activities. She may have a closed exhibition to which only Jews may be invited. She may sell only to Jews Etc. Etc.

5 December 1936 [Braunschweig]

Sausages in *Bierstube*. HH [Heil Hitler!] without ceasing. Reunion of *WH* [Winterhilfs] *Werkers*. Damned again. Read the rotten guide that is the only one (I thought there was a *Grieben*). Dead tired to bed. What a *Schererei* this trip is becoming.

15 January 1937 [Berlin]

Go to Pschorr about 3 + eat hash + read about the bloody new *Glaspalast* in Munich, *Haus der deutschen Kunst* + the coming Exhibition open to high + low, all + sundry. Now that the period of Nolde, the *Brücke*, Marc etc. has been *"uberwünden"* [*sic*]. Soon I shall really begin to puke. Or go home.

3 March 1937 [Regensburg]

Look again at N. door. Completely different world from 13th century in Naumburg + Bamberg. In its naiveness (formal) + freedom from naturalism more modern. I know it is wrong to be concerned with what it means, but when one knows one is wrong it is diverting. Walk away past *Dominikanerkirche*, that I don't look at, except to see on N. door notice *Grüss Gott* crossed out + replaced by *Heil Hitler*!!!

A Race of Thieves

After he left his native France, Jean Genet traveled around Europe as a vagabond. He went to Spain, Italy, Albania, Yugoslavia, Austria, Czecho-slovakia, and Poland. From Poland, in the summer of 1937, he traversed Germany for a few weeks—a short stay that featured in a brief, but important, passage in his *Diary of a Thief*. Genet's narrator had, in the course of his "existentialist" project, styled himself as "the Other" of French society, the complete counterimage of bourgeois civilization. He had flirted not only with vagrancy and criminality but, over and over again, with fascism. In Berlin, it became clear to him that to be a criminal in Germany, or to be involved with fascism, meant conforming with the majority. If he were to maintain his individuality, he would have to return to the very position against which he had originally rebelled—namely that of Western bourgeois society. He quickly leaves the country and returns, via Belgium, to France, where his long journey had started.

In order to get to Antwerp I had just gone through Nazi Germany, where I had stayed a few months. I walked from Breslau to Berlin. I would have liked to steal. A strange force held me back. Germany terrified all of Europe; it had become, particularly to me, the symbol of cruelty. It was already outside the law. Even on Unter den Linden I had the feeling that I was strolling about in a camp organized by bandits. I thought that the brain of the most scrupulous bourgeois concealed treasures of duplicity, hatred, meanness, cruelty and lust.

I was excited at being free amidst an entire people that had been placed on the index. Probably I stole there as elsewhere, but I felt a certain constraint, for what governed this activity and what resulted from it—this particular moral attitude set up as a civic virtue—was being experienced by a whole nation which directed it against others.

"It's a race of thieves," I thought to myself. "If I steal here, I perform no singular deed that might fulfill me. I obey the customary order; I do not destroy it. I am not committing evil. I am not upsetting anything. The outrageous is impossible. I'm stealing in the void."

I would feel a kind of uneasiness after stealing. It seemed to me that the gods who govern the laws were not revolted. They were merely surprised. I was ashamed. But what I desired above all was to return to a country where the laws of ordinary morality were revered, were laws on which life was based. In Berlin I chose prostitution as my means of livelihood. It satisfied me for a few days and then wearied me.

The Germans Really Are Too Good

On completing his first year of study at Harvard in the summer of 1937, John F. Kennedy undertook a private educational trip to Europe with his friend LeMoyne Billings. After they had explored France and Italy by car, the two students went to Germany for a week in mid-August. They traveled with a German girl whom they seem to have picked up while entering the country. Kennedy and Billings ended their "Grand Tour" in Great Britain, where, in the following year, Kennedy's father took up the post of ambassador of the United States. Among the later president's effects is the roughly ninety-page handwritten diary of the journey in which, on almost ten pages of dated entries, John F. Kennedy describes his stay in the National Socialist Reich. This extract is fully reproduced in what follows.

August 16, Monday

Venice to Innsbruck
Due to the rain, decided to leave for Munich. Picked up a bundle of fun to take with us in addition to Heinz and set out. Bad driving and by the time we got to the Brenner Pass, it was pretty cold. The Austrian people impressed us very much as they were certainly different from the Italians. Stayed at a youth hostel in Innsbruck which caused "her Ladyship" much discomfiture. It was none too good as there were about 40 in a closet and it is considered a disgrace to take a bath.

August 17, Tuesday

Innsbruck–Munich
Up early, though not from choice. Her Ladyship stated that her night had been far from pleasant. Started over the Alps to Germany after exacting money from Johann who was rather upset. Stopped at Garmisch where the Olympic games were held, then to Oberammergau where I saw the Christus — Anton Lang. Arrived in Munich around eight and went to the Hofbrau house which was very interesting. Hitler seems so popular here, as Mussolini was in Italy, although propaganda seems to be his strongest weapon.

August 18, Wednesday

Munich
Got up late and none too spry. Had a talk with the proprietor who is quite a Hitler fan. There is no doubt about it that these dictators are more popular in the country than outside due to their effective propaganda. Went to see the Deutsche Museum in the afternoon which is terribly interesting, as it outlines the different steps in mining and shows the development of aviation, etc. A great job and shows the German sense of detail. That night went to see *Swing High Swing Low* for the 2nd time and enjoyed it more than the first. Probably because we haven't seen a picture lately. When we arrived back at the car found a note from Pourtalis + Iselin and met them at the Hofbrauhaus with Ann Hollister + Joe Garrety from Harvard. Went to a Munich night club which was a bit different.

August 19, Thursday

Munich–Nuremberg
After the usual amount of cursing and being told we were not gentlemen we left the Pension Bristol for the American Express. Saw Pourtalis and Iselin there. Broke — lent them 20,00 and then started out for Nuremberg. Stopped on the way and bought "Offie," a dachshund of great beauty for 8,00 as a present for Olive. Immediately got hay-fever, etc. So it looks like the odds are about 8–1 towards Offie getting to America.

August 20, Friday

Nuremberg—Wurtemberg
Started out as usual except this time we had the added attraction of being spitten on. Due to the cold stopped short of Frankfurt. Offie is quite a problem because when he's got to go—he *goes*.

August 21, Saturday

Wurtemberg–Koln (Cologne)
Started out for Cologne by way of Frankfurt, where we stopped to look for more dachshunds, Offie being so attractive. However, no luck, so continued on our way up the Rhine. Very beautiful as there are many castles all along the way. All the towns are very attractive, showing that the Nordic races certainly seem superior to the Latins. The Germans really are too good—it makes people gang against them for protection . . .

August 22, Sunday

Cologne–Amsterdam
Got up in the worst day we've had yet and parted on good terms with the woman for about the first time. The women seem to be the more honest—strange as it seems. Went to mass at the cathedral which is really the height in Gothic architecture—the most beautiful really of all we have seen. From there headed for Utrecht on one of the new autostradas that are the finest roads in the world. Really unnecessary though, in Germany, as the traffic is so small, but they would be great in U.S. as the speed is unlimited. Looked around for some more dogs and then went across the border into Holland where everyone looks like Juliana + Bernhard. P[ai]d a tax on entering for the roads instead of having it added on to the gasoline which I think is a very good idea, as it makes gasoline so much cheaper and makes travelling cheaper, at least for tourists. I suppose the small size of the country has something to do with it though. Slipped in at Doorn and saw where the Kaiser lives—although his place is entirely surrounded by barbed wire.

A Visit to Heinrich Heine

Born to a German-speaking Jewish family in what is now Croatia and growing up in Budapest, Maria Leitner studied in Switzerland and wrote for left-
wing papers during the First World War. After the destruction of the Hungarian Soviet Republic in 1919, she fled to Vienna and from there to Berlin.
In the 1920s, traveling in the United States, she was sending reports critical
of American society. Her novel *Hotel Amerika* appeared in 1930; in 1932,
she published a collection of her reports, *Eine Frau reist durch die Welt* (*A
Woman Travels through the World*); and in 1937, the novel *Elisabeth, ein
Hitlermädchen* (*Elizabeth, a Hitler Girl*) was published in Paris. After the
Nazis seized power, Leitner left Germany, going first to Prague and then
to Paris. Apparently, the dedicated communist returned unrecognized to
the Third Reich on several occasions, carrying false papers, to report on
her impressions for exile newspapers (1936–39). This was when her "Visit
to Heinrich Heine"—referring to a secret sojourn to Düsseldorf—appeared,
under the pseudonym *Mary L.* in the Moscow periodical *Das Wort*. Leitner
was interned in France in 1940, but initially managed to escape. She was
last seen in Marseille in the spring of 1941 (by Anna Seghers). Presumably
she was carried off to a concentration camp and murdered.

Today, Düsseldorf has only *one* "major" son: Schlageter. Eternal
flames burn in his honor. Monuments to him are built. His cenotaph stands on the Königsallee in the midst of music cafés. In the

provincial and municipal library on the Friedrichsplatz a large sign proclaims: "Schlageter-Museum."

I ask the porter: "Where is the Heine room, please?"

He looks at me blankly. Then he calls to an older man. He informs me darkly, "The Heine room is permanently closed at present."

I am not satisfied with his answer and go into the library's cataloging area. "Could I see the Heine room, please?"

Everybody present, men and women alike—they are employees of the library—stop working and look at me in astonishment. One of them snarls, "Don't you know that the Heine room is closed? Where on earth do you come from?"

"From America," I say, "and I made a stopover in Düsseldorf just to see the Heine room."

They all stare at me as though I were some sort of mythical animal: So she comes from America and has no idea what's happening in Germany! But weren't there also people in the war who didn't know anything about it?

I looked straight ahead cheerily and ingenuously. The employees put their heads together, they whisper, consulting one another.

Then a gaunt man comes up to me, "Wait!"

I sit down and wait. The gaunt man has left the room, probably he has to consult with the director. After a while, he returns and says curtly, "Come with me."

He goes ahead of me, with his key, not saying a word, through dark passages, through corridors in which the card catalogs are stored. No, it isn't just recently that the Heine room has been banished to a back room: even in the days of the republic it was half-hidden and people were a bit ashamed of it.

The key rasps in the lock. The door is hard to open, as though it were stuck fast by dust. Dust also lies thickly on the cabinets that run along the walls. The walls are bare.

The gaunt man begins to open the cupboards. He carefully takes a few volumes out of their prison. A layer of dust lies on the frayed leather bindings that bear the author's name in golden curlicues on their backs.

The books are covered in dust; but when they are opened it is as though someone is talking with a very fresh youthful voice: *The city of Düsseldorf is very beautiful, if you happen to have been born there, and I feel as if I have to go straight home. And if I say go home, I mean the Bolckerstraße and the house in which I was born. This house will one day be quite remarkable—*

The house in the Bolckerstraße really does look remarkable now: with the inscriptions that have been scratched out and the empty niche from which a statue has been ripped off.

"We must make haste now," says the gaunt man, but his hands are still stroking the lot of the volumes in the cupboards as though to determine that they have not yet disintegrated into dust.

Books in Japanese, Chinese, Spanish, Greek, Hindustani, Indo-Chinese—books in a hundred languages! All these peoples thought it was a German poet that they were reading in their own language, and loved . . . The Third Reich wants to teach them otherwise.

The gaunt man quickly opens a few more cupboards and looks into them; there is Heine's bust, there are drawings in which he looks like a real dreaming German poet, and here is a stuffed parrot, his favorite bird . . .

"He wrote to Laube about this parrot, saying that only he and Mathilde kept it alive," the gaunt man explains, but then suddenly clams up as though he had already said too much. He looks at his watch and quickly starts to close the cupboards up again.

"*There's no sense in any of that,*" he says, and I don't know *what* he is referring to.

Then we are outside. The key rasps again.

Downstairs, they are already waiting for our return as though we had ventured into a far distant, forbidden land.

"Ah! There you are again," says a friendly woman, and she opens a guest book in front of me, as though we were living in the old days.

And I wrote a name in it.

Translated by **KENNETH NORTHCOTT**

The Yellow Face

Hidden behind the pseudonym "Shi Min" is a Chinese student who was living in Berlin in the 1930s. His "German Travel Narrative" appeared in 1938 in a collection of autobiographical and pseudo-autobiographical texts written by Chinese who were studying in Europe and America and pursuing their literary ambitions: *Oufeng Meiyu* (literally, *European Wind and American Rain*; freely translated as *Our Tempestuous Life Overseas*). The account reveals the ambivalence of a follower of the Kuomintang—the movement organized by Chiang Kai-Shek (1887–1975)—who sympathized with fascism, but who also found himself the object of the racism prevailing in Germany. In another text that appeared in the same collection, "Chinese Students in Germany," the author describes how he and his compatriots lived to the hilt the sort of life that they believed was European: "There was scarcely one among us who did not have at least eight to ten outfits in his wardrobe; today you wear a dark blue suit with highly polished black leather shoes, tomorrow a light gray suit with yellow patent leather shoes. Once a week you go to the hairdresser and have a thick layer of hair cream applied, you shave twice a day and before going out you look at yourself three times in the mirror. That's a fact: for the students it all boils down to the honor of our country!"

The streets of Berlin impress everyone with their spacious breadth and their spotless cleanliness. In addition, both sides of them are planted with lovingly tended rows of trees, all of uniform height;

not a single horse dropping spoils the middle of the road and there is no
dirty wastepaper on the sidewalks: An unimaginable state of affairs for
a Parisian. [...] We Chinese can do nothing but lift the yellow face full
of admiration and in devotional astonishment. [...] Must we not admit that we members of "Race category third grade" are not entitled to
enjoy the solid fortune of the "race of supermen"!? (Just think of the dirt
on the streets of Beijing, soot and wastepaper everywhere; in the evening
every family pours out its bucket of urine and the contents unite into a
yellow stream. To say nothing of the stench emanating from the bodies of
dead dogs, rotting cats, decaying rats, and the heaps of "golden pagodas"—
human excrement—that are produced overnight.)

Translated by **KENNETH NORTHCOTT**

Göring's Cup

Richard Hillary was shot down in early September 1940 during the Battle of Britain. He was uninjured and quickly returned to duty. A week later, when his plane was hit again, he bailed out but suffered serious burns. The Royal Air Force officer then wrote a book, *The Last Enemy: The Memoir of a Spitfire Pilot*. In the first part, Hillary—who had started his studies at Oxford University in 1937—describes a trip he took to Germany in the summer of 1938. Hillary and his travel companions take part in a rowing regatta—for, of all things, Air Marshal Göring's cup. Its course is interpreted as a symbolic anticipation of the war. The Germans are well trained and eager, whereas the British look at the race from the point of view of gentlemen; at first behind, they finally win. The book describes airmen's training, the battles against the Luftwaffe, the comradeship of the RAF, and the sorrow at the death of friends. The title quotes a verse from the Bible (I Corinthians 15:26): "The last enemy that shall be destroyed is death." Hillary was still not fully recovered when he set off on his last flight at the beginning of 1943.

We wrote to the German and Hungarian Governments expressing the hope that we might be allowed to row in their respective countries. They replied that they would be delighted, sent us the times of their regattas (which we very well knew), and expressed the wish that they might be allowed to pay our expenses. We wrote back with appropriate surprise and gratification, and having collected eight others, on July 3, 1938, we set forth.

Half of us went by car and half by train, but we contrived somehow to arrive in Bad Ems together, two days before the race. We were to row for General Goering's Prize Fours. They had originally been the Kaiser Fours, and the gallant General had taken them over.

We left our things at the hotel where we were to stay and took a look at the town which, with its mass of green trees rising in a sheer sweep on either side of the river, made an enchanting picture. Down at the boat-house we had our first encounter with Popeye. He was the local coach and had been a sergeant-major in the last war. With his squat muscled body, his toothless mouth sucking a pipe, the inevitable cap over one eye, his identity was beyond dispute. Popeye was to prove our one invaluable ally. He was very proud of his English though we never discovered where he learned it. After expressing a horrified surprise that we had not brought our own boat, he was full of ideas for helping us.

"Mr. Waldron," he said, "I fix you right up tomorrow this afternoon. You see, I get you boat."

The next day saw the arrival of several very serious-looking crews and a host of supporters, but no boat. Again we went to Popeye.

"Ah, gentlemen," he said. "My wife, she drunk since two years but tomorrow she come."

We hoped he meant the boat. Fortunately he did, and while leaky and low in the water, it was still a boat and we were mighty relieved to see it. By this time we were regarded with contemptuous amusement by the elegantly turned-out German crews. They came with car-loads of supporters and set, determined faces. Shortly before the race we walked down to the changing-rooms to get ready. All five German crews were lying flat on their backs on mattresses, great brown stupid-looking giants, taking deep breaths. It was all very impressive. I was getting out of my shirt when one of them came up and spoke to me, or rather harangued me, for I had no chance to say anything. He had been watching us, he said, and could only come to the conclusion that we were thoroughly representative of a decadent race. No German crew would dream of appearing so lackadaisical if rowing in England: they would train and they would win. Losing this race might not appear very important to us, but I could rest assured that the German people would not fail to notice and learn from our defeat.

I suggested that it might be advisable to wait until after the race before shooting his mouth off, but he was not listening. It was Popeye who finally silenced him by announcing that we would win. This caused a roar of laughter and everyone was happy again. As Popeye was our one and only supporter, we taught him to shout "You got to go, boys, you got to go." He assured us that we would hear him.

Looking back, this race was really a surprisingly accurate pointer to the course of the war. We were quite untrained, lacked any form of organization and were really quite hopelessly casual. We even arrived late at the start, where all five German crews were lined up, eager to go. It was explained to us that we would be started in the usual manner; the starter would call out "Are you ready?" and if nobody shouted or raised his hand he would fire a gun and we would be off. We made it clear that we understood and came forward expectantly. "Are you ready?" called the starter. Beside us there was a flurry of oars and all five German crews were several lengths up the river. We got off to a very shaky start and I can't ever remember hearing that gun fired. The car-loads of German supporters were driving slowly along either bank yelling out encouragement to their respective crews in a regulated chant while we rowed in silence, till about quarter-way up the course and above all the roaring and shouting on the banks I heard Popeye: "You got to go, boys, you got to go. All my dough she is on you." I looked up to see Popeye hanging from a branch on the side of the river, his anxious face almost touching the water. When Frank took one hand off his oar and waved to him, I really thought the little man was going to fall in. As we came up to the bridge that was the half-way mark we must have been five lengths behind; but it was at that moment that somebody spat on us. It was a tactical error. Sammy Stockton, who was stroking the boat, took us up the next half of the course as though pursued by all the fiends in hell and we won the race by two-fifths of a second. General Goering had to surrender his cup and we took it back with us to England. It was a gold shell-case mounted with the German eagle and disgraced our rooms in Oxford for nearly a year until we could stand it no longer and sent it back through the German Embassy. I always regret that we didn't put it to the use which its shape suggested. It was certainly an unpopular win. Had we shown any sort of enthusiasm or given any impression that we had trained they would have tolerated it, but as it was they showed merely a sullen resentment.

A Demonstration against the War

William Shirer was active as a correspondent in Berlin from 1934 to 1940—for the press (*Chicago Tribune*), for news services (Universal News Service, International News Service), and finally for radio (Columbia Broadcasting System). He sees Nazism as a bitter enemy. However, Shirer seems less interested in the movement's historical causes; rather, he explains its dominance by a presumed predisposition of the German people. He confronts racist ideology with racist terms. Shirer's diary contains numerous entries about the "character" of "*the* German": "the Nazi regime has expressed something very deep in the German nature and in that respect it has been representative of the people it rules." "Surely the Germans must be the ugliest-looking people in Europe, individually." It is only for the censors with whom he has to work ("decent") and the armed forces ("business-like," "very correct," "I get along all right with German naval people") that he seems to have a strange preference. Anticipating German reunification in 1990, in the newest edition of his historical study *The Rise and Fall of the Third Reich* (1959), Shirer writes, "Europe will be faced again with the German problem." Shirer is skeptical in his answer to his own question: "Have the Germans changed? Many in the West seem to believe so. I myself am not so sure." One of the few observations that relativizes Shirer's picture of the German population is that they were far from enthusiastic in their acceptance of the war.

Berlin, September 27

A motorized division rolled through the city's streets just at dusk this evening in the direction of the Czech frontier. I went out to the corner of the Linden where the column was turning down the Wilhelmstrasse, expecting to see a tremendous demonstration. I pictured the scenes I had read of in 1914 when the cheering throngs on this same street tossed flowers at the marching soldiers, and the girls ran up and kissed them. The hour was undoubtedly chosen today to catch the hundreds of thousands of Berliners pouring out of their offices at the end of the day's work. But they ducked into the subways, refused to look on, and the handful that did stood at the curb in utter silence unable to find a word of cheer for the flower of their youth going away to the glorious war. It has been the most striking demonstration against war I've ever seen. Hitler himself reported furious. I had not been standing long at the corner when a policeman came up the Wilhelmstrasse from the direction of the Chancellery and shouted to the few of us standing at the curb that the Führer was on his balcony reviewing the troops. Few moved. I went down to have a look. Hitler stood there, and there weren't two hundred people in the street or the great square of the Wilhelmsplatz. Hitler looked grim, then angry, and soon went inside, leaving his troops to parade by unreviewed. What I've seen tonight almost rekindles a little faith in the German people. They are dead set against war.

Kristallnacht

A Swiss merchant reports on his experiences in Germany between 1923 and 1943. He tells of the Hitler putsch in Munich (1923) and of a meeting with the later "Führer" in a Munich restaurant. The South German firm for which he worked (whose location is obscured in Juvet's reports) and his group of colleagues (whose names, like his own, are concealed behind pseudonyms—the Latin *juvet* means "may he help") become a microcosm of German society and can serve as examples for the study of different behavioral patterns during individual phases of National Socialism and the Third Reich. They cover the period after the Great Depression, when the Nazis became the strongest party in the Reichstag (1930); the crisis of the Weimar Republic (1932); the time after Hitler's coming into power (1933); the Anschluss of Austria and the annexation of the Sudetenland (1938); the outbreak of war (1939); and the period when the campaigns in Russia and North Africa took a critical turn (1942/43).

Waldmeyer had sent me to Northern Bavaria to call on clients and I had spent the evening of 7 November with friends in Nuremberg, Jews. They belonged to a family that had lived there for centuries, and that had been converted to Christianity for generations. The master of the house, the owner of an old and respected firm, had been a Bavarian officer in the artillery in World War I; he had lost a leg and an eye and had been decorated with the Iron Cross, Classes I and II. The evening had passed quickly with music and a bottle of good Rhine wine; we had scarcely mentioned politics, I knew what bothered my friends. At that time Streicher—the man who had made a pathological religion out of the hatred of the Jews—was still gauleiter of Nuremberg. His periodical, *Stürmer*, was on sale on every street corner: it was full of repellent and distorted caricatures that were mostly occupied with the Jews' allegedly insatiable lust for blonde German girls. Franconia, Streicher's district, was admittedly a rewarding field for his propaganda. Before 1933 almost the whole of rural trade had been in the hands of the Jews, and as a result of the depression, the peasants were all, more or less, in the Jews' debt. But a creditor is always disliked, especially if he has the natural tendency to demand his money. Thus the hatred of the Jews had arisen here, quite automatically, from the dislike of creditors, and Streicher found a rich soil for his immoderate propaganda.

My friends had long since prepared for their emigration to America. But there were huge difficulties; the waiting periods were lengthy and so, for the time being, they had to contain themselves in patience. They did not complain about their fate, they clung to Germany with a touching affection and were completely supportive of the German action in the Sudetenland— they could not understand my sympathy for the Czechs. They gave Hitler great credit for having saved world peace at Munich, but almost more than that for having succeeded in realizing the pan-German dream of his people.

A shadow lay over the evening. On the day before, news had come from Paris that a young Polish Jew named Herschel Grynszpan had made an attempt on the life of Ernst vom Rath, an officer at the German embassy. I had more understanding for the motives behind the insane act of this desperate young man whose parents had been forcibly deported from Hanover than my hosts, who vigorously condemned his behavior, but we said little about the affair because we did not want politics to spoil the beauty and harmony of the evening.

In any case, I could not stay for long, because next morning I wanted to go on to Bayreuth. The wine ensured that I had a deep and dreamless sleep and thus I had only vaguely heard noises on the street, some time after midnight. Since this was nothing unusual in a large city, I did not think the noise was in any way significant and went back to sleep.

I reached Bayreuth quickly via the new autobahn. I had never liked the town with its vanity and all the Wagnerian theater pomp, but the experiences of that day eternalized my dislike of it.

At a bend in the road, I saw a crowd of people, and as I approached, I noticed that they were standing in front of a house out of which firemen were carrying charred pieces of furniture. The house looked somehow different from all the others and the waiting crowd, too, had a different face from what one expects at a fire. They were quite obviously excited and happy.

I got out of the car and asked a woman what was going on. "Ha! We burned the synagogue down last night." Why in God's name? "Don't you know that the Jews killed our Herr vom Rath?" I took a chance and asked whether it had been Bayreuth Jews or whether the unfortunate Herr vom Rath, "our" Herr vom Rath, as my informant had said, had perhaps come from Bayreuth. But it was rather inadvisable to go on talking like this; the faces of the bystanders, at first astonished and then threatening, told me enough.

I gathered from snatches of conversation I had heard that the Jews had been quartered in a warehouse and were awaiting their transportation. I drove to the warehouse. On the way, I passed several Jewish shops, all of which had their windows shattered; the shop windows were all empty— they had been looted—and the shops' furnishings had all been thrown out on to the street. A large gaping crowd was gathered in front of the ware-house. I was reluctant to add myself to the assembled crowd but I had to see with my own eyes what was happening there. Through the great windows you could see perhaps fifty people in a bleak, empty hall. Most of them stood against the wall, staring gloomily, a few walked restlessly about, others were sitting—in spite of the severe cold—on the bare floor. Almost all of them, incidentally, were inadequately dressed; some only had thrown on a topcoat over their nightclothes. The SA people who had picked them up during the night had apparently not allowed them time to put on more clothing.

Compared with what happened later, this was only a small beginning. I had lost all desire to do work that day. If this could have happened in Bayreuth, which was not part of Streicher's gau, what must have happened in Nuremberg! I was worried about my hosts of the night before; I needed to have some assurance. But I did not want to telephone, I preferred to drive back the seventy kilometers.

I did not need to drive through the city in order to get to my friends; they lived in a northern suburb that lay in the direction of Bayreuth. Thus, for the time being, I did not see any of the destruction in the shops. But what had happened to their house looked all the worse for that. The front door had been torn off its hinges, furniture lay in the garden. The whole staircase was soaked, the nocturnal intruders had had the playful idea of turning on the taps in the bathroom and letting the water run out. The staircase and almost all the doors had been shattered with axes, and the magnificent Steinway grand piano that I had played a few hours before had suffered no less. The valuable pictures on the wall had been slit with a knife; in short, anything that could be damaged and destroyed had fallen prey to the mob's lust for destruction. I looked for my hosts, but the house was empty. As I turned to leave, the lady of the house appeared. She was covered in bruises; I won't even describe her mental state. Her husband was in the hospital; he died the day after from the wounds he had received.

I have described things as I saw them. I don't want to talk about my feelings, because they are not important. What seems more important to me is what the small section of the German people with whom I was in contact said about the events of 8 November 1938.

To the credit of my Augsburg colleagues, I can report that they—with the exception of Neder, who took part in the operation in his role as an SA Führer—disapproved of the excesses. Some more, others less. Waldmeyer said nothing, but he was very thoughtful in the ensuing days; Hofmann, who could almost count himself as one of the old guard, made no attempt to conceal his horror from me. I also heard that the workers were outraged. I have spoken about it to no one. Neder gave other people drastic accounts of his heroic deeds. They were not much different from what I had seen in Nuremberg and what had gone on in every other German city. In the venerable university city of Würzburg, the very rector of the university led the pogrom in person.

A little while after this I met our Nuremberg representative, a harmless and industrious person. He was a member of the SA but was, by chance, kept away from home that evening. According to his report, Streicher had drummed up the whole of the Nuremberg SA, had made an inflammatory speech, and had divided the army of destruction up to express the organized popular anger according to a preconceived plan. Everyone was assigned a district.

"I am happy I was not in Nuremberg that evening, it certainly would have rubbed me the wrong way," said our representative.

I asked him whether he would have taken part if he had been there. "Of course," he said, "orders are orders."

His words clarified a whole lot of things for me.

Translated by **KENNETH NORTHCOTT**

Berlin in the Summer of 1939

Heinrich Hauser (who often gave contradictory information about his own biography) underwent some strange political changes in the course of his life. After hovering for a long time on the far right of the political spectrum, belonging to a Freikorps and being on close terms with the Nazis, he dissociated himself from them in 1942 (with *Time Was: Death of a Junker*). Since 1938 he had been living, for the most part, in exile in the United States and was publishing both there and in Germany. In the winter of 1938/39, he returned on occasion to Germany. The first chapter of his book *Battle Against Time*, "Berlin in the Summer of 1939" (which he published in the same year in New York), deals with a journey from the point of view of an American tourist. In the foreword Hauser writes: "It is out of the conviction that Adolf Hitler is leading the German people to destruction, out of the recognition of the duty to rebel against this, that I have written this book." Nonetheless, *Battle Against Time* contains many elements of Nazi ideology and a friendly "profile" of Hermann Göring. In 1945, Hauser went further and formulated a reactionary critique of the United States (*The German Talks Back*). Heinrich Hauser published novels (*Brackwasser* [*Brackish Water*], 1928), travel books (*Feldwege nach Chicago* [*Country Roads to Chicago*], 1931), and industrial reports (*Im Kraftfeld von Rüsselsheim* [*In Rüsselsheim's Field of Force*], 1940—one of the first specialist books to contain color photographs)—as well as documentary films (*Die letzten Segelschiffe* [*The Last Sailing Ships*], 1930). In 1949, he was for a short time editor-in-chief of the magazine *Stern*.

When Hitler came to power, many apprehensions were voiced that he might make another city his capital—Munich, perhaps. These fears were groundless. It is true that Munich is still the capital of the Party, but no other city would have been as suited to the dynamic will of the Fuehrer as Berlin. If the Prussian kings had achieved the impossible in its development, Hitler was just the man to step into their footprints.

Let us suppose that the American traveller in the summer of 1939 goes sightseeing one day with a member of the Nazi party for his guide, and on the following day with an ordinary citizen who has not yet accepted the Hitler idea. Our tourist will thus see the city from two totally different aspects.

The Nazi guide—the chances are that he will be quite an intelligent young man—will not limit himself to showing the stranger only the beautiful sides of the city. As a true German, he will be very thorough in his explanations:

"To understand Berlin, you should know that the city counted only 170,000 inhabitants in 1870. Since then it has grown at a mad tempo, almost too fast. A chaos of building followed, practically without any plan. The wealth of the eighties and nineties had come too suddenly. The large majority of houses in the big business centers date from this period. You will see for yourself that though they were called palaces at that time, they were palaces in poor taste. For an example of planless and bad architecture, I will show you a typical apartment house in Berlin East. You observe that the five-story block of houses, with its hundreds of small flats, is like a fortress closing in on half a dozen narrow back yards without light. Unfortunately, a large part of Berlin's population is living today in houses like these. There should have been streets instead of back yards. Do you know how these blind courts came about? Because an architect submitted to the king his blueprint for this section of the city without drawing in the necessary side streets; the king okayed them and the architect did not dare add the side streets which he had planned.

"I am purposely showing you first what I consider bad, so that you may understand how greatly Berlin needed the Fuehrer's reshaping. The street 'Unter den Linden,' for instance, is a disappointment to every foreigner who sees it for the first time. The houses are almost all of unequal height and are built in different styles. It can't stand comparision with the Champs Élysées in Paris or with the Ludwigstrasse in Munich. It is Berlin's misfortune to have been built not by kings and great lords but by greedy speculators.

"Our 'Dom,' opposite the imperial castle, is a poor imitation of St. Peter's in Rome. You seldom see anybody walk into it. The castle itself is a potpourri of styles from seven centuries. The unsightly Emperor William Memorial Church only interferes with the traffic of an already crowded square. On the Kurfuerstendamm the structures look as if they have trousers on, as a witty Frenchman said—which means that the frightful architecture of the business buildings is dressed up part way by the lower stories of shops.

"However, all this will very soon be changed by the building energy of the Fuehrer. Look at these new buildings: the air ministry, the chancellery, the new home of the propaganda ministry, the giant Tempelhof airport, the arena of the Olympic games, the East-West axis—the widest, most beautiful thoroughfare of any city in the world. Look at the city plan and I shall show you how we are bringing order into this chaos: We are rechannelling the Spree River to make it navigable for 1000-ton barges. We are transferring the railroad stations; we shall build new subways and entirely new suburbs like Legebruch near Oranienburg, which has grown in two years from 400 to 5000 inhabitants. We have the biggest building program Berlin has ever known, except that not everybody is allowed to build as he wants to. It is the Fuehrer and, after him, the general building inspector for Berlin [Albert Speer], who does the deciding as to what shall be built and how it shall be built.

"You have noticed here and there, distributed all over the city, the giant building excavations and plots, the soaring steel structures. At night you are kept awake by the booming of the pile-drivers in front of your hotel; you look down into the foundations of a new construction and see the forms of the workmen diminished as in a mine, amid the flaming of acetylene torches, the rattle of riveting hammers, the growling of concrete mixers and the sputtering of engines. The work goes on day and night.

"And yet you cannot say that the Fuehrer has everything that is old torn down indiscriminately, if it is not to his taste. Neither the Fuehrer nor we think of the *Siegessäule* (the victory column) as a thing of beauty, and we find the monuments of the Victory Avenue in atrocious taste. Nevertheless we concede their right to endure in a place specially reserved for the memory of the epoch of William II."

By now the American tourist will no doubt have been impressed, and reasonably enough, by this enormous building activity. He will have perceived that the great new constructions of the Fuehrer are executed in a clear, appropriate, and simple style, a style as much in keeping with the character of Berlin as the best new skyscrapers are with that of New York. But next day he goes sightseeing again with another guide, let us say a business man who is not a special friend of the Hitler party:

"The big buildings? Yes, they are colossal, I would say *too* colossal.

Do you know how much the converted area is costing the state per cubic meter? One thousand marks! Take, for example, the chancellery, with a length of 422 meters, a height of over 20 meters, and a depth, roughly, of 60 meters. Figure out yourself what it must have cost! We estimate, together with the inside furnishings, an expenditure of at least half a billion marks. When you look at the building plan you will notice on the corner of Wilhelmstrasse, fitted in with this giant construction, the old imperial chancellery of Bismarck. Today it looks as small as a doll's house. Yet Bismarck governed a great empire from that doll's house. We don't think that this giant new construction was actually necessary. And it's said to be too small already!

"Perhaps you've heard the story of the two workmen who pass by the chancellery and one says to the other: 'What do you think Hitler would have built if he had had means?'

"When you go to Munich you must visit the exhibition of architecture, and see the models of all the colossal buildings that the Fuehrer plans. You'll be overwhelmed. The program comprehends 60,000,000 cubic meters of converted area, but the entire production capacity of the German building industry is only 12,000,000 cubic meters per year of converted area. That means that the entire German building industry would have to work six years in order to carry out the Fuehrer's program, and not a single private house could be built.

"King Ludwig of Bavaria was locked up as insane for having spent 10,000,000 marks for three castles. And Hitler . . . ?

"Look at this pile of demolition which some day will be a street, and here again, this crater which will be a public square. The land in this section is worth 200 marks per square meter. Formerly there were tenement buildings here. They weren't good-looking, but they brought a yearly income of so and so many million marks. They were torn down, at a time when the housing shortage in Berlin was already acute—a shortage of at least 300,000 apartment houses, mostly small apartments. For that reason the little man is now forced to pay excessively high rents. Of course the housing market is regulated by the State—the rents must have authorized figures and may not be raised—but in practice it works this way: The agent of the apartment or flat puts a few pieces of old and worn furniture into it and forces the tenant to rent a furnished flat at an exorbitant price. Or he will force him to pay too much for the old stuff unless he will prepay the rent for a year. When you look at the newspaper advertisements you will find dozens of ads of big firms wanting apartments for their employees.

"Our best residential district in the old West section, between the Tiergarten and the Landwehrkanal, no longer exists. On all private houses you will see signs of hundreds of 'official bureaus.' There are government bureaus, economics societies, bureaus of the army and of the air force. In front of them you will see the official automobiles in long files—you can easily recognize them by the celluloid flags they carry on each side of their radiators.

"In front of the rising buildings which serve officialdom are stacked piles of precious bricks, sacks of concrete, steel girders, which a private individual is no longer able to get. Do you know that a citizen, after making numberless applications and filling in dozens of forms, receives only one ton of steel for his house? He is told to use wood instead, but wood can also scarcely be had. The windows of the new houses are to be arched in order to save the iron carriers above. The architects are told to convince their clients not to have open fireplaces built because of the limited wood supply.

"I don't want to say anything against the barracks, the airports, the motor highways, the bridges; perhaps they are necessary and in some way or other will serve the welfare of the whole nation. But why these colossal buildings, these stadiums for 200,000 people, to be used only during a few days in the year? And then, and above all, there are the palatial houses of the Party leaders, each of which has cost many hundred thousand marks, to embitter us. How have these Party leaders grown rich so quickly? Where does the money come from? Why do they get the building material which is refused to the private citizen?"

The American tourist has now seen Berlin from two different points of view, but he has gained no conception of Berlin as the greatest industrial city of Germany.

There are 2,400,000 people in Berlin earning a living. Of them, 145,000 are in the electro-industry. The textile industry has 2,000 factories and workshops in the city. Ninety-five per cent of all German films are made in Berlin. The breweries have a capital of around 100 million marks. The port is the second largest in Europe, handling 10 million tons a year. Berlin is the seat of the most important German banks. The share of the Berlin machine industry in the entire German machine industry amounts to 12 per cent.

The budget of the Berlin city administration amounts to almost a billion marks. The annual tax receipts are 524 million marks.

The American industrialist will naturally be most interested in the large representative industries. But they are not typical of Berlin as an industrial city. Far more characteristic are the thousands of small business concerns, dwarf factories with from two to twenty workmen. Properly speaking, they are not factories at all; their activities extend through all the stories of a building in a tenement block intended for living quarters. Although they do not pay as high wages as factories engaged in mass production, the Berlin workman quite often prefers them. For he is an individualist: he likes to have his coffeepot beside his workbench, or to send the apprentice to the near-by saloon for a bottle of beer for his second breakfast. That would be impossible in a large factory. He also likes to have personal contact with his boss.

The employee or business man who goes to his job in his own car encounters no parking problem—one of the agreeable surprises for the tourist from the United States. Even in the business sections a man can park his car anywhere, never more than one block from his destination. There are no skyscrapers, hence no large crowds so typical of the business centers of American cities. The streets of Berlin are wider than those of New York or London or Paris, and the traffic runs more smoothly. In contrast to Manhattan, Berlin will always have space enough to expand in all directions. Today it covers an area of 900 square kilometers, and yet you can cross the city from one end to the other in half the time it takes to travel the length of Manhattan island.

Berlin is a "green" city: it has as many trees as inhabitants, and the balconies, so typical of the Berlin apartment houses, are covered with flowers all summer long. One might expect life in such a setting to run in more leisurely fashion than in a large American city. But Berlin is a working town; work proceeds under pressure, and the typical Berliner is proud of never having a moment's time. From five o'clock in the morning the working classes flock to the factories by the hundreds of thousands. Most of the big industries work in several shifts; the first begins at six o'clock. In factories with only one shift, work begins at seven. From eight o'clock on, the cream-colored street cars, the two-story buses, the red-and-white trains of the elevated and subways, the dark red-and-cream-colored suburban express trains, are crowded with a second army, the horde of office employees. The street cars are still the most important means of transportation. They carry more than 40 per cent of the traffic, the elevated trains and subways 15 per cent, the express trains 33 per cent, the buses 11 per cent.

Work in offices begins promptly at nine, usually for employer as well as employee. After nine the traffic slows down, and one sees the housewives in the residential districts out shopping, or marketing with big bags to stock the family larder.

Few business people, employees, or workmen have occasion to lunch at home. In the large factories of today the workmen are supplied, almost without exception, with an ample, warm lunch, really their main meal of the day. This is one of the measures of the Labor Front movement, designed not only to make the workman more efficient but also to economize on fats for the sandwiches which he formerly ate for his lunch. For the warm luncheon, prepared in the kitchen of the workshop, the workman pays between 30 and 50 pfennigs, let us say about 20 cents. Since the canteen is not able to furnish an adequate lunch for this sum, the deficit is carried by the factory.

Stenographers and minor employees usually lunch in their offices. Milk bottles and containers of frankfurters are brought in by circulating dealers, and sandwiches are carried from home. As typical as the Londoner's umbrella is the Berlin employee's briefcase, except that it is more likely to hold bottles and sandwich parcels than business papers. The business man and the higher employee take lunch in one of the innumerable restaurants in Berlin; Aschinger takes the place of Lyon's in London and of Horn and Hardart in New York. There are also many hundreds of saloons, most of them belonging to the brewery concerns. Here the man of medium income drinks his "kleines Helles," his small glass of light beer, for 15 pf. The dishes most favored are pea-soup with bacon for 60 pf., bockwurst with potato salad for 50 pf., and sandwiches for from 10 to 50 pf. apiece. The man who can spend more may order a three-course lunch, with soup, a meat dish, and dessert, at a cost, in these cheap restaurants, of about one mark.

High-class stenographers with an income of more than 250 marks a month prefer a light lunch in the coffee-houses, in an atmosphere more refined than that of the automat or Aschinger's. They can afford to spend 1.20 to 1.50 marks for a pot of coffee, a dish of cold cuts, and two soft-boiled eggs in a glass.

The well-to-do man lunches in one of the big hotels or good wine restaurants, where, depending on the bill of fare and the drinks he chooses, he will pay between 4 and 10 marks for his lunch.

At five o'clock in the afternoon the rush-hour begins again, to last until night. Most offices close at five, although many in the recent years of intense business work until seven and even later.

From six o'clock on, the chart for the consumption of gas and electricity rises sharply: the housewives are cooking supper. Because the main meal of the day is taken at noon, Berlin families used to have the cold-supper habit. Two years ago a big change set in: in order to lessen consumption of butter and meat, the government made strong propaganda for a warm evening meal, of which the main substance must be potatoes, one of the few food products always abundantly to be had.

Government propaganda is effective in all provinces of human life, to an extent not dreamed of in other countries. Step into a Berlin apartment house and your eye will first be caught by a series of colorful posters next the entrance. There is an appeal for contributions to the "Mother and Child" fund, another appeal for the *Winterhilfswerk* (winter-relief fund). A third is a Party exhortation to visit either an anti-semitic lecture or an anti-semitic film, or perhaps a meeting where the colonial question will be discussed. A fourth poster, in screaming red, bears the urgent question: "Fellow-countryman, have you bought your gas mask?" A fifth warns you not to throw away such garbage as tinfoil, empty tooth-paste tubes and other metals, even old razor blades, and to collect them in special containers.

Every one must join the Air-Defense League; it is "a citizen's duty." Every apartment house has its air-defense monitor, with police powers. The attic of every house contains air-defense implements—spades, hatchets, shovels, piles of sand. Every kitchen must have fire extinguishers and pails. All the windows must have light-proof curtains. Detailed instructions tell you how to put out fires in the house in case of attack: the gas jets must be turned off, the windows pasted over with paper to keep them from cracking under the pressure of explosions. Signs point the way to the cellar, which, if it is deep and well protected, is fitted up as an air-defense room with steel doors, ventilators, portable toilet-pails, emergency lamps. In case of attack one is enjoined to take milk along in thermos bottles for the children.

State propaganda does not stop at apartment doors. Each door carries from one to half a dozen small posters, labels, and signs. One, for example, has the letters "NSV," which means that the resident is a member of the Party organization for the welfare of the German people. He contributes a regular monthly sum of two marks on the average. Another sign reads "Collecting forbidden": the tenant has paid a certain amount to exempt himself from the very frequent collections for all sorts of Party purposes. This exemption does not extend, however, to solicitations for the "Winter-Relief Fund," a weekly collection for mitigating the winter hardships of the poor. Neither does it protect the tenant from collections for the "Pound fund," into which he is supposed to pay not money but food products in pound packages, such as sugar, flour, farina, and rice.

Although all these contributions are nominally "voluntary," they are practically enforced. A family which could not paste on its door proofs of contributions to several collections would quickly get a bad reputation in the house and would run into all sorts of trouble. On Sundays, for intance, when collecting for the Winter-Relief Fund is going on in the streets, no one would dare walk abroad without a badge pinned conspicuously to his coat. Usually all members of a family, children included, wear such a badge, which costs 20 pfennigs.

If we were to visit a Berlin family in their apartment we should have to concede that it is far more spacious than an apartment for the same income group in New York or London. In every respect this is a spacious city; by American standards there is even a waste of space in Berlin apartments. The kitchens in particular are very large; a kitchenette is unknown. Cooking is done predominantly on gas stoves; the electric stove has gained ground only in the last few years. The government favors the installation of both gas and electricity, in the hope that in case of war one or the other will still function. The double installation is a guarantee of double safety.

Generally speaking, you will find the furniture of a Berlin apartment more solid and elaborate than in a corresponding New York home. The Berliner, like the average German, prizes his home *Gemütlichkeit*, his comfort. He spends a larger part of his income on furniture than does the average American. A "substantial" set of furniture is the principal and proud dowry of the bride. On the other hand, far less importance is ascribed to modern conveniences than in America. The cheapest automatic refrigerator in Germany still costs over 300 marks and is entirely inaccessible for the poorer classes. Washing-machines and vacuum-cleaners are rarely owned by families. They are more apt to be owned by the apartment house, and are found in the laundry in the cellar, where housewives may use them in turn. The radio, however, is as much a matter of course as in an American family. The cheapest "people's receiver" costs 45 marks, the next size 65 marks. These two types are manufactured by the entire German radio industry on government orders, since German broadcasting is one of the most important vehicles of State propaganda.

In modern Berlin apartment houses—those built since the war—almost all apartments from three rooms up have bathrooms. Hot-water boilers with gas heaters are most commonly used. The rent for a three-room apartment varies according to the neighborhood, ranging between 75 marks for east Berlin and 130 marks for the best section in west Berlin. The better residential sections used to have only large apartments of six rooms and up, but during the depression many large apartments stood empty because they were too expensive, and the owners remodelled them, making two small apartments out of a big one. The intensified Jewish persecutions of recent years can be traced back to the housing shortage: as the wealthy Jews were forced to give up their large apartments, thousands of smaller apartments became available for Aryans.

Supper is over, the children are put to bed. What next?

The majority of Berlin families spend the evening at home, which is cheapest and generally in keeping with German tradition. The housewife takes up her sewing; the radio is turned on; the husband reads his Party newspaper. They go to bed early, around ten, at the latest half-past-ten, for they have to get up early. The weekly visit to the movies—oftener than that is impossible for the income-group under 250 marks per month—is usually postponed to Sunday. The entrance fee averages one mark. Once a week the husband will treat himself to an evening in his favorite saloon or *Stemmkneipe*. In two cases out of three, he belongs to some skat-club or to a singing society. If he has children, he cannot afford on his night out more than three or four *Mollen*—a larger glass of beer for 20 pf. Relatively little strong liquor is taken.

It doesn't follow that the father of the family spends the rest of his evenings at home. If he belongs to some Party organization, which is likely, he will be "on duty" at least one evening a week. If he is in the SA, he will have to put on his brown shirt and go to a "drill," a duty which will also claim him on Sunday forenoons. Or he may be a blockwarden—the lowest rank of Party officialdom—an air-defense attendant, or merely an ordinary member of the Party, but in all certainty he will be called to a meeting, a lecture, a training evening, or a demonstration. He must go collecting at the doors of other tenants or "voluntarily" offer his evening to help build some new home for storm troopers. In a word, he must do service of some sort for at least a few hours a week, for the good of the Party. It goes without saying that all these duties are "honorary," without pay.

The wife of this man must also meet her share of Party demands. She will have to attend a lecture of the "National Socialist Women's Organization," where she too will have to contribute pennies for something. She may be taking a course in "The Training of Mothers" or "The Art of Fatless Cooking." If she is still young, she will probably devote one evening a week to a class in athletics.

When their children are over ten years old, these German parents will have to give them up almost every Sunday and at least one evening a week, for the children will have duties to perform in the "Hitler Youth." [...]

Before Hitler came to power the night life of Berlin had the reputation of being even more gay and frivolous than that of Paris. Its amusement centers had an international style about them; the majority of night-clubs flaunted English and French names. The orchestras played the international hits that one heard in London and Paris; the movie theaters showed the same pictures seen on Broadway. At that time Max Reinhardt felt justified in prophesying that German films would soon be done in English because the whole German nation was making rapid progress in English by way of the American film.

What made this night life so fascinating for the foreigner was its hectic atmosphere. One could sense instinctively that one was dancing on a volcano; that the shining hardwood floors of these brilliant dance palaces were shaking from the underground pressure of gravest economic despair; that one stood on the brink of a revolution. The foreigner found himself playing the agreeable part of a spectator in a theater; he could enjoy the drama without being involved in it.

The Hitler revolution at first swept away all this somewhat spectral internationalism of Berlin's night life, and for the next several years the amusements were decidedly dull. But now a new dance on the volcano has begun, a craving for pleasure and a night life no less febrile than that of the past. Berlin is swimming in money. No government measures have been able to prevent certain industries from making enormous sums in the past three years, the war industries particularly. It is evident that nobody believes in the durability of these quickly made fortunes, and the night life of Berlin is again experiencing an abnormal, tropical flowering such as it has not seen since the inflation. Money is of no account. In the State theaters seats which cost up to 25 marks are sold weeks ahead. If you wish to go to one of the big vaudeville houses like the Skala and the Wintergarten, you will do well to book your seats at least one day ahead; the same holds true of the well-known cabarets. It is useless to try to go to one of the fashionable restaurants after nine o'clock in the evening unless a table has been ordered in advance. From 11 o'clock on the night clubs are overcrowded; champagne and wine flow freely. While champagne is relatively cheap because the government made it tax-exempt at a time when it was important to stimulate its consumption, good wines have doubled and tripled their prices since 1935. For a cocktail or a whisky-and-soda in a fashionable place one must pay two or even three times as much as in the United States.

In this summer of 1939 night life is just as international as before, except that far fewer Americans, Englishmen, and Frenchmen are to be seen. Instead there are many more Rumanians, Hungarians, Greeks—the entire diversified crowd of the "upper ten thousand" of southeastern Europe. For all these nations Berlin has taken the place of Paris, not only because Berlin has become the economic magnet of southeastern Europe, but also because the currency laws of these countries have made the French franc inaccessible and the Reichsmark readily available.

Berlin has also become, more than ever before, the Mecca of the pleasure-loving German. Except for a few other large cities like Cologne, Duesseldorf, and Hamburg, the original puritanical spirit of the first years of the Hitler regime still prevails in the provinces, and Berlin offers the chief outlet for the spirit of recklessness. Moreover, the entire economic life of the nation is becoming increasingly dependent on the governing powers in Berlin, with the result that the business man from the provinces who used to visit the city four times a year is now obliged to come every week. This class too has ample means.

The observer of Berlin night life cannot rid himself of the impression that the people are consciously trying to drown themselves in indulgence. The Germans in general are a sober nation, and drunkards on the street were once a rare sight. Today, however, alcoholism is spreading to such an extent that the government not long ago started a campaign against it by imposing severe penalties. The emphasis on nudity is another narcotic. In 1937, German illustrated papers were still contrasting the modesty of the well-draped German dancers with the American nudist type. Thank God we are better than they, was the inference. In the last half year this has changed completely. The Berlin shows are now nuder and more daring than those almost anywhere else in the world. Even the Fuehrer, German's number-one puritan, applauded a nude ballet in Munich, giving approval to the tendency toward more nudity on the stage. In the humorous magazine *Simplicissimus*, for example, there is more indecent nudity than in the notorious *Vie Parisienne*. What Party organs formerly referred to as despicable Jewish sensuality is now called a healthy exuberance disposed to stimulate the birth-rate—and therefore of political value!

Probably the most interesting feature of Berlin night life is the cabarets. Here the entertainers crack political jokes which convulse German audiences with laughter. Though these witticisms seem tame to foreigners, they furnish a real outlet in that they hint at things which every one knows but no one dares mention. Time and again reckless humorists have been sent into concentration camps or banned from the stage, but there have always been other men willing to take the risk because they could rely on the gratitude of their audiences. One of the most recent to go was the comedian [Werner Finck]. He said: "We Germans too often use the plural instead of the singular. For instance, take the proverb: 'Lies have short legs.' Why don't we say simply: 'The lie has a short leg'?" It was an allusion to Goebbels, the minister of propaganda, who has a clubfoot.

There is only one man in Germany who can tell political jokes without fear of punishment: the humorist Weiss-Ferdl in Munich. He is often called to Haus Wachenfeld, Hitler's mountain retreat, to entertain the Fuehrer. He plays the role of court jester, and his indiscretions are overlooked. [. . .]

Very few American business men go to Hitler's Germany solely for amusement. Most of them come either to study this new comet in the European skies at first hand or to do business. Since everything spectacular emanates from the government, and since every large business deal with Germans depends directly or indirectly on the approval and assistance of the government, the American business man can do nothing more useful than to make official contacts.

It is much easier than a foreigner would suppose; one might even say that it is almost difficult to avoid these contacts. For if an American does business with Germany it means dollars, and if there is anything Germany needs more obviously than the Fuehrer's principles, it is dollars. That is why many doors closed to the average citizen are ajar for the visitor blessed with foreign exchange.

The massive gates of the new chancellery open to every more promising letter of introduction. The enormous building seems to have been designed specially to overwhelm the visitor by its size, its splendor, its dignity. And this it most certainly does.

When the Fuehrer received the foreign diplomats in his new office for the first time, you could see in the newsreels the next day the awe with which these men walked through the "great hall." It is 146 meters long and 12 meters wide, with windows 6 meters high on one side, opposite three enormous doors set into the marble walls. The center door leads into the Fuehrer's study, which is 27 meters long, 14½ meters wide and 10 meters high.

Outside the door of this sanctuary, sentries—tall, black-uniformed Élite guards—are posted night and day, regardless of whether or not the Fuehrer is in Berlin. Two sentries remain on duty for an hour at a time, completely motionless, a thing that is possible only after long, hard training. These statuesque, heavily armed soldiers provide a strange contrast to the splendor of the dark red marble columns, the enormous candelabras, the soft carpets and costly foliage plants that mark the room. Should they ever have to defend the Fuehrer with their weapons, they will inevitably shoot holes in the costly tapestries or smash something else that cost a lot of money.

It is an amazing spectacle to watch these sentries being relieved, for the first requisite outside the door behind which the Fuehrer is working is— Silence!

With mechanical precision the relief guards cross the large hall and wheel about abruptly toward the Fuehrer's door. The black-uniformed soldiers face each other with masklike, immobile features. Suddenly a sharp hiss comes from the mouth of one: the sentries at the door step four paces forward, past their relief. A second hiss: the relief watch march to the columns beside Hitler's door. At a third hiss they turn about, facing out; at a fourth hiss the relieved soldiers march off like marionettes, seeming to dwindle in size as they fade into the deep background.

The real mysteries of this building, in which the might of the Third Reich is presented to the world, naturally are not shown. They include subterranean air-raid shelters into which whole fleets of automobiles can be made to disappear—it is said that there are five stories underground—provision rooms from which Hitler's staff could be supplied for months on end, and subterranean tunnels which are believed to lead into the subway tunnel, thus providing emergency exits.

The guide has amazing things to tell—the history of the enormous rug in the Fuehrer's reception room, made on specially constructed looms. Proudly he will show some of the technical devices with which the studies of the higher officials of the chancellery are fitted. He will open for you some of the doors of rare woods set in the walls, giving you a view of the safes where the secret archives are housed. He will press a button, and suddenly a mysterious machine built in the wall will begin to buzz: it is an archive-destroying machine. "If an official wishes to do away with secret documents, he simply stuffs them into the machine as if it were a wastebasket. And here you see the result: minute paper strips, on which not a single letter remains legible."

No less impressive though distinctly comic is a gallery on one of the upper floors which is a storeroom. Here are the works of art, chiefly sculptured, about whose fate the Fuehrer has not yet made his personal decision. Imagine, if you can, some 150 busts of der Fuehrer, each with its own expression of strength, dignity, or exaltation. Imagine also about a hundred busts of Mussolini in comparable poses. Imagine 200 nude warriors, with and without helmets, with and without sword or shield, and some 150 nude women in marble or bronze, with and without figleaf. Now imagine this whole formidable group arrayed in perfect military precision, so that the Fuehrer may pass them in review as if they were a regiment of soldiers!

Still larger, though less luxurious, is the air ministry with its 3,000 offices, known colloquially as Goering's "cubby-hole." Not all the government bureaus, however, are provided for in such a grand manner. They grow like mushrooms, and the new buildings are by no means able to house them all. Thus the offices of the propaganda ministry are distributed through at least a dozen different buildings. Like innumerable other government offices, they seem to be constantly on the move. Should it be your misfortune to have to seek out a certain official, you will seldom find him under the address listed in the directory. Since the last issue was published he has probably moved several times, and the chances are that even in the bureau where he now is, the receptionists know nothing of his presence. State bureaucracy in Germany is the most frightful, cancerous growth imaginable. It grows and grows, seemingly without rhyme or reason, simply in response to an inward urge to expand and expand, without restraint or opposition. Whoever enters bureaucracy is lost in a jungle.

Private bureaus—one might call them semi-governmental—also grow like mushrooms. Examples are the German economic societies which are located in Berlin. Since the State has undertaken to direct and influence the entire life of the nation, the nation must keep in close contact with the State.

There is hardly a large enterprise in Germany which does not keep an office in Berlin for close representation in government bureaus. An entirely new profession has sprung up: that of contact-man with the government. It takes men who understand the complicated mechanism of the State apparatus as well as is humanly possible, and who also understand the principles and mechanism of government regulation of industry. Their chief requirements, however, are [the] ability to deal with officials and a long-standing membership in the Party; their chief duty is to maintain good relations with government officials whose decisions are important for their firm. Former officers are especially favored as go-betweens; they have social position and understand government language, which differs from that of the civilian [...]. This contact-man is often the most important figure in his firm. On his cleverness depends whether his firm can obtain enough steel for an expansion project, or even sufficient raw materials to maintain production.

It would be untrue, however, to assert that this system leads to unlimited corruption. On the whole, the official of the Hitler government is not corrupt in the sense that he can be bribed. But it does make a great difference whether the contact-man has to cool his heels in an anteroom in the hope of being granted a few minutes of an overburdened official's time, or whether he can call up his friend, Director "Soandso," and make a lunch date.

This lunch date will doubtless take place in a good restaurant and the bill will doubtless be footed by the expense account of the firm. Business can be transacted so much better over a good glass of wine and an excellent demitasse than in the frigid atmosphere of a government bureau.

That is the situation today—a situation against which Doctor Frick, Minister of the Interior, has recently issued severe decrees, forbidding officials to accept invitations to hunting or weekend parties. There is no rule that cannot be evaded, however, and the contact-man will have to prove his indispensability in new ways.

Let us suppose that in the midst of this new and exciting commotion the business man from America has become somewhat acquainted with two men—a government official and a contact-man. It need not be a friendship; it will be enough to have lunched together a couple of times or to have sat together over a few glasses of beer or wine. Eventually, confidences will be made to him, and he may hear the following from the government official:

"I'm sure, Mr. Z, that you must have good connections in the German business world. Couldn't you put in a good word for me to help me get out of government machinery and into private business? I can hardly endure this life any longer. Like many of us, I was most enthusiastic about the new State, and I hoped to find a task in which to live up to my National Socialist ideals. I lost that hope years ago. This isn't the Third Reich of which we dreamed; it's a regular war business gone mad, a red-tape war, and we're in it up to our necks. Add to that the fact that every position is being undermined from half a dozen sides by people envious of you. Fifty per cent of my energy is wasted in holding off intrigues directed against me—and that's true of any one who occupies a responsible position. Furthermore, as a young government official I'm making only 400 marks a month, which has to cover a lot of representation expenses. With my ability, I could ask for a salary three times as high in a private concern and would have no other official expenses. It's true that as a State official I'll be entitled to a pension—but to hell with my pension! Who can guarantee that the State will ever be in a position to pay me anything when I've reached the retirement age?"

That is one story. Next day the American may listen to confidences from the contact-man:

"Haven't you good connections in the U.S.A., Mr. Z., and couldn't you get me a job over there? I can't go on like this any longer. My nerves are shot, my energy gone. Every expenditure of good will I've offered the Third Reich—like so many others—has gone for nothing. Do you think it's been fun for me, an old army officer, to flatter the young greenhorns who are sitting in the government bureaus today? You understand that joke about Goering's asking the government councillors to get their discharge from the Hitler Youth? There's some bitter truth in it. These young officials on the average are uneducated, inefficient, and not even intelligent. The present-day product of our national education and our universities differs very unfavorably from the former product. Once the German official was, if not always intelligent, at least conscientious in every matter he had to deal with. He judged his cases to the best of his knowledge, and on their merits. Nowadays the referee asks himself first: 'I wonder what my colleague decided when he looked at this? How will my chief think about this matter? Will I harm him, will he harm me?' A large circle of officials are involved in these apprehensions. Everything that passes through the government bureaus becomes a matter of importance for the personal advancement of the referee. A case is no longer handled according to its merits; it is just 'skipped over.' We have the most dangerous form of red tape that you can find in any country except Russia.... By the way, do you know this joke: What's the difference between Germany and Russia? Well, Russia is colder.

"In the firm where I work, fifty per cent of all the office work is concerned with government negotiations. And it's the same everywhere. We have in Germany today, aside from the army, approximately six times as many government officials and employees as in 1932. This cannot go on...."

They are recurrent refrains: "This cannot go on."... "Do you know of a private job?"... "Don't you know of a job for me abroad?" A foreigner hears them from his best German friends. At first he will be inclined to think that they exaggerate. Possibly they do, to a degree, for such utterances break from a depth of suppressed feeling.

And when an American encounters such outbursts he senses the deep need to throw off these shackles, to speak freely or with one word to become free, and he begins to look more skeptically at the magnificent façade which the new Germany has erected.

Then he will probably feel the desire to look behind this façade, to go to the very bottom of German problems, and carefully to weigh and balance against each other the "good" and the "bad" in Hitler's Germany.

1939 to 1945

Counterattack

William Shirer was in Berlin at the outbreak of World War II. Soon after he left Germany, Shirer's *Berlin Diary* appeared in the year 1941, and became a bestseller. Shirer returned to Germany with the victorious U.S. forces at the end of October 1945. He attests to this in a continuation of his Berlin diary, *End of a Berlin Diary* (1947). Shirer's radio reports from the capital of the Reich (1938–40) were published in book form under the title *This Is Berlin*.

Berlin, September 1, later

It's a "counterattack"! At dawn this morning Hitler moved against Poland. It's a flagrant, inexcusable, unprovoked act of aggression. But Hitler and the High Command call it a "counter-attack." A grey morning with overhanging clouds. The people in the street were apathetic when I drove to the *Rundfunk* for my first broadcast at eight fifteen a.m. Across from the Adlon the morning shift of workers was busy on the new I. G. Farben building just as if nothing had happened. None of the men bought the Extras which the newsboys were shouting. Along the east-west axis the Luftwaffe were mounting five big anti-aircraft guns to protect Hitler when he addresses the Reichstag at ten a.m. [Max] Jordan [NBC] and I had to remain at the radio to handle Hitler's speech for America. Throughout the speech, I thought as I listened, ran a curious strain, as though Hitler himself were dazed at the fix he had got himself into and felt a little desperate about it. Somehow he did not carry conviction and there was much less cheering in the Reichstag than on previous, less important occasions. Jordan must have reacted the same way. As we waited to translate the speech for America, he whispered: "Sounds like his swan song." It really did. He sounded discouraged when he told the Reichstag that Italy would not be coming into the war because "we are unwilling to call in outside help for this struggle. We will fulfill this task by ourselves." And yet Paragraph 3 of the Axis military alliance calls for immediate, automatic Italian support with "all its military resources on land, at sea, and in the air." What about that? He sounded desperate when, referring to Molotov's speech of yesterday at the Russian ratification of the Nazi-Soviet accord, he said: "I can only underline every word of Foreign Commissar Molotov's speech."

Tomorrow Britain and France probably will come in and you have your second World War. The British and French tonight sent an ultimatum to Hitler to withdraw his troops from Poland or their ambassadors will ask for their passports. Presumably they will get their passports.

LATER. *Two thirty a.m.*—Almost through our first black-out. The city is completely darkened. It takes a little getting used to. You grope around the pitch-black streets and pretty soon your eyes get used to it. You can make out the whitewashed curbstones. We had our first air-raid alarm at seven p.m. I was at the radio just beginning my script for a broadcast at eight fifteen. The lights went out, and all the German employees grabbed their gasmasks and, not a little frightened, rushed for the shelter. No one offered me a mask, but the wardens insisted that I go to the cellar. In the darkness and confusion I escaped outside and went down to the studios, where I found a small room in which a candle was burning on a table. There I scribbled out my notes. No planes came over. But with the English and French in, it may be different tomorrow. I shall then be in the by no means pleasant predicament of hoping they bomb the hell out of this town without getting me. The ugly shrill of the sirens, the rushing to a cellar with your gas-mask (if you have one), the utter darkness of the night—how will human nerves stand that for long?

One curious thing about Berlin on this first night of the war: the cafés, restaurants, and beer-halls were packed. The people just a bit apprehensive after the air-raid, I felt. Finished broadcasting at one thirty a.m., stumbled a half-mile down the Kaiserdamm in the dark, and finally found a taxi. But another pedestrian appeared out of the dark and jumped in first. We finally shared it, he very drunk and the driver drunker, and both cursing the darkness and the war.

The isolation from the outside world that you feel on a night like this is increased by a new decree issued tonight prohibiting the listening to foreign broadcasts. Who's afraid of the truth? And no wonder. Curious that not a single Polish bomber got through tonight. But will it be the same with the British and French?

Audience

The Swedish world traveler Sven Hedin visited Nazi Germany regularly between 1935 and 1943. Honors were heaped upon this prominent sympathizer. He gave speeches, and his books were very popular (*The Silk Road*, 1936; *A Conquest of Tibet*, 1940). Alarmed by the Soviet Union's attack on neighboring Finland (1939) and fearing that the Red Army would push on into his homeland, the Swede pursued a sort of private diplomacy with the "powers of the Third Reich." He reports—not without some personal vanity—on meetings with the propaganda minister Joseph Goebbels (1897–1945), the Reichsführer SS Heinrich Himmler (1900–1945), the foreign minister Joachim von Ribbentrop (1893–1946), and many others. Hedin met with Adolf Hitler four times, in 1936, 1939, and twice in 1940. The following extract describes his second meeting with Hitler on 16 October 1939 in the Reich Chancellery (Otto Meißner, who attended the meeting, was the leader of the presidential chancellery). Hedin's memoir appeared in 1949 in its original Swedish in Stockholm as well as in German in an émigré publishing house in Buenos Aires.

Meissner took me now by the arm and we passed through the Festhalle, decorated with German marble, where foreign Ambassadors were generally received, on through the rotunda and the 512-ft. long "Great Gallery." Barely half-way down it we swung to the right and entered a waiting room with a round table and several armchairs in the middle. When the clock struck twelve Meissner went in to the Führer's reception room next door, and came back at once to fetch me.

The large, oblong reception room was furnished with sober and solid good taste but without any unnecessary luxury. The left-hand, lengthwise wall ran along the Great Gallery, on the right were the huge windows. Beside the nearest window, and standing out at right-angles to it, was a long sofa. After greeting me warmly Hitler invited me to sit down in the left-hand corner of this, the corner nearest the window. He himself took an armchair, so placed that he had the daylight behind him while I had the light on my face from the window on my left. Meissner sat in another armchair and [Walther] Hewel, the Legation Counsellor, on an ordinary chair. Meissner and a Foreign Office representative were present at all interviews with Hitler. Presumably they acted as witnesses in case distorted accounts of what Hitler had said should be published after an audience. Besides that, Meissner had a phenomenal memory and could sit down at the end of the interview and write down everything that had been said straight off the reel. These notes were afterwards preserved in the archives of the Reich Chancellery.

One can hardly say that there was a connected thread running all through our conversation. Whenever a fresh idea occurred to him Hitler would suddenly switch over from one subject to another and start off on some completely different tack. But he always answered the questions I put to him clearly and straightforwardly. The statement that is often made that when he gave an audience he did all the talking himself, and his visitor was merely expected to listen patiently and quietly while he held forth, is probably true enough. He was dictator, he decided everything and there was no other will in Germany than his. His Ministers, who were supposed to be his advisers, each in his own special branch, were merely there to obey orders. And if he received a stranger his policy was to inform him how he wished things to be—what the stranger might think and feel did not interest him in the very least.

I had already had sufficient contact with Hitler to have a pretty clear idea of his mentality and make-up.

Fevered German Dreams

When the Swiss writer Meinrad Inglin crossed the German border in
February 1940, he was en route to accomplish several missions. He had
been invited by the association of Swiss expatriates to give a series of
readings; he wanted to talk to his German publisher and, besides this,
he had been entrusted with a diplomatic packet for the Swiss embassy
in Berlin. The government had also asked him to "keep his eyes open"
while he was staying in the neighboring country, which was now at war.
A notebook disguised with fictional titles for literary projects (*e Dichter
hed immer Plän* [*A Writer Always Has Plans*]), which he started for making notes about troop movements at railway stations and other con-
spicuous activities, has unfortunately not been preserved. A typescript
of his travelogue (1943) written after a first short report (1940) was only
marginally edited for its first publication in the *Schweizer Monatshefte*
(1963). Thomas Hürlimann treats the attitude of the Swiss ambassador
in the Third Reich—which Inglin criticizes at the close of the accounts
of his travels—in a play, *Der Gesandte* (*The Ambassador*, 1991).

I was warned about this trip. Foreigners were no longer well liked
in Germany and would scarcely survive unscathed if they did not
think along Nazi lines or would not, at least, deny their own political
views. I knew Germany from previous trips and stays in the country
and was not worried. On crossing the frontier at the end of February
1940, I enjoyed the advantage of being a courier, and, later on, I was

able to call upon our consulates for assistance; the expatriate secretariat of
the New Helvetian Society, which had sent me on the trip to give a series
of readings, had announced my arrival and referred me to all and sundry.

Members of the infamous SS appeared at the German passport control, and I already recognized that I myself was not free of the prejudices
that arise out of generalizations; I was instinctively expecting to see harsh,
aggressive types in the black-uniformed representatives of the National
Socialist elite corps and was surprised to meet harmless-looking, polite
men. A customs officer took my private luggage out of the train and requested me to accompany him. I identified myself as a courier, but he insisted, and I followed him into the customs shed, where the first of the
two dozens travelers were producing the contents of their luggage in the
pointedly trustworthy manner that one adopts on such occasions. Here,
I explained to an official that I could not wait but was going to return to
my diplomatic bags in the train. He stopped short, disappeared, and after
a few minutes returned to make a formal apology; unfortunately there had
been a mistake, my private luggage would be brought back to me immediately—unopened—in the train. I nodded to accept his apology and left,
unhurriedly, watched by my fellow travelers; I was edified by their respect
and felt inclined, when the next opportunity should present itself, to perform this pleasant service for the confederacy again. To my pleasure, when
I returned to the compartment I found that the giant sealed package that
had been sent to me from Bern was lying untouched where I had left it. I
did not imagine that it contained any important files beyond the usual pile
of newspapers and printed matter, but it was strictly not to be tampered
with and had been entrusted to me.

I read German newspapers on the journey. Swiss newspapers were
for the most part held at the frontier; they were not considered favorable
enough and their sheer neutrality—that was irreconcilable with the system
of unified and purposefully directed public opinion—was already a source
of mistrust. To the democratic foreigner, this paternalism that deprived individuals not only of the right but also of the ability to form for themselves
an opinion beneficial to the people as a whole was one of the most striking
characteristics of the new form of government. You were constantly aware,
however, of the extraordinary need felt by this awakened people to hear
an opinion other than the official one. Wherever you went and identified
yourself as a Swiss, the same eager question was to be answered: "What do
people in Switzerland say about it?"

The German press reported only superficially on the actual state of the
great conflict. The tempestuous rise to power of the Third Reich, and the

first warlike reaction to it by England and France, were interrupted at that moment by an uncanny pause. The powers faced each other across a fron-tier that was strongly fortified; the Allies were still insufficiently armed but burdened with international obligations that finally had to be fulfilled. The Germans were fully conscious of the superiority of their military might, but allegedly were prepared to avoid open warfare if their goals could be achieved by other means. Probably only the Reichskanzler, Adolf Hitler, knew all the facts about these goals and their extent, and it was already more than doubtful that there could be any negotiations about them. In any case, the Allies did not seem prepared to accept the German violence against Poland and Czechoslovakia and to make new concessions. Their own future was at stake and, for Europe, the future of western democracy itself. A victory of the dictatorships would inevitably change the whole face of the world. The passionate need to foresee the course of events could be felt everywhere, but the United States and Russia—in spite of the Russo-German mutual assistance pact—were still regarded as great unknown quantities, and there was not so much as a crack in that terrible curtain.

At about four o'clock in the morning, half awake, I began to feel very cold. The compartment was blacked out, the fellow passengers were sitting asleep in their seats, and I tried, without moving, to fall asleep again in my window seat. I woke up fully between Leipzig and Berlin, still freezing cold, and raised the curtain to discover a coating of ice on the inner frame of the window pane, through which, in the early light of dawn, the snow-covered plain was visible. It was February, it was fiercely cold outside, and the train was unheated. Germany was saving coal. The passengers began to stir and were obviously as cold as I was, but no one complained or put on a coat; they seemed unwilling to admit to weakness in the face of circumstances created by the war.

On the platform in Berlin, I looked in vain for a porter and carried my luggage myself out to the front of the Anhalter station, to one of the few taxis that were still permitted to run. At the Swiss embassy, the diplomatic bag was taken from me as nonchalantly as though I were a delivery boy, I was not asked for any identity papers and noticed with amusement that the importance of a courier was here viewed quite differently from what a neophyte imagined. After I had waited for a while, unnoticed, in the ante-room together with a number of other people, and because time was get-ting on, had made myself very obvious, I was received most courteously by the chargé d'affaires, who was representing the ambassador in his absence.

In the afternoon, I was in a police station, jammed among a crowd of about fifty other people, waiting to get a visa for the rest of the places I was to visit, as it had yet to be entered in my passport. In the large office space behind the counter, a couple of dozen officials were working at comfortable tables so calmly and so deliberately taking their time as if determined, in this artful way, to upset the fifty impatient people who were waiting to get some urgent authorization from the police. People started to make a scene. A Dane who had to leave by the next train was desperately asking for his passport, a working-class woman left the place in a fury remarking, as she went, that she had now been waiting two hours and could not leave her children at home alone any longer. Besides impatient and angry looks one could see that expression of fatalistic endurance that was later to make the face of the German public so inscrutable and to have so much to hide. The officials did not for one moment abandon their agonizing composure.

After an hour, I went up to an official—who had a slight limp and had taken my passport—mentioning for the second time the police inspector who had been suggested to me by the embassy; the man gave me a quick glance, remained silent, and continued, with deliberate slowness, to sort through some control cards. I asked him politely how long it was still going to take; he shrugged his shoulders and said nothing. After two hours I had to leave, I gave the man my card with the necessary notes and left—without my passport—for an appointment at which I was impatiently awaited.

At five o'clock in the afternoon, I went into a police station in the west of the city and asked the duty officer to call Police Inspector X at the Alexanderplatz and let me talk to him. When I told him why, the other officials looked at me amusedly, and the duty officer asked me brusquely what I was doing running around the west of Berlin without a passport—by rights he was obligated to arrest me. However, the inspector was called, and he explained curtly that I should collect my passport at once. I took the overcrowded Stadtbahn, standing, to the Alexanderplatz.

Two policemen armed with carbines, who were guarding the entrance to the massive police station that towered high into the twilight, told me that office hours were long since over and that there was no one there. When I assured them that Inspector X had told me to come there, they somewhat mistrustfully let me go in, without being able to tell me where the inspector's office was. I entered a long dark corridor at the end of which the office I was looking for had to be located, but I did not find it and began haphazardly knocking on a number of different doors, all of which were, however, closed. A gray figure came prowling towards me, I approached her and asked about the inspector. She was a cleaning woman, she knew nothing about an Inspector X, but told me I should look in the other wing, up two flights of stairs, then along the corridor to the right, then down another flight of stairs, and along the corridor to the left. I followed her directions but failed to find the office and started once more knocking on closed doors, found no one, and finally, at a complete loss, went down to the ground floor, where I started looking for the nearest exit; I found it, but the door was bolted. I retraced my steps and began looking for the cleaning woman and the proper exit, but the woman had disappeared and I didn't find the exit.

I went on looking, walking along narrow passages, up a flight of stairs, down a flight, round the corner to the right, around the corner to the left, now in semidarkness, now in subdued light filtering here and there through an outside window. Since I had caught a cold in the night train and by this time was already running a temperature, my strange situation reminded me—not without cause—of a feverish nightmare. Curious as to where this would lead, I wandered about for a while in the lower stories of the rambling building, sometimes interrupting the echoing and reechoing of my footsteps with shouts and standing still and listening, or trying to open doors. One of the doors yielded, I walked out under an archway and saw once more the dark figures of the two policemen, who turned to look at me.

After a short parley it turned out that I should apparently be looking for Inspector X in another building, number so-and-so in such-and-such a street, but I would be unlikely to find him there at this time. I set out and it was only then that I noticed that the city was blacked out; the blue light of the few guide lights made it impossible to read either the street names or the numbers. I went back to the Alexanderplatz, got into a taxi, and in a few minutes I was in front of the right building. Again I was gathered up into a long dark corridor, I walked along it to the end, knocked on a door, and went in.

At the back of a large, dimly lit room, in the light of a small floor lamp, someone was sitting with his back to me. "Heil Hitler" was the prescribed greeting, but I said, "Good evening" and approached the man. Only after I had been standing next to him for at least a minute without saying a word did he acknowledge me, he turned slowly towards me, looked me up and down, and asked, "What are you doing here?" After I had explained what I wanted and had informed him of my referral to Inspector X, I learned that the person I was looking for was sitting there in front of me. My satisfaction at having finally found him, which I presumably expressed too openly, made no impression on him; he spoke very ungraciously and again left me waiting. Then, without a word but with obvious annoyance, he thrust my passport at me, now containing the new visa.

I went back to the taxi stand in the Alexanderplatz, but the stand was now empty. I was told that the last cab had left five minutes before, but that

I could try to hail a passing one. I tried doing this, although with the dim, shrouded headlights it proved very difficult. It was raining, cold, and dark, I stood in the road shivering, without a flashlight, and signaled passing cabs to stop, but the ones that passed closely by me were mostly full; through the window of one of them I glimpsed some officers who, in the pale blu-ish light, looked, as they stared at me, like some strange creatures out of an aquarium. After repeated, and vain, attempts, I rang my hotel from a phone booth, but could not get through, I then followed a man in uniform and on his advice descended somewhere into the depths and got into a subway train. Since by now everything had been transported into the realm of the bizarre, I nursed very little hope of reaching my goal in this way, but I did get there, found my hotel, and went, in my fevered state, to bed.

My temperature dropped in the night and the next day I went to Leipzig, looked round the city again, and walked round the famous book district, which, with its gigantic stock of scholarly works, music, and literature—with, among other things, works of Othmar Schoeck and eight thousand copies of books of mine that had been published here—was, before the end of the war, to go up in flames under allied bombs. After an animated evening with my publishers, whom I had come to know and respect on earlier occasions, I was accompanied to my hotel and fell confidently asleep.

I spent the next evening with the Swiss consul who had invited me to dinner. In his stylish and stately apartment I came to know him as a regu-lar Bernese fellow and, at the same time, as a sophisticated and cultured man, who had occupied a similar position in the Far East. The Swiss, as a man of the world, remains a very attractive sort, as long as his traditional character has not been polished up into an international showpiece but has merely, as in this case, assumed cosmopolitan form while retaining its original characteristics.

After dinner, I went with him to a Swiss colony event, for which a small and crowded room in an inn had to suffice, as there was no permit to be had for heating larger ones. I read passages that could serve to remind our compatriots that at home we lived in an old established democracy and had no need to wait for a people's state, which had been praised so loudly in recent times. During the presentation, I drank wine instead of water in order to soothe my dry, hoarse throat, warmed up, and read very respect-ably. After some rather complicated preparations, there was a showing of a 16 mm film from the mountains and finally, by pure chance, an advertising film for a North Sea shipping company that had nothing to do with the tenor of my reading.

I had been introduced as the "ambassador of the homeland" and I ended up, at the conclusion of the event, in a crossfire of question-and-answer that, for better or worse, I had to stand up to. Why were people in Switzerland so very opposed to Germany and why did they permit any old writer to talk publicly about conditions that it was impossible for him judge at a distance? Expatriate Swiss, throughout the Reich, sometimes had to make amends for that; for their part they tried to maintain a good relationship with this powerful country that had offered them hospitality and allowed them to work there, while people from their little homeland were, so to speak, shooting them in the back with their short-sighted and presumptuous attitude. If you want to be neutral, then you should act accordingly. That was the common opinion of a large number of Swiss living in Germany. In the following year, on the other hand, there was a growing number of timid souls who had no hope that this "dirty little country in the Alps," as Göring contemptuously dubbed it, this democratic relic in the midst of a superpowerful political and military structure, could continue to exist or had any future but to capitulate. The worst among them were those who had been infected and seduced, who advocated a Swiss National Socialism or even Anschluss, but I did not get to know any of them, as they formed their own circles and regarded the colony merely as a hunting ground. On the other hand, I met fellow countrymen everywhere I went who said— with human as well as political indignation—that the course of events in Germany was a catastrophe, but who were compelled to keep quiet about it in public. However, all but the really renegade Swiss whom I met revealed, in the final instance, an attachment to their dirty little land that sprang from a deeper source than their particular political opinion.

I tried to formulate the point of view of the home country as well as I possibly could, and pointed out, above all, the difficult and delicate necessity of remaining neutral on the one hand but, on the other, of recognizing that National Socialism was the possible aggressor and of strengthening an attitude that would under no circumstances permit making a pact with it.

In order to get rid of my cold, I stayed in bed in my Leipzig hotel for forty hours. [. . .]

Early in the morning of the day that I was due to read in Hamburg, I still felt no better and would, for my part, have gladly abandoned the rest of the trip. However, our expatriate Swiss secretariat had arranged the tour for important reasons and so I had agreed to do it. The arrangements for the whole undertaking had involved long and painful preparations, the secretariat had spent money and had smoothed my path; in Hamburg, Frankfurt, Mannheim, Stuttgart, and Munich people were waiting for me, my lectures had been announced, the venues had been reserved, and programs had been printed. How could I in these circumstances have canceled the tour just because of a fever? I went to Hamburg and, an hour before my lecture, had dinner in my hotel with our consul general, Zehnder, and the president of the Swiss association. I was feeling hot and cold by turns and did not enjoy my meal. The consul general put his hand on my arm and said that I had a temperature and advised me to go to bed straight away instead of giving my talk. I refused, but had to agree at least to take my temperature, and as it was 39,5 [103], there was no point in further argument. I was angry at my failure and depressed at the possibility of having to give up the lecture tour, but—already shaken and weakened—I went to bed in my hotel.

The first person to enter my room on the following morning was consul general Zehnder, an elderly, outgoing, friendly man who abhorred Nazism and who, sadly, was killed in an air raid just before the end of the war, while still in office. I could not tell him that I was feeling better, and he discussed with me in his quiet, cheerful manner all the necessary arrangements that were to be made. I owe it to him that later in the same day a competent doctor came to see me, an advantage that a foreigner could not necessarily expect, given the prevailing lack of doctors and the strong demand for them. The doctor, a captain in the medical corps, apologized for turning up in uniform and quickly gained my confidence, which, as things turned out, proved quite justified. After he had examined me, the question as to whether or not I had pneumonia was still an open one, but he forbade me to continue my tour and said that, instead, I could at least take a proper look at Hamburg. When I remarked that I was most attracted by the harbor, the coast, the sea, he told me that in this harsh winter the North Sea was, most unusually, iced over for a long way out from the shore.

During one of the following nights, a storm awakened me out of my confused doze, a severe storm from the west, which growled and rattled the windows for hours. I thought immediately of the frozen border of the sea and was seized by a vision of the waves alternately breaking over the edge of the ice and diving beneath it, splitting it; the waves swelled out of the towering sea into breakers that cracked up the ice, tore it open, and flung it around wildly, creating a turbulent, foaming crest of ice and water that crashed and thundered in the roaring storm, gradually moving on a broad front towards the coast. The following day, I read in a Hamburg newspaper that this, or something like it, had actually happened, and I was sorry that I lived through this exciting drama only in my imagination.

In the meantime my temperature had gone up; it was regularly 40 [104] or higher, and the doctor's next examination revealed that I had pneumonia. The consul general, who called me on my bedside phone to ask how I was, and occasionally came to see me in my room, now told me that he would have to telegraph my wife in Switzerland. I imagined what a shock this would be for her and recommended strongly that he not do so but, in the end, I had to agree to a telegram that would at least tell her what was going on but would leave it up to her whether or not to come to Hamburg. When she got the news, she dropped everything, made the complicated arrangements which were, most helpfully, speeded up by the Expatriate Swiss office in Bern, and left at once.

I tried to keep a clear head, but slowly a change came over me, which I was powerless to control. According to instructions, I took my temperature again and found that it was over 40,7 [105]. I then lapsed into a state of quiet composure, no longer bothered by customary thoughts and feelings, nor even bodily sensations. It seemed to me as if I were enclosed in a transparent, glowing red ball that preserved me from anything inessential or disturbing. I felt deeply secure inside it and was ready to become extinguished without putting up any resistance.

I had no idea how long this state continued; I saw and heard the doctor come to me and ask whether he might give me a new medicine that was highly recommended, but that he himself had not yet tried. I took the medicine and, to my astonishment, within a few hours my temperature was normal. When the doctor next came to see me, he was amazed, and thought the medicine wonderful. It was Cibazol, a Basel product that had just been introduced into Germany under the name Eubasin and into France as Dagénan and because of its striking effect—in the most diverse cases—was soon recommended universally. However, my doctor emphasized that all that had happened was that the danger had been lifted, but that the process of healing had only just started and had to be furthered with a careful stay in hospital. It turned out that all the beds in Hamburg's hospitals were full, but after a long search the consul general, with his truly fatherly concern for me, which I shall never forget, did find a place for me in a Lutheran hospital run by an order of deaconesses, a branch of the Bern deaconess house. The hospital made room for the Swiss citizen who had been taken ill, and in fact—such was the strange mode of my trip—I was placed in the section for women with newborn babies.

On the sixth day of my illness, two strong men put me on a stretcher and carried me down the secret back staircase, which was also the way that corpses were carried out of the hospital. The employees who encountered us looked at me in a part curious, part sympathetic manner, while I myself was in a cheerful and confident mood.

The well-regulated care given by friendly sisters, and a rigid daily regime that I followed not without demur, put an end to my somewhat haphazard existence as a sick person in the hotel room. The sisters shook their heads in amusement when I did not want to wake up and have breakfast until eight o'clock rather than at six in the morning, or when I started to read as night was falling rather than putting out the light. The doctor, who also came regularly to examine me here, explained that I had already passed the crisis, but that I was by no means cured and had to stay in bed for at least ten days longer. When I was reading I noticed how much the fever had weakened me, I often grew tired and could fall asleep in broad daylight. When I could neither read nor sleep, I would have liked most of all to go for a walk; but since this was also impossible, I could at least sit, half propped up, looking out of the window. But outside a cold, gray day was creeping by, and my eyes looked out over a chaotic courtyard at the back of some bare brick buildings. In the midst of some ugly sheds in the courtyard, there was a garbage dump to which a cart would often drive up and scare off a flock of gulls and hooded crows. I was at first glad to watch the birds and what they were doing, but after a couple of shabbily dressed men had been engaged for several hours doing some unimaginable and repulsive work on the garbage, and the crows were just waiting, squatting on the roofs of the sheds, while the gulls, flying greedily about, realized that they could only hope to seize the odd scrap from the dump, and while the same cold wind kept ruffling the birds feathers and the same dirty grey mist was hanging over everything, I was glad to turn my eyes away from this dreary urban spot, so far removed from the spring. At home, at this same moment, *Märzenglöggli*, lilies of the valley, may already have been peeping through the snow on the meadows, and the hazels were standing full of catkins under a warm blue sky. I saw it in front of my eyes as an indispensable reality, and longed for it as I had never done before.

On the evening of my third day in the hospital, I was told that my wife had arrived. A few minutes later she stood on the threshold of my room, her troubled, questioning eyes were still filled with the torment of the long journey and the even longer uncertainty about her husband's condition. But when she saw me, she breathed a sigh of relief, or rather started to, since she had been carrying no ordinary burden, and in spite of my confi-

dence, she only gradually learned to laugh again. From now on, I had nothing more to complain about.

After my furlough abroad, at home I would soon have to put on my
uniform again: the Swiss army had been mobilized for active duty for
months. [. . .]

Before settling down for the night, the door of my room would, from time
to time, be softly opened and, from outside, I could hear the sisters' pious
evensong, after which a quiet face would appear in the doorway and give
a friendly nod; the door would close and a rarely interrupted and peaceful
night would begin.

One day the door opened at an unusual hour and stayed open, and
the harsh sound of a speech forced its way into my room: the Führer was
speaking on the radio. Even abroad, people had sometimes listened to this
weirdly intense man. In Germany, his effect was astonishing. The broad,
uncritical mass of the population to whom he was primarily speaking was
seized and infected by the tone of his speech, by the controlled, passionate, and harsh pounding, the threatening crescendo, and the furioso. Our
nurses did not resist him. These gentle, pious women, who certainly bore
in their hearts a hundred reservations about the violence of the movement, allowed themselves—at least for the moment—to be convinced by
a mentality that contradicted their whole way of life. What wonder then if
young people, ready for the military, who were predisposed to that mentality, endorsed it with enthusiasm? Those who understood and those who
resisted had to keep quiet or be ruined; those who at first wavered were
carried along. Anyone who wishes to call the attitude of the broad mass of
people to account later on will first have to ask whether they themselves
did anything against it in good time and, even then, they will only avoid
reaching a wrong verdict if they apply a very humane psychology and not
a strict morality. And who would want to retrace those admittedly blurred
borderlines within which people who had not yet been educated to take
political responsibility would betray what they had believed until then and
believe in the new order, or convert an original indifference into an oppor-
tune adherence. The Germans will one day have to come to terms with this
on their own. Their allied opponents, however, the future victors, will have
to grant a general absolution to the unfortunate nation after those who are
responsible have been found guilty.

After ten days in hospital, I went out of doors for the first time, with
my wife, but I found a short walk to the nearest park so tiring that I was
glad to sit and rest on a bench. Trenches that had apparently been built by

the schoolchildren who played here ran through the sparsely grassed-over surfaces under the leafless trees, but the connecting passages with their breast- and shoulder-high defenses bore witness to a knowledge that was more than playful. A little urchin with a toy pistol suddenly jumped out at us, took aim, shot, and immediately took cover. Two days later, I saw a street urchin looking with a frown at the consul general's car, looking at the license plate that bore the letters C. C.—with which he was probably familiar. He shouted angrily, "And that lot still have gasoline!" He shouted it out, spat, and marched off.

As soon as I was properly on my feet again, we went—fulfilling an old and urgent boyhood wish of mine—out to Stellingen, to Hagenbeck's [the famous zoo], which my poor wife had the greatest difficulty getting me to leave in good time. Before the trip back, the local president of the Swiss association showed us as much of storm-swept Hamburg as the short time at our disposal would allow, enough at least to make our farewell to the strange and remarkable of this city a difficult one. We promised to return in more peaceful times, when we would want to drive around the harbors and the canals, between wharves, cranes, and ships of all kinds, to the steamers that, shrouded in the magic of foreign lands, would once more come here from fairytale countries, we wanted to go down the Elbe to the immense mouth and to the lonely coasts by the open sea.

In the dark of the early morning we left for Berlin from Altona, where the train that quickly grew overcrowded in Hamburg still had a few empty seats. Here we checked in at the Swiss embassy, and I told the minister, who had in the meantime returned to his post, the essentials of my unsuccessful trip. While he was showing us the imposing rooms of the embassy, we got into a conversation about the unavoidable theme. He too complained about the antineutrality stance, especially of the smaller Swiss newspapers, which was by no means overlooked by the responsible German offices but was carefully recorded. He emphasized that the only tolerable and fruitful relationship with this immensely powerful new Reich was one based on friendship. I reminded him that you could not count on more generally friendly feelings for the Third Reich in Switzerland and that in certain political circles people were actually aggrieved at him because he was purported to maintain friendly relationships with prominent Nazis and did not come across as a sufficiently determined exponent of democracy. He replied bitterly that he would like to see a Swiss ambassador who, without such relationships, could achieve as much economically as he had done. Of course, he knew better than anyone what he owed to his duty, a duty of the most delicate nature, which had to be done in the context of the present circumstances and not with a vague view to developments that might be quite different in the future.

In the afternoon we browsed around in a few bookshops. There were heaps of Nazi literature on display without, as it appeared, being much in demand. I asked, on the quiet, what they were no longer allowed to keep in stock, and it really did not seem to be available, but I did find—among stocks of remainders that had been set aside—a few individual copies of the works of Hofmannsthal that I immediately bought, among them the incomparable *Andreas*. Only the first page of Wassermann's afterword was to be had—it had been carefully glued to the preceding page—the rest of it was missing. By no means all of Ernst Jünger's works were on hand. [...]

We sat in a well-known café on the Potsdamer Platz—one that I had frequented on previous occasions—and quietly made do with the awful ersatz coffee, which was all that was to be had. No one spent long over it; enjoyment was no longer in tune with the times—deprivation spoke for itself.

We arrived at the Anhalter station in the late evening, an hour before our train was due to depart, just early enough to get a seat in a compartment. Eight days before, we had tried, in vain, to get sleeping-car berths and had been told that we should have tried fourteen days earlier or else put off our journey home. There were only civilians in our compartment, except for a captain in uniform, a middle-aged man with stern features and a tight-lipped demeanor. He was sitting upright in his seat and, when the train left, he did not make the slightest movement to emulate his fellow passengers and—in view of the long journey ahead—take up a more comfortable position.

As I could not read by the dim blue light in the compartment, I thought back over my trip and realized, once more, that I had really seen very little of the heavily armed, extremely tightly organized Germany that was keeping the world on tenterhooks. It was hidden from the foreigner, it no longer paraded itself as it did before 1914, but it was there, in remote training grounds and airfields, in official buildings, in barracks, in the omnipresent consciousness of preparedness in the west, and it kept a pressure on German life that no one could avoid, unless by an inner escape. I had also seen little of German art on this occasion, but I had met new people and had had a few personal experiences that are not vouchsafed to you between your own four walls.

Towards midnight, people in our compartment finally tried to fall asleep—with the usual signs of discomfort—or else they were already asleep and forgot for a time what they looked like, only to be shaken awake again, to stretch their legs out in a different position, and then, feeling relaxed once more, to forget themselves again. The captain sat there, still upright, leaning gently against the cushions, and did not forget himself for a moment.

At three o'clock, on a great gloomy station concourse, a special edition of the newspapers was being sold announcing the end of the war between Russia and Finland. There was a lively discussion about this in our compartment, one of many events to mark the beginning of the world war in such a vague, rapidly changing light. The captain listened attentively, but when an attempt was made to draw him into the conversation, he so obviously backed off after muttering a few polite words that the attempt was not repeated. For the rest of the journey he again sat there at ease, but upright and saying nothing, and it was not until Stuttgart that he left the compartment with a short military salute. He had traveled through the whole night without relaxing his posture, and betrayed no sign of that stale overnight condition with which the other passengers finally greeted the morning. It was the attitude that the German soldier, an officer, assumes towards the public and the world, independent of the political destiny of the day that is availing itself of his service. He survives every test, never lets go, and will never spontaneously engage in conversation. It is the outer form of a weird discipline and soldierly efficiency. This attitude is older than the Nazi one, though that is certainly influenced by it, and in many cases, even today, there is still more to it than there is to be found behind the metallic severity of the face of a Jünger soldier. The old Prussian virtues have—in the eyes of the world—been compromised by militarism and now, again, by National Socialism. Those who truly bear those virtues feel a reverence for discipline and bravery that involves not only one's own honor but also, in knightly fashion, that of one's fellows, and they alone might still possess the capability—brought into disrepute among Nazis—of accepting defeat.

The benevolent presumption that aside from Nazi Germany there still exists another Germany, a better and more humane one that is condemned to silence, has lost more and more ground in the opposition camp. But the presumption is right, this other Germany did exist, and still exists, just as there has always been another Italy aside from the fascist one. This more humane Germany will one day have to return its soldiers to peaceful toil, lead its youth back into the classroom, assume political form, and embrace the European cultural community to which it belongs.

Translated by **KENNETH NORTHCOTT**

At Göring's Table

As early as the First World War, Sven Hedin was publishing books from a German perspective: *A Nation under Arms* (1915) and *To the East!* (1916). The Swede continued this partisanship under the Nazis as well, with the only exception being that his book *Germany and World Peace* (1937) was actually printed by Brockhaus in Leipzig, but never distributed because Hedin refused to erase some critical remarks that were objected to by Walther Funk (1890–1960), who was secretary of state in the Propaganda Ministry since 1933 and minister for economic affairs since 1937. The Swedish travel writer talks about this, among other things, in his *In Berlin with No Orders* (1949). The following extract describes a visit to Hermann Göring on 6 March 1940.

Whenever I went to see him I always used to take Goering a bottle of Swedish brandy, which he loved. He took the bottle in his arms and caressed it like a baby. The party was in high spirits, the meal Lucullan. There was butter and real Gruyère cheese, caviare, lobster, fresh asparagus, hot dishes and delicacies of every sort. The restrictions in Berlin were not observed at Goering's table.

Frau Emmy was sweet, dignified and unassuming. She confided later to my sister that she detested all this luxury at a time when millions were living in poverty and want, and she was appalled at this unnecessary war which could lead to nothing but destitution, disappointments and sorrow.

Little Edda tripped in and greeted the guests very prettily. And then began a tour of inspection of this original dwelling, which was a sort of cross between a manor-house and a farmstead. A positive museum of gifts that had been presented to Goering by colleagues, organisations and communities was displayed on tables and in cases—valuable goblets, cups and beakers of gold and silver, chests, statuettes and articles of every description. The walls were covered with carpets and paintings by old Italian masters. But what he himself valued most highly was his collection of Cranach's masterpieces, which he said was the largest in existence.

One wall was hung with framed photographs taken on various historic occasions. One feature they all had in common, and that was that Hitler appeared in every one. The library was richly stocked with *de luxe* editions. In one of the large drawing-rooms the outer wall was composed of a single pane of glass, the largest in Germany.

We were also taken down to the kitchen department, which was enormous and clearly showed that the owner by no means despised the culinary arts. In the basement we were shown the bathing-pool, whose crystal-clear water was 8 ft. deep and was kept at a temperature of 82°. Nearby was also a miniature railway that was supposed to be Edda's, but was obviously just as highly appreciated by her father, who gave us a demonstration with evident pleasure of the way the small electric trains tore round through the hilly landscape, vanished into tunnels and rattled on over bridges and viaducts.

After several pleasant hours at the Goering home we drove back to our old Kaiserhof.

Half Moon and Swastika

The Danish writer Karen Blixen flew to Germany on 1 March 1940 to write a series of reports for the Copenhagen newspaper *Politiken*. She was to write them from the capitals of the three warring countries, Germany, France, and England. A few days after her departure from Berlin on 2 April, German troops occupied her homeland (9 April 1940). Blixen's *Letters from a Land at War* was not published until 1948 in the Danish literary journal *Heretica*. Besides her stay in Berlin, the traveler describes an excursion to Bremen, where she visited the former commander of the German colonial units in East Africa, Paul von Lettow-Vorbeck (1870–1964). References to Africa and Arabia are very important for Blixen, who for seventeen years had centered her life in Kenya, which she treats in her best-known work, *Out of Africa* (1937). Blixen's account of her travels in Germany is full of surprising associations: she relates the Nazi organization to Tibetan yak oil; she compares fascist aggressiveness with that of the early Islam; a German whom she met "had the same attitude as my black people in Africa"; and Hitler's subordinates behave like deep-sea fish—who are only viable when they feel immense pressure.

GREAT UNDERTAKINGS IN BERLIN

The stranger who comes to acquaint himself with the Third Reich meets a surprising and impressive courtesy here in Germany. The day after my arrival in Berlin, an official from the Ministry of Propaganda paid me a visit to give me advice regarding what I should see during my stay here. He—so to speak—attached to me a young Ph.D. from the Ministry and an amiable, Danish-speaking lady, and placed an automobile at my disposal. I put myself in the hands of my guides—their choice of things for me to see was instructive. "Look freely about for yourself," they said. I am grateful to them for their solicitude and their pains—and therefore I looked out for myself.

In a totalitarian state, I suppose, there must necessarily develop in addition to the body of officials a kind of political clergy, a staff of social and spiritual advisors. Here those in the higher ranks have salaries, but most have only "honorary appointments." They have a power of the same sort as the Catholic church when it was at its most powerful. The private, spiritual welfare of the people, and in particular its education in the proper faith and its continuance in that faith has, to a large extent, been put in their hands, and is felt by them as a responsibility. They are, I believe, recruited from what we call the middle class. It is difficult to imagine that this social clergy can have, to any degree appreciably greater than the Catholic clergy, any private life; for the private life of other people makes up the content of their existence—they assist, direct, guide, and restrain it. From the nature of things, it is this active social, domestic, home-missionary work I have some knowledge of. Its men and women all resemble one another—their faces radiate their faith; they are untiring, zealous unto death, without any doubt or hesitation in their souls. What the great masses of passive people say—"the people to whom things are done"—of that I have no knowledge.

The *Reichsfrauenbund* was the first of the large, voluntary social organizations with which I was made acquainted. The society has fourteen million members, and over all of them stands Frau Scholtz-Klink, who in turn is responsible directly to the Führer. I had the honor of being presented to Frau Scholtz-Klink, an erect, typically German woman with long blond braids around her head and a pair of light-colored eyes. The Reichsfrauenbund's assignment is, first and foremost, the education of German women, old and young. It is divided into branches, according to the same system as other large institutions of the kind, by *Gau, Kreis, Ort, Zelle,* and *Block,* down to the very basis of the population, the individual families. The Block, which is the smallest unit in the system, consists of thirty to forty families who live in a single neighborhood—either in a large complex in the city or in a district of private homes or in a village. For its welfare the Block-guard, the representative of the women's organization, is responsible. She does not expect that those who need it will seek out her help; it is her job to know where there is material or spiritual need and to step in at once. She gets mothers to nurse their children; she places girls as maids in the homes of right-thinking housewives; she sends sickly children out into the country and difficult children to a home; in particular, she admonishes the women in her Block to show "neighborliness," so that each one feels responsible for the others' affairs; and she can order the childless woman in the Block who has a large apartment or a small garden to take on her overworked neighbor's seven children while the latter is expecting her eighth. I never really found out what means the Reichsfrauenbund has up its sleeve to get its way in case someone refuses obedience. The fault was perhaps mine, for I lacked the prerequisites to understand the consequences of such a thing. When I asked about it, they answered, "It never happens," and this answer was perhaps in itself quite as enlightening as any explanation.

I ate dinner in the canteen of the women's organization at one of the long white-scoured tables, together with advocates from all parts of the Reich, lively, sturdy young girls who chattered like a flock of sparrows and work-tanned veterans with something strangely childish in their glance. It struck me that the women who are now governing the entire German femininity are a type which, until the arrival of the Third Reich, had little opportunity to wield power. It is strange to think that the being of a single man, just like a magnet which is dragged past a collection of bits of iron, can regroup and change a society.

The *Volkswohlfahrt* and the *Arbeitsfront* are organized in the same way throughout the nation. This society is not picturesque nor even melodic, but, God knows, it has a structure. Not without reason have they made their greatest aesthetic contribution in architecture. I have seen some of the mighty architectonic works: the Chancellery, the new Reichsbank, the Stadium. The architectural style of the Third Reich, which they call neoclassical, maintains itself in contradistinction to what was built in the years just preceding it, but achieves its effect by its very dimensions. I have also seen a city plan for Berlin, showing what the city will become once the work of demolition and construction, which even during the war is going forward under full steam, has been completed; at least as far as area and mass of materials are concerned, it is an incomparable achievement. All the German handicraft in stone, wood, or iron which I have seen here is beautifully executed.

It is impossible not to be impressed the whole day through by the will and the immeasurable capacity of the nation. "Do you think," they ask in Berlin, "that any other nation would be in a position to produce all this in seven years?" "No," one answers, "and God knows I never would have believed it if I did not have the direct, sure testimony of my own eyes." To me, even after having seen it, it is inexplicable: how has it been possible to create these things in so short a time? And further, why was it important to create them so quickly? It is a superhuman and inhuman tempo. It is not a growth, it is a *tour de force* and there is fear somewhere, one doesn't know where, whether in the viewer or in the architects.

None of these things could have been constructed without the German people's unique ability for organization. Of everything I have observed here, that is the most remarkable. One could almost believe that in this people there is a peculiar sense of life as a mathematical problem which is known to have a solution. We people of other nations may, while we marvel, get an impression of something spectral, as if one could organize a cause so that the entire matter would end like the national economy of Tibet, of which I have read that lamps burning yak-oil are placed on the altars in order to insure good crops, but that the number of lamps has in the course of time been multiplied so many times, and yak-oil has become so expensive, that all of Tibet's annual income must now be used to pay for feeding the lamps.

But so it is with the Germans. When I have sat here together with representatives from the various projects, I have felt as if it were the organization of a cause, as such, of any cause whatsoever, that delighted them; to it they dedicated themselves as in religious worship. They have a pure and unadulterated love for statistics, in which they wallow and compete to surpass each other by large numbers, with which they deal cheerfully and without ulterior motive, as if the concepts to which the statistics refer had departed from their consciousness.

There was a very intelligent young Ph.D. from the Arbeitsfront who attempted to introduce me to its financial system. All German workers and employers belong to the Arbeitsfront; it has twenty-eight million members. They each pay specific monthly dues, which for none of them is less than twenty-five pfennig or over fifteen marks, and which amounts in sum to an average dues of two marks. I was told that this is fifty percent less than a worker previously paid to his union treasury, but I do not know the relationship of what he got from the one and what he now gets from the other. "Now you can yourself figure out what that is in yearly income," said the young Ph.D. Yes, I could, it would be six hundred and seventy-two million Marks. "And how do you think," he asked me with his serious eyes looking into mine, "one could most reasonably distribute this amount?" For them rationing and restrictions seem to be pervaded by the same harmony and exaltation: the people's hardships are over, they have been recorded on paper, classified, and made divine.

Other nations have interpreted the Germans' sense for system and willingness to permit themselves to be systematized as signs of defective individuality. It is not certain that this is the case. Perhaps the average German has his own source of individuality so deep-seated that he can submit himself to all laws without, as a consequence, suffering in the nature of his being. The average Englishman, who demands a greater latitude in practical life, does not really seem to use any greater effort to form his own opinion about life and the world. Particularly when confronted with the ordinary German woman, the housewife with whom one speaks on the street and in shops and who, on the whole, is a strange and remarkable member of the human race, one has the feeling that she, despite all prohibitions, guards her own life pretty well intact. Perhaps, I reflected, the Germans resemble the sedate, unruffled deep-sea fish about whom I have read in my natural history, who swim along their own paths under many thousand tons of water pressure. If it is true that they explode when they are brought to the surface and the pressure is released, that does not happen because they are empty.

I wonder if there has ever been anything comparable to this Third Reich? Of all the phenomena which I have known personally during my life, the one that approaches it most closely is Islam, the Mohammedan world and its view of life. The word *Islam* means *submission*, which is the same thing that the Third Reich expresses with its upraised arm. Yours in Life and Death.

Of the two, Islam is the more elevated ideal because it is better to serve God than to serve a country or a race. The cry from the minaret, "There is but one God and Mohammed is His prophet," is more nearly eternal than any watchword about a chosen people. The half-moon is a nobler symbol than the swastika (which, for me in any case, possessed something restless and broken, spasmodic, in its movement, unless, as on the towers at the entrance to the Stadium, the hooks are bent so that they create pieces of a periphery, so that they unite the figure and bring it to rest).

The two worlds have many things in common. But we must not think of senescent Islam, as we know it today, long after it found a *modus vivendi* with the other religions of the world. One must go back eleven or twelve centuries to the young Mohammedan movement when it arose and expanded like a flag and went forth to conquer the world. Then the clouds must have been full of lightning and thunder and the neighboring kingdoms must have felt ill at ease. Whence did the people of the desert acquire such power?

The Mohammedan view of the world, like Nazism, generates tremendous pride: the true believer confronts all disbelief; the soul of the true believer is worth more than all the gold in the world. It is intrinsically without a class system, like the Third Reich; one Mohammedan, whether he be a water-carrier or *emir*, is just as good as any other. Islam possesses a mighty solidarity and great helpfulness among the believers—ten percent of your assets you must give to the needy of Islam, and this is not alms but a debt which you pay. In its rituals, Islam resembles the Third Reich: the true believers do not have an opportunity to become strangers towards one another. Some things in *Mein Kampf* resemble chapters in the *Koran*.

Islam was propagated by the sword; this is a charge leveled against it by other religions, though in this matter they do not themselves all have the cleanest conscience. I shall quote, insofar as I can remember it, since one cannot buy English books here in Berlin to look something up, what Carlyle said in his book *Heroes and Hero-Worship*, which, incidentally, shares much of the outlook of the Third Reich: "of the sword," he writes. "Indeed, but where did the prophet get his swords? Every new religion begins as a minority of a single man—he is on one side, all the others are on the other side. It would not help him much to disseminate his faith by his own sword alone. Let him acquire his swords."

Even Islam's representation of Paradise was created as a warrior's fantasy; it is an ideal for an army on the march. "As long as you are marching, you must accept all hardships and maintain yourselves by abstinence, having been tested and made ready for battle. But when the city is taken and we have left our camp, then it will be something quite different." That is a five-year plan of monumental dimensions.

Islam bears the imprint of its desert origins; it has its sandstorms and great mirages. In contrast, I think, the Third Reich has a quite ecstatic respectability, *honnête ambition*, as a matter of life or death, in Heaven as on Earth. Which of the two mentalities is the more dangerous, it is not easy to know.

Verily, as they say in the Koran. Mohammed used the word as a sentence in itself: Verily. But Islam was a belief in God. It could both give and take away; with all its power it would save the entire world, if the world would only receive it. The conquered peoples who accepted Islam became one with it. Through this, Islam went forward carrying and bestowing greater human rights than any other victorious race; through it, Islam and the surrounding world came more easily to terms with one another than the Third Reich and the surrounding world seem able to do. [...]

[T]he cultivation of race gets nowhere, for even its triumphal progress becomes a vicious circle. It cannot give and cannot receive. Despite all strength and joy, and despite the great hopes for the future which have been praised here, the vista of Nazism has a limited perspective. For this reason, there is a tragic component in the being of the Third Reich; its most celebrated rôles are tragic rôles. The people, or the masses, have risen in a new, surprising, and frightening way. They lour against the heavens like a monumental force; they cast a mighty shadow and none of us knows how far the shadow will extend or over whom. Nevertheless, the viewer thinks that, in the last analysis, this people is standing in its own light.

When for some time one has tried to understand the Third Reich and has heard about its organization, its social undertakings, its art and architecture, its philosophy and ideals, one sometimes stands still on the street and, with a feeling of release, watches the soldiers who are marching westward and who are to deal with people of another kind. Possibly, a race which has its ideal and goal within itself and which in its credo forbids the mixture of bloods, needs in time to conduct a war, to conduct some kind of a war, in order to keep its blood in circulation. It is, after all, a sort of relationship to other people to fight with them. "Nazism is not an article for export," they often explain here—another people cannot "embrace," as one says in English, this people's gospel. Nor does the Third Reich concern itself with the spirited importation of ideas from without. It wishes to be self-sufficient. There is no more respectable ambition; one must take one's hat off to a self-sufficient man; he seems to be on the safe side. But there are some areas in life and in passion where self-sufficiency can get on one's nerves, undermine one's constitution, and lead to hysteria—where it may become fatal. [...]

STRENGTH AND JOY

I have come here at a time when Berlin has lost its luster, like some gorgeous bird in the molting season, for the army is at the front.

Here there is no music in the street, there are no flying flags, no footsteps thousandfold—anything that marches, resounds, or strikes the eye is out of the picture and there is no opportunity to be deceived. I remembered what my friends and acquaintances who attended the Olympics four years ago told me about the storm of victory and exhilaration which the Third Reich exuded and how they lost their own footing—of that I have noticed nothing. I can only say that the city is now a sorry picture. The streets are everywhere dirty beyond description; just enough time has been taken to push the snow to one side, but it has not been removed because trucks are otherwise occupied. People walk cautiously in their last-year's clothes; if I have seen no rags, neither have I seen any elegance. In a large city, more than other places, is "le superflu le nécessaire," and without a cultural élite the city seems insufferably monotonous, like despair itself. When I sit in the lounge of the Hotel Adlon—a typical product of the first decade of the century, with heavy, tactful effects of gold and bronze, marble, mosaic, and glass—I think that the only people who look as if they belong there are the *portier* and the cashiers. The public here makes a totally alien impression and, if other kinds of people didn't exist, it would occur to no one to construct such buildings for them to sit in. The food-ration cards, which one must guard with care and produce when one orders dinner, create an intensely frugal and preordained, anxious impression—this is not the sort of grace that can be said to introduce a festive meal. *La dure nécessité, maîtresse des hommes et des dieux*, seems to hover over Berlin.

But when one has been here for some days, the mood changes imperceptibly. Great works are indeed being continued; hammer-blows resound from immense scaffoldings, and from the ground where mighty roads are being laid. This society has not been plundered but is anxiously practicing self-denial for the sake of a purpose. It acquires a kind of elegance in the second degree, like a man who has an important piece of work to do, who takes off his jacket, rolls up his sleeves, and is now correctly clad for the occasion. The will, the collective, conscious feeling of duty, gives to winter's slushy Berlin an attitude and a bearing.

The first time one experiences it, the blackout seems frightening in the March evenings. Strangely enough, it seems as if one were sinking, and there are accompanying sensations as if one were drowning. One soon becomes accustomed to moving about in the dark; but for all that, one does not escape an intermittent horror. It is no longer the darkness which is oppressive but the knowledge that about one in all directions are four million people who have determined to be invisible and deathly silent in the night. Their silent singleness of purpose is as clearly expressed as through words.

Everywhere the stranger in Berlin is impressed by tremendous exertions of the will. The force of will is the Third Reich's achievement—there where will suffices, it suffices, and insofar as one believes in the power of the will, one is able to accept its gospel. [...]

Then I thought, "Nemesis, thou art a mighty goddess and it is awesome to see thy countenance! Thou hast appeared!" The cause of the great difference between Germany and England today, more decisive than any political opposition, is that England had good fortune while Germany suffered unhappiness and injustice. Though it is difficult in this year of the Lord, March 1940, to imagine England subdued by a superior power and forced to accept what to the nation itself necessarily seems an unfair judgment, it is more difficult perhaps to imagine that England, even under such conditions and with all its forces concentrated upon reconstruction, could be made to give up that peculiar faith in the grace of God which is called humor. Here, humor itself is anathema, a heresy directed against the sole means of salvation—that is, belief in the omnipotence of the will. Those who have wind in their sails trust in the grace of God, but those who sit in the galleys at the heavy oars must trust in the will. The united, victorious nations decided twenty-two years ago to divest the Germans of their faith in God's grace towards Germany. And this people which, everywhere one meets it, is marked by the deprivation, has determined to depend upon the will as God's only grace towards it.

"Do not," I thought, "do not take belief in *la grace de Dieu* away from a conquered enemy."

Here one may observe a remarkable and significant phenomenon of our time: propaganda—which to be sure, is not art but an art, and one in the service of the grand design. "Propaganda is the salt of the Third Reich," a young German told me. I believe, however, that the propaganda artists may sometimes, after the fashion of the depraved, democratic nations' motto, *L'Art pour l'Art*, carry on propaganda for propaganda's own sake. It generates something like an obsession; it seems a kind of magic. It is a precarious thing, like a business which is using up its capital and possesses no reserves. [. . .] The propaganda that has here reached such a state of perfection covers all aspects of existence and constantly surprises one by finding new fields of endeavor. But once a new generation has grown up that has wholly emancipated itself from the tradition of a union between word and fact, the substance of the word will have been juggled out of it, and it will be like paper money which is nowhere backed by gold, and the propaganda itself will have lost its savor. And with what shall it be salted? It will no longer be good for anything . . . (*Matthew* 5:13).

The film is an ingenious and powerful tool of propaganda. Here I have seen many brilliant propaganda films. I regret that I do not have a sense for films (because I do not like photography at all and certainly do not see things the ways the camera sees them). In Germany they presumably photograph as well as can be done, and long series of pictures are ably and lavishly created; but the films are apparently directed at a public which either completely lacks fantasy itself or, at least, is not disturbed by the fact that it knows in advance what everything is going to lead to and end with.

I have also been in the UFA ateliers at Babelsberg and walked through its tremendous buildings there. It was an ice-cold day and snow had fallen during the night. I had the honor of greeting Zara Leander and Willy Birgel, who were playing Mary Stuart and Bothwell. We arrived at UFA's open-air stage just as the queen, in a carriage drawn by six horses, was surrounded by Bothwell and his men on horseback. One might suppose it difficult to execute a scene from the Scottish highlands in the middle of Berlin, but the camera was buried deep in the earth so that its horizon was very low, and in the background some sand had been piled up and planted with small fir-trees, all of which, I was told, would look like highland landscape in the film. The horses were having difficulty pulling the carriage through the deep mud and slush and would not rear up as they should when Bothwell's group came galloping; they probably had become accustomed to the surprise attack. While we watched, the scene was taken three or four times. Zara Leander and a young lady of the court who was with her in the carriage complained that they were freezing. Inside the studio, in rooms as high-ceilinged as a cathedral, they were arranging large, magnificent interiors from the eighteenth century, and it was interesting to see how carefully and conscientiously all the details were designed and assembled by UFA's scene-painters and laborers; it was a handsome piece of craftsmanship, though the material was of an ephemeral nature. To my surprise, it was *Jud' Süss* that was to be filmed there. Count Schönfeld from the Ministry of Propaganda, who was with me as my guide, explained to me that not the hero of the novel (by the exiled writer, Feuchtwanger) would be presented, but the historical Süss, and I understood it would be a sort of propaganda film. I do not remember much about the historical Jew Süss; here, it seemed that his life had taken place chiefly in bed, for there were three pompous Louis XV beds in various rooms where the film was to be made—at the foot of Süss' own bed I saw the star of David, the holy Jewish symbol. In other studios they were practicing scenes a half-minute long from a Bavarian peasant comedy and a drama set in a fishing hamlet on the North Sea coast. When we emerged, we saw Mary Stuart once more being stopped and captured by Bothwell.

I stood and watched and thought, "Here I see with my own eyes Dante's hell on earth. No man or men could have thought this up; only the spirit of the time could do it. The poor queen of Scotland once made a fatal mistake, and in that unhappy moment her life was decided—and now here she must, three hundred years later, experience that dread moment in a more dreadful manner. Among tall suburban apartment houses, in the raw and cold Berlin air, she proceeds to a tragic meeting in a carriage with a curtain of painted cardboard through a pile of sand which represents the moors and glens of her native land. Her own beauty, which was her pride and joy, is recreated in hellish fashion with heavy orange-colored makeup and stiff, inch-long eyelashes suitable for a doll; she wears ermine and silk that are not ermine and silk. And yet she must believe—from the evidence of print—that the place is the highway at Dunbar and the day the fateful 28th of March in the year 1566. And when the inescapable moment is reached, when the group of riders springs forth, takes her horses by the bits, and stops the carriage, when swords fly out of their sheaths, when Bothwell, alongside one of the carriage wheels, cries 'Marie!' to her face—then an order comes drily from the black-clothed technician surrounded by machinery down deep in the earth, 'Do it again.' Here we have the twentieth-century's form of justice in judgment, the modern, stylish costume of the goddess Nemesis." Time and again, since I visited Babelsberg, I have, without wishing to do so, seen the heroes of the Third Reich as they would appear in the makeup of film stars, in the wings, at the great moments of their lives and careers. And which moments will the public of the future call the most important and demand be made eternal? Moments that the heroes, on the orders of a director, must repeat again and again? That we cannot know. [...]

THE STAGE

In Berlin the theaters are full, which redounds to the honor of the Berlin public, considering the blackout and the slush of the winter months. It is difficult to buy a ticket to any theater, and I would not have got to see much if the Ministry of Propaganda had not kindly obtained seats for me.

There are few modern plays in the repertoire; they play classical things. Many foreigners in Berlin complain about this, and wait impatiently for the new theatrical art which is to be created by the force of the will of the Third Reich. It may be that this dutiful, harshly tried people unconsciously makes its way to the theater in order to be encouraged, strengthened, and kept on the right path for a few hours, and, in order, without any design, to put themselves at the disposal of great spirits:

> And when all else fails,
> there is solace to be drawn
> from tragedy and the sorrows of great men.

Here one hears much talk about popular art. Not a small cultural élite, but the great German people itself will, they say, now create the art of the Third Reich. Very well, and if the great German people could speak for itself, what would it say? I have looked at a number of works of art here that have been described to me as the people's own art. Exhibitions of paintings I have not seen, to be sure, and as far as I know there has been none, but I have had a taste of graphic art in the great decorative works, ceiling paintings and mosaics, in the tremendous new public buildings. All these are pervaded by the gigantic respectability of the Third Reich. The great naked, flat figures are as respectable as they can be; the respectable naked young man, with a hand on a plow or a sword and wide-open blue eyes, has by his side a respectable, heavy-limbed, naked young maiden with a pale, pious face, who in some spaces further along has developed into a physically abundant, happy young mother, respected by all, who exudes milk and honey. It is an heroic idyll, ever-repeated. It is in this way that the people see themselves. I should imagine that the people are secretly a bit embarrassed when they are encouraged to recognize themselves in the figures—for their own sakes, or for the artists'? These are people seen through the eyes of the middle class, or rather, they are the wish and the dream of the middle class: how people should be. They do not resemble the original much more than did the figures in eighteenth-century pastoral poetry, which was a sensitive and witty idyll, an aristocratic culture's picture and dream of the people. Neither the heroic nor the idyllic mood suits the common people. I believe that their own art is or will be satiric—a kind of tragic satire that absorbs in its domain all the misery and horror of life, and laughs piously and caustically. Most of the Negro art that I have seen has embodied such tragic satire, like the fairy tales about *Big Claus and Little Claus* and *The Swineherd*, and like *Tom of Bedlam's Song*. Common people do not favor hyperbole either as heroic epic or caricature; they are soft-spoken even in passion. They deemphasize—if one may use the word—on purpose, and say of those human beings to whom they would give the highest praise that such persons are really something, or that they are no fools—which, taken literally, is a reserved recognition. [. . .]

At the same time that they were playing *King Lear* at the Deutsches Theater, they were playing Bernard Shaw, Musset, and Ibsen in Berlin. It does not look as if the Third Reich thinks it has anything to fear from those classical works. The Germans indeed appropriate foreign classical art in their own way, like a great power; and a stranger from a little country who sits and listens to them while they talk about the matter can feel a bit ill at ease. Shakespeare, they say, is in reality Germanic, by virtue of his mighty humanity; Shaw is Germanic in his clear understanding of problems; Ibsen is Germanic in his search for truth and bitter idealism. It is not only the dramatic classical art alone that the zealous Germanic hospitality embraces, but the entire history of art and deed. Hans Christian Andersen is invited in; he is of course German in his spirit; Søren Kierkegaard is the same because of his depth of mind; Rembrandt, in his artistic earnestness; and Michelangelo is Germanic by virtue of his very size. Such a faith can move mountains, and one looks about fearfully—how much will be buried here under the landslide? Behold! Germany carries on a conquest after the manner of Alexander the Great—let them prove to the world that Alexander and the old Greeks were German in spirit and in truth.

The Germans' Mood Swings

Howard K. Smith worked in Berlin from 1940 to 1941 as a correspondent for the United Press, the *New York Times*, and Columbia Broadcasting System. The title of his memoir is *Last Train from Berlin*. Smith did literally succeed in catching the "last train" across the border into Switzerland. After the Japanese attacked Pearl Harbor, Hitler declared war on the United States, and as an enemy alien Smith would have been interned. After he arrived in Switzerland, he wrote a report of his experiences. Parts of the book were translated into the languages of occupied countries—as Smith reports in his afterword to a new edition published in 1982—and dropped from Allied bombers. The Danish underground circulated brochures. The material was even supposed to be filmed in Hollywood, with Gary Cooper playing the lead. The book is not just a report on his experiences; it develops a number of sharp analyses drawn from everyday observations—for example, the mood swings of the German population that depended on what hope of peace there was at any given moment.

The graph of German morale is not a graceful, snaky thing which slithers upwards in long rises and downwards in slow, calm declines like the graph of almost any people living in peace. It is a low, jagged line which leaps spasmodically upwards in one instant and collapses into sharp depressions in the next. The reason for its abrupt contours is the unmitigated fear of this war which afflicts the German people, and their gullible readiness to believe anything, however fantastic, which indicates an early end to it. [...]

The graph has never been on a high plane, even in peacetime. From my days of travelling constantly back and forth between England and Germany, I am convinced that, however effective Hitler's nerve-war was against England, really the first victims of the war of nerves were Hitler's own people. The British were worried, extremely worried at the time of Munich; I know because I was there and I was worried too. But when I went to Germany a short while later, the signs of strain there were far greater than any I, personally, had seen in England. A dear friend of mine in Munich told me she fainted from the strain and could not get the family doctor to come because he was visiting two other people who had collapsed from strain. At the pension I usually stayed in when I was in Cologne, I found, after Munich, the manager had given up his lease and moved outside town because he feared living too near the railway station. The general reaction was, I think, best summed up by a German student I knew in Munich who had studied in America. When I asked him how it felt being a young German in Hitler's Reich, he said: "It's like being married to a daring young man on a flying trapeze. There's never a dull moment, but it's disastrous to your nerves."

The morale-graph, from what colleagues told me, dropped and steadied at a new low level when war was first declared. In the second month of the war it suddenly leapt to a record height. The occasion was that amusing day when some miscreant, believed to be a Jew, a Bolshevik or a plutocrat who dropped with a parachute, started the rumor moving through Berlin that Chamberlain had resigned as Prime Minister, and England had agreed to talk peace-terms with Hitler. On that occasion, hundreds of Berliners gathered outside the Fuehrer's chancellery singing "*Wir wollen unseren Fuehrer!*"—We want our Leader!—to thank him for the early peace which had not occurred. In such a mood drops are always more severe than rises, and the discovery that there was no peace induced a fit of depression.

The invasion of Denmark and Norway caused a mild flurry, but no noteworthy change in the progress of morale. The indifference of the populace to this singular, bold leap over water to occupy a mountainous land was registered brutally in the stacks of unsold extra editions by the side of which newsboys stood idly all that afternoon. What little enthusiasm there was, was offset by the knowledge that conquest might be a strategic gain but it did not decide the war, and that is absolutely all the German people were and are interested in. I remember the characteristic reception of this historic event by a couple of old-timers I encountered going into the

Berlin zoo that forenoon. One was an old man with turned-up moustaches who apparently took his Dachshund for a walk in the zoo every day, and the other was the zoo doorman. The latter, taking the ticket of the old man, said:

"'*Morgen*. See we invaded Norway this morning?"

"*Ja*," said the visitor, removing his cigar from his mouth, "and Denmark too."

"*Ja*," said the ticket-taker handing back the punched ticket.

"*Auf Wiedersehen*."

"'*Wiedersehen*." And the old man and his Dachshund went in to observe the strange manners of the animals, both wild and domestic.

The opening of the campaign in France, on the other hand, brought a decided reaction: a severe drop. One of the most dangerous features of the German consciousness is to think in parallels to the World War. The mention of names of places bloodily fought over in the last war invariably conjures up images of a similar outcome. The news of the crossing of the Belgian border on May 10 did this. In a pension on Kurfuerstendamm where I lived at that time, another pensioner, an ageing Prussian, came to my room as soon as he had read the headlines on his paper. He sat down and looked worriedly and intently at me.

"It's begun," he said. I acknowledged it had.

"Now it will really get started," he said, peering again at his folded newspaper.

"We didn't want this war. We really didn't." Tears welled in those hard, old eyes as he proceeded to argue the oft-repeated German case. This was typical of the World War generation: no faith in German strength, believing more fully than any Englishman or Frenchman in German inferiority, praying for mercy to the only foreigner within reach. It was a pathetic little show, but it was hard for me to work up sympathy. Those who cower first also become the haughtiest and most overbearing when triumph comes.

The early victories moved the graph upward: the taking of Eben Emael, Liége, Brussels, Dunkirk. But it is an astounding record of how little faith the German people had in their army that, after Dunkirk, when the German armies halted temporarily (one day) to recoil for the final blow at France, most of the Germans I talked to still felt they were licked. Their faith in ultimate victory had been in no way strengthened. The old vision of Moltke's drive up to the Marne, the stabilization of the front there and the long four years' misery of a war of attrition was conjured up by the parallel of the sudden halt at the Somme in 1940. The graph rose to a rather high peak when the armistice was signed. Strangely, though this event represented one of the greatest military triumphs of all time, there were no demonstrations on the streets, no open signs of elation anywhere in Berlin. (Shortly before, when Italy chose a safe moment to become involved in the war, the first and only demonstrative "march" through the streets of Berlin in the entire war was stupidly gawked at from the kerbstones by a few Germans. The march was organized by the handful of Fascist black-shirts in Berlin and comprised about fifty German students who looked teutonically ill-at-ease at thus parading themselves behind three or four uniformed Italians in black Fascist uniforms.)

About a month later, an extraordinary thing happened. The graph reached its all-time high. It was the only occasion in the better part of six years I have spent in Germany that I saw real, uninhibited enthusiasm, with Germans weeping and laughing from pure, spontaneous joy. It has never happened before and it has never happened since. A division of Berlin infantry had returned from France. It was to march from the East-West axis through the Brandenburg gate of victory down Unter den Linden. Then the whole division was to be demobilized. This was, at last, a real, tangible sign of victory and the end of the war Germans detested and feared. Sons, husbands and fathers, sun-tanned and healthy after long military training, happy as kids after the great triumph, were returning home to their families to stay. The buildings on Unter den Linden were veiled in great red and white pennants forty yards long and ten feet broad. The thoroughfare, and all the streets running into it were jammed with cheering thousands. The soldiers marched past the reviewing stand on Pariser Platz before the American and (ironically) French embassy buildings, where Goebbels and the commander of the local garrison received their salute and returned it. Then they marched on down Unter den Linden in clouds of confetti. Children broke through the police cordon and carried little bouquets of flowers to the marching soldiers, while a dozen military bands, punctuating the ranks of the marchers, played martial music. It was truly a glorious day. And in every happy heart lived the belief that this was the end of it all. Perhaps as symbolic as the fact that the triumphal reviewing stands on the western end of Unter den Linden were erected in front of the old French embassy was the fact that the eastern end of Unter den Linden, the route of march, runs straight into the front portal of Kaiser Wilhelm's palace, from which the first world war was directed. But that escaped notice.

The triumphal reviewing stands remained intact on Pariser Platz, mounted by the eagle of the German army, for another month. Obviously more divisions were coming home to be demobilized. Then, from the centre of the stands, the army eagle was removed, and the golden, stylized spread eagle of the Luftwaffe, the air force, was set up in its place. Obviously, there would be a few irresistible blows at England, another victory, and the Berlin Luftwaffe units would be brought home to march in the path of the infantry through the Victory Gate, to freedom from war duty. England would quickly see the sense of the Fuehrer's promise of peace and his desire to "spare the Empire," and the whole thing would be over.

It is no mere newspaperman's creation that Germany, the People and the Leaders, expected Britain to talk peace at this time. From a highly reliable source, I learned at the time that the Propaganda Ministry issued contracts to decorating firms to line the main streets of German cities with Victory Pillars for the triumphal march homeward of all German troops. The source is the director of one of the firms which received a contract and whose firm actually began working on the street decorations in July, 1940. Also, from trustworthy sources, I heard Hitler called to Berlin one of his leading architects to build a new, special Arch of Triumph outside Berlin. The arch was to be slightly bigger than the *Arc de Triomphe* in Paris.

What happened to these hopes is history. Churchill was not having any that season. The gilt on the wings of the stylized eagle tarnished in the first snows of winter, and late one evening when I was walking up Unter den Linden, I stopped to watch a squad of workers knocking the planks of the triumphal stands apart and carting away these tissues of hope, in trucks. They worked swiftly, and next morning Pariser Platz was clean and open again. Morale sank steeply after that. And like the graph of American prosperity after 1929, it never again really rose. The whole show was repeated on smaller scales all over Germany. In villages, crude little triumphal arches were set up over roads at the beginnings of towns. On an automobile trip through South Germany I saw them, neatly frilled with boughs of pine and with little bouquets of flowers hanging by gilded ropes from the centre. The legend across the top read: "Rothenburg (or Nordlingen or Dillingen) Greets its Triumphant Heroes!" I also saw them later when the pine boughs were turning brown and the needles were falling off the branches and the flowers had faded in the rain.

In the Wild West Bar

Harry Flannery went to Berlin in November 1940 as a correspondent to relieve his predecessor, William Shirer. In his book *Assignment to Berlin*, Flannery describes his ten-month mission in Germany, from his arrival (via Portugal and Spain) to his departure in September 1941. The following extracts, in chronological order, recount events from the end of November 1940 to the fall of 1941.

During a bombing on the night of November 26 I was caught, for the first time, in a public air-raid shelter. I was wandering along the busy Friedrichstrasse when the alarm sounded. As the siren wailed, the strolling crowds suddenly hastened their steps, the low conversations quickened, and there were shouts here and there in the darkness. I stopped, whirled about, and joined those rushing toward Unter den Linden. Some swept on. A policeman stopped me.

"Get in a shelter," he said.

"But my hotel is only two blocks away, the Adlon."

"Doesn't make any difference. Get into a shelter."

I turned around and walked slowly in the other direction. A young man in one of the many Nazi uniforms came by; he wore that of some kind of air-raid official. I asked him about the nearest shelter. We walked together. He recognized my accent and fumbling manner of speaking German, told me he had studied English eight years before in school, and suggested we talk English. He spoke it as badly as I did German, but it was interesting as we mixed the languages. One of the yellow signs, with the word *"Luftschutzraum"* upon it, was around the corner. We walked toward it and stood in the doorway of the shelter talking. The raid had begun. We watched the long ribbons of searchlights climb the skies, the sparkle of the anti-aircraft, and the glare of the flares, listened to the low rumbles in the distance and the pandemonium that came when the action neared. As we stood there, the air-raid warden came up.

"You'll have to go below," he said. "I'm responsible for this place and no one can stand outside. Someone might see you and report me."

We hesitated a moment, then fumbled through a long dark hallway and down a stairway lighted with blue globes into a basement room. It was fitted with unpainted tables and benches, much like those used for picnics in parks. A few poorly dressed men and women were at the table just before us, some talking, others resting their heads on their arms on the table. Young Storm Troopers and their girls were at the other tables, laughing and talking. A few sat on the tabletops, one girl to my right swinging her legs as she talked. Others were on the benches with their arms around one another. It was evident that some of the soldiers had been drinking.

The young air-raid official and I stood by a pillar talking. One of the young soldiers staggered up.

"I heard you talking English," he said; "I want to apologize first for some of us having been drinking. We had a hard day and we had some wine and beer. That's all right, isn't it?"

I had no objections.

"I used to be in England," the soldier continued. "I was there for a year— played a piano in an orchestra. I liked it, liked the people, had a grand time."

Then he stiffened, leaned toward me, shook his finger in my face.

"But now," he cried, "it's war, and I hate the English. I don't want anything to do with them, except kill them."

The conditions, in an air-raid shelter surrounded by drunken Storm Troopers, were not the best in which to defend the English. I merely answered that I could understand his feelings, and tried to determine toward which wall to move. Then, to my relief, the all-clear sounded, a single long piercing note. Everyone jumped from his seat, yelled with joy, and began hastening toward the stairway. The Storm Trooper forgot me.

The air-raid official, in the meantime, had become solicitous. He insisted on walking back to the hotel with me.

===

[T]he Nazis showed United States motion-picture films of the raids on London. These were included in the regular *Wochen[c]hau*, the German news weekly. This part of the film began with the pictures of Nazi ground men loading ponderous bombs, ten feet long and so heavy they had to be pulled by a tractor and six men and were hoisted into place on the planes by steel cords on special cranes. The Nazi planes were then shown in the clouds. The outlines of the Thames appeared below. The bombs were released from their racks. Mountains of earth were thrown high in the sky. Clouds of smoke arose. Then came the United States pictures of London ruins. At one point King George and Queen Elizabeth looked upon the devastation. No accompanying voice identified them, and I do not believe the German audience knew who they were. At any rate there was no reaction in the audience.

The attitude of that German audience was, as a whole, revealing. The bombing of London ended with a large close-up of Winston Churchill, upon which a voice in German cried: "Winston Churchill, the cause of it all!" Almost any other audience, especially in a country at war, would have hissed the leader of the enemy, probably cried out in angry vengeance, at least mumbled, but the Germans sat silent and still.

One other part of that same film was also interesting. It showed a contingent of the Japanese army marching by. An American audience, seeing a scene of its allies, would have cheered, but the Germans again did little more than make inaudible remarks and cough nervously. I suppose that was principally because the Germans, as some had remarked to me, thought it at least inconsistent that they, presented as the superior people, white, blond, and Aryan, who were admonished to preserve the purity of their race, should have the little brown men as their principal allies. That was partly the reason for the lack of reaction to this part of the news weekly, but the attitude was one of the many incidents that were to demonstrate to me that the Germans were not enthusiastic about the war, or about anything much since it had come, that they accepted it as a grim serious business for which they could offer no cheers except when inspired by one of their orator leaders or when commanded by cheer-leaders.

===

EXCEPT for the outbursts from the Nazi orators, over the radio and in the press, and except for the reports of feverish diplomatic activity and rumours of troop movements, we in Berlin hardly knew a war was on during the early part of 1941. There were no air raids to disturb our rest, and the conflict seemed far away.

Snow that had fallen in November remained on the ground as the new year arrived, with snow flurries every few days. One Sunday, before dinner with Joe Harsch [a fellow journalist] on the Budapesterstrasse, we walked along the wooded paths of the Tiergarten watching the strolling soldiers with booted girls on their arms, families striding briskly by, children coasting without benefit of sled down slippery mounds of snow, skaters on the ponds, and wild ducks still waddling about the ice on the streams and swimming in the open places made by barges.

Crowds milled up and down Unter den Linden, stopped to look in the store windows, and slowly wandered on their way. Almost every Sunday there were men and women on the streets rattling their little red boxes in collections for Winter Relief—a fund for the needy in a country where, with no unemployed, it did not seem logical that there should be anyone who required State aid. It was whispered that most of the money was used to pay the costs of the war. In any case, the Winter Relief collections were made for three days a week beginning Friday about every other week.

As I walked down Unter den Linden on this Sunday, German bands played on the island spaces between the two roadways, and figures in character, including comic cows and horses, danced to the music. Even hot wieners were offered for sale, if you surrendered fifty grams of meat marks to the women attending the temporary booths. People dressed in old-time costumes rode by in carriages and stopped at street corners to collect. Along the Linden, as I went by, the collectors were tall men dressed in tall hats and tight-fitting black clothes, carrying brooms, to represent the German good-luck character, the chimney-sweep.

To add variety to the occasions, each collection was in charge of a different group. One week it would be the police, another the army, the labour front, the Red Cross, or the Hitler Youth. The tags also were changed so that you might get tiny flowers one week, miniature books on the war, another small tanks, anti-aircraft guns, flamethrowers and other weapons on still another, and, on the day of the police, little traffic signs. I remember that the pins on January 19 were curious little figures of picturesque Berlin types, the quaint flower women of the Potsdamerplatz, the milkmen who went by in the old days ringing their bells, the *Dienstmänner* in their long white aprons, and such individuals as Erich Carow, characterful tavern-keeper in Berlin's north end. One time you were tagged with signs of the zodiac, with the idea being that you would choose one for your birth-date. Usually I tried to dodge the tags, but I did get one on this occasion. I found that it was intended for one of twins. The tags on another day were small glass badges on which were relief heads of Germany's prominent men: Hitler, von Hindenburg, Bismarck, Goethe, Schiller, and others. As a publicity manœuvre, the Nazis turned out less of the Hitler heads so that they became more scarce and brought a higher premium—as much as two hundred marks. In my script that day I managed, despite the censors, to say that the Germans were offering high prices for the head of Hitler.

Buying a tag did not protect you against further solicitations, as it usually does in the United States. Instead, a tag appeared to brand you as a possible victim, and some people wore the whole set for the week flapping from their coat lapels. Sometimes, too, the collectors were bothersome. I had been in a subway when a lusty German workman came in with his red can, made a speech at the end of the car, and then set out to shake the box under each nose. I was once in a night club when a collector accosted me. I was polite at first.

"Nein, danke," I said.

He appealed again.

"Nein, danke," I said, louder this time.

He continued to beg.

"I don't want any," I cried in English.

The man looked at me with his mouth open in surprise. He left.

Afterwards I adopted that idea. An answer in English almost always made the collectors slink away staring in bewilderment.

===

The buses, street cars, and subways were crowded, especially on Sunday, when transportation was curtailed. Among those who rode were families going to the beer gardens and concerts, the theatres, the cafés and restaurants. On almost every subway train and bus moving west were groups of young people carrying their skis and bound for the Grunewald. Sightseeing soldiers rode in old horse-drawn ten-seat carriages along the Wilhelmstrasse and under the Brandenburg Gate. Long streams of trucks carrying soldiers, and sometimes tanks and guns, frequently rolled by.

On week-days the streets were filled with tiny motor-cars that operated on motor-cycle motors, small trucks with but three wheels, and motor units that pulled two and three trucks. Horse-drawn vans were common and I saw even old mail-vans from the turn of the century brought back into service because they could be drawn by horses. Large limousines stood only in front of the offices of main officials and the leading hotels, such as the Adlon, for no one except those highest in Nazi circles, or their guests, were permitted to ride in them.

Of the common people none was permitted to drive a car unless he was able to prove his absolute need for one, and that was never to be used unless it was impossible to get where he was going on any public conveyance. The mere fact that a man was a merchant did not entitle him to own a van, and if he handled the kind of goods that required a motor vehicle he must never use it to aid a friend unless he wanted to risk a fine of from 50 to 300 marks, the loss of his licence and perhaps his car.

No one was permitted to go to the theatre, a restaurant, or the home of a friend in a taxicab. Their use was restricted to the sick, the lame, the old, and travellers with heavy luggage coming from or going to a railroad station. Early in 1941 it was decreed that all taxicabs must be off the streets by nine o'clock, so that anyone who wanted one after that hour had to call the police. I saw the police on many occasions stop cabs and check to see whether the passenger was riding contrary to law. If the driver had failed to ask the destination when the passenger was travelling illegally, he, too, was subject to a fine and the possible loss of his licence and cab.

Those who were permitted cars were allotted only enough petrol to travel between the necessary points. Bill Shirer was given the use of a car on the plea that he often had to travel to the radio station during hours when there was no other means of transportation. Generally the Nazis were more liberal with foreign correspondents. They did not require a new licence for the first year, provided you had been issued one in some other country, but it was stipulated that you must carry a German translation of the foreign licence. Mine had been issued in University City, Missouri, written "Mo.," on the card. My translation sheet, stamped by the German Automobile Association, came back with the "Mo." translated as "Mexico." Petrol allotments varied from 25 to 500 litres a month, or as little as five and a half gallons. The price of petrol was fixed at 44 pfennigs a litre, or about 3s. 2d. a gallon.

Germans with cars were warned not to be careless with the tyres on the risk of being fined. When a tyre wore out, a new one could not be obtained for weeks, and when repairs were needed, one had to apply to a special office for a permit and be certain to submit it the same day. Then, since the military had priority, and labour was scarce, one would have to wait at least eight to fourteen days before the work was even started.

Many private cars operated on wood gas, with a stove in the car, or on a small trailer behind. Wood gas was fairly successful although it was necessary to clean the cylinders every day. It was so much in use that there were two hundred filling stations for wood gas in and around Berlin alone.

Buses and some vans operated on a gas made from refuse material, with a big tank to be seen on the front by the side of the driver.

All German cars were required to have red-illuminated signal indicators on each side to warn the driver behind of a turn to right or left. The indicators were operated from the dashboard.

The German highway system, of wide roadways with islands separating opposite lines of traffic and with clover-leaf branches at intersections to avoid cross traffic, was the finest I had ever seen. The roads connected all important German cities and were actually planned not so much for passenger traffic as, like all else in Nazi Germany, to facilitate the speedy movement of mechanized troops.

===

The Day of the Army, one of the Winter Help collection periods, intervened. In preparation for that occasion, the Armistice car from Compiègne was set up in the Lustgarten, a fee being charged as people moved on a special platform past the dark-finished car and peered into its windows: German light and heavy tanks, airplanes, anti-aircraft and other guns were stationed in the open place between the Staats Opera and one of the palaces of the kaisers off the Linden, with boys permitted to crawl all over them, turn the cranks, and look into the sights; German army field kitchens were stationed in the park strip on the Linden to serve food; and barracks, drill grounds, naval bases, and airfields all over the Reich were made the scenes of military demonstrations, games, and entertainments in which celebrities of the motion pictures, vaudeville, and opera took part.

===

I visited one of the barracks in Berlin where rooms were made into cafés representative of Spain, Rumania, Russia, the Netherlands, Scandinavia, Italy, the Balkans, and even the United States. That interesting fact recalled that the unemotional Germans, unlike the people in the United States, despite the propaganda in the newspapers against the United States, did not react against American citizens and things American—except in isolated cases. The Stars and Stripes were still on the Haus Amerika out by the Adolf Hitler Platz, in the mosaic on the wall of the Braun store on Unter den Linden, a British and an American flag were entwined in a bakery-shop sign on the Friedrichstrasse just off the Linden, and the Stars and Stripes were still on the wall of the Haus Vaterland in the Potsdamerplatz.

The Haus Vaterland, like the barracks, had rooms set aside for different countries. The Wild West Bar had log-cabin walls, pictures of Lincoln and Jefferson over the booths, one of Bill Hart over the bar, and an Anheuser-Busch print of *Custer's Last Stand* beside the bar. Off at one side was a window arranged as if looking over a scene in the West, with hills in the background and a lighted lone cabin in the valley. The big blond waiters, with bandanas around their necks, and wearing cowboy shirts and chaps, were incongruous in their costumes, but by no means as amazing as Germany, ready to war with the United States, completely without emotional reaction to that country.

Outside the door of the Wild West Bar I stopped beside a light-gun machine, by which the operator could aim and shoot at pictures of passing planes. Two young anti-aircraft soldiers were busy there. I watched them. One fired intently and then stepped back, patted himself on the chest, and boasted of his perfect score.

"Give me my *Ritter Kreuz* (Iron Cross)," he cried.

In Potsdam, on the Day of the Army, soldiers stood on guard at the gates of the Kaserne Barracks, in the colourful uniforms of the Kaiser's *Garde de Corps*, and some marched and rode by in these uniforms and those of the Hussars, Uhlans, and Dragoons. Other people rode through the parks in the carriages and tallyhos of their ancestors. In one barracks there was trick riding on horses and motor-cycles, tanks staged a sham battle, children were given rides in army motor-cycle sidecars, in armoured trucks, and in tanks, small boys lay behind a machine gun to fire at a suspended model airplane, and German girls spent ten pfennigs to talk on the telephone with an unknown soldier.

===

We in Berlin also were becoming used to alarms again. Demonstrations on the proper way to fight incendiaries were to be seen on street corners, where the general crew wore masks, and those fighting the fire had on overalls and helmets. One of the group filled buckets with water, another manned a pump, and a third, with a board as a shield, turned a hose on the fire. Posters appeared showing a woman fighting an incendiary bomb, and a boy at the door bringing her a bucket of water. One of the papers suggested that a washtub lid could be used as a shield in fighting the bombs and recommended that one be added to the buckets of water, sand, broom, and shovel on each apartment landing. The people were told that the sand should be in ten-pound bags. Articles on proper air-raid precautions were carried in the press. The people read that the temperature in shelters should be about sixty degrees and that, for comfort, it was advisable to cover the floors and walls with old rugs or paper. The populace was reminded that no insurance damages for death or injury would be paid unless the victim had taken refuge in a shelter, and everyone was advised to have a box containing all valuable papers handy to carry with him into the cellar. German editors were taken on a tour of anti-aircraft emplacements so they could write stories about the protection. One of the articles mentioned that because of the noise of the guns, officers gave their commands over microphones carried around their necks.

There was a warning that almost any crime committed in a black-out meant beheading. In Leipzig two were sentenced to death because of burglaries. In Berlin one man was executed for snatching a woman's purse, and another for the theft of a ton of coal, all during black-outs. A Berliner who had left his house with a light lit had to pay the cost of the call for the fire department which broke into his place and a fine in addition. A poster warning people to "*Verdunkle*" — "Blackout" — showed the skeleton of Death riding in a plane and tossing a bomb at a building where a light still showed.

===

Before I left on the trip to Crete, Plack insisted that I see a few night clubs and have dinner with him. On Saturday night, May 21, he took me to the Jockey Bar, where I found pictures of United States motion-picture stars on the wall, including Leslie Howard, who was on the B.B.C. at that time. The orchestra played American dance music in modern tempo for what was apparently a sophisticated crowd. The atmosphere was about the same at the Carlton. Both were astonishingly like night clubs in New York except that there was no dancing. None is permitted when a campaign is in progress.

On Sunday night Plack took me to Horcher's, the select restaurant in Berlin to which no one but leading officials of the Reich had entrée since the war began. Anyone else who called for reservations was told all the places were taken. That was partly because Horcher's, even with the war in progress, was given the means of trying to maintain its reputation from the days when no prices were printed on the menus because it was said, after you had enjoyed the food you would not care what it cost. Horcher's during the war was a place to which Nazi leaders could take their friends and strut. We had *hors d'œuvres* that included *pâté de foie gras*, pickled herring, and lobster salad. There was fried spring chicken, ice cream with real chocolate sauce, and real coffee. Horcher's also did not count the ration cards as you surrendered them. They put a box on the table and trusted you to be honest. The prices were probably staggering; I did not learn what they were because the bill was not brought to the table.

===

All week long the reports had been scattered and without definite information. The High Command itself had said practically nothing, and all that could be learned was in the less reliable PK reports. On Sunday, June 29, the Nazis unleashed their propaganda. They had erected loudspeakers at intervals along all the main thoroughfares, such as Unter den Linden and the Kurfürstendamm in Berlin. From these and over radios in all parts of the Reich they began early in the morning to release communiqués. An announcer would interrupt whatever programme was on the air to tell the people that a communiqué would be heard in *zehn Minuten*. Military band music and marching songs followed. Five minutes later the announcer said the communiqué would be heard in *fünf Minuten*. Finally, after the stirring music, came a fanfare, a blare of trumpets and a roll of drums, and the dramatic announcement beginning:

"Aus dem Führerhauptquartier gibt das Oberkommando der Wehrmacht bekannt:" ("From the headquarters of the Führer, the High Command announces:")

After that, of course, the communiqué, and *Deutschland über Alles*.

Everyone was ordered to stand in silence during the reading. Along the Kurfürstendamm the milling crowds halted and those at café tables rose. During the first several of these communiqués the enthusiasm of the people returned. I listened and heard them remark:

"Fantastic! Unbelievable! Wonderful!"

One communiqué said that 322 Red planes had been shot down by Nazi fighters and anti-aircraft on the first day of fighting, and that since that time the Soviet had lost 1,811 machines, while the Nazis had lost but 35.

Another raised the ante and said that since June 23, 2,582 Red planes had been lost.

A third said that Brest-Litovsk was in Nazi hands. Another that Vilna and Kovno (Kaunas) had been taken. Each was brief.

After the first several announcements had been made, single-sheet extras of the newspapers appeared on the streets. The *Völkischer Beobachter*, in huge letters, underlined with red, shouted: "Victory March." Above were the words: "Overwhelming Beginning of German Operations." Underneath, in part: "Advance of the Soviet Army Broken. 1,300 Armoured Cars Destroyed. The Dvina Crossed, Dünaburg (Dvinsk) Taken." Sound-trucks began to go up and down the streets playing recordings of the announcements and new PK reports. The show went on all day long, with more and more communiqués, additional extras, and continued blasts from the sound-cars.

The Russian war was being presented as a spectacle, but, as might have been expected, the people began to react against it before the day was over. It was not long before the men and women of Germany knew that the whole thing had been planned, and they resented it.

"Why," I heard one German say, "it is obvious that they have saved these communiqués for today. Why didn't they tell us during the week how the war was progressing? They are making a show of this war."

Even Nazis admitted to me that the skeleton of the scheme was too plain. Goebbels, supposed to be a propaganda expert, had again revealed himself as a blundering amateur.

===

For the first time since I had been in the Reich, I was able to find a seat in the train going to Hamburg. The German people were not travelling toward bomb targets. As I made this journey, I tried to discover the fabled fake Berlin. Two Americans and a number of Germans had asserted that they had seen it north of Berlin on the route to Hamburg, but it eluded me. The idea was fantastic, but possible. After all, the Germans, who spent long months and vast sums for camouflage, could have built what would look like Berlin in a blackout. If the night were dark enough, planes flying at great heights could see little of the real Berlin except occasional glints of light and the outlines of the lakes and rivers. There was reason to believe there was a false city since the British reported twice in the autumn of 1941 that they had flown over Berlin when I knew they had not. Perhaps they were over the phantom capital.

Fake Berlin or not, the Nazis worked hard in the summer and autumn of 1941 to make it more difficult to hit objectives in the real city. The most pretentious undertaking was along the East-West Axis. That five-mile-long street, so wide that five cars could pass abreast on either side of the centre island, was a guiding arrow to the heart of the capital for the men in the clouds. As it passed through the Brandenburg Gate, the Reichstag, the Kroll Opera House, and a railway station, the Lehrter Bahnhof, were off to the left; the Wilhelmstrasse with the Chancellery, the Foreign Office and the Propaganda Ministry, and two railway stations, the Potsdamer and Anhalter Bahnhof, were to the right, and the old palaces and the Friedrich-strasse Bahnhof almost straight ahead.

West of the Brandenburg Gate, for more than two miles the Tiergarten lay on each side of the Axis. In this section workmen erected steel poles fif-teen feet high, stretched over them wire netting covered with green shreds of cloth, and here and there placed rows of the tops of pine and other trees.

Traffic could continue under the netting, but the Axis, as far as bombers was concerned, had been blended into the Tiergarten. The other three
miles of the Axis had not been covered when I left, but it was likely that
the Nazis would blot it from bombing eyes by erecting covered scaffolding
to represent buildings.

That had been done elsewhere. A lake, the Li[e]tzensee, which shone
as a guide to aviators, had been covered in that fashion. It was interesting
to note that the wild ducks which had swum on the Li[e]tzensee in other
days were still there under the fake buildings. Deutschland Halle and other
prominent landmarks in that region were covered with netting so that they
appeared as parks with paths running through them. To further the illusion, open spaces, as in the Adolf Hitler Platz, and a park near the Axis,
were filled with the pseudo structures.

Hamburg also was camouflaged. The railway station into which I came
had become a park to planes overhead, and other buildings in the vicinity
also were either blotted from view or given new outlines. As I came into the
centre of the city, I saw even more ambitious changes. It happens that there
are two lakes in the centre, the Binnen Alster and the Aussen Alster. The
former smaller body of water was covered with scaffold buildings, with but
a narrow water lane retained for necessary traffic. To make the air picture
more deceptive, the outlines of the Binnen Alster were reproduced in a part
of the larger Aussen Alster, and the bridge that runs between the two was
represented in the new position. Later, as I took the boat down the Elbe
into the harbour, I looked casually on what appeared to be a hilly island,
with rocks and trees, and paid little attention until, when almost past, I saw
the end of a factory jutting from the uncompleted part of what, at a few
hundred yards, was a convincing deserted bit of land.

===

It was while I was in Frankfurt that the Nazis first enforced their require-
ment that all Jews wear the word *Jude* and the yellow star of David on their
coats. There, for the first time, I realized how many Jewish people remained
in the Reich. There had been more Jews in Frankfurt and Berlin than in
any of the other cities of Germany before the Nazis came into power, but it
was hard to believe that thousands could remain despite the fact that they
were denied almost every means of life. I recalled that the *Deutsche Zeitung
in den Niederlanden* had said not long before that there were still 200,000
Jewish people in Germany, 170,000 in Bohemia and Moravia, 60,000 in
Vienna, and 160,000 in the ghetto created at Litzmannstadt in Warthegau,
but those were elusive figures until the new order came.

I had visited the old Rothschild mansion in Frankfurt. It was a large, beautiful home located on a vast estate in which were long garden paths, fountains, and a lake. The Nazis had converted it into a park and put a sign upon the gates: "*Juden Verboten,*" forbidding Jews even to enter. Jews could go into other parks, such as the Tiergarten, although none could loiter there or rest on the benches. Jews also were denied entrance to the leading hotels, theatres, and restaurants, and were not permitted to walk on some streets.

As I waited for a street car near the Rothschild mansion, almost every tenth person was Jewish, some surprisingly well dressed. Riding on the car, I saw children with the star upon their coats, and an old Jewish couple pushing a cart. It was interesting to note that most of the German people, even on this first day, paid no attention to the Jews. At no time, in Frankfurt, Berlin, or elsewhere, did I see a German Aryan stare at a Jew. None paid any attention to the sign that proclaimed the religion of the wearer, and Jews wore it with visible pride.

Everyone knew that the Nazi edict presaged more harsh measures against the Jews. Some party members, such as Krauss and Lessing [the censors whom William Shirer and Harry Flannery had to deal with at the broadcasting station in Berlin; both of them had lived in the U.S.A. for a while], were bitter against the Jewish people, but most of the other Germans were sympathetic. Many Germans secretly patronized Jewish doctors because they knew there were no better and others did what they could to aid old friends. Since Jewish doctors and lawyers were permitted to deal only with their own people, and most Jews were able to make a living only in menial tasks, it was hard to understand how many could live. "Works that are especially fit for Jews," said the *Börsenzeitung,* "are digging, street-cleaning, sorting rags, labour work in factories, and similar employment." Otherwise, Jews had no opportunity to earn anything.

Even when they did make a few marks, the Jews found it difficult to buy. No store could sell to Jews except within a few certain hours a day, and some stores refused to sell to Jews altogether. The Jews had only the fundamental ration cards, each marked with the word *Jude,* and were denied fruits, most vegetables, cigarettes, chocolates, and all other special allotments, even for children. They were not eligible for payments for illness or pensions for old age and could not collect air-raid insurance.

As Berlin became more crowded with foreign workers and officials of the party and the military and lodgings were difficult to find, Jews were forced to move into apartments already occupied by one or more Jewish families, into wooden shacks on the outskirts of the city, or were shipped to Poland.

When they were required to move, no Jew could take more than a hundred pounds of baggage, and if he was sent to Poland, no more than a hundred marks, or ten pounds, ninety marks of which had to be surrendered to the authorities to pay for his passage. He thus left with one pound and meagre personal belongings. Some were taken to Litzmannstadt, where they made uniforms for German soldiers at wages of half-a-crown a day. Others were transferred to a place in East Poland, a large enclosure occupied only by Jews, who were behind a barbed wire guarded by soldiers and left to starve or in whatever way possible find a means to bare existence. Such Jews were actually in what was a huge concentration camp, which differed from any other only in size and in the fact that they were furnished no food.

"Jews are to blame for the war," said Dr. Goebbels. "They are suffering no injustice in the treatment we give them. They more than earned it."

Somehow, perhaps because they have the spirit to carry on under persecution, the ability to stand firm despite their sufferings, the Jews, in Germany, as I saw them, still held their heads high. They proved themselves worthy of their ancestors.

Special Press Conference, 9 October 1941

Before live broadcasts foreign radio journalists like William Shirer, Harry Flannery, and Howard K. Smith had to submit the manuscripts to the German censor. Because of censorship, propaganda, and disinformation, the correspondents were forced to draw political conclusions from petty details of everyday life and read between the lines of official German communiqués. Smith analyzes the coverage of the Russian campaign and observes the way in which the German propaganda machine squandered any degree of credibility. Hitler's troops attacked the Soviet Union on 22 June 1941. They destroyed large parts of the enemy's armies in gigantic encirclement battles, and conquered huge stretches of land. The offensive against Moscow, which was to seal the final victory in this blitzkrieg, began on 30 September. On 7 October, the enemy units were encircled at Briansk and Viasma; however, at that moment, worsening winter conditions and increasing resistance brought the attack on the capital to a standstill, just when the Germans were in view of the outskirts of the city. The Soviet counterattack started on a broad front at the beginning of December.

One date stands out over all other possible candidates for designation as the Great Watershed—that point in time before which all was rising and after which all fell, in the history of Hitler and National Socialism. It is Thursday, October 9, 1941. Since that day the morale of the German people has fallen into a black abyss from which nothing on earth can ever resurrect it except a complete, final, decisive military victory in the war. There can be no substitutes of propaganda and no substitutes of bold military successes which are astounding but not decisive. On that day, German propaganda destroyed itself as an effective means of moulding opinion, spirit and morale; and a callousness to military victories set in which nothing less than a real, tangible *decision* in this war can remove. If the decision does not come soon, I hazard the prediction that Germany will lose the war. In that case, I believe the perspective of history will call October 9 not only the watershed of Nazi History but of the entire conflict determining—to borrow a leaf from Hitler—the destiny of the world for the next thousand years. The world took little note of the occasion, principally because its ultimate consequences turned out to be exactly opposite to every indication at the time. The story is an interesting one. This is it:

Known circumstances permit a chronological reconstruction. The Russian war had hit the doldrums. The Red Army simply refused to collapse under a series of mighty blows. Winter was approaching. The situation inside Germany was, as a result of overlong strain, not so good. In a month of quiet on the central front before Moscow, Hitler, secretively as possible, drew up every soldier and every gun, big and little, which he could extract from the Reich and spare from the other fronts. He compressed millions of men and weapons tight up against the Russian lines, like the spring of a giant catapult, for a final blow no army in the world could withstand. This was the consummation, the concentrate of all Prussian military skill and power. The might with which he blasted holes in the Maginot Line was not to be the equal of this. To quote Hitler's own official newspaper of a later date, writing of this occasion, "This time, it was really all out!" (*"Diesmal ging es aufs Ganze!"*) On October 2, Hitler drew the latch and the mighty mass sprang forward. Already on the first day, the advance was impressive, but the issue was not yet certain. On October 4, Hitler went from his eastern headquarters to Berlin to make a speech at the opening of the Winter Relief Campaign. The occasion was a melancholy one. At the beginning of the year Hitler had promised victory in 1941; and here he was back in Berlin opening the third war-time Winter Relief Campaign. The Fuehrer had ordered total silence about the new offensive. But the occasion demanded a branch of hope; so the Leader made known to his people, for the first time, the fact that this mighty new offensive had been launched, and he prophesied that it would bring the Eastern war to an end before winter. That was helpful, but, after he had returned to the front, the people became restive for specific news. On October 8, the Fuehrer issued a High Command communiqué, the first news, telling of progress. And on the morning of October 9, after poring over his maps and pronouncing what he saw on them good, he called in his lipless little press chief, Dr. Otto Dietrich, from an adjoining hut in the headquarters. Removing his horn-rimmed glasses which he wears in private but sedulously guards from the range of court photographers, the Fuehrer became expansive before the Doctor, bidding him to go to town and reveal all. The period of "strategic silence" had ended. Dietrich caught the bright, "historical" mood of his Leader and returned to his hut to order an underling to contact Dr. Goebbels in Berlin on the telephone, and instruct him to gather the world press; there was history to be made. Then Dr. Dietrich put on his grey great-coat, kicked the first light eastern snow off his polished boots, and enplaned for Berlin, important as the good horse Roland who carried the joyous news from Ghent to Aix.

When the telephone rang, I was lying in bed with a miserable cold and a skull-splitting headache. It was the secretary of Dr. Froelich, the Propaganda Ministry's liaison officer for the American press and radio. She was excited, and told me I should come to an important special press conference at noon sharp; something of extremely great importance. No, she did not know what it was about, but be there on time, for at five minutes after twelve the doors would be barred and guarded.

I had no broadcast that afternoon. And besides, after two years packed with repetitions of Nazi full-dress shows, I was inured to "history" and indifferent, anyway, to the further progress of a world which has never discovered an effective remedy for the common head-cold. So I turned over and tried to go to sleep. The telephone rang again. It was Guido Enderis, the chief of the *New York Times'* Berlin office, for whom I had been writing on occasion. His man, Brooks Peters, had gone home to escape the Berlin blues, so, would I cover the special conference for the *Times*? He had been assured of its historic import. Reluctantly, I yielded.

I put on my clothes, stuffed two handkerchiefs in my pocket, and took the underground to the Wilhelmstrasse. The red-plush Theatre Hall of the Propaganda Ministry was filled with reporters from everywhere, guessing in a dozen different languages what it was all about. My head throbbed. Before the audience was a long conference table, and around the table in little clots stood a bevy of gorgeous uniforms—green, brown, grey and two shades of blue, well stuffed with Prussian officers, party officials and just bureaucrats of the Ministry, beaming with joy at an opportunity to appear before their daily *Publikum* in costumes which lent glamour to waistlines and limbs made for mufti.

As on all Nazi "historic" occasions—except those in which Hitler is the leading man, for he can afford to risk non-conformity—the central show-piece was impressively and precisely late. At 12:30 on the dot, a few officers

rushed through the door into the room, indicating the coming of the Leader's emissary. The clots dissolved into one fine phalanx and in walked little
Dr. Dietrich, flapping his right palm back over his shoulder in imitation
of his Fuehrer's salute and grinning as if fair to bursting with the tidings
he bore. There was profuse handshaking, sandwiched each time between
stiff-armed salutes. Cameras snapped and flashlight bulbs flashed. On the
great stage behind the central figure, Dietrich, the red velvet curtains were
drawn apart to reveal a monstrous map of European Russia thrice as high
as the speaker. The effect was impressive.

   Dietrich was introduced briefly and oilily by Dr. Brauweiler, a musty
old Nazi party wheel-horse who had been appointed leader of the foreign
press section of the Ministry after the arrest of Boehmer, and given a natty
blue uniform for having kept his mouth and head shut for eight years. Then
the little doctor rose and held forth. I regret I cannot quote him directly.
But it is a strange, strange feature of this grand occasion that the text of
what Dietrich said has never been published. Unlike most other important
utterances of Nazi leaders, his words were never rebroadcast to the German people—a feature which caused inquisitive whispering in German
and foreign circles alike. It is just possible that somewhere among the roses
of enthusiasm which blossomed out in uniform that happy day, there was
a little, inconspicuous thorn of prudence, some little bureaucrat, who cast
the vaguest shadow of a doubt over the mind of Dr. Goebbels, the producer
of the show, with dampening references to the uncertain space between the
cup and the lip, and with that hateful phrase which is anathema to the best
laid plans of mice and men: "But, suppose it doesn't turn out that way?" If
there was such a bureaucrat, you may be sure that, however much he may
have been considered an unwelcome cold douche on that merry day, he has
since been promoted and given a new uniform for his counsel.

   For Dietrich said bold words and cast moderating and conditional
phrases to the four winds. In the vernacular of the diplomatic correspondent, Dietrich put himself away, away out on a mighty high limb. With an
air of finality, Dietrich announced the very *last remnants* of the Red Army
were locked in two steel German pockets before Moscow and were undergoing swift, merciless annihilation. This was sensational. To understand
how big the story was one must remember the circumstances. This was
the first substantial news about the mighty, new offensive. It came directly
from Adolf Hitler himself, and could not be doubted. Dietrich continued:
behind the two pockets there stood between the German armies and Moscow just so much space and nothing more. As one correspondent later put
it, Dietrich indicated that between Germany and the complete conquest of

the untold riches of Russia there remained only "the time it takes man and machine to cover the given distance." After seven short days, the Fuehrer's offensive had smashed the Red Army to splinters, the decision was reached and the eastern continent lay, like a limp virgin, in the mighty arms of the lustful, hungry German Mars. " . . . And on that, Gentlemen, I stake my whole journalistic reputation!" Dietrich shouted, swinging his fist high in the air in a dramatic gesture.

Now nobody will contest the contention that the Nazis tell lies, and great big ones. But it is true that Hitler himself has never told a lie about a specific military fact which can be checked. There are two good reasons for this. First, he does not have to lie about them; you don't have to tell a fib when you're winning. Second, a specific military fact can be so easily checked, and if it were found out that the "Almighty" had told a blunt untruth, especially about something so big as this particular event, it would be disastrous to his position. So we of the fourth estate had no choice but to believe these dramatic assertions were gospel truth. Behind his unrecorded words there arose, in the minds of his listeners, inevitable images. Russia, with her rich resources in Hitler's hands: an increment of almost 200,000,000 units of slave labour to make implements of war, bringing the total of man-power at Germany's disposal to a figure greater than that of England, and North and South America combined. Hitler's armies, ten million men, flushed with victory, eager for more of the easy, national sport, were in the main free to return west and flood England, at long last, with blood and Nazis. The American news agency men, in the first row, were sitting on the edges of their seats, tensely eyeing the door behind which were telephones, leading to more telephones to America and the world. My headache receded in my consciousness and in its place settled the more painful conviction—common to all there—that the eastern war was over; and, perhaps, the decision in the entire conflict already lay in Hitler's hands.

When Dietrich finished tense excitement prevailed. The uniforms gathered round him and pumped his hand as a sort of mutual congratulation on the German victory. The agency men had burst through the doorway and were giving short, hot bulletins over the phones to their offices. Axis and Balkan correspondents applauded and cheered, then stood and raised their arms in salute to Dietrich, who sped out of the room to return to the Fuehrer's headquarters and be on hand for the last terrible blows, the *coups de grâce*, the Grand Finale.

I walked down the marble stairs from the Theatre Hall and talked briefly to [Fred] Oechsner [United Press], who had just returned from his breather in America, and [Louis] Lochner [Associated Press]. The mood was grim all round. I went alone, then, up the Wilhelmstrasse to the Adlon bar for alcoholic reinforcement against my cold. The bar radio announced a special communiqué could be expected from the Fuehrer's headquarters in a few minutes; when it came the barman turned up the volume and the specifically military report Dietrich had made in his speech, minus the trimmings and predictions, was announced. I scanned my notes and began writing a tentative lead on the back of an envelope; but it was one of those insidious stories whose implications grow on you as you think more about it. I left the hotel, took a taxi to the *Times* office to get that accessory which is indispensable to clear thinking on my part, a typewriter; although my deadline was still hours away.

My insidious "growing" reaction was apparently universal. Several American bureau chiefs had been invited the day before to leave on October 10 on a trip to the eastern front—the juiciest journalistic plum the German High Command could offer. But so strong was the conviction among us that the end was perhaps a matter of only hours away that Louis Lochner, of the Associated Press, telephoned the Propaganda Ministry, after studying his notes, and informed the proper official that he had decided to relinquish his place on the trip and remain in Berlin. It was too hazardous leaving his base of communications at a moment like this. Then Pierre Huss, of I.N.S., phoned and delivered, with regret, the same message. Oechsner, of U.P., wavered but ultimately decided to take a chance on going to the East. That afternoon powerful pieces, "situationers" reeking with historic implications, went over the wires from Berlin.

But what escaped almost every correspondent was the reaction of the German people themselves. At this time, in the atmosphere of triumph, that feature was, after all, secondary to considerations such as the new strategic and economic advantages the total conquest of Russia offered Hitler. But when that atmosphere dissolved, when the true consequences became clear, the main, and, for Hitler, disastrous feature was: the People.

The little thorn of prudence kept the full strength of Dietrich's predictions from them. The papers published no direct quotations. But they did publish condensed, expurgated, indirect summaries of the "epochal" conference which were strong enough to make German hearts beat faster. Headlines shouted: "The Veil over the New Offensive is lifted!"; "Dietrich: 'Campaign in East Decided'"! The *Voelkischer Beobachter* headline read: "The Great Hour has Struck! Army groups of Timoshenko, Voroshilov encircled—Budyenny Army-group in dissolution." Quoting the Fuehrer's order of the day to the army at the beginning of the offensive, to "strike the last mighty blow, which will crush this enemy before the beginning of winter," and to complete "the last great battle of decision of this year," the official Nazi newspaper commented in bold language, only a few degrees less perilously committal than Dietrich's own words: "That order has already essentially been carried out. In the sense of the Fuehrer's order, the strategic decision has already been gained. If ever the concept 'Blitzkrieg' was realized, it is here!—Seven short days have sufficed to deal a deathblow to the largest war machine in the world, a blow from which Russia can never, never recover."

The response was electric. There was visible alleviation in faces that for weeks had been dismally drawn. In Baarz' beer-restaurant behind Unter den Linden, people stood and saluted when the radio, after repeating the High Command communiqué, played *Horst Wessel* and *Deutschland ueber Alles.* Rumours, which are the dangerous daily diet of people in any totalitarian country where news is twisted or kept from them, spread over Berlin like wildfire. In Baarz', a waiter whispered to me, had I heard, Stalin had requested an armistice. At home, the janitor in my apartment house stopped me in the hall to tell me he had it from reliable sources who had good friends high up in the party that Moscow had fallen this noon. The civil population were hanging wreaths of roses on German tanks in joy at being liberated. It would be announced in a special communiqué tonight or tomorrow. In the days that followed, bookshops got in new sets of Russian grammars and simple readers for beginners in the tongue, and displayed shop windows full of them; the eagerness to get a job in the rich, new colony was everywhere. The economics minister of the Reich, Dr. Walter Funk, sat himself down and wrote a fine speech about Germany's colonial mission in Russia, entitled "The contribution of the East to the New Europe," and next day the papers published it under the heading: "Europe's Economic Future Secured."

The horrible slaughter of Germany's best sons was nearing an end. The boys were being taken out of the Panzers by Christmas. To parched desert-dwellers, the rains had come. Even as God had promised, and his apostles confirmed. And grateful worshippers were wallowing joyously in the coolness of it.

It is hard to realize what this meant to the German people, unless you have lived through those two years of war with them, and watched them suffer. As the core of a strong, steel-willed leadership, they have been remarkably timid and sensitive to trends. They have detested this war from the moment it broke out, and they, the People, have been willing to end it at any juncture. Before it came, they feared it far more than the peoples their leaders and their army threatened with annihilation. On the few occasions on which the end appeared to be in sight, they have been gleeful as children. Dr. Goebbels has not distinguished himself on the score of telling the truth. But when he said, "The German People did not want this war," he knew, for once, what he was talking about.

===

Those were the balmy days, if I ever saw balmy days. It's almost too bad they did not last longer. But they didn't. The awakening was quick and harsh. Here is a genuine sequence, without a day missing, of frontpage headlines in the *Voelkischer Beobachter* on the days following the Dietrich episode. See if you can feel the draught:

October 10: (commenting on Dietrich's speech in big red letters spread all the way across the front page):

> The Great Hour Has Struck
> CAMPAIGN IN EAST DECIDED!

October 11: (in black letters)
> EASTERN BREAKTHROUGH DEEPENS

October 12:
> ANNIHILATION OF SOVIET ARMIES
> ALMOST CONCLUDED
> Horrible Terror in Odessa; Soviet Deserters being Shot in Back

October 13:
> The Battlefields of Vyasma Bryansk Far Behind Front

October 14:
> Operations in East Proceed According to Plan [!]

October 15:
> Operations in East Proceed as Foreseen

And on this same day, the main headline read: SPEEDBOATS SINK BRITISH FREIGHTERS FROM CONVOY! Within two weeks after the greatest military blow in Hitler's history, one week of the Decision being Reached, and four days after Stalin's last armies were in dissolution, the sinking of a couple of British freighters in the English channel had become more important than the biggest military conflict in the world! [...]

Dr. Dietrich was always a bold spokesman, given to hazarding his reputation, or goodly parts of it, cheaply. He loved to make daring statements and bold predictions; and revelled in superlatives. Once he made the famous declaration to a public gathering that the German press was the freest press in the world, and the German public the best informed of peoples; an utterance which, early in the war, established him as an unconscionable ass with the foreign correspondents' corps. [...]

For him, however, the disaster lay not in losing it with the foreign press and radio, but in losing it with the German people. The disaster was all the greater, for into his personal *débâcle* the whole reputation of Nazi propaganda was drawn. In the wake of it followed a flood of those little *Witze*, those political jokes and three- or four-line oral *feuilletons* which circulate over Germany by word of mouth faster and broader than any of Goebbels' newspapers. In private homes, people took to the little quip of raising their hands in a clenched fist salute at the mention of the Dietrich speech, and saying: *Der Bolschewismus ist tot! Es lebe der Bolschewismus!* ("Bolshevism is dead! Long live Bolshevism!") Another was a crude but clever mimeographed cartoon which was secretly circulated over Berlin, showing a German propaganda soldier standing above a trench across the Russian lines and holding up a big placard to the enemy which read: "Russians! You have ceased to exist!" It was signed "Dr. Dietrich." [...]

After Hitler's little press chief had raised the spirits of his people to the skies and then let them fall again down into the abyss of despair German propaganda could never again influence to any important degree the morale of the German people. From now on a wall of distrust separated the Ministry of Dr. Goebbels from his people. The shepherd-boy had hollered "Wolf!" too often.

This was more than a cogent little analysis suitable for table talk. The evidence for its truth is overwhelming. The first sign was the decline in newspaper sales. To test word-of-mouth reports that a decline had occurred, I asked my newspaper vendor in a large kiosk on Wittenberg Platz, and was told that sales of newspapers had fallen off in all the kiosks operated by her particular concession-holder. In her kiosk the drop had been greater than forty per cent. [...]

More important still, because it was a positive sign people were seeking news elsewhere, rather than the negative one that they were ceasing to look for information from Nazi sources, was the rapid increase in listening to news broadcasts from foreign capitals—especially London and Moscow. An official of the Propaganda Ministry told me arrests for this "crime" in Germany tripled after the Dietrich speech.

[. . .] On November 23, the *Voelkischer Beobachter* got out its red-ink pot again to publish a big two-word headline. It was: "ROSTOV TAKEN!" But it didn't raise sales any at all. The people read much more closely an inconspicuous little notice of the High Command which appeared in the *V.B.* two weeks later. Then, it was getting on to Christmas. The shops were empty, except for the toy shops where there were lots of cardboard games, like one called "Bombs on England." There was no liquor for Christmas punch, and there were no geese or rabbits for Christmas dinner. On the streets at dusk, queues before shops were getting longer. The notice in the papers was to the effect that a Russian town named Rostov, situated at the mouth of the Don River, had been evacuated by the troops of the Fuehrer in order to prepare reprisals against the civil population in view of their inhospitable attitude. It was in black ink.

The Heaven of Nieflheim

The Nazis pursued a cultural foreign policy during the war. They tried to use European writers for their own purposes. In October 1941 and in October 1942, they organized tours, each of which ended in an international convention of writers in Weimar. Numerous participants published reports afterwards. Jacques Chardonne, a Frenchman who took part in both tours, wrote a long literary essay, *Le Ciel de Nieflheim* (*The Heaven of Nieflheim*, 1943). The title refers to the "Misty World" of Nordic mythology, a primeval region in the far north and subsequently a realm of the dead. In his text, Chardonne quotes a sentence from *Le Génie du Rhin* (*The Genius of the Rhine*, 1921) by Maurice Barrès (1862–1923), which Barrès, in turn, ascribes to Goethe: "Ah! je n'aime pas le ciel de Nieflheim." Individual impressions of his journeys through Germany are combined with pictures of rural France to form a reactionary vision of a cultural Europe that was to be collectively protected against the Soviet Union. This was Chardonne's theme when he visited Marshal Philippe Pétain (1856–1951) immediately after his return from Germany in December 1941. He tried, in vain, to persuade Pétain to enter the war as an active participant on Germany's side. Under the German occupation, Chardonne was the head of a publishing house (Édition Stock). After the liberation, he was called to account as a collaborator, taken into custody in 1944, and subsequently sentenced to house arrest. The case against him was discontinued in 1946. Today Chardonne is mentioned in histories of French literature as an important author.

Together with Marcel Jouhandeau, [Ramon] Fernandez, and [Gerhard] Heller, I went to Bonn, where the Bürgermeister held a reception for writers from a number of countries. He had invited, for the evening, functionaries from the region, some officers, and some notable people who had come from Berlin. Afterwards, I was often invited to gatherings of this sort; but Bonn revealed everything to me.

There were notables of a new sort here. Traits that formerly indicated class distinctions, the student's dueling scar, the officer's arrogance, a certain Wilhelminian exterior, have disappeared. These men all have an air of being related to one another. The majority comes from modest backgrounds, but some belong to the aristocracy. This is difficult to recognize: almost all of them were of the same young age, all were poor and had grown up in the midst of a tragedy. The impression they made on me, and this has not changed, I would call "elegance," and, later on, I discovered why: these men live to the height of their capacity. This rapture is National Socialism.

===

Our traditional ideas about Germany are wrong, or they have ceased to be right. It is a nation that has created a revolution, and I believe that occurs only once in a nation's history. There is still private property in Germany, there are still workers, bosses, noblemen, members of the military, but the relationships among people have changed. The new society has not been built on ruins and hatreds. It is strong because it is fraternal. Its power and its beauty do not derive from force. A nation in thrall does not do such great things; it is a nation that is inspired.

German socialism reveals that Germanic spirit, feudal and religious, which nothing purely material can satisfy, which is at ease in the greatness that allows its contrasts to harmonize. It has achieved its full expression at the moment of world renewal. What is truly new in Germany lies in the human being.

===

The revolution has profoundly changed German society and its spirit. Some remain attached to those delicate forms of life that do not survive the high temperature of social overhaul. Changes in art and civilization have caused outrage at every period, and our libraries are full of the sighs of old people who have watched things that they thought to be good, change. Neither our senses nor our thoughts are suited to life.

The feeling I have when I consider German society as a whole is aesthetic in nature. It is a question of moral beauty (courage, will, self-denial, decency, and various forms of health) and also of style and creativity. This society has style even in its smallest expressions; it exudes a high-toned atmosphere.

Baldur von Schirach held a reception for writers from various countries in Europe in the Vienna Hofburg: the dress was informal. This troop of foreigners, among them some Viennese notables, recognizable by their yellow tunics, did not make a very good showing in the royal apartments.

We were seated at about twenty round tables, each lit by a circlet of red candles and decorated with a bouquet of autumn leaves, amidst splendid china from an earlier age. The electric light was extinguished. We listened to a Bach chorale, a song hummed by children's voices; then a Mozart quintet, after which the pure song with its restrained resonances was repeated. The general silence, the half-darkness that shrouded the participants, the flickering of the red candles, the autumn foliage, and the really beautiful music united to create a sort of spiritual spectacle. There were no speeches that evening.

I always sensed a certain splendor in these gatherings, full of nobility and good taste, which derived not only from the décor and the music but also from a certain quality of mind.

One Sunday in Freiburg (I remember it because, in the morning, I had visited a church full of true believers) we were invited to a harvest festival in a neighboring village.

A huge hall, brand new. A platform that seemed to have been raised on a bed of flowers. The village people were celebrating the harvest with chorales, the most exalted of music, an invocation to nature sung very articulately, and with great authority, by a boy's voice; the whole thing done without merriment but with a kind of serious enthusiasm. It was presided over by a very young man with the face of a soldier-apostle whose function was to watch over the district, to advise the farmers, to explore their abilities, and to support them.

All this seemed admirable to me, but I sensed a certain embarrassment on the part of the Germans who were accompanying us, and I can guess what they were feeling: They were shocked by the religious tone. Excessively scrupulous. This nation, which saw the foundations of its society disappear (in an upheaval that others will come to experience), has reconstructed them by restoring their sacred character, wiped out by familiarity. The gratitude to the earth can be expressed by this fervor, without disquieting forty million German Catholics, much more persnickety than our own, who have not themselves experienced the humiliations visited upon believers by our republic.

National Socialism has broadened the notion of the sacred without altering it. The nation is steeped in religion.

===

It is possible to live in Germany for a long time without meeting a single being who embodies the idea of the SS—a totally new Germanic creation drawn from this people's most ancient substance but unlike the Germans. It is like an order of militant monks, completely foreign to present-day mankind.

They assemble at daybreak in the town square, make a few well-regulated movements, then disperse: they go wandering through the streets, wearing green woolen gloves, or playing ball. They are all tall, in elegant uniforms, they are surprising because of their youth and their joyous appearance. Yet they are bored and they miss Russia; where "there was always something to do." They were in all the battles, in all the countries of Europe, always the victors; but there is nothing of the traditional warrior about them. Their youth reflects their soul; they have a faith. Their courage is not an accident; it is like a constantly practiced hygiene that confers on them a healthy appearance of strange purity. The model of a fully realized man, but simplified, who has been known before and who at once achieves perfection—that absolute that is called heroism. They live ingenuously, in total self-denial, there is nothing personal about them, they do not seem to feel sorrow, or fear, or hunger, or desire: they are the angels of war come down for a moment from the heaven of Nieflheim to help people perform a task that is too difficult for them: to save what can be saved.

Translated by **KENNETH NORTHCOTT**

"The Enemy Is Listening!"

József Nyírö, a Hungarian born in northern Transylvania (Siebenbürgen), spoke German. He was ordained a priest in Vienna in 1912. After the First World War, he left the priesthood and married. He worked as a journalist, publisher, and novelist. In 1942, he was elected a member of parliament for his native region in Hungary. When the war ended, Nyírö lived in Bavaria and later in Spain, where he died. In October 1941 and October 1942, like Jacques Chardonne, he took part in the two Weimar conventions of the "Association of European Writers" founded by the National Socialists in 1941. In the association's journal, *Europäische Literatur*, he casts a "Look at Fighting Germany" (1942). He reports on the first of his two stays in Weimar and Berlin. Nyírö observes everyday life looking for the signs of the war. While alleging that what he wants to show is how little the country has been affected by the war and the air raids, he describes a few details that from today's point of view sound critical: disabled soldiers and food rationing. A Jewish shop seems to hold a magical attraction for him. But above all, he realizes that he, the foreigner, is met on all sides with secretiveness, rejection, and enmity: "The enemy is listening!"

Whole libraries have already been written about the Reich. But for me, there was still one secret left. That secret was the power that makes this people capable of waging a victorious struggle against the whole world.

I was wondering about this and eventually could hardly wait to get into the Reich. "I shall see miracles," I said to myself. And I did not see any "miracles." I did not see any because once you have crossed the border, you see absolutely nothing of Germany at war. I saw only a few signs and traces. I made a note of them.

A small printed panel in my compartment in the train caught my eye. "Attention! The Enemy Is Listening!"

I shrugged my shoulders. People don't worry much about a thing like that. We aren't allowed to talk to anyone we like on the train? Give me a break! What are the Germans thinking of? The railroad compartment is, at least for us, a sort of confessional, where you tell your worries, sins, and secrets quite openly and force them, so to speak, on the person opposite. It is the place where you can best discuss all the questions to do with the government, where it is easiest to give directions to the army command.

That surely must be the same here, I thought. I only need to keep my ears open and in half an hour I'll know exactly what the "situation" is, just as if I had grown up in Germany. [...]

: : :

I was wrong in my expectations. I traveled a few thousand kilometers round the Reich, but no one talked about the war. Not a single word. The little panel was enough for ninety million people! Awareness that the enemy might also hear what was being said was enough.

That is Germany's secret: it can be great even in little things.

: : :

Somehow, order, punctuality, self-control, willpower, self-respect, security, organization, and some unwritten law are all in the air and the foreigner too cannot escape them.

Why did I draw the curtain in the compartment? True, there is a warning notice up there. But why don't I wait until the conductor does it? The way it's done at home! It's his job! Why didn't I resist, at least inwardly?

Why didn't I enter the Jewish shop when I came across the notice "By Jews for Jews!" It was this shop that really interested me. I was curious. I stopped in front of the shop and wanted to persuade myself, convince myself, that this provision did not apply to me. No one can take me to task if I go in. Yet in spite of that, I walked on. Something held me back.

Something. That secret force, that invisible spirit standing guard over the Reich.

: : :

Finally, a wounded soldier. I am almost glad to see him. The war cannot be hidden. I knew that I would meet him. He got onto the train here, in Leipzig. His arm was in a plaster cast, but that didn't bother him. What struck me was that I had met a total of only three war-wounded. And they were on the train. There is not one on the streets. Not like the First World War. I well remember what it was like then; you met them at every turn. They were in style. They reveled in women's sympathy, love, and friendly glances. Later on, the romanticism wore off, so to speak. People had grown used to them. The sight of wounds, of cripples, of suffering irritated civilians. The dreary realities entailed in the war came to the forefront; in the wounded men, people saw the ghosts of hard times. The wounding of the soul followed the wounding of the body. The poor soldiers did not deserve that.

Nowadays, they are cured. They are sent to health resorts to convalesce. They are taken care of in all respects. They do not parade around as living advertisements for death and destruction. The wounded soldier is also not tormented by worry about himself and his family. He is certain of the nation's respect, its thanks, and its help. And he will continue to be, as long as there are Germans on this earth. This certainty and this security are worth every sacrifice.

: : :

And the dead?

I visited them in Berlin as well. They are at rest inside the Reich cenotaph, symbolically, in the shadow of the cross in the circle of wreaths that surround the huge granite block. Parents, wives, siblings, fiancées lay wreaths here to embrace their loved ones, whose earthly shell lies somewhere on a foreign battlefield in the great unity and history of the nation. The names and brief phrases comprehend destinies that proclaim the beauty and the grandeur of the sacrifices that have been made for the Fatherland. This depth of feeling, this warmth of soul, this self-awareness, and this happy pride are the very core of German history. Anyone who looks at these signs of remembrance feels elated. He almost yearns for such a wreath for himself, so that his name too shall be inscribed in the Book of the Nation. You feel no terror here, no fear, no rebellion against death, against the cold blows of fate, but self-assurance, simplicity, depth, and height.

For they are not victims, they are blessed of the Fatherland.

: : :

But I think that what the cenotaph represents is the war that was: it is, in a certain sense, the past, whether ancient or recent. What I would like to see is something of the war. Frankly speaking, I would like to see the destruction wrought by the air raids. Let's have a look at the opera house. I know it suffered a few direct hits by British bombs. The Germans even reported it. Indeed, it is fenced off. Sand, stones, building materials are piled up all round it. Over the way, they are working on a corner of the cathedral. And on one bank of the Spree, I saw a building whose windows had been shattered by blast. But, compared with what I had imagined, it is all so improbably trivial that I doubt my own observations. What is being done here is merely the building and repair work that can be seen in any city. All right, I'll make sure. I latch on to a pedestrian, point at the opera house, and ask: "Tell me, what happened to this building?"

He looks me up and down suspiciously. I notice that for a moment he toys with the idea of handing me over to a policeman. Then he snaps, "Burned down!" and walks off, tight-lipped. His whole being is nothing but rejection. I stare after him with my mouth open—enviously, in fact.

Is it not admirable that this simple, anonymous German man, this one among the ninety million, should behave like this, as though all the secrets and troubles of the Reich were confided to, and laid upon, him alone? He doesn't gossip, he doesn't gabble, doesn't spill the beans to the first person he comes across. His mistrust is the Fatherland's protection. It is a duty that is not imposed on him from outside, but one that is imposed from within. What is happening here and elsewhere in the Reich is an internal matter that can be handled without my help.

All this lay in the two words, "Burned down!"

Everything is incorporated in this wonderful organizing of life. The war as well, it can only be won in this way. Everyone knows that. Not only the Reichsminister but also this person here who, forgetting himself, is leaning on the statue of the Kaiser and fishing in the Spree. I look upon him as an emblem of German tranquility. Nothing symbolizes this tranquility better for me than this man fishing. While the Reich is performing the most spectacular deeds in the whole world, he stands there, a picture of peacefulness, and fishes in the Spree with complete peace of mind.

It was only while I was having my lunch that I realized that the man who was fishing was not fishing for pleasure. He was working. Whether professionally or not, I do not know. The waiter said something similar when I told him the story.

"It's not possible" that he is just loafing about.

: : :

"Not possible," said the waiter or, more correctly, the Herr Ober [*senior waiter*, the customary address for a waiter in Germany], because every meal here starts with the Herr Ober's taking a note of the orders, cutting out the necessary ration coupons, and then seeing about the dishes. This happens with everyone. At first, I was not used to it and I was not ready to accept it. Partly because I came with the motto "Do not extol the rationing system!" Although we realize that, in unusual times, rations have to be worked out and allocated, we are inclined to regard ration coupons as our enemies, simply because they rob us of our comfort. Thank heavens the people in charge have more understanding than we do, and assert their will and enact the measures that the time and the situation call for.

"There will be exceptions here," I thought to myself when I was in Weimar, eagerly awaiting the banquet that the minister had ordered in honor of the foreign writers. And my jaw dropped when I saw that the waiter was cutting out the minister's coupons just as he was mine.

That's one more thing to which all you can say is: Hats off!

: : :

But why don't they finally bring me my supper? What a mess!—I grumble to myself, as I'm accustomed to at home. I look around angrily but then see a little notice on the table: "My colleague Friedrich Müller serves this table."

"Good Lord," I think, dumbfounded. "*Colleague?*"

So, not "Now listen, waiter!" Or "Man alive, you're fired, you ass, or whatever you are . . ." No! Honor labor, and respect the laborer! "Colleague!"

You even have to be aware of "trivialities" like that.

: : :

And similar trivialities:

I was surprised to find a radio built into the wall in a hotel. The set was, however, only tuned to the German wavelength. The guest must not be infected by London.

In another hotel, three books awaited me on the table. Hitler's *Kampf*, Bruno Brehm's *So fing es an* [*That's How It Started*], and a beautiful illustrated book on the history and sights of the town.

You pick them up and then you forget yourself.

I am forced to take note of the history of the town and the historical changes that have taken place in it. It was sneaked into my cognizance by a subtle gesture. Next day you are well oriented as you go into town.

: : :

"Now," you sigh on your way home—"Now, indeed, home again!"...

It would be good if it were like that in our country, even so. You make comparisons instinctively, out of concern for your own country. Conflicting feelings struggle with one another. One minute you come to the depressing conclusion that we still have a lot to learn at home, the next you start making plans to join in the great competition in which the European countries are engaged. You are filled with responsibility and concerned about your own country. The soul struggles and vacillates.

You have no idea that all this is the way it is because the true Hungarian abroad becomes even more of a Hungarian. It is only when he hears the first words of Hungarian on his arrival at the frontier that he shivers to the core with an unfamiliar feeling. He stands up and sits down again. At this moment it becomes clear to him that we also have strengths, capabilities, and values that have allowed us to remain strong in the face of humanity's bitter struggle. We alone are responsible for our continued existence in the future, for being able to stand, unbroken, before the judgment seat of history, and to receive the verdict that will allow us to assume a worthy place in the new Europe. [. . .]

Translated by **KENNETH NORTHCOTT**

At the Lion's Tail

Howard K. Smith could not take any notes with him when he left Germany at the end of 1941. He wrote his book *Last Train from Berlin* in Switzerland and immediately published it in the United States and Britain (1942). In the 1960s, Smith became an eminent reporter for the American TV network ABC. In the following passage, he sketches out his theory of the inner corruption of Nazi German society, and he develops the thesis that the Germans did not have the courage to refuse allegiance to the regime because they feared retaliation for their transgressions, of which, even at the time, they were well aware.

To see Berlin, you take a walk. To see the people you take a subway. You also smell them. There is not enough time nor enough coaches, for coaches to be properly cleaned and ventilated every day, so the odour of stale sweat from bodies that work hard, and have only a cube of soap big as a penny box of matches to wash with for a month, lingers in their interiors and is reinforced quantitatively until it changes for the worse qualitatively as time and war proceed. In summer, it is asphyxiating and this is no figure of speech. Dozens of people, whose stomachs and bodies are not strong anyhow faint in them every day. Sometimes you just have to get out at some station halfway to your destination to take a breath of fresh air between trains.

People's faces are pale, unhealthily white as flour, except for red rings around their tired, lifeless eyes. One would tend to get accustomed to their faces after awhile and think them normal and natural but for the fact that soldiers ride the subway trains too, and one notices the marked contrast between young men who eat food with vitamins in it and live out of doors part of the time, and the ununiformed millions who get no vitamins and work in shops and factories from ten to twelve hours a day. From lack of vitamins in food, teeth are decaying fast and obviously. My dentist said they are decaying all at once almost like cubes of sugar dissolving in water. Dentists are severely overworked as most of them must spend half their time working for the army, and take care of a doubled private practice in the rest of the time. They have raised prices tremendously to discourage the growing number of patients; he said they simply had to do this. This winter there has been the most severe epidemic of colds in Berlin in many winters, and doctors predict it will get worse each year and probably assume dangerous proportions if something cannot be done about food and clothing, especially shoes, which are wearing out fast.

Weary, and not good in health, Berliners are also, and consequently, ill-humoured. That is an understatement; they have become downright "ornery." All lines in faces point downwards. I can recommend no more effective remedy for a chance fit of good humour than a ten-station ride on a Berlin tube train. If the packed train suddenly lurches forward and pushes your elbow against the back of the man standing in front of you, it is the occasion for a violent, ten-minute battle of words, in which the whole coach-load of humanity feels called upon to take part zealously as if their lives hung on the outcome. They never fight; they just threaten ("*Ich zeige dich an, junger Mann!*"—That's the magic phrase these days: "I'll have you arrested, you imprudent young man," that and "I have a friend who's high up in the Party and *he* will tell you a thing or two!" They're like children threatening to call my Dad, who's bigger'n yours). Berliners have always been notorious grousers. They always complained about anything and everything. But it was a good-natured kind of grousing you could laugh at. What has happened in the past year is something new and different. It is not funny; it is downright morbid, the way people with pale, weary, dead-pan faces which a moment ago were in expressionless stupor can flash in an instant into flaming, apoplectic fury, and scream insults at one another over some triviality or an imaginary wrong. You could watch people's natures change as the war proceeded; you could clearly watch bitterness grow as the end of the war appeared to recede from sight just as you watch a weed grow. It has been depressing to watch and it leaves a bad taste in your mouth. Partly it's the jitters and partly it's a national inferiority complex. But mostly, it is because people are sick; just plain sick in body and mind.

It may be just an impression, but it seems to me that the sickness has hit the little middle-classes hardest. Take those little family parties I've been to time and again where middle-class people, bred on middle-class Respectability, used to play *Skat* all evening and maybe open up a bottle or two of cool wine for refreshment. Recently, I've been to several, and the whole atmosphere has changed. They do not play *Skat* any more at all. They round up all the old half-filled bottles of anything alcoholic they can find (this was before the December Drouth set in with a vengeance), and just drink. They do not drink for the mild pleasure of drinking, not to enjoy the flavour of what they drink nor its subtle effects. They drink to get soused, completely and unmitigatedly; to get rollicking, loud and obstreperous, pouring down wine, beer, sweet liqueur and raw *Ersatz* cognac all in an evening. The general atmosphere is that of a cheap, dock-side dive. I'm not trying to make a moral judgment, but there are grounds for making a social one. The atmosphere is one of decay. And that atmosphere seems thickest among just those strata of Germany's population which have always formed the basis of German society, the *Kleinbuergertum* (lower middle classes). Any type or form of society exists because broad sections of the people have an interest in it existing. In Germany, the petty middle-classes are the ones who have always had an interest in *Bourgeois* society being maintained. They brought Hitler to power in the hope of maintaining their society against the airtight caste of privilege maintained by the classes above them. Now, it seems to me that the little middle-classes are losing interest, and drowning their disappointment in alcoholic lethe, or lethe of any other sort. Superstition has grown apace. There has been a wave of morbid interest in all sorts of quack sciences and plain superstitions, phrenology, astrology, all kinds of fortune-telling. I am sure one reason Goebbels banned all soothsayers from the German stage was that they were becoming too influential among the people. I am always inevitably reminded by these things of another society where a man named Rasputin gained influence and power in a higher circle but for the same reason, shortly before that society collapsed. People who are either unwilling to admit they know what is wrong with them, or are unable to do anything about it—i.e. get rid of Hitler—are seeking escape in *Ersatz* directions. That is psychological, but it has its physical complement. People who are suffering from nothing else but the inevitable effects of bad nourishment, are inventing fancy names for their ailments and buying the patent-medicine houses out of wares. Outside the armaments industry, the only business which is making big money in Germany is the patent-medicine industry. Every woman carries a full pill-box of some kind along with her almost empty vanity compact, and no man's meal is complete without some sort of coloured lozenge for the belly. A substance known as *Okasa* for sexual potency has become almost a German national institution. Young girls welch boxes of *Pervitin* from air-force officers to reinforce energy that should be natural. The general atmosphere smells strangely like that of an opium dive I once visited in New Orleans many years ago.

If I had to describe Hitler's Reich in one figure, I would compare it with a fine looking fat apple with a tight, red, shiny skin, which was rotten in the core. The strong, polished hull is the army and the Gestapo, which has become the main constituent of the Nazi Party. It is a strong, very strong cover. The rotten inside is *the whole fabric of Nazi society.*

[. . .] Nazi society is rotten from top to bottom and in all its tissues, save the strong hermetically closed hull. The people are sick of it. The general theory of society denoted by the name *Fascism*, of which Nazism is a form, has had its flare of popularity in Europe, and so far as popular following is concerned, its day is over. It will never again be an attracting force as it was before the world discovered its meaning.

In Denmark, the Nazis are opposed to parliamentary elections being held because they know that elections would result, as certainly as sunrise, in the Danish people throwing out the three measly Danish Nazis who are in Parliament. In Norway and Holland, the Nazis do not dare even to support a planned "plebiscite" for fear of the evidence it would give of how dead their philosophy truly is. As an idea, Nazism is dead as a door-nail. As for the German people, they are attached to the Nazis like the man who unexpectedly found himself holding on to a lion's tail, and kept right on holding on, not because he enjoyed the lion's proximity, but because he was scared speechless at what might happen if he let go. Or like the little boys who were having a fine ride on a toboggan until it hit a slippery place and started zipping down curves on one runner; they were scared to jump off and it got more impossible every second. Don't get me wrong. I don't mean only that the German people are afraid of the Gestapo and that all they are waiting for is for someone to weaken the Gestapo, and then they will revolt. Though the Gestapo is certainly a big element in the fear complex, it is not the biggest. The main reason the Germans cling to the lion's tail is that they are terrorized by the nightmare of what will happen to them if they fail to win the war, of what their long-suffering enemies will do to them; of what the tortured people of their enslaved nations, Czechoslovakia, Poland, France, will do when there is no longer a Gestapo to hold them down. The German people are not convinced Nazis, not five per cent of them; they are a people frightened stiff at what fate will befall them if they do not win the mess the Nazis have got them into. Take note of the new tone of Nazi propaganda of late. For two years Goebbels blew the shiny, gilded horn of how beautiful Victory was going to be, in order to urge his people on to battle. Suddenly in autumn, the tone changed to that of what will happen to Germany if Germany *fails* to win. If you read the dispatches from Berlin by American correspondents at that time, you will recall that famous editorial written by Goebbels and published in *Das Reich* entitled, "When, or How?" In that leader, for the first time, Goebbels admitted to Germany and the world that conditions had grown extremely bad inside Germany, and he ended by warning his people that however miserable things might be now, they would pale beside what would happen to Germany if Germany lost the war. This tune is now being played long and much in the German press. In all its forms, the incitement of Fear in the hearts of Germans, is the only strong weapon in Goebbels' armoury since Dr. Dietrich played hell with the others.

People in the outside world who know the Nazi system only from photographs and films; from dramatic shots of its fine military machine and the steely, resolute faces of its leaders, would be amazed at what a queer, creaky makeshift it is behind its handsome, uniform exterior. It is not only that the people who support those stony-faced leaders are timid, frightened and low-spirited. It is also, the government, the administration of those people and their affairs. [. . .] It looks roughly like a Rube Goldberg invention, inspired by a nightmare, but it is more complicated and less logical. And there are no A, B, C directions under it to show how it works. The men who work it have no idea how it works, themselves.

Don't Throw Stones at the Pianist!

In the First World War, Gösta Block had voluntarily served in the German military. He returned to Stockholm with his decorations and completed his studies, which had been interrupted by the war. He became a journalist. In the twenties, Block—whose family had roots in Germany—edited two volumes of *Sueco-germanica*, a journal for German-Swedish cultural and trade exchange. He then became editor-in-chief of the tabloid *Gnistan* (*Spark*). In addition, he worked as a public relations consultant for an actor and headed a textile firm. Block broke with the Swedish Social Democrats over the disarmament policy, which he opposed. He turned to the far right and became a National Socialist representative at the local level. From 1940 to 1942, he worked in the press department of the German embassy in Stockholm. Finally, he took up a position with the Reich broadcasting system in Berlin, where he lived from February to September 1942. Block worked as head of the Swedish radio program (known as "Königsberg Radio" because of the frequency on which it transmitted) as an announcer and reporter. After six months, he returned home, and in 1943 he published—privately—a critical book in which he gave an account of his "views from within" Germany. (The cover page shows the Swedish family in front of the Berlin broadcasting house, which is covered with camouflage nets.) He resumed contact with the Social Democrats. Because of his Nazi sympathies, Block was kept under observation by the Swedish security police—both before and after his trip to Germany.

It is clear that in the Third Reich, it is neither productive nor healthy to speak out and work for what is right. This means that so much that is wrong in Germany is allowed to stay wrong. No one wants to burn his fingers in vain, and it is an indisputable fact that this is exactly what you do, severely and painfully, if you aren't careful about whom you touch. In today's Germany, people only intercede in the rarest and most exceptional cases in order to prevent abuse or other violations of the law, since one can never know ahead of time who the lawbreaker might be. For it is not always evident from their outward appearance what position people have within society and the Party, and for that reason one could quite easily happen to make the wrong choice out of imprudent enthusiasm. And to make the wrong choice in the Third Reich is more dangerous than in most other places in the world. This fear of confronting right and wrong is expressed in other areas as well; for example, within civil service departments and businesses. If someone has a supervisor or an employee who carries out his work in such a way that it might cause everything to go wrong, it is better to let everything go wrong than to acquire an enemy. It is also possible to acquire friends and merits through such behavior, but this means less, because friends for the most part have shorter memories than enemies, so the one who pokes his nose into other people's business is still always the stupid one in the end, no matter how right he is!

Conditions in the Third Reich have been and are such that people become blunted. There is no point in making unnecessary trouble for oneself; rather, he who does the least and does this as unnoticeably as possible, goes the furthest. There is no point in trying to get high up, for then you just get hurt even more when you tumble down again. Of this we have seen evidence. The less visible one is, the less one is seen, and the less audible one is, the less one is heard! And to be unseen and unheard is, in the Third Reich, the safest position and the most desirable one at the moment. The effect of this on efficiency and progress is obvious, but such qualities are not currently necessary, since people will be driven to where they are supposed to end up anyway; the Party and "Gestapo" will see to that.

===

THE GERMANS, THE JEWS, AND THE FOREIGNERS

If conditions in the Third Reich are anything but heavenly for most people, for certain categories of people they are completely hellish. This is especially true for the Jews, but in many cases foreigners as well are reminded that they do not belong to the "master race," and this in spite of the fact that they work for Germany.

Jews in today's Germany are truly hunted animals. They lack all the rights of citizens, and they are reminded every day, in both speech and writing, that the Jew is the enemy of the German people. Wherever they go, gigantic posters scream this in their face; and the looks they receive, from Party members of greater or lesser prominence, do not bode well for the future—at least, if the future turns out as these Party members hope and try to believe.

As is probably well known, Jews now have to wear on the left side of their chest a palm-sized, yellow, six-pointed star, on which the word "Jude" is emblazoned in Fraktur. Even little children only a few years old must wear this decoration, and it is truly depressing to see this sign that a person does not belong to the Third Reich—something that in itself, of course, is no tragedy. The tragedy lies in the fact that the Jews must live in the Third Reich and put up with all the notions—and there are many—that those who are in power at the moment might come up with.

Germany's Jews have been thrown out of their professions. Some doctors, dentists, and lawyers have been allowed to continue with their professions, but they are only allowed to offer their services to those of their own race. The Jews may purchase food and other things only between four and five in the afternoon, and it is easy to imagine what is left by then. The Jews do not receive any rationed items that are not considered absolutely essential, such as candy and chocolate, for example. Nor do they receive extra rations of food, so that it is no exaggeration to state that Germany's Jews are now suffering bitter deprivation.

The Jews are not allowed to visit theaters or movie houses, and a great number of German shops have signs announcing that they do not serve Jews. There are even newspaper sellers who display such signs. The Jews may use trains and streetcars, but they may not sit if other travelers are standing. This means that most Jews never bother to sit down, for they would rather remain standing than risk being made to get up by some child or half-grown teenager. But every now and then it happens that you see people tell seated Jews (men or women) to stand up, so that they can take their seats. You will then also see many disapproving expressions on the faces of the other passengers, but it is very rare that anyone intercedes, because, as I have already said, the inhabitants of the Third Reich have had to learn that you should not get mixed up in anything that does not directly concern you, however wrong it may be. However, sometimes this has occurred, and here I will relate a few episodes that cast a glaring light on the mainstream German attitude toward this matter. I have not witnessed them myself, but they have been told to me by persons whose trustworthiness I have no reason to doubt.

One episode took place recently on the "Untergrundbahn" [underground] in Berlin. A small Jewish woman of about sixty sat hunched over in a corner of the train car, which was full of passengers. There were a lot of men who were standing, but none of them made the old Jewish woman get up. Suddenly a large, well-fed gentleman in a shining new Party uniform pushed his way toward the old woman and told her gruffly to get up because he wanted to sit in her place. The woman became completely paralyzed and could not immediately bring herself to stand up. But a captain who was sitting in the opposite corner of the car did so. He was wearing a well-worn field uniform and a wrinkled cap, and it was easy to see that he had not been away from the front for long. He tapped the Party gentleman on the shoulder and offered him his seat. The latter then explained stammeringly that he had not meant it that way at all, that he did not at all want the captain's seat, but that it was necessary to keep one's eyes open regarding the Jews, "to sweep the house clear of this rabble who had destroyed our land." Whereupon the captain measured the fine Party functionary with his eyes from head to toe and then said, "I wonder whether we combat soldiers should not instead sweep the house clear of the rabble who are now busy destroying Germany." The whole carload of people laughed loudly while the Party dandy slunk out onto the platform and hid in a corner, for it is not always true that "the strong man is most powerful alone."

The other episode is quite similar to this one and took place a year or two ago on a streetcar in a town in southern Germany. A little old Jewish woman there happened to get in the way of a uniformed "SS" man, which caused him to berate her loudly because she and the likes of her had started the war, because they were draining the life out of Germany, and much more in the same vein. Their fellow passengers listened with interest, but did not take any action, save for a combat soldier who was standing nearby. He made his way to the "SS" man and told him that if he didn't keep his dirty mouth shut and get himself off the streetcar as soon as possible, he would be kicked out quicker than lightning. The "SS" man looked around the streetcar for help, but when no one made the least move to step in, he got off at the next stop. And then the passengers reacted by applauding loudly. The combat soldier then patted the Jewish woman on the shoulder and said "that there was no intelligent person in Germany who believed that she had started any war, but that it had been completely different people who had done so and that she shouldn't worry, because their day would surely come in a not too distant future." [. . .]

But it is not only the Jews who are treated badly in Germany today. Various categories of foreigners, as well, are treated like pariahs by the German "master race," and this is completely irrespective of whether they are working for Germany or not. The only exceptions are made for diplomats and newspaper correspondents, and this is not out of any affection for these people, but rather out of fear. On the other hand, people are not afraid of those foreigners who can be assumed to be dependent on Germany, and they are treated accordingly. [. . .] For example, there are a lot of Polish workers in the German farming industry. These are all marked with a "P" in the same place where the Jews wear their stars, and the fact that they are not treated much better than the Jews is something for which we hope the German people will not have to suffer someday, because the people are mostly innocent of what their rulers have been up to since the year 1933. Of course it is the German people's fault that National Socialism came into power in the first place, but what has taken place thereafter has not happened with the approval of the fine German people. Nor have they voluntarily placed themselves at the service of the system, but this has been forced upon them, for the Third Reich has the means to soften people up. It is now a given in Germany that the man who does not obey an order will not grow old, and perhaps that is neither so remarkable nor dangerous; but then there are wives and children, and people are reluctant to get them into trouble. But that is what you do in the Third Reich, if you don't howl with the wolves, and that is why so many people today are howling along with those that they would so gladly turn against. The Third Reich's leading men know this, which makes them even more rabid, and in this way the tension is heightened more and more.

To be a foreigner in Germany today is not pleasant, and this is due to many factors. First of all, the Germans feel that they do not have more food than what they themselves can eat, and this much we have to concede. It is also true that foreigners in Germany, aside from the class of workers performing purely physical labor, are paid according to a completely different scale than the Germans, and that they are exempted from certain taxes, and this fans the flames of envy toward them. It is also a fact that the deeper layers of the German people are jealous of those lucky ones who have a foreign passport and are not at the mercy of the Nazis, for better or for worse; and people who are envied usually do not have an easy time of it. If nothing else, then there is a tendency to misinterpret the sidelong glances. There is yet another factor that makes many Germans angry with the foreigners who are working in Germany, and that is that they feel that these foreigners, through their contributions, are prolonging the war and extending the regime of the National Socialists. For people in these circles see the war that is going on now as the evil that will drive out the worst evil, namely, National Socialism itself, and it is clear and understandable that people do not feel kindly toward those who get mixed up in this situation for no particular reason and delay the catastrophe that they see as their only possible salvation.

These are the reasons for the antipathy of sectors of the German people from whom something different might be expected. The reason that the rest of the German residents are not friendlier toward foreigners is just as easy to understand. First and foremost, they despise all those who do not belong to the German "master race." Individuals belonging to the "lower races" might be forgiven for this, but when people of Germanic origin do not immediately embrace National Socialism (this "ancient Nordic teaching") and its blessings, this is absolutely impossible to understand, and especially to forgive. Today one meets Germans with whom it is impossible to exchange so much as a word about Sweden without being scolded severely. Dutch people, Danes, and Norwegians have similar experiences, and the number of those Dutchmen, Danes, Norwegians, and Swedes who would not abandon Germany to its fate, if they had the possibility to do so, is not large. I dare suggest that of those announcers who are now making propaganda for the Third Reich, and its modernities and inventions, not a single one would turn down a modest, considerably less well paid occupation in their homeland, if any such were to be had. Anyone should be able to understand what it must feel like to get on the radio and propagate for a cause that you no longer believe in yourself, simply out of concern for your family and your livelihood, so don't throw too many stones at the pianists!

Translated by **SONIA WICHMANN**

In the Dying City

Before he returned to Berlin in November 1943, Konrad Warner spent a few months in the countryside. The greater part of his book *Schickalswende Europas?* (*Europe's Fatal Turning Point?* 1944) is devoted to a description of the air raids and the destruction of the German capital between 1943 and 1944. Parts of his book had previously appeared in the magazine *Weltwoche*. The French edition bears the highly expressive title *Dans la Cité mourante...* (*In the Dying City...*).

On 1 March 1943—Göring's Tag der Luftwaffe [Day of the German Air Force]—there was a fairly heavy raid. Although people were expecting heavy raids on national holidays, this "raid"* came as a surprise in which, admittedly, the weather also played a part. It so happened that I was in the Swiss café Josty on the Kaiserallee when the sirens went off at half past nine in the evening. The antiaircraft guns started firing a quarter of an hour later. Stupidly, like many other people, I stood under the porch of the Wilmersdorf town hall and watched the drama of the aerial warfare. The heavy guns thundered, the light flak whirled over the sea of houses in curving arcs of different tracer ammunition, reminiscent of prewar nighttime lake festivals, when things looked and sounded quite the same.

But this was serious. One plane after another flew over the city, slowly and undeviatingly, at a great height, always in the light of the searchlights, and from time to time I could see eight or ten of them at once as they flew on their way. The flak raged and barked up into the sky. An English bomber suddenly burst into flames, bright against the night sky, spun down, a wing broke and flew off in a different direction, while the burning fuselage fell straight down into the city. While I was watching that, twenty or thirty incendiary bombs in a row suddenly clattered down in front of me onto the street and into the houses opposite. An extremely strong wind was blowing, and the upper stories of the houses that had been hit were soon in flames.

The flak went on incessantly. Shrapnel rained down, smashing windows, roof tiles, and metal roofs, bounced off the walls and sides of houses, and buzzed like dangerous hornets through the night. Suddenly, an indescribable droning sound that not only the ears but the whole body sensed, came closer. All the buildings began to shake slightly, windows rattled in their frames, metal plates on their mountings, the roofs must have started vibrating. And then a swarm of airplanes flew low over the housetops, so low that you might have thought they would hit the chimney pots. At the same time, I felt a great increase in air pressure and heard the muffled "plop-plop-plop" of the impacts. Window panes burst and, because of the ear-splitting noise all around, the details could only be vaguely differentiated.

Next day, it turned out that the Prager Platz, which lay in the immediate vicinity of where I had been standing the night before, had been bombed. With a single exception, all the houses round the square, and in the streets that radiated from it, had been completely destroyed. It had been cordoned off, and you had to make a wide circular detour around it if you wanted to get a full view of the destruction. I went into all the streets leading to the square; thick clouds of smoke were still issuing from all the cellars. Little more was standing than crumbling walls.

From March to August 1943 Berlin had not been damaged to any appreciable extent by air raids, but in August a few heavier night attacks were the prelude to the destruction that lay ahead. Things grew quiet again, however. From time to time, there was an air raid warning in the evening or at night. Mosquitoes [light RAF bombers] buzzed around in their rapid zigzag flight, sometimes caught in the searchlights and accompanied by them for a short distance. The antiaircraft guns fired into the dark sky, no longer heaven. It had become the arsenal of hell, from which phosphorus, gasoline, mines, and high-explosive bombs were hurled down.

But the nightly visits of the Mosquitoes were only a minor skirmish, reconnaissance, deception. True, there was always some damage, but it was spread over a large area and not much attention was paid to it. You could hear the thunder and the barking of the heavy and the light antiaircraft guns and, in the distance, the sound of bombs bursting. When the planes got nearer, then was the time to hurry off the streets, to which curiosity had drawn you, and return to the cellars. True, the Berliners were jolted, but they neither wanted, nor were able, to believe that their city would suffer the same fate as so many other German cities before it.

Translated by **KENNETH NORTHCOTT**

"Tomorrow I Have to Go Back to the Camp"

Numa Tétaz, alias René Juvet, was born in Frankfurt am Main and grew up in Munich as a bilingual Swiss expatriate. Besides the report on his time in Germany, he published, under a pseudonym, the short work *Die Deutschen im kommenden Europa* (*The Germans in the Europe of the Future*, 1945). After the war, he wrote—under his proper name—a book about suicide, *Du darfst leben* (*You Are Allowed to Live*, 1970) and became involved in Swiss telephone counseling. The following scenes from the book *Ich war dabei* (*I Was There*, 1944) describe Juvet's experiences in Bavaria in March 1943.

Of the seven hundred thousand volumes destroyed in the burning of the state library—whose smoke-blackened walls, devoid of their roof, stare sadly into the sky—several thousands had only been available in Munich and are completely irreplaceable. After months, smoke-blackened scraps of paper still swirled through the air. I picked one up once as it lay at my feet; it was a page from an early edition of Voltaire's *Candide*. At the top of the page stood the words: "And as he looked at everything, he found that all was for the best in the best of all possible worlds."

$$===$$

I was traveling home to Augsburg late one evening on a small local line. At one station, an SS man got into my compartment. We were alone, and it was so dark that it was impossible to make out one another's faces. He had obviously been drinking and was very talkative. "You know," he said, "in my profession you have to have alcohol, otherwise you can't stand it and you can't sleep." He was on leave, the son of Catholic parents, and had been conned into signing up for SS service as a "volunteer." He was serving in a concentration camp near Linz, which contained only Jews and foreigners from the East. These people's work consisted of the Sisyphean task of carrying heavy stones uphill and almost collapsing under their weight. If someone did collapse, he was whipped, and forced on. The path along which the stones were to be transported was fenced in on both sides by wires charged with a high-voltage electric current. If someone had to be disposed of, he was driven at gunpoint onto the wires. Officially he had committed suicide. "Tomorrow, I have to go back to the camp," said my SS man, "but I don't know whether one of these days I won't run up against the wires myself. I can't stand it any more. How are things going to turn out? There must be a God; the Führer himself is always talking about the Almighty, especially when things get nasty. Do you think God will let everything that lot has cooked up go unpunished? It's true they're wearing gloves so as not to get their hands dirty, but they're turning us into murderers."

I said no more. "That lot"—if the SS was already talking like that, what were the others saying?

Translated by **KENNETH NORTHCOTT**

"Will Exchange Skillet for Picture of the Führer"

In several chapters of his book *Schickalswende Europas?* Konrad Warner describes in great detail the air war and the destruction of the city of Berlin: "Prelude to Hell," "The Destruction Goes On," "A Metropolis Dies." Although he is concerned with giving a plain account, his style becomes more literary as the horror he is depicting grows more unbearable.

War and fear and tedium, fatigue and sickness, poverty and hardship smirked at me from many a face. The time I had spent reflecting while in the country had reopened my dulled eyes, and I saw the gloomy backs of the houses alongside the railroad line, saw the crumbling exterior plaster and the cheap beds, the pale faces of careworn women and the serious eyes of undernourished children, mature before their time. I saw the worn-out clothing of my neighbors, their tired faces, their hunger for bread, light, sun, and peace. I saw the oppression, and resignation to fate, indeed, the almost detached calm of the inhabitants of the city spreading everywhere like an invisible fluid, and it was eerie and shocking at the same time to have a presentiment of what the unavoidable fate of them all would be.

===

CHILDREN PLAYING AT WAR

There were a few children playing "air raid" in the street. They were little kids, not yet of school age. Their childish faces were distorted with the pugnacity with which they would confront the enemy, risking their lives on the front line if they were soldiers. The boy holding the paper airplane ran round in a circle, imitating the sound of a bomber's engine with a deep-toned humming. With sharp cries he marked the release of the bombs, and then everyone shouted to mark direct hits on the city. Another child started up as a night fighter and shot at his comrades with a machine gun, which he imitated in his childish voice with a high-pitched rat-a-tat. A third formed the firefighting crew, another the salvage corps. Others imagined themselves manning antiaircraft posts and shooting up into the night sky. At the end of the "game," they all stood around in a circle and looked at the damage that had been done. In their imagination they pictured the fires, they saw the devastation caused by the high explosives; there a mine had exploded; here people were still buried under rubble.

===

After one air raid, I saw the owner of a burning shop that sold household goods trying to save his stock. The whole street was chockablock with all sorts of household items. Women were taking what they most urgently needed, and, as they did so, they were cursing the merchant, who had always turned them away and assured them that he had received no deliveries, that his store was empty, and that they must be patient. He too had hoped that the time would come when the stock he had stashed away could be unloaded at greater profit and with fewer taxes to the state.

===

Shortages took the most incredible forms. Heavy smokers collected their cigar and cigarette butts for reuse in their pipes or in hand-rolled cigarettes. People who were worried about hygiene boiled the butts and dried them on blotting paper on the radiator. Then they chopped them up and mixed them with lavender, rose, and sour cherry leaves, with peppermint, chamomile, or lime-blossom tea, which could still be bought at the drugstore. In the late evening hours, I had often noticed shabby figures scurrying from table to table in restaurants to empty the ashtrays. In the subway stations, the station staff swept up the platforms after the last train had left, and they always had two buckets with them, one for the dirt that they had swept up and the other for butts that had been thrown away.

At the terminals of the subway, children tipped over the ashtrays, and when I asked them what they were going to do with the cigar butts they had sorted out, they replied, "We're going to take them to mother, she'll make new ones out of them and then sell them." I saw addicts on the streets, slinking along the ditches at the side of the road, bending over attentively and, from time to time, picking up their precious findings. It was not unusual—and it no longer attracted anybody's attention—for even better-class people to carry a can around, in which they picked up the remains of their butts. Only rarely did you catch them glancing bashfully at their neighbors.

===

JEWS AND SS

It is shocking to hear what a single tormented heart will pour out if it can open itself up to you. Someone I know told me a story about one of his friends, a high-ranking officer in the "Waffen SS," who had been driven mad by pangs of conscience after he had been in the occupied countries in the East for months and had continuously been ordered to execute Jews: not singly but en masse. He had come home and prostrated himself in front of his wife and confessed everything. Since he had really lost his mind, he was admitted to an institution.

My friend also told me how the Jews were made to kneel on the edge of a gully and would fall into it after they had been shot in the neck. "An explosion would cover the scene of the horror with rubble, and the murdered victims were never seen by human eyes. But in the consciousness of their fellow believers they will live on in an indomitable desire for revenge.

"In other places the Jews were gassed. In the cities they were fetched from their homes under cover of darkness and taken away in trucks. The children were grabbed by SS men and tossed in. The SS men stood around with their rifles at the ready. I could often witness this sight when I was walking home at night, after endless conversations with friends about the war and politics. The city was asleep, darkness was creeping through the streets. The trucks would appear, and black figures dashed into the houses. Hunched figures waited under the eyes of their guards for what was to come, while weeping and screams could be heard from the hallways. But they were soon silenced."

===

When people find it too expensive to place an advertisement in the newspapers, they post notices about things they wish to exchange on the many trees that adorn the streets of Berlin. On one such notice was written, "Because of shortage of cooking fat, will exchange almost new skillet for picture of the Führer." On the trees in Grunewald you could see pictures of leading personalities just as they are placed in every office, home, and pub, but with their eyes blanked out. On the walls of the subway you can see, over and over again, the words "Stalin is winning!" written by anonymous hands.

===

IN THE ANTIAIRCRAFT TOWER AT THE ZOO STATION

Catastrophe descended on the capital on 22 November 1943. Until then, air raids had mostly taken place in good weather, but that day was dark, heavily overcast and wet. No one expected an air raid warning, let alone an attack. It was misty and drizzling. "Well, they won't be coming today," people would say when they ran into a friend or were chatting with their neighbor. "No, the weather's too bad, we shall be left in peace."

[. . .] We were just about to start eating the food from our field kitchen when, punctually, at the expected moment, the sirens began howling. We reckoned that at worst it would be a so-called nuisance raid, but we went to the shelter at the Zoo station, which had room for fifteen to eighteen thousand people. Until then, when the warning sounded I had always walked home without giving it a second thought, but today I hurried to the shelter on account of the bad weather and also out of interest, because until then I had only seen the outside of the fortress-like building, with its four gun towers.

A broad flight of stairs led to the second of five stories, but there were no seats left. As if in a church, there were rows of benches, occupied by people who had been passing by and had been surprised by the air raid warning. We stood against a wall and waited for what was to come. At first people conversed animatedly, speculating on the coming raid, but as everyone expected to go outside again quite soon, no one was very worried.

Immense quantities of reinforced concrete had been used in the construction of this antiaircraft tower, and since the walls and the ceilings were extraordinarily strong and thick, no sound penetrated them from outside. Soldiers regulated movement, distributing people among the floors and into the many rooms; electric lighting made it possible to read or do needlework. Some people had brought their valuables and most important possessions with them in small suitcases. Others came from nearby cinemas or pubs where they had been disturbed as they were enjoying their evening off.

The raid must have begun at about eight o'clock. You could hear the guns firing above our heads, as though off in the distance. At times the muffled thunder grew louder, and you suspected that it was more than just a nuisance raid. Then there was a severe impact, and the massive building was shaken to its foundations. From somewhere you could hear a metallic clattering, the lights went out in a wink—then a deathly silence. Immediately afterwards the guns started firing again, and you imagined you heard the drone of aircraft engines. People roused themselves from their torpor and started talking again. Now and again a flashlight could be seen in the darkness. Then someone lit a candle. A few people took advantage of the darkness to light a cigarette, but the fine noses of the guards noticed at once, and the sinners had to put out their burning ember.

A woman fainted, people called for water, then everything was quiet again. People conversed in whispers. Again there was a crash outside the shelter and the sound of wood splintering. The gunfire was exceptionally heavy, it could be heard more readily now because everyone was quieter. [. . .]

You couldn't hear the "all clear," but suddenly everyone noticed that it must have sounded. Streams of people slowly began to flow downwards, people left the room at a snail's pace, and walked along the corridor to the forecourt, which was already getting crowded by people from other areas. Tightly packed together, everyone felt their way down the stairs. There had been a direct hit down below in the entrance hall, which was only surrounded by a flimsy wall.

A flight of wooden steps had collapsed, doors had been burst open, and the reflection of a fire flickered from outside. Smoke filled the hall, and everyone started coughing.

We had finally reached the outdoors, but what a sight greeted our eyes! The shelter is located in the middle of an extension of the zoo between trees, lawns, and shrubberies. The railroad embankment runs along the opposite side. Trees and shrubs were burning; behind the embankment the flames blazed up into the rain clouds. Black smoke filled the air and blotted everything out. Because the structures were all aflame, people did not know, at first, where to turn. Then, in the immediate vicinity, with a loud bang, time bombs began to explode, one after the other, so that the crowd of people flooded back towards the entrances, where there was an indescribable crush. The blast from the bursting bombs could be felt this far away. People then began appearing, carrying one or two small cases, among them many from Charlottenburg, who reported that everything was burning over there, their houses had been destroyed, the whole district had been demolished. I found out afterwards that this was an exaggeration, but, in the midst of that sea of fire, you would have thought the whole city was ablaze. [. . .]

I hurried first to the Zoo railway station, which had apparently not been hit. But the buildings all around it were burning. The Kaiser-Wilhelm church was engulfed in flames, the Ufa Palast am Zoo was nothing but a ruin. I went farther down the Joachimsthaler Straße as far as the Kurfürstendamm. Here, too, individual houses were burning, the sky was red, but because of the rain clouds and the hovering smoke, visibility was very poor. I looked down the side streets but could see nothing through the impenetrable black curtain from which, here and there, tongues of flame were licking. I ran into the Kaiserallee, where I was greeted by a strong gust of wind filled with a rain of sparks that roared out of the buildings that were burning on either side. Streetcar wires were lying on the ground, trees had been torn up, branches had been flung to the ground. The road crunched under my feet because it was completely covered with bits of broken glass. I hastened and stumbled on, holding a handkerchief to my mouth and my eyes, my hat pulled down over my face and the collar of my topcoat turned up.

But I had to stop for a moment and take a breath. Across the road, two old people, a man and a woman, were dragging their suitcases along. They turned at the street corner. The building there was burning from the ground floor upwards. Above, a balcony, looking almost like a tower, slowly began to break off. I thought I was watching one of those familiar slow-motion shots that show the collapse of a smokestack in its individual phases. And at the same time I saw the old couple who had dropped their suitcases for a moment so that they could catch their breath. But they quickly picked them up and were already on their way again. Before I could shout out, the walls fell, enveloped in a cloud of dust, but these two old people groped their way out, just when I believed they had been crushed to death. They had barely escaped.

===

The fire storm gradually assumed unbelievable proportions, and it became more and more dangerous to move on the streets between the burning houses. We fought our way forward in the middle of the road to avoid being hit by pieces of falling masonry. The fire roared, it boomed and howled, it crashed, crackled, exploded and imploded, arching itself, in great billows, out of windows, doors, and collapsed walls. A black vault loomed over the sea of flames, as if embracing all the horrors in the world.

===

As time passed, you grew used to the destruction, and no one paid attention any longer when they were passing a field of rubble. The eye registered the frightful sight as an everyday phenomenon, almost without missing a heartbeat. Also the feelings, of horror, of sympathy, and fear are blunted with time. And that is just as well if you have to lead a shadowy existence in the realm of death, for otherwise you would go mad.

People wandered about as though they didn't belong to this world. Two old people were pushing a serving trolley on which were piled the remains of their possessions, to get them to "safety" somewhere. Others were searching through the ruins of their houses. I saw people crawling into cellars that were partially under water, still trying to salvage something. The security and aid services, the rescue teams, and the military were digging for those who had been buried and were removing rubble and traffic obstructions. All over the place, signs were chalked up on the facades of buildings, giving the new addresses of those who had been bombed out. Paper signs saying "Business as usual. We are open at such-and-such an address" hung in the burned-out shop windows, or "We shall go on working until we have won the war!"

I talked to people everywhere—in food shops, pharmacies, and tobacconists—and again and again I heard people ask, with a bitter undertone of doubt, "What on earth is going to happen?"—"When are we going to fight back?" "How much longer can this go on? Is the whole of Berlin going to be destroyed?" And a lot of people said, "If *everything* got destroyed, then at least we'd have some peace!"—"You're always happy if you're still alive in the morning and have a roof over your head."—"You've got to write off everything you own, we're going to lose everything anyway!"—"If only it would all end!"

===

The destruction of Berlin is a catastrophe of historic proportions. It will be spoken of for centuries to come. And who knows what this ruined city will symbolize? We can see the signs of collapse, but we cannot yet interpret them. We can see the remains of the walls in aerial photographs. Black and dead, they stare up like the empty eye sockets of a mutilated corpse. And all the other cities look up, in the same way, into a merciless sky. These wounds cry out for peace and healing in every country. But their cries of despair are not heard. The destruction will go on until the world has bled to death.

One district after another is reduced to rubble and ashes. The death of cities spreads like the lava of a volcano. That is man's work. But sometimes it seems as though events burst upon us like natural phenomena, independent of the human will. Are governments still in control of what is happening? Once unleashed, history unfolds like a horror show at the Grand Guignol puppet theater. But the show turns into reality. The audience itself is tortured and loses blood, while the directors sit in the box office and count the receipts.

I just happened to be in Berlin. I could just as easily have experienced the same things in London or in Bucharest, in Sofia or in Leningrad. A metropolis dies! No. A world comes to an end. Anyone with eyes to see, and with ears to hear, experiences this end, day in day out.

Translated by **KENNETH NORTHCOTT**

Carpet Bombing

The Norwegian Theo Findahl was a reporter in Berlin for his country's newspaper *Aftenposten* from 1939 to 1945. In his book *Undergang: Berlin, 1939–1945* (*Collapse: Berlin, 1939–1945*), Findahl describes the devastation of the German capital—by bombing and by the entry of the Red Army—in the last year of the war. The narrative and reflective chapters of the work include extensive diary entries. The book was published in 1946 in a German translation. After the war, Findahl was a correspondent for *Aftenposten* in New York. In what follows, Findahl describes the air raid that took place on 22 November 1943, which Konrad Warner also experienced.

Journal, 22 November 1943

There was a telephone call from Oslo at 6:15 p.m. on the dot. When I hang up, it's 7:30. ALARM! Well, maybe nothing is really happening. I'm alone in my apartment in the Hanseatic Quarter, at 33 Klopstockstrasse, so I go through the rooms to make sure that all the lights are out, that the bathtub is full of water, and that the windows are open so the air pressure from the bombs will not smash the glass. There has often been an alarm at exactly this time in the evening for the past week, but there hasn't yet been an attack. Goebbels has partially convinced the Berliners that the RAF cannot make it all the way to Berlin, thanks to the city's exceptional anti-aircraft defense. I don't even bother taking my little suitcase with a change of clothes and toiletries as I walk through the pitch-black streets to our old haunt at the Grosser Stern, where a large group of colleagues and friends usually meets in the underground passage when the British bombers fly in over Berlin.

Tonight there aren't many people I recognize in our famous bunker. I'm sitting with some Hungarians, the Slovakian press correspondent, and other foreigners. The blasts begin; we look at each other. This is really serious, much more serious than any other air raid we've experienced. The air pressure shakes the heavy metal doors and makes our ear drums hurt. The lights go out—a thundering crash of explosions surrounds us. A bomb must have fallen very close by, perhaps right over our heads. The dark bunker gets quiet. A few women start to get hysterical, but they are quickly brought under control—luckily the eastern bunker at the Grosser Stern is never very crowded; it's good to be here and not in the western one, which is always full.

We realize *how* terrible the attack has been only after we emerge on the plaza by the Victory Column after the blasts have ended. The vast circular plaza is totally covered with bomb splinters, branches, and limbs from the trees in the park. Along the sidewalk there are rows of cars engulfed in flames; on the pavement a bus is flaming like a giant torch. Our faces are whipped by black smoke from the storm above the sea of flames. *Carpet bombing*—like in Hamburg? Yes, this must have been the first carpet bombing of Berlin, right over this very area.

From the plaza it seems like the whole city is burning. Behind the park the entire Hanseatic Quarter is in flames. I have to get home to see if anything can be salvaged! The water main on Altonaerstrasse has sprung open, and the whole street is like a lake. It's impossible to reach Hansa Platz that way. The Tiergarten is now a jungle; branches and brushwood stick you in the face as you struggle over fallen tree trunks—Händelallee—a sea of fire!

I walk farther along and turn onto Klopstockstrasse. The street is hot as an oven—in some places people are trying to salvage things, here and there pieces of furniture have been thrown onto the street, but most people have just given up and are letting it all burn. There is no chance of reaching number 33—a red-hot wind is whipping through the street, the house is a heap of flames. A bunch of confused women come running out of the large house across the street, which has the largest cellar; a half-grown girl is crying hysterically, but most people are fairly calm, almost as if drugged—in a flash I see before me the pale, moaning French woman crawling along the houses in Bergues three years ago, when the Germans bombed that city to gravel and ash. It's best to turn around as quickly as possible and try to reach the park again, where the air isn't full of burning soot and smoke, like here—rush away from this place that was one's home for three years.

Another alarm! The stream of people on the axis heads towards the Grosser Stern; long lines have already formed at the entrances to both bunkers. It's better to be alone, to find somewhere in the park to crawl under a bench like an ostrich, to lay flat on the ground, just to be alone, not crushed to death or blown to bits with the masses. I drift through the dark park as if in a daze. It's not easy to find a way through. Fallen trees form obstacles all over the pathways, but at least there is no scorching hot wind here. The air is relatively clean and clear; many trails are empty of people and good to walk on. The sirens blare, signaling that the danger is over. Presumably there were some scout planes there to photograph the damage and confuse the rescue workers—once again it is possible to move ahead slowly, but where to go? There is no home anymore.

Towards the city, towards Wilhelmstrasse out of habit, to the workplace. The Adlon Hotel stands like a dark wall against the fire-red sky. I could go in there, maybe get a room, or at least rest in the hall. I wasn't the only one with that idea—the great hall in this old luxury hotel is crammed with temporary guests. Not a bed available, but you can sit in the hallway. People covered in soot are packed in everywhere, on chairs and benches; suitcases, bundles, and packages are all over the marble floor—like in a refugee camp. The revolving doors are in constant use, but it is still incredibly quiet in the hall. Everyone speaks softly and looks dead tired; everyone has been through the same thing so no words of explanation are needed. A strange and oppressive mood of destruction fills the atmosphere. Indeed, a metropolis is falling right in front of us. Scenes from novels about the fall of Rome or Carthage come to mind. But this is much faster, just as the machines of the West are so much faster than those of any other civilization. The mind cannot grasp such a cruel fate ...

===

27 November 1943

The scene is hectic in the bar at the club by Leipziger Platz. Two prominent German journalists are outdoing each other with jokes and puns and adventure stories about "the Battle of Berlin" on November 22. The burning train full of dead people careening madly over the railroad "circle" around the city, the puma from the zoo that jumped through a sea of sparks and was killed on Lützow Platz, the tortoises and crocodiles that were boiled alive in the aquarium at the zoo—pure Edgar Allan Poe! Is it really true, even in these apocalyptic days, that the art of making clever and entertaining chatter out of everything is the heart of journalism? "An earthquake is better than no news at all." In any case, one of them says, these attacks don't mean anything *politically*. The British are mistaken if they think an attack will incite dissatisfaction with the regime here. People have enough with their own troubles that they don't have any time to think about politics, he continues, and then he begins humming "Sous les débris de Berlin" to the tune of "Sous les ponts de Paris." The new Berlin, says another journalist, will not rise from the ruins, it will live under them. Cheers!

It's strange how all the commotion here makes people forget about everything else—Gomel, Kiev, Vitebsk—but for how long?

Translated by **DEAN KROUK**

Leipzig Is Dead!

In his "factual report" *Ein Schweizer erlebt das geheime Deutschland* (*A Swiss Experiences the Secret Germany*), René Schindler describes a journey he undertook in 1944: the crossing of the frontier, the train journey, the food situation, the ruined cities, the effects of the air war on human beings, the "big wheels," the power of the party, the first defections to other countries, foreign workers, the newly arisen "proletariat of the bombed-out," changes in language, the extermination of the Jews, and the dilemma faced by many Germans caught between reason and patriotism, concern for existence and fear of the future. While Hitler is making his last New Year's address, Schindler is on his way home to Switzerland. (Apparently, however, the journey and the report had already been finished earlier.) The excerpts that have been selected describe the beginning of the journey, his arrival by train.

"Secret Germany" refers to the allegedly numerous Germans who remained silent in the face of the terror imposed by the regime and who only confided their accusations to a foreigner they could trust. It alludes to a concept that had been used in the circle of the poet Stefan George (1868–1933) since 1910; it finally surfaced as the title of a poem by George himself, "Geheimes Deutschland" ("Secret Germany"), which is included in the volume of poetry *Das Neue Reich* (*The New Empire*, 1928). While the term originally applied to those belonging to George's circle as "the real Germany" (as opposed to the official, imperial one), it was later criticized as "pre-fascist." After 1945, George's disciples countered that it was a code name for "inner emigration." There is a myth that when Claus Graf Schenk von Stauffenberg (1907–44) was dying, he cried out "Long live the *secret* Germany!" (and not the "*holy*" Germany, as historiography claims). Schindler, for his part, in the last year of the war, still rested his hopes upon an inner resistance to the Nazi regime or a revolt of the foreign forced laborers.

The man behind the pseudonym "René Schindler" was Franz Wolfgang Rieppel. He was born in Weimar in 1917 and lived largely in Germany until 1934. He attended schools in Germany and England and received his doctorate in Zurich in 1942, as an economist, with a dissertation entitled *Die Entschuldung der schweizerischen Landwirtschaft* (*The Debt Write-Off of Swiss Farming*). He then joined the staff of the commercial college in St. Gallen. After the war, he worked for the chemical industry in Basel. In the 1990s he published some volumes of poetry.

The compartments are filthy, the upholstery worn to shreds, the windows covered in soot. There is an indefinably unpleasant odor, a smell of decay. A typical smell that was to stay with us and, at times, became intolerable. Still, we do manage to find a good seat, the last time we do until we get home, for as soon as we get to Bregenz the train is besieged and in a few minutes our two coaches are filled to overflowing. Two civilians get into our compartment together with a Red Cross nurse and three uniforms. There are eight of us with our luggage in a second-class compartment on our way to Munich. We are traveling through a country engaged in a life-and-death struggle. Signs are posted displaying blackout regulations, instructions on how to behave in the case of air raids, and the ever repeated warning, "Be careful what you say! The enemy is listening!" The uniforms and the conversations constantly remind us of that.

In Lindau our coaches are attached to the train for Munich, which is just as crowded. Here too, as in Bregenz, placards and banners proclaim, "Victory first, travel after!" and "Wheels must roll for victory!" If you are traveling more than a certain distance you must produce certification of the military importance of your journey in order to get a place in an express train. In spite of this, every seat is taken. The corridors are jam packed with passengers and luggage, and it is not uncommon to see someone leave the train by climbing out of the window. Every German dialect is to be heard, but you can hear just as much Italian and French—and the Balkans are also abundantly represented.

The travelers' conversations are primarily about food. The conductress, when asked at what time we arrive in Munich, does not even know how far the train will be able to go today. There is talk of bombings, and not one of the passengers has not been affected in some way or another.

One traveler says that a basket of apples was left standing on a wall in Stuttgart for quite a long time, bearing the invitation, "Please take one, they're free!" and the basket had always been anonymously replenished. Someone had written "Thank you!" underneath. This was while there wasn't a single apple to be bought in the whole city—a mute protest against the *Ablieferungspflicht* ["compulsory delivery," the rule whereby farmers had to surrender their produce to the authorities for distribution]?

===

Traffic in the midst of these ruins varies. During one air raid on Munich, a streetcar depot and a large part of the rolling stock were destroyed. The blue Munich cars were joined by green ones from Katowice and yellow ones from Verona. But the native of Munich is no hero when it comes to organization. You have to cover long distances on foot because the overhead wires or the streetcar rails could not be repaired. This is what you had to do, for example, if you wanted to visit the "Brown House" that had been hit, or the "memorial" on the Odeonsplatz, which is still standing, but without the guard of honor that used to ensure so scrupulously that everyone who walked past it raised their arm in the Hitler salute to honor the victims of 9 November [1923]. Today the guard of honor would have to be standing on a pile of debris and staring at the ruins of the residence across the road.

It wasn't always the case. After previous air raids the debris extended, on one occasion, right up to the guard of honor at the "memorial." But with an enormous effort involving trucks, bulldozers, and innumerable prisoners the debris was removed within a few days. All so that the guard of honor could march up in goosestep again, while a few blocks away the population, without any help, was trying to dig up those who had been buried alive.

===

"NO ENTRY. DANGER OF COLLAPSE!"

The ruins take on a ghostly aspect against the night sky. In places, the smell of burning is especially noticeable, but the city seems dead, seems extinct, no one takes any notice of the smoldering fires, no one takes any notice of us.

And it is the same picture everywhere. In Munich, and Augsburg, Stuttgart, Darmstadt and Frankfurt, Leipzig and Berlin. Ruins and rubble everywhere, debris and broken glass.

In the midst of all this wreckage there are pieces of furniture, and suitcases, a rusty typewriter, candelabras and files, radiators and bathtubs, pipes, cables, burnt-out and rusted safes, parts of a sewing machine, splinters of glass, and roof tiles.

Individual houses, entire streets, whole blocks of houses: "No Entry. Danger of Collapse!"

I couldn't say which of the cities I've seen has been the worst hit, which one today, after new attacks, has not suffered more severely than it had when I visited it.

What do numbers tell us any more? Can the most vivid imagination envisage what lies behind the statement that, for example, in Leipzig during that first terrible air raid, which lasted barely half an hour, 260,000 people were rendered homeless, that the number of people buried under the debris was said to be well over 2,000? And that was only one attack, just on Leipzig, which has since been the object of many more attacks.

And since then how often has "Leipzig" been repeated! In Leipzig, the raid "only" claimed 2,000 victims; in Freiburg, the number is said to have been more than 30,000! To date, no figures at all have been announced for Ulm and the Rhineland, Munich and northern Germany.

And with the people, their cities are stricken. Munich is probably the German city best known in Switzerland. After all, before the war, according to your temperament, you went to its university, its Oktoberfest, or to the carnival in Schwabing. And Schwabing itself, the jolly, easy-going artists' quarter, has been the worst hit. Mars and Death had a rendezvous here and slaughtered a whole epoch, a piece of Munich that had become familiar worldwide. But not only Schwabing, in the inner city too, around the main railroad station and along the tracks that run through the city, in the valley and in Mittersendling, in the Au and in Bogenhausen, everywhere you see the sign "No Entry!"

In Augsburg there is no point in looking for the "Drei Mohren" any longer. The Königsstraße in Stuttgart is one vast expanse of rubble. The "Goethe-Haus" in Frankfurt, the "Römer," and all the other places that the foreign visitor knew from before the war are now just unrecognizable ruins. "Darmstadt-Rest" ["the remains of Darmstadt"] is what, with bitter humor, a once-flourishing city is now called. And if you were to assemble all the houses that remain standing in Berlin, the capital of "Greater Germany," you would probably have no more than an insignificant little provincial town.

And finally Leipzig.

Leipzig is dead! What is left of the city made famous by its great organist and choirmaster, Johann Sebastian Bach, of the trade-fair city, of what was probably the greatest music- and book-publishing center in Europe, is not worth listing. Leipzig is dead, is extinguished, and it will take generations for the city to recover from the downpour of steel and fire that the war has showered upon the town and its rubble.

I found the whole of the inner city, the east and south of Leipzig, in ruins. It no longer exists, it is obliterated, flattened the way Coventry was. All the theaters, including vaudevilles, cabarets, and cinemas have been closed down by the bombs, even before Goebbels ordered the closing down of these establishments throughout the Reich as a token of the total war effort, exempting only cinemas from this regulation. All the large banks, several churches, the university, the main railroad station, the old city hall, the main post office, the museums, all hotels except for one, and also that one was severely damaged, lie in dust and ashes. The book- and music-publishing quarter is totally destroyed. Not a single building remains standing in the main shopping streets of the city, so well known to trade-fair visitors.

The number of homeless in the whole Reich has meanwhile risen to the millions, the victims of air raids into the hundreds of thousands.

Still other notices carry the warning "Caution, rat poison sprayed on this site!" and newspapers publicize the "War on rats!" For the rats in these unhappy cities can find plenty to feed on, and have become a dangerous plague.

And everywhere, debris and rubble, debris and ruins; piles of rubbish, meters high, extend along the sidewalks, and signs are posted on them as well, signs and notices, too, on what is left of garden fences, facades with notices chalked on them telling you the new addresses of the former occupants.

For somewhere, and somehow, people have to go on living, even though there are many who don't see the point of going on living today.

Translated by **KENNETH NORTHCOTT**

The Sky Is Red

Occasionally, the paths of foreign observers crossed in Germany. Thus Theo Findahl, a Norwegian, met his Danish colleague, Jacob Kronika. And he quotes Howard K. Smith's *Last Train from Berlin* ... All these observers share a common theme: the destruction of German cities by the Allied air raids.

3 February 1945

A huge attack on Berlin, the largest yet in the air war. Young American pilots come sailing in as if on parade; the weather is so lovely, mild as an April day with sunshine and light clouds across the fresh blue sky. Snow-white contrails linger in long fluttering paths after the shiny silver machines that rush forth smoothly and evenly, like a speed train on its tracks. While the good citizens in their residential suburbs may enjoy this sight, everyone in the city must rush into the cellars and underground stations. Seven heavy bombs fall on the area between Potsdamer Platz and Anhalter Bahnhof. Seven times in the subway tunnel we are startled by the loud explosions and the air pressure. The lights go out. The tunnel is dark as night, filled with soot and smoke, as eerie as the kingdom of the dead. Every so often, the suppressed panic breaks out in a chorus of nervous voices shouting for calm after the harshest explosions. Women call out for doctors, but no doctors come, and no nurses come, and the patient, whoever she is, has to manage as best she can. I too am sick, with a fever and sore throat, and I'm going straight home and getting into bed, if only we can survive this.

Outside on the street it's the same mood we know so well from the other big attacks. Streetcar tracks torn apart, wagons burned out. Traffic at a standstill. Everyone must trudge on foot through a chaos of rubble, around craters filled with greenish brown water. Smoke. Soot. The smell of fire. A strong wind sends sharp dust burning into our eyes. We aren't the least bit curious to see more ruins and fires, just exhausted. Everything looks ugly and horrible. The lovely Esplanade Hotel, one of Europe's best, received a direct hit and is now a flaming ruin. The Volksgerichtshof (People's Court) next door is also engulfed in flames—yet another consolation.

No one today has heard the Germans cry, "Down with the Americans! Down with the Russians!" or anything like that, which one might expect, given what happened in previous wars. But I wonder whether the first cry of "Down with Hitler!" wouldn't spread like wildfire? It feels like it would. It's in the air like the coming spring. Ach, sighs an honorable colleague, what will become of us in Europe? We don't believe in economists any more, or in politicians, and certainly not in the military. Where is the "church militant"? If only it would rise up again and lead a crusade against all false prophets and seducers of the people, who promise all the power in the world to their supporters if only they follow blindly.

All is well at home on Kielganstrasse. The house was jostled slightly by a bomb that fell nearby. The maid is hard at work with her dust cloth, quite annoyed that plaster dust from the roof has fallen on the furniture. I'm starving, and I eat before going to bed and sleep until seven o'clock in the evening. When I get up, the sky is gleaming red from all the fires. I close the curtains and turn on the lamp, with its reassuring glow under the milky white shade, sit down in the armchair, and listen to some light music humming on the radio. Then a strange feeling comes over me, as if I'm sitting in a padded nutshell of a boat and sailing through frightful infernos past gaping abysses. I made it through with my life again this time. A deep feeling of gratitude comes over me in this strange little twilight hour.

5 February 1945

In the huge concrete bunkers like this one on Karlstrasse, the feeling of safety alone produces a kind of everyday mood—the buzz of small talk is everywhere, the ladies sitting together discussing prices of food, three teenage girls on the bench behind me laughing and giggling, putting their heads together to look at pictures of actors. The soldiers, who aren't the worst at moving through the crowd of women and children, are also laughing and chatting. The elderly among the people here are the most serious, looking exhausted and ill tempered. There is not much sorrow or sense of tragedy about the fate of Berlin to be noticed among these common people—their major concerns are the workshop and the store, the kitchen table and the beds at home—as long as *those things* remain, everything is fine, and for the time being they're pleased to be in the safety of the bunker. A recent bitter joke: According to a message on the wire service, the heads of the party have reached the bunker!—of course they have: Goebbels and his fellow party members are down in the safest bunkers of all, governing from beneath the ruins.

8 February 1945

Frau von Sowieso is chatting endlessly with her friends in the bunker, who shiver every so often when they hear explosions nearby. What pain and hardship she has experienced; nearly all her shoes were destroyed by fire in one of the air raids, and she had such a magnificent collection: blue, red, brown, white, black, most of them from Paris, and now they're all gone, burned up, just two pairs left, life is not worth living . . . What time is it? asks a dear friend of hers, interrupting her constant chatter. Frau von Sowieso looks at her watch, the alarm has lasted almost an hour now, it's about time it stopped. Isn't this watch just lovely? Look at this one, she takes another out of her bag, I have so many watches, all my friends in Paris send them to me. She sighs, how tiresome these alarms are . . .

A bomb can quickly put an end to all that boredom. I wonder whether French noblewomen during the revolution chattered on about such trivia while the earth was shaking under their feet, their privileges and possessions drifting away from them, without the slightest understanding of what was happening . . . ?

Translated by **DEAN KROUK**

Children's Games

Jacob Kronika was the spokesman for the Danish minority in South Schleswig and, from 1932 to 1945, the German correspondent for the Danish and Swedish newspapers *Nationaltidende* and *Svenska Dagbladet*. He published several books in the 1930s. *The Downfall of Berlin* was compiled mainly from "the pages of a diary kept during the collapse of Berlin" interspersed with additional subheads, and it describes the period from February to May 1945. Religion serves as the leitmotif; Kronika sees fascism as the "rebellion of paganism against Christianity." On the other hand, he sees Catholicism as the "powerhouse of renewal." He describes, in an allegorical manner, church services held in the ruins, church bells that have survived the destruction and still ring, the Memorial Church in Berlin, a cemetery, representations of the crucifixion, and the half-destroyed monument to a Hohenzollern ruler holding a crucifix in his hand.

25 February 1945

Children are everywhere in Berlin. They play cheerfully in the bombed-out streets between the alarms, but their games have been influenced by the war. When they dig with their little shovels and spades now, they're nearly always building bunkers. In play, they compete to see who can build the strongest bunker. Young children speak precociously about the explosive power of the various bomb calibers; they've become experts with two-tons, four-tons, six-tons, super bombs.

: : :

An American bomber crashed into a corner building in central Berlin, a house that had already suffered bomb damage. Only a few broken walls were still standing, at about the height of the second floor. Everything else was in ruins. There was once a large flower shop on this corner; amid the destruction a sign "Flowers" was still hanging.

Now an American bomber sat on the blackened and pulverized ruins of the flower shop. People stopped for a moment and stared at the scene. They explained knowingly that the bomber must have been flying very low when it was hit, or it wouldn't have been preserved in such good condition!

A crew member was lying on top of the wreckage. Strangely, the dead pilot's body appeared not to have been mutilated or injured. However, it was only the pilot's solid, tight-fitting uniform that gave this impression.

The pilot was lying on his back, with one arm pointed toward the sky. His face was completely black.

One day a boy, ten to twelve years old, climbed up onto the ruins of the flower shop. None of the bystanders were bothered by this, and no one said anything. There was no way of knowing what the boy was up to. He looked furtively to the left and the right, and then he made his way carefully to the dead pilot. He got down on his knees and started to grab at something in the wreckage of the plane. A few moments passed, and then the boy stood up again. He tried as best he could to hide his loot, looking cautiously down at the people on the street. Still no one said anything. The boy crawled down from the ruins carefully. He had barely set foot on the ground before he ran off, holding his loot tightly in his arms.

"He took the parachute!" a man shouted.

"Stop the boy!" yelled another.

"That's strictly forbidden!"

"Just let him go," said a young girl. "His mother will be happy to have all that nice silk."

: : :

There is an old water pump in the middle of a bombed-out street, an iron one of considerable size.

Luckily, there are many of these pumps in Berlin. In normal times they seemed prehistoric, but now, in the days of air war, Berliners are happy to have their pumps. Where else would they get water, now that the underground pipes have been destroyed?

Men and women stand in long rows at the pumps. It takes a while to fill the buckets with water, but people have a great deal of patience. They should be glad and thankful, being among the few who are still fetching water for their *own* houses!

Near the old pump there is a demolished streetcar on torn-up tracks. All the windows are shattered; the coaches are full of holes and dents. The power lines are in pieces on the ground.

Two little girls are climbing up and down on the stairs of a streetcar. One of them is holding a shabby doll in her arms. She has fixed a handkerchief around its head, just like the way women in Poland and Russia wear them. The other little girl has used a piece of a dirty sheet to make herself an apron, which reaches down to her toes. Both girls have deeply serious expressions on their faces. Much too serious for when they're playing. But I wonder what kind of game this is?

"*I* am a refugee from the east, and *she* is an NSV" (a member of National-Sozialistische Volkshilfe, the so-called People's Aid), the girl with the doll explains when I ask them.

"This streetcar is the train station's soup kitchen for refugees, and I'm getting food for my child. We haven't eaten in twenty-two days . . . We're going to Thüringen on that other streetcar. We'll have a new house there, with a garden. There will never be any alarms, and the Russians won't come anymore, and father will come home from the war . . ."

"So your mother is going to Thüringen with you?" I interrupt the little "refugee."

"*Mother?*" she asks slowly.

There is a moment of silence, and then she says, "My mother was taken away on the refugee transport . . ."

"Her mother was shot," says her friend.

"And now we only have an NSV mother," the little "refugee from the east" adds gravely, looking down at her doll.

"She's over there getting water at the pump . . ."

Translated by **DEAN KROUK**

Nineveh Is a Great City

Theo Findahl presents historico-mythological patterns of interpretation of the destruction of Berlin. He connects the fall of the European metropolis "Germania" with the downfall of the legendary cities of Jerusalem, Carthage, Rome, and Pompeii, as well as Nineveh. By the end of January 1945 the Red Army had reached the Oder. While British and U.S. squadrons continued their bombing, the inhabitants of the Third Reich's capital were awaiting the final massive assault of the Russian divisions.

18 March 1945, Palm Sunday

There is a pale green glow over the lovely old willow trees down by the water outside the Norwegian rowing club in Wilhelmshagen. In the surrounding gardens, crocuses and snowdrops are in bloom, the sun is shining blessedly, the first days of spring are near. Just before church time, the radio starts to send threatening messages. Numerous formations of bombers—two entire "groups," which means over a thousand planes total!—flying eastward, toward Berlin. An American daytime attack in the current phase of the war is usually in the grand style; it will certainly be serious. The neighborhood women make haste preparing to depart for the bunker in Rahnsdorf, an hour-long drive from here. The housekeeper at the club sighs: I can't take it anymore, life isn't worth living, every single day in the bunker, it surely can't be worse for the Russians,

if only the war would end ... In the next breath: a woman at the office in
the AEG [Allgemeine Elektrizitäts-Gesellschaft, General Electricity Com-
pany] told me recently that the new weapon is ready for use, it's supposed
to begin on 27 March, she said, they've put together some electric machines
that can shoot the American and British planes down from the sky, maybe
that would mean the end of the war ... ? The hint of hope in her voice
dies away: I don't know what to believe, we've heard so many stories like
that ... if only the war would end ...

It is indeed true that Goebbels has fed his countrymen countless stories
about new miracle weapons. They haven't heard much about that in Berlin
lately; instead, they've started to spread stories about new offensives in the
east and west, but out here in the suburbs the stories about miracle weapons are still going around ...

Alarm! The Norwegian businessman, the only one still living at the club
since the last students left, heads with me to one of the neighbors', the coal
seller S., who has a small private bunker in his garden. It's always better
than the rowing club, which doesn't have a cellar and offers about as much
safety as an open umbrella. The coal seller is a calm and reasonable man,
100 percent anti-Hitler, and in his bunker people can talk about whatever
they want, unlike in the communal Splittergraben [splinter grave], where
two men were arrested by the police just the other day for speaking carelessly. That sort of thing only makes matters worse, remarks the coal seller,
the hate and outrage grow. We chat about all kinds of issues as we stand in
front of the entrance to his little cave. In this war, he says, it's the civilians'
turn to crawl around in trenches. If fate has it in store for the bomb to reach
you here, you'd be nicely buried in an instant. A little wooden cross above
the cave could show where you were laid to rest. In a strange way, I find
that consoling, much more so than being crammed together in a mass grave
deep under Berlin, under a hundred tons of rubble and crushed sewage
and water pipes. These small caves in suburban gardens are in fact much
better than cellars in Berlin; they are secured against anything, except, of
course, a direct hit. The coal seller continues: I don't bother listening to the
propaganda anymore, he says, all that about the violence and the Russian
atrocities in the eastern provinces. I turn off the radio, it's mostly lies, I'm
sure of it. For my own part, I have nothing to hope for; I'll live out the last
third of my life in bondage ... His honest blue eyes take on the distant
expression of a man contemplating a mystery. *Who is to blame for it all?
Is it just this one man?* The entire age is to blame, he answers quickly, as if
telepathically; people have had it too easy, they have only asked and taken,
never been thankful; the steak wasn't juicy enough, the cakes weren't sweet

enough, the coffee wasn't strong enough, the rolls weren't white enough, they stepped on the bread . . . now God's punishment is upon them . . .

There's no time for further reflection, now the *attack* begins! From here it looks like a stage production with the strange power and majesty of judgment day. The American four-engine bombers show up in groups of twelve, rushing at the heart of Berlin like quick snakes. The plane itself is the little silver snake's head, after which the long snow-white contrail forms an arc over the blue of the sky. From north, south, and west the planes come rushing; white stripes cover the heavens. Now they give the signal to drop the bombs—rockets that release giant snowy trails that form the strangest shapes. The antiaircraft artillery crashes, bombs explode far in the distance, the mighty organ music of the attack roars more and more wildly. It's time to go into the bunker, where we can take turns looking out carefully through the opening. A young Pole who works for the coal seller goes first; he has sharp young ears and eyes, and he gives a brilliant reportage, pointing and explaining. Look, he shouts with excitement, here come eight German fighter planes, the new kind—Mein Gott, they're so fast! They're heading straight at twelve of the closest American planes—it's a real air battle! There's an American bomber on fire in the air out there—the others are spreading out of the way, look! look! The burning plane is swaying and wobbling, but the pilot is still in control, Mein Gott, what heroes . . . Maybe they're going to try to reach the Russians, he says, but they're not going to make it, look! look!—and, indeed, the burning machine falls like a torch to the earth. We duck down involuntarily, even though the plane is much too far away to do anything to us . . .

The German antiaircraft defense seems to have improved, says the coal seller, but what's the use now? . . . The planes are flying much closer to us. Cannons roar high up in the heavens and on the ground, a *furioso* that forces the earth to shake and sigh, to writhe in pain. Smoke from burning Berlin begins to appear on the horizon in dark gray banks of fog. The sun is gradually eclipsed; it shines only as a bleak moon through a heavy veil before it is blocked out completely. A strange and unreal yellowish gray light covers the earth. There's nothing to be heard except the roaring of explosions, every living thing has crept into hiding, dogs are wailing, and only the foolish hens are still moving around undisturbed, hacking at the grass. It goes on and on. A new wave of bombers rushes in, but we can only discern a few of them through the clouds of smoke. We can hear a third wave, but we can't see a single plane anymore. The entire sky is covered with gray and white clouds . . . It's lasted for over an hour now . . . Finally it quiets down, it's over for this time . . . Now we feel the wind that always comes after bomb fires, throwing more ash into the air, which soon falls like quiet, fine rain. After such an attack it always seems as if the heavens are weeping over Anti-Jerusalem.

In the Bible it is written, "Nineveh is a great city of three days' journey." It's a good twenty-five kilometers from Wilhelmshagen to the center of Berlin, a six- or seven-hour march. The subway and streetcars are certainly out of service, the busses stopped driving a long time ago due to the lack of gasoline. Luckily I have a piece of Danish sausage with me, which can always get me a ride of some sort if I just stand by the side of the road and wave it. It works again this time, and in an hour I'm with a group of other stranded people in a covered cart pulled by two white horses. They take off and trot at an even pace until we reach the railroad that runs around the city, where the streets have been made impassable by the bomb craters and fallen rubble, and the driver refuses to go any further. We're in eastern Berlin, in an area that was hit the worst. Burning smoke gets in your eyes; the fire department is working hard to put out all the flames, but they can't deal with everything. Orange flames burst from windows and rooftops, while people in other buildings look out curiously from behind the hyacinths and lilies blooming in the windows of their petty-bourgeois living rooms. Some people are gathered on balconies to get a better view of it all. Wreckage from the burning houses covers the sidewalk; the finest furniture looks truly worn out and wretched when it's thrown on the street, ravaged by fire and water.

There are no signs of distress among the people, no screams or cries, no tears. Complete apathy. No one has the strength to rebel against Hitler and the total state, let alone against war and fate.

The air is cleaner in the west. The wind kept the smoke away, and no one noticed much of the attack. Was it really so bad? In the west, the subway lines and streetcars are still working. "Nineveh is a great city . . ."

19 March 1945

The engineer asks how thick the concrete is in the bunker where I'm staying. I tell him 1.8 meters, and find out that this is not nearly thick enough for the new kind of bombs. It seems our bunker is hopelessly outdated. The engineer says that the effect of the bombs depends on their kinetic energy plus their explosive force, and bunkers must be designed to have a corresponding power of resistance. Then he tells me about the effects of a six-ton American "earthquake bomb" in Duisberg—or was it Düsseldorf? After a direct hit on a large concrete bunker, which held twenty thousand people, there was nothing left on the site except concrete powder, tattered clothing, and shreds of flesh. And blood was streaming through the middle of it all. Considering that each human body contains about five or six liters of blood, said the engineer, the twenty thousand people who were killed in that bunker had a total amount of blood of over one hundred thousand liters. Clearly some of this was bound to trickle out . . .

The engineer inhales smoke from his pipe before continuing: let us take a few moments to contemplate the unfathomable brutality and horrific soullessness of machine warfare.

Translated by **DEAN KROUK**

"I Must Speak to the Führer!"

Jacob Kronika was present during the Russian attack on Berlin. On 16 April 1945, the Red Army began its great offensive on the Oder front, with 2.5 million men. On 20 April, German resistance on the Oder collapsed. When the Soviet vanguard troops met on 25 April in Nauen, in the west of the city, Berlin was surrounded. On 26 April, Soviet troops entered the capital from different sides. On 30 April, Hitler committed suicide in the "Führer's bunker" under the Reich Chancellery. The city capitulated on 2 May 1945.

20 March 1945

A moving scene on Voss-Strasse. A woman comes clambering out of the ruins of the Wertheim department store, screaming and flailing her arms. At first she appears to be drunk, but the poor thing has lost her mind. She runs across the street to the entrance of the Reich Chancellery; a police officer follows her.

"My son is dead! My son is dead! I must speak to 'der Führer'!" the unhappy woman shouts.

The officer takes hold of her. A soldier is sent to Linkstrasse to get a car. People crowd around and stare at the scene with bleak and despondent faces. The woman keeps trying to break loose from the police officer.

"You've taken my son from me," she shouts wildly. "Let me in to see 'der Führer' . . . !"

In a few moments the car arrives and takes the woman away. Where is she going? The Berlin Hospital, which has so far escaped all the bombardments, has no more room for patients; it's full up.

:::

Millions of German mothers have experienced this woman's pain and sorrow. Several years ago I attended a little going-away party at the studio of a very talented young painter, Harry E., who was leaving for the eastern front the next day. The mood was dismal. Everyone in the painter's family hated the war and Hitlerism.

At one point the painter's mother blurted out: "I swear to God in heaven I will kill Hitler with my own hands if Harry doesn't make it back from the war . . ."

Harry *never* did return. He, who was born in Vladivostock, spoke Russian, and loved Russia, was shot by Russian partisans. His mother never fulfilled her promise of revenge. She just broke down in nameless despair.

===

28 March 1945

Last night there was a dance at the Press Club in Dahlem. To be sure, it was not public entertainment, but still! In these times! The Germans were at least as eager to dance as any of the foreign guests. There were top officials, well-known German editors and their wives, all dancing on the floor of the library. A gramophone was playing music. Among the favorite records, played numerous times, was "Mrs. Miniver," the famous English waltz. This, during the downfall of Berlin!

===

10 April 1945

You would think that the stifling atmosphere of destruction that has weighed down on Berlin for so long would eliminate most of the erotic life in the city. That is not the case; it is rather the opposite. The soldiers are showing an insatiable appetite. In the evenings, the dark quarters near the zoo, Wittenbergplatz, and Kurfürstendamm are all wildly erotic. There is yelling and screaming, mating calls the likes of which were not heard in normal times in the past. Women are not holding back at all.

The hunger for men makes many of them completely uninhibited.

Young soldiers don't have to make an effort to find women; soldiers are sought after. Women offer cigarettes and meals to have their desires fulfilled. During nighttime alarms in the large bomb shelters, where thousands of people are crammed together, the people are not only weary and despairing in silence; there is also a net hanging over them, made with the trembling threads of erotic sensuality. Very young people have obviously given in early to their erotic drives. Boys and girls in uniform have gained adult knowledge at all too young an age. Nothing is holding them back. Their home life has dissolved. The camp life encourages them. Doctors in Berlin have told about the devastating frequency of sexually transmitted diseases and about very young girls becoming pregnant. Frantic lust has been released during the downfall of Berlin.

"We want to do everything, because we might be killed tonight or tomorrow!"

That seems to be the motto these days.

===

19 April 1945

I witnessed a bloody scene on Nollendorfplatz. A young man of seventeen or eighteen came running out of the subway station. It was clear that he knew he was being followed. He threw a bundle of clothes aside and ran like a hunted animal into the park by the station, but he didn't make it very far. Two men in civilian clothes ran after him. They ordered him to stop, and when he kept running, they shot at him. The young man was killed. They searched his pockets, but there were no papers on him.

Other people came out and formed a small crowd around the young man and the civilians with pistols. Some people were explaining the episode in hushed voices:

The two civilians were actually plain-clothes officers assigned to watch for deserters. All male civilians of a certain age were forced to show their papers. When the officers asked this young man for his papers, he ran away, and this cost him his life.

"Is he a foreigner?" people wondered as they stood staring at the dead man.

"Couldn't be," said an elderly man. "If he were a foreigner, he would have had valid civilian identification with him. He must be one of our own who couldn't take any more war . . ."

"He's only a boy," remarked one woman. "Did they really have to shoot him so quickly?"

===

21 April 1945

Russian Shturmovik aircraft are flying over the city constantly. They are especially interested in the Reich Chancellery. They are not bombing anything, and it is very interesting to monitor their actions.

It's impossible to get a telephone connection to the Propaganda Ministry. I went over there and found out that Dr. Goebbels is to be relocated without delay to a bunker deep underground.

There are no evening papers. The usual press correspondents are also missing. Things are falling apart very quickly.

Strangely enough, it is possible to get a telephone connection to Copenhagen and Stockholm. While I'm talking on the telephone with the newspapers, grenades are falling on Leipziger Platz and Potsdamer Platz. They say they can hear the artillery noise on the other end of the line.

Refugees are streaming in from the east. It is a dreadful sight. Where are they going to find room for these people? Long processions of refugees come walking down Leipziger Strasse. They have furniture, horses, and cows with them. Where are they going to find food for these poor animals? A ten-year-old boy from Freienwalde ties his cow to the gate at the Press Club.

===

22 April 1945

Dr. Goebbels spoke this evening on the radio. He assured everyone that he would remain in Berlin with his wife and children until victory is achieved. Additionally, he made a bunch of new threats against deserters and defeatists. The foreigners staying in Berlin received a special flood of abuse: the consequences would be dire if they tried to do anything to sabotage the defense effort. Goebbels went on to say that houses displaying white flags of capitulation would be considered "plague bacteria," and that new precautionary measures were to be introduced at once.

All the barricades are now off limits. Men from the *Volkssturm* are standing guard with old rifles in narrow openings that someone could squeeze through.

Loads of heavy German military vehicles are patrolling along the east-west axis and on Tiergartenstrasse. They are camouflaged with spruce twigs. The Tiergarten quarter and the area around Bendlerstrasse, near the OKW [Oberkommando der Wehrmacht, German Army Command], have been rapidly transformed into a regular military camp.

Russian bombers mount a series of attacks on the two immense anti-aircraft defense towers by the zoo. The towers are Berlin's most powerful defense position. The giant cannons on their corner platforms fire at the Russian attack forces with deafening blasts.

People are going mad trying to get hold of some extra provisions and supplies. This is certainly not an atmosphere of Sunday relaxation. Long lines have formed outside stores. According to a decree by Goebbels, it is now possible to get meat, sugar, and canned goods without stamps, but the supplies are very short. Shop owners are worried about the possibility of chaos and looting.

::::

I was over at the Propaganda Ministry again. The work there is now being done in the underground bunkers.

Dr. Goebbels is still continuing to the bitter end with his insane propaganda. Today he was spirited and hopeful, because—according to him—international political sensations are underway: Molotov is not going to San Francisco! The Allies are in disagreement about the Polish question! The alliance between East and West is coming to a decisive end! Ambassadors will be called home!

But even his closest associates down in the bunker can hardly swallow his attempt to make the awful situation seem better.

::::

More and more people are heading to the subway stations early in the afternoons to get ready to stay overnight. Young children go around wearing heavy steel soldier's helmets on their heads. It's a heartbreaking sight; these children's faces have nothing childlike about them.

::::

The Hitler Youth have become a kind of police authority. They patrol the streets in groups of six with rifles over their shoulders. No adults are watching over them, so they do whatever they want. The people are indignant, but they keep quiet.

The armed youth patrol officers search for bicycles and confiscate them whenever they can get hold of them. They certainly have enough money, because they'll pay forty to seventy marks for a confiscated bicycle.

===

23 April 1945

Last night the Adlon Hotel opened the doors of its wine cellars, and guests could drink as much as they wanted. A wild symposium ensued, with the accompaniment of Russian and German grenades.

: : :

No one is allowed in the blockaded area except soldiers. Red telephone wires have been laid out on the sidewalks and all over the piles of ruins. Or perhaps they are electric cables attached to explosives? At this point, Hitler probably doesn't want the Russians to find a single building intact in Berlin!

Translated by **DEAN KROUK**

Crispbread from Stockholm

Theo Findahl leaves a villa in Dahlem, an elegant part of Berlin where he had taken shelter from the approaching Soviet units, and ventures into the ruined center of the city at the end of April 1945.

23 April 1945

This, our final car ride through Berlin, was an unforgettable journey. There are four of us in the car, and one person must constantly be on the lookout for the Russian Shturmovik planes, which swoop down like hawks at cars and other vehicles. When we spy a Russian plane, the car has to pull over quickly, preferably under a tree, and we sit as quiet as mice until the plane is over our heads, then the danger is over and the car drives on at top speed. We make it without misfortune to Güntzelstrasse in Wilhelmsdorf, pick up some vital packages there, and then we try to make it to the apartment in Kielganstrasse, near Nollendorfplatz, and then, we hope, all the way to the Finnish bunker to save our clothes and other possessions, but we're too late. The main streets are barricaded, so the car must wind its way forward, taking the oddest detours. Grenades are falling constantly on Lützowplatz, it's mad to try to make it through—we do an about face and head back to Dahlem. The few cars we pass are all driving at the same breakneck speed, and the danger of collision has never been greater, but luck is with us and we reach Dahlem in good shape. No castaway could be happier to have reached a blessed green isle than we are when, a short while later, we are sitting in the freshly blossoming spring garden, which seems twice as peaceful and beautiful after all the thundering cannons in the gray city center. Meanwhile, a cozy evening meal is simmering in a pot on the hearth between green bushes.

Eggs, butter, and canned goods are nice to have, but we have access to a small supply of something even more important: *bread.* In Lichterfelde West, at the residence of one of the Royal Norwegian government's secret trustees in Berlin, there are packages from the Royal Norwegian Legation in Stockholm, which contain large amounts of crispbread, among many other good things. If there's a hope of getting some of it, the attempt must be made this afternoon, as quickly as possible. The thunder from the artillery is getting louder; more and more Russian planes are racing through the air. War is clearly approaching Dahlem. The road to Lichterfelde West is not long, a half-hour by foot, but it's no walk in the park. I pay a short visit to my colleague Huitfeldt, from the Danish newspaper *Socialdemokraten,* to ask him to come along. It's better to travel with someone in such circumstances. On several occasions we have to press ourselves into a doorway, our hearts in our throats, as bombs from Russian planes explode in nearby yards, and shrapnel from the German defense artillery rip through the leaves of the trees on the avenue. But we make it there, get the packages, and make it back. Now we have bread and other food to last for two or three weeks, boiled water in bottles, regular water in buckets and bathtubs, and enough wood for the garden hearth. We're not dependent on gas, electricity, or water provision. We arrange mattresses to sleep on in one of the rooms of the cellar, and set up another room with outdoor chairs to make a combined living room and dining room. We are as well prepared for the Red Army's advance on Hitler's capital as it's possible to be for a few unfortunate civilians in a fragile villa in the garden suburb of Dahlem.

Translated by **DEAN KROUK**

Twilight of the Gods

A Swedish volunteer in the Waffen-SS describes his experiences in the "Nordland" Division during the last months of the war on the German eastern front. Beginning with New Year's Day, his book, which appeared in Sweden in the same year, treats the battles in 1945 against the Red Army as it advanced on Berlin: first in Kurland (in Latvia); then in Pomerania, around the Stettin bridgehead, on the Oder front, during the retreat to the suburbs of the German capital; and eventually in the city itself—the *Endkampf*, the "final battle." The title of the Swedish original, *Ragnarök*, means "Twilight of the Gods." Nazi ideology persists, expressed from an immediate postwar perspective. The author's identity is not revealed in the German edition, which appeared in Buenos Aires after the war. The book is based on the recollections or tales of Erik Wallin, known as "Jerka." The stories were recorded by Thorolf Hillblad, who, until replaced by Gösta Block, worked on the Swedish program of the Reich radio service. Before the war, Wallin was a member of the Swedish National Socialist movement. Between 1939 and 1942, he was a volunteer in Finland and joined the Waffen-SS in January 1943. After the war, Wallin was idolized by the neo-Nazis. The selected passages are all concerned with the end of April 1945, in and around Berlin. The actual *Endkampf* lasted about two weeks, from 20 April to 2 May 1945.

We were getting closer to Berlin. The landscape changed character. We drove into the pine forests of Mark Brandenburg, where small

lakes glittered between the trees. Weekend cottages, taverns, and small refreshment inns for cyclists and motorists who used to come from Berlin
on Sunday trips became more and more numerous. Now they were empty,
or temporarily lodged wounded and exhausted soldiers. On the gable of
an idyllic little tavern close to the highway, we met the blazing words *Berlin bleibt Deutsch!* ("Berlin remains German!") They were painted over the
bleached wall-advertisement for the beer brand *Berliner Kindl.*

===

The expectation of being able to stop the Red Army in front of Berlin, and
of having the co-operation of the western enemies, had faded. In fact we
were already standing just outside Berlin, and could see yellow and blue-red
trains of the metropolitan railway, standing there and being shot to pieces
on demolished embankments. Time after time we saw railway-stations
with names that are associated with Berlin. Over and over again we saw
signs for *Commerz-Bank, Lokal-Anzeiger* and *Berliner Morgenpost.* This
was all extremely depressing. From more and more gable walls the words
Berlin bleibt Deutsch! stared down on us. But now we began to ask ourselves with despair in our hearts "Will Berlin really remain German?" The
last hope was now with *Obergruppenführer* Steiner and his northern army
which, we were told, was on its way to our rescue.

===

Now the real battle of Berlin began! The final struggle against the giants in
east and west, the "Twilight of the Gods," had reached its peak and passed
into its last phase. We found positions, already prepared, that the civilian
population had dug and built ever since the Russian breakthrough on the
Vistula at the turn of the year.

At important road junctions the blockades against Russian tanks were
standing ready to be dragged into positions with tractors or tanks. There
were trams, filled with paving stones, and big freight wagons with well-
known names such as *Knauer, Berliner Rollgesellschaft, Schmeling* and others. Small foxholes, which had been dug in on almost every street crossing,
were mostly already manned by some *Volkssturm* men armed with a couple
of *Panzerfäuste.* Everywhere *Volkssturm* soldiers could be seen, most of
them with just a helmet and a badge as identification.

Among them were lots of young boys from the *Hitlerjugend,* aged between eight and twelve or thirteen years. After a mercilessly cruel war of
bombs they were just as hardened as old frontline veterans. In the middle
of the worst bombardments they showed a confidence and a balance of

mind that scared us. We thought that these boys should be playing harm-
lessly in the schoolyard. As the enemy became visible or could be located
by his firing, the faces of these small boys assumed the same grim, hard
resolute look as those of hardened veterans.

Added to the confidence in battle of these warlike children, came a ran-
corous frenzy and a boundless contempt of death, which we grown-ups
could not muster. With the agility and speed of weasels they climbed and
struggled their way into completely impossible positions, to knock out a
Russian tank with a *Panzerfaust* or to finish off one or several advancing
Red Army soldiers with a hand-grenade. There were quite a number of
Russian tanks put out of action by small boys in their early teens during
the battle of Berlin.

===

Public transport was at a standstill. With only a wheelbarrow, or a rickety
bicycle those poor people did not manage to get far with their children
and their most necessary belongings. First they had to force themselves
through the giant city's ruins, past blockages, over horse cadavers and human corpses that had already begun to pile up in the streets.

The people who decided, or had, to stay went down into the shelters.
After all it was a life they had already gotten used to. They were cave-
dwellers in the 20th Century! Down there they grouped together, waiting anxiously, agonising, listening to the constantly approaching sounds of
battle. They felt the vibrations of the shell impacts and heard the houses
collapsing above them.

Tens of thousands of these terrified people were crushed under the falling masses of stone. Or they were closed in from the outer world by a
collapse, to face an agonising death by thirst and starvation that first drove
them insane, before death came and relieved them. Those who survived had
to save every drop of water and every piece of bread as long as possible. To
run up from the cellar to bring water from the tap on the nearest street corner was like running to meet Death. In this city there hardly remained any
silent spot. Merciless shells always seemed to find an unfortunate victim.

===

Filled with concern for the fate of our comrades, we drove along Her-
mannstrasse northwards. The gathering-point was U-Bahn Stadtmitte,
where our Division Nordland's new command post was to be set up. For
about an hour we zigzagged hither and thither on almost impassable
streets. On a house wall we for the first time saw in hastily painted letters

SS-Verräter—Kriegsverlängerer! ("SS traitors and extenders of war!") German communists had been at work. Was this the way it would be? Would they start to emerge from now on? Perhaps the civilian population's morale, which so far had stood up well under all the hard tests of the bombing war, had started to give way? Still we were saluted with "Heil Hitler!" when we sometimes stopped on a street to ask some water-carrying civilian the way to Stadtmitte. But perhaps it was only because of fear of the "death's-head" soldiers that they saluted that way. Were we going to be forced to fight an inner enemy, too?

We had hardly completed this thought when right in the middle of Hermannplatz we had bursts of bullets sweep over the half-track from a roof. There, German communists with red armbands were lying shooting, with machine-guns that they had stolen from the *Volkssturm's* stocks. Soldiers from another SS unit came running, rushed up into a building on the other side of the square and put the roof over there under fire with their machine-guns, while some other men ran into the Communist house and set the upper floors on fire. Then they waited down by the front door, to see if the commies up there would prefer to die in the fire or try to get out, just to be caught and hanged from the nearest lamp-post.

We watched other depressing signs of disorganisation on our roving way to Stadtmitte. Numerous *Wehrmacht* soldiers were standing loitering, weapon-less, in doorways. As they caught sight of our half-track, they quickly stepped back into the dusk. The respect the *Wehrmacht* had for the Waffen-SS was without limit. How many times out at the front had we been sent into action to get them out of trouble, trouble that only the SS could solve? We also met *Wehrmacht* soldiers who, helplessly drunk, staggered around in the streets, without caring about the howling shells or air bombs. In a doorway, a woman surrendered herself recklessly to a *Wehrmacht* soldier. On the opposite side of the street an old man and some women were just tearing large pieces from a swollen dead horse. A whistling shell approached. They threw themselves to the ground behind the horse for a moment, awaited the impact, stood up again and continued with bloody hands to tear, scratch and cut in the cadaver. They paid no attention to the two in the doorway. What had been only cultural plaster was beginning to crumble in larger pieces. Here and there, alarming signs of moral decay were seen.

The Final Days

A few days before the Red Army entered Berlin, the Danish observer Jacob Kronika watches the SS soldiers from the Nordic countries march past, those whose experiences Wiking Jerk describes in *Twilight of the Gods.*

24 April 1945

We are standing by Hauptstrasse, a major thoroughfare, watching the fallen regiments pass by. A truck full of wounded SS soldiers from the Wiking Division passes by; there must be some Danes among them. But of course we stay passive and quiet.

On the corner of Hauptstrasse and Reppichstrasse, where there is the busiest traffic, they just hanged a man from the bus stop post. A shudder runs through my body. The Nazis dare to offer this to Berlin when they are mere hours from their downfall!

===

25 April 1945

As we walk back across Lützowplatz, German soldiers are setting up two enormous cannons. One of them faces northwest, the other southeast.

===

26 April 1945

The Victory Column is the German commando center. We see messengers coming and going. The east-west axis is being used as a runway for small airplanes. A red-and-white signal system has been set up on the wide street.

Translated by **DEAN KROUK**

The First "Amerikanski" in Berlin

When U.S. and Soviet troops met at Torgau on the Elbe, the journalist Virginia Irwin, her colleague Andrew Tully, and their driver, John Wilson, seized the opportunity, on their own initiative, of taking a jeep and driving behind the Red Army lines. In 1945, the three were the first Americans to reach Berlin while fighting was still going on in the city. Irwin had come to Europe in 1943 with the Red Cross and had, since 1944, been reporting on the war in France, Belgium, the Netherlands, Luxemburg, and finally Germany. The following text forms the first part of a three-part article that did not appear until two weeks later in the St. Louis Post-Dispatch. Irwin's report, like that of her colleague, was submitted to the Soviet censors by the U.S. High Command. Their deletions can be recognized on the typescript that was returned. They were not, incidentally, respected when the article appeared in the newspaper on 8 May, the day of the German capitulation to the Soviet army. In the following passage, the censored portions are underlined. The U.S. military authorities rescinded the resourceful journalist's permit as a war reporter. From 1946 to 1960 she worked in the New York office of the newspaper, for which she had been writing since 1932.

BERLIN, 27 April 1945

I am one of the first three Americans to enter Berlin.

After a fantastic journey northward after we crossed the Elbe

River, where the Russians and Americans made contact this afternoon, I arrived in Berlin at dark tonight with Andrew Tully, reporter for the Boston Traveller, and jeep driver Sergeant John Wilson of Roxbury, Massachusetts.

The air is heavy with smoke. Everywhere around us is the crackle of small arms fire. Russian artillery is pouring an almost constant barrage into the heart of the city.

But in this Russian Command Post, where we are guests of Guards-Major Nikolai Kovaleski, there is a terrific celebration going on. The arrival of three Americans in Berlin was the signal for the Russians to break out their best vodka and toss a terrific banquet in our honor.

I have just finished eating all sorts of strange Russian concoctions and being toasted by every officer in this Command Post. I have danced with at least a dozen Russians of various rank and degrees of terpsichorean ability. I have even been initiated into that great knee-bend brand of acrobatics which the Guards-Major says is "Russian Kosachec."

We arrived in Berlin a few minutes before 8:00 o'clock tonight after the strangest journey I have ever taken. It was a nerve-shattering experience. We "ran off" the map and had to navigate by guess.

None of us understood Russian. All German road signs had been removed and replaced with their Russian equivalents. We got to Berlin on the strength of a crude, hand-made American flag flying from our jeep, several hundred handshakes and repeated assurances to fierce Russians who repeatedly stopped us that we were "Amerikanski."

And everywhere, as soon as we had convinced the Russians of our identity, we were mobbed. Russian infantry piled out of their horse-drawn wagons and crowded around. Refugees of all nationalities closed in around us and time after time, the road had to be cleared almost by force before we could proceed.

Shortly after noon today at Torgau, east of the Elbe, we dined with Major General Emil Rheinhardt, Command of the Sixty-ninth American Division; Major General Clarence R. Huebner, Commander of the American Fifth Corps; Major General Gleb Vladimirovitsch Baklanoff, Commander of the Thirty-fourth Russian Corps, and General Vladimir Rusakov, Commander of the Fifty-eighth Guards Infantry Division. The dinner was the official celebration of the meeting of the American and Russian troops at the Elbe River.

From Torgau, we started north, behind the Russian lines, traveling sometimes over deserted roads, through dark forests. At other times, we hit highways clogged with the great body of the Russian Army, [beating along in its motley array of horse-drawn vehicles of all sorts.

There were Russian troops riding in American 2½-ton trucks. There were Russian troops riding in two-wheeled carts, phaetons, in old-fashioned pony carts, in gypsy wagons, and surreys with fringed tops. They rode in everything that could be pulled.

The wagons were filled with hay and the soldiers lay on top of the hay like an army taking a holiday and going on a great mass hayride. It was the most fantastic sight I have ever seen. The fierce fighting men of the Red Army in their tunics and great boots, shabby and ragged after their long war, riding toward Berlin in their strange assortment of vehicles, singing their fighting songs, drinking vodka, were like so many holiday-makers going on a great picnic.]

Before eight tonight, we were well into Berlin with the forward elements of the Russian troops in the German capital.

German dead lay on the sidewalks and in the front yards of the bomb-shattered homes of the Berlin suburbs.

All streets were clogged with Russian tanks, guns, infantry, men in their shaggy fur hats, and everywhere the horses of the Russian Army ran loose about the streets.

But the Russians were happy—with an almost indescribable wild joy. They are in Berlin. In this German capital lies their true revenge for Leningrad and Stalingrad, for Sevastopol and Moscow.

And the Russians are having their revenge. All along the road into Berlin, the fields along the roadways are littered with the carts and belongings of the Germans who tried to escape from the German capital. But the Russians are not polite as the Americans are to Germans who clog the roads in the path of army traffic. Americans wait while the Germans pull off the road to let traffic pass, but the Russians either drive over the German carts or push them off the road and upset them.

In the territory over which I travelled to reach Berlin, I saw very few Germans. They fear the Russians as no nation has ever feared a conquering army.

The Russian Red Army is a mad, wonderful lot of fierce fighting men. They are also wonderful hosts.

American prisoners of war liberated from the great prison camps I passed on the way to Berlin told me today that the Russians insist on sharing their last morsel of food and their last drop of drink with every American they encounter. And tonight here in Berlin I am sampling Russian hospitality at its best.

This command post is what is left of a German home in the shattered city of Berlin, almost leveled by American bombers. There are no electric lights and there is no running water. But the Guards-Major is the kind of host who can rise above such difficulties. The minute I arrived he had his Cossack orderly, a fierce Mongolian with a great scar on his left cheek, heat a dishpan full of water. And after I had washed my face, the Guards-Major produced some German face powder, a quarter-full bottle of German perfume and a cracked mirror.

I made myself as presentable as possible and sat down to a candle-lit and flower-bedecked dinner table. The candles were upturned milk bottles and the flower vase was an old pickle jar. But the dinner was served with all the formality of a State function in Washington. At each toast, the Russian officers stood up, clicked their heels, bowed deeply and drained tumblers of vodka. Besides vodka, there was cognac and a drink of dynamite strength the Major described simply as "spirits."

The food was served by a German woman and the Russian laundress attached to Artillery Headquarters. The "appetizer" was a huge plateful of something that tasted like spiced salmon. Then came in huge platefuls of a strange dish that tasted like mutton cooked over charcoal, huge masses of mashed potatoes with meat oil poured over them, a huge Russian cheese, and for dessert, platters of Russian baked pastries.

After each course there were toasts to "The late and great President Roosevelt," to Stalin, to President Truman, to Churchill, to "Capt. Andre Tooley," to "Capt. Veerzeenee Erveen," to the "Red Army," to "the American Army," to "Sarjaunt Wilson," and "to the American jeep."

As we drank our toasts, the battle of Berlin raged only a few blocks away. As the artillery roared, the house shook and the candles fluttered. The candles are still fluttering as I write this story—the story of the most exciting thing that could ever happen to a newspaper reporter. It is all unreal.

The Russian officers in their worn military tunics bedecked with the medals of Leningrad, Stalingrad, and all the other great Russian battles, are unreal. The whole battle is somehow unreal.

And the thought keeps coming into my mind that here is the greatest city dump in the world—with the remains of a world capital all dumped into the same place with a whole city of dead.

I asked the Guards-Major if Berlin was his greatest battle.

He smiled and said sadly in French that I could understand: "No. To us there were greater battles. In those we lost our wives and children."

And then the Guards-Major told me the story of the strange staff [he

<u>has gathered</u>] around him. Every officer on that staff had lost his entire family to the Germans.

In that Major's story, I thought, lay the answer to the success of the fierce battle the Russians are waging for a Berlin that is almost all now in Russian hands.

The Propaganda Minister's Corpse

When the fighting for the inner city in Berlin was moving towards its close and Red Army soldiers were penetrating deeper and deeper into the government district, Adolf Hitler killed himself, on 30 April 1945, in his bunker beneath the Reich Chancellery. One day later, Joseph Goebbels committed suicide. The body of the Reich Chancellor was totally incinerated by his remaining followers; that of his short-lived successor, only partially. Wiking Jerk reports on how he was able to conceal his identity as an SS man when he was taken prisoner by Red Army soldiers, and how he succeeded in escaping from the prisoner-of-war camp. On his way through the center of the city, in front of the Reich Chancellery, he claims to have seen the body of the propaganda minister and gauleiter of the capital.

Having reached Wilhelmplatz I stopped dead. On a gallows in front of the Reich Chancellery a male corpse was hanging. I went closer. It looked like Goebbels! Although the Bolsheviks had crushed his nose and given the corpse a deep bayonet stab in the throat, it was impossible to be mistaken. Civilians who came walking turned their heads away as they passed the gallows. But Red Army soldiers stopped in groups, pointed at the hanging body, and laughed.

Cry for Vengeance

It was not only the remaining correspondents, like Jacob Kronika, who were seeking refuge in the building and the air-raid shelter of their embassies in late April and early May 1945, but also scattered SS soldiers from the Scandinavian countries. Wiking Jerk (the narrator of *Twilight of the Gods*) describes how he went into hiding for a time in the Swedish embassy.

3 May 1945

The Russian commissar spoke fluent German. He took a great interest in the German legation's employees in the Danish bunker. The younger women, who had been kept out of sight by curtains, empty cardboard boxes, and so on, were told to come out and take a spot on the mats with the men and children. I was requested to sit next to the commissar; I had no idea what his intentions were. He gave a fairly long speech:

"If I were to ask you individually, I am certain that not one person among you would be a Nazi. We know this already; now that the German army has been defeated, all Germans are suddenly opponents of Hitler and have always been anti-Nazi . . . I am a Russian, a Communist, and a Jew. I have seen the German atrocities in my country. My mother and father were murdered by the SS, because they were Jews; my wife and my two children have disappeared; my home is destroyed. Millions of people have gone through what I and my family have gone through. Germany has murdered, raped, plundered, and destroyed . . . What do you think we'd like to do now that we have defeated the German armed forces?"

The Germans crouched down, trembling with fear. The commissar stared at Carl's oldest son, a twelve-year-old boy. [Carl was the caretaker of the Danish Legation.]

"Stand up!" he ordered. "How old are you?"

"Twelve years old," answered the boy.

"That's around the age my boy would have been today. The SS criminals took him from me . . ."

His hand disappeared under his uniform. He brought out a revolver and pointed it at the boy. Carl leaped up; his wife grabbed for the boy.

"But commissar, this boy cannot be made responsible . . ." I began. The tension was dreadful.

"No, no, ladies and gentlemen," continued the commissar. "I won't shoot. But you must admit, I'd have reason enough. So many people are crying out for revenge . . ."

He put the revolver back under his uniform.

===

4 May 1945

Today's walk gave us more disturbing impressions of the Berlin battlefield. The devastation is impossible to describe in words. The entire city center, including the government quarter and the area around "Fortress Tiergarten," is utterly destroyed. The streets are littered with the burned-out wreckage of cars, tanks, motorcycles, cannons, and so on. The major roads have been cleared enough for the Russians to come through with their incredible numbers of cars and horse-drawn carriages. Very young female traffic officers with rifles stand watch on the street corners. At this point people still have not had time to bury all the dead, though they're beginning to do so. The Russians are taking care of their own casualties, but the Germans have to bury German soldiers. The Berliners have to clean up everything, remove barricades, and so on. All young men have to show their papers to the Russian patrol officers to prove that they are not soldiers in disguise. The Russians are searching for fifty thousand Germans who managed to avoid imprisonment by disguising themselves before capitulation. Foreigners wear their national flag on their arms; it's not uncommon for them to get arrested and forced to work.

The first army orders have already been posted on walls everywhere. No civilians are to be outside between the hours of ten at night and eight in the morning—Russian time. Radios, cameras, and weapons must be handed over to authorities.

Throngs of Berliners are constantly on the move. Most of them have no place to go. Many people are camping, in the open air, in the Tiergarten, which is cluttered with instruments of war. There are long lines at all the water pumps; hungry people are hunting for food. Their searches are often successful, as they find provisions on fallen soldiers, in abandoned vehicles, and in bombed-out houses.

Translated by **DEAN KROUK**

Eighth of May 1945

Theo Findahl saw the end of the war in Berlin. On 7 May 1945, in the Supreme Headquarters of the Allied Expeditionary Force in Reims, Colonel General Jodl signed the unconditional surrender of the German armed forces. On 8/9 May, Field Marshal Keitel repeated the surrender in the headquarters of the Soviet Army in Berlin-Karlshorst. The last German units capitulated on 11 May.

8 May 1945

This is the first time I've come this far into the city, where the appalling destruction defies all description. Budapester Strasse, with the Hotel Eden, Elizabeth Arden's beauty institute, and all the elegant specialty shops and comfortable boarding houses, has become a stinking jungle. Russian trucks kick up clouds of brown dust wherever they force their way past bomb craters and ruined buildings. Dead horses with swollen bellies lie on their backs, legs in the air. Severed human hands and arms, limbless bodies, and fragments of corpses have been flung by the explosions onto the streets and against the houses. It looks like this throughout the diplomatic quarter and all around. It takes us hours to walk home, seeing the same everywhere: ruins, burned buildings, death, and destruction.

Translated by **DEAN KROUK**

CHRONOLOGY

6 November 1932	Reichstag elections. NSDAP gains 33.5 percent of votes.
30 January 1933	President Paul von Hindenburg appoints Adolf Hitler, formerly the leader of a coalition government, to the post of Reich Chancellor.
27 February 1933	Reichstag fire.
5 March 1933	Reichstag elections. NSDAP gains 44 percent of votes.
1 April 1933	Organized boycott of Jewish businesses.
20 July 1933	Concordat between German Reich and the Vatican.
30 June 1934	Assassination of Ernst Röhm. Hitler's purge of the SA.
25 July 1934	National Socialist putsch in Austria. Assassination of the Austrian fascist dictator Engelbert Dollfuß.
2 August 1934	Hitler becomes Reich president after Hindenburg's death. Armed forces swear allegiance to Hitler.
13 January 1935	Plebiscite in Saarland. Ninety-one percent in favor of amalgamation with German Reich.
16 March 1935	Reintroduction of draft.
15 September 1935	Nuremberg Laws are passed.
3 October 1935	Start of Italian colonial war in Abyssinia.
7 March 1936	Remilitarization of the Rhineland.
18 June 1936	Military revolt under Franco.
1 August 1936	Opening of Olympic Games in Berlin.
13 March 1938	Anschluss with Austria.
29 September 1938	Munich Conference.
1 October 1938	Invasion of the Sudetenland.
9/10 November 1938	Kristallnacht.
15/16 March 1939	Invasion of Czechoslovakia.
28 March 1939	Entry of Franco troops into Madrid.
23 August 1939	Russo-German non-aggression pact.

1 September 1939	German invasion of Poland.
9 April 1940	Start of occupation of Denmark and Norway.
10 May 1940	Attacks on Luxemburg, Belgium, the Netherlands, and France.
22 June 1940	Armistice in Compiègne.
6 February 1941	Intervention of the Afrikakorps in the war in North Africa.
6 April 1941	Campaign against Yugoslavia and Greece.
22 June 1941	Attack on Soviet Union.
31 July 1941	Heydrich assigned to the "Final Solution to the Jewish Problem."
9 October 1941	Hitler's press chief, Otto Dietrich, announces victory over the Soviet Union.
5 December 1941	Start of the Russian winter offensive.
20 January 1942	Wannsee Conference on the "Final Solution to the Jewish Problem."
28 June 1942	Start of the German summer offensive. Advance to the Volga.
23 October 1942	Start of British counteroffensive at El Alamein.
19 November 1942	Start of the Russian winter offensive.
22 November 1942	Encirclement of German forces at Stalingrad.
31 January–2 February 1943	
	Capitulation of German forces at Stalingrad (Sixth Army under Field Marshal Paulus).
18 February 1943	Joseph Goebbels declares "total war."
6 June 1944	Landing of Western Allies in Normandy.
20 July 1944	Unsuccessful attempt on Hitler's life in the Führer's headquarters (the "Wolfschanz").
13/14 February 1945	Destruction of Dresden by Allied bombers.
19 March 1945	Hitler's "Nero Command" to destroy areas lost by Germany.
16 April 1945	Start of final Russian offensive on the Oder.
30 April 1945	Hitler commits suicide in the air-raid shelter beneath the Reich Chancellery.
7/8/9 May 1945	Signing of unconditional surrender of German armed forces in Reims (by Jodl) and Karlshorst (by Keitel).

SOURCES

SAMUEL BECKETT
(1906–89)
German Diaries [manuscript, 6 notebooks, ca. 600 pages], Archive of the Beckett International Foundation at Reading University Library. Transcription: Mark Nixon, with the help of James Knowlson. Entries of 28 October 1936 (notebook 1); 24 November and 5 December 1936 (notebook 2); 15 January 1937 (notebook 4); 3 March 1937 (notebook 5). © The Estate of Samuel Beckett. Extracts from Samuel Beckett's *German Diaries* reproduced by kind permission of the Estate of Samuel Beckett c/o Rosica Colin Limited, London.

KAREN BLIXEN
[Tania Blixen, Isak Dinesen]
(1885–1962)
"Breve fra et Land i Krig," in *Heretica* 1:4 (1948), pp. 264–87; and 1:5 (1948), pp. 332–55, here: pp. 277–84, 285–86, 332–34, 337–38, 339–42, 342–44, 348. "Letters from a Land at War," in *Daguerreotypes and Other Essays*, trans. P. M. Mitchell and W. D. Paden, foreword by Hannah Arendt (Chicago: University of Chicago Press, 1979), pp. 88–137, here: pp. 102–10, 111–12, 113–15, 119–20, 120–23, 124–26, 129–30. Reproduced with the kind permission of the Rungstedlund Foundation.

GÖSTA BLOCK
(1898–1955)
Tyskland inifrån. "Königsbergsradions" förre programchef har ordet (Stockholm: Blocks Förlag, 1943), pp. 146–47, 156–60, 161–64. © Henning Block, Sweden.

ALBERT CAMUS
(1913–60)
L'envers et l'endroit (Algier: Charlot, 1937), p. 45, in *Essais*, Bibliothèque de la Pléiade, vol. 2, eds. Roger Quilliot and Louis Faucon (Paris: Gallimard, 1990), pp. 1–50, here: p. 36. © Editions Gallimard, Paris. "The Wrong Side and the

Right Side," in *Lyrical and Critical Essays* by Albert Camus, trans. Ellen Conroy Kennedy (New York: Vintage, 1970), pp. 40–51; here, p. 47. Translation © 1968 by Alfred A. Knopf, a division of Random House, Inc. © 1967 by Hamish Hamilton Ltd. and Alfred A. Knopf, a division of Random House, Inc. Used by permission of Alfred A. Knopf, a division of Random House, Inc.

JACQUES CHARDONNE
[Jacques Boutelleau]
(1884–1968)
Le Ciel de Nieflheim (n.p.: self-published, 1943), pp. 14–15, 15–16, 150–53, 173–74; Bucharest, 1991, pp. 17–18, 18–19, 116–17, 132–33.

MARTHA DODD
(1908–90)
Through Embassy Eyes (New York: Harcourt, Brace, and Co., 1939). *My Years in Germany* (London: Victor Gollancz, 1939), pp. 21–27, 28–30, 31–32, 58–62; 124–26, 128–29, 130, 131–32, 132–33, 134–36; 80–85. © Martha Dodd 1966.

W. E. B. DUBOIS
(1868–1963)
"Forum of Fact and Opinion," in the *Pittsburgh Courier*. Excerpts from the following issues: 26 September 1936, 7 November 1936, 24 October 1936, 19 September 1936, 17 October 1936, 31 October 1936, 9 January 1937, 10 October 1936, 14 November 1936, 5 December 1936, 12 December 1936, 19 December 1936, 2 January 1937, 26 December 1936, 9 January 1937. (The titles of the individual newspaper contributions are void.) Reproduced with permission of the *Pittsburgh Courier* archives.

GUNNAR EKELÖF
(1907–68)
Letter dated 16 December 1933 to Agnes von Krusenstjerna: *Brev 1916–1968*, ed. Carl Olov Sommar (Stockholm: Bonniers, 1989), pp. 50–51. Taken from *Der ketzerische Orpheus. Essays, Skizzen, Briefe. Zur Autobiographie und Poetologie*, ed. and trans. Klaus-Jürgen Liedtke (Münster: Kleinheinrich, 1999), pp. 207–8, here: p. 207. © Kleinheinrich Verlag, Münster 1999.

THEO FINDAHL
(1891–1976)
Undergang: Berlin, 1939–1945 (Oslo: Forlagt Av H. Aschehoug & Co., 1945), pp. 69–72, 74; 83–85, 85, 86; 86–91, 91–92; 156–58; 185–86. © H. Aschehoug & Co. (W. Nygaard) AS, Oslo.

HARRY FLANNERY

(1900–1975)

Assignment to Berlin (London: Michael Joseph Ltd., 1942), pp. 52–53, 86–87, 110–11, 112–13, 151–52, 152–53, 199, 214, 262–63, 293–94, 295–97. © Patricia A. Yoder, U.S.A.

MAX FRISCH

(1911–91)

"Kleines Tagebuch einer deutschen Reise," *Neue Zürcher Zeitung*, 30 April 1935, 7 May 1935, 20 May 1935, 13 June 1935, in *Gesammelte Werke in zeitlicher Folge*, ed. Hans Mayer and Walter Schmitz, 6 vols., vol. 1, 1931–44 (Frankfurt am Main: Suhrkamp, 1976), pp. 84–97, here: pp. 84–86, 88, 89–93, 95–96, 97. © Suhrkamp Verlag, Frankfurt am Main 1976.

JEAN GENET

(1910–86)

Journal du voleur, self-published [1948] (Paris: Gallimard, 1949), pp. 138–39. *The Thief's Journal*, trans. Bernard Frechtman (New York: Grove Press, 1964), pp. 123–24. © 1964 by Grove Press, Inc. Used by permission of Grove/Atlantic, Inc. Used with permission of Faber and Faber Ltd.

HEINRICH HAUSER

(1901–55)

"Berlin in the Summer of 1939," in *Battle Against Time: A Survey of the Germany of 1939 from the Inside* (New York: Charles Scribner's Sons, 1939), pp. 1–27, here: pp. 2–15, 17–27. © Huc Hauser, U.S.A.

SVEN HEDIN

(1865–1952)

Utan uppdrag i Berlin (Stockholm: Fahlcrantz & Gumælius, 1949), pp. 52–53; 98–99. *Sven Hedin's German Diary: 1935–1942*, trans. Joan Bulman (Dublin: Euphorion Books, 1951), pp. 40–41, 82–83. © The Sven Hedin Foundation, Stockholm.

RICHARD HILLARY

(1919–43)

The Last Enemy: The Memoir of a Spitfire Pilot (London: Macmillan, 1942), pp. 19–23. © Richard Hillary, 1942. Reprinted by permission of A.M. Heath & Co. Ltd.

MEINRAD INGLIN

(1893–1971)

"Missglückte Reise durch Deutschland," typescript, 28 pages, Meinrad Inglin Archive at Kantonsbibliothek Schwyz; here in *Schweizer Monatshefte* 43:3 (June

1963), pp. 246–61, here: pp. 246–51, 251–55, 257–59, 259–61. © Ammann Verlag, Zürich.

VIRGINIA IRWIN
(1908–80)
"Story Number 1," typescript, 5 pages, dated "Berlin, 27 April 1945," National Archives II, College Park, Maryland. "A Giant Whirlpool of Destruction," in *Reporting World War II*, part II: *American Journalism 1944–1946* (New York: Library of America, 1995), pp. 709–19; here, pp. 709–12. Originally published in the *St. Louis Post-Dispatch* as: "Post-Dispatch Reporter Gets into Berlin" (part 1), 8 May 1945, pp. 1A and 2A; "Post-Dispatch Reporter Stopped by Gunfire in Heart of Nazi Capital" (part 2), 9 May 1945, pp. 1A and 3A; "Virginia Irwin in Berlin Finds Russians Dance and Drink in Midst of Battle" (part 3), 10 May 1945, pp. 1A and 3A. Reprinted with permission of the *St. Louis Post-Dispatch* © 1945.

CHRISTOPHER ISHERWOOD
(1904–86)
"A Berlin Diary (Winter 1932–33)," in *Goodbye to Berlin* (London: Hogarth Press, 1939), pp. 285–317, here: pp. 311–17. "A Berlin Diary (Winter 1932–33)," in *The Berlin Novels* (London: Vintage, 1992), pp. 464–90, here: pp. 484–90. Reprinted by permission of Donadio & Olson, Inc. © 1939 Christopher Isherwood.

WIKING JERK
[Erik Stig Wallin]
(1921–97)
Ragnarök (Stockholm: Den Svenskes Förlag, 1945), ghost written by Thorolf Hillblad, pp. 92, 106, 109–10, 113–14, 120–22; 138–39. *Twilight of the Gods: A Swedish Waffen-SS Volunteer's Experiences with the 11th SS Panzergrenadier Division Nordland, Eastern Front 1944–45*, ed. Thorolf Hillblad, trans. Jackie Logan with Thorolf Hillblad (Solihull, Eng.: Helion & Company, 2004), pp. 76, 88, 90–91, 92–93, 98–99; 112. Reprinted with permission of Helion & Company.

RENÉ JUVET
[Numa Tétaz]
(1903–86)
Ich war dabei. 20 Jahre Nationalsozialismus 1923–1943. Tatsachenbericht eines Schweizers (Zürich/New York: Europa Verlag, 1944), pp. 76–82, 151–52, 152–53. © Europa Verlag AG, Zürich 1944.

JOHN F. KENNEDY
(1917–63)
German Diary, in personal papers; box #1; series 2: Early Years; folder: *Diary European Trip*, 7/1/37–9/3/37, John F. Kennedy Presidential Library and Museum (Boston), here: 16–22 August 1937.

JACOB KRONIKA

(1897–1982)

Berlins Undergang (Kopenhagen: Hagerup, 1946), pp. 11–14; 60–61, 68–69, 90, 114–15, 120, 121–22, 123–24, 124, 125, 127, 129; 137, 140, 145; 165–66, 168–69.

MARIA LEITNER

[here: Mary L.]
(1892–1941)

"Besuch bei Heinrich Heine," in *Das Wort* [Moskau] 3:1 (1938), pp. 145–46. Taken from *Elisabeth, ein Hitlermädchen. Erzählende Prosa, Reportagen und Berichte*, ed. Helga W. Schwarz (Berlin/Weimar: Aufbau, 1985), pp. 224–26. ©Aufbau-Verlag, Berlin und Weimar 1985.

OLIVER LUBRICH

"Journeys to the End of the Night," "About This Anthology," "Bibliography," and "Chronology," introductions to the fifty-two chapters in this volume. © Eichborn AG, Frankfurt am Main, 2004.

JÓZSEF NYÍRÖ

(1889–1953)

"Blick auf das kämpfende Deutschland," in *Europäische Literatur* 1:2 (June 1942), pp. 2–3 (slightly abridged). © Heirs József Nyírö.

DENIS DE ROUGEMONT

(1906–85)

Journal d'Allemagne (Paris: Gallimard, 1938), pp. 9–10, 12–15, 32–33, 41–42, 44–49, 49–50, 51, 61–63. © Editions Gallimard, Paris.

JEAN-PAUL SARTRE

(1905–80)

Entry of 28 February 1940, in *Les carnets de la drôle de guerre. Novembre 1939– Mars 1940* (Paris: Gallimard, 1983), pp. 319–42, here: pp. 338–39. © Editions Gallimard, Paris. *War Diaries: Notebooks from a Phoney War, November 1939— March 1940*, trans. Quintin Hoare (New York: Verso, 1984/1999), p. 279.

RENÉ SCHINDLER

[Franz Wolfgang Rieppel]
(1917–2000)

Ein Schweizer erlebt das geheime Deutschland. Tatsachenbericht (Zürich/New York: Europa Verlag, 1945), pp. 7–8, 10–13, 16. © Europa Verlag AG, Zürich 1945.

ANNEMARIE SCHWARZENBACH

(1908–42)
Letter to Klaus Mann dated 8 April 1933, in *Wir werden es schon zuwege bringen, das Leben.*" *Annemarie Schwarzenbach an Erika und Klaus Mann, Briefe 1930–1942*, ed. Uta Fleischmann (Herbolzheim: Centaurus, 2001), pp. 101–3. © Centaurus Verlags-GmbH & Co. KG, Herbolzheim 2001.

SHI MIN

[Pseudonym]
"Deguo youji" [German Voyage], in *Oufeng Meiyu* [literally: *European Wind and American Rain*; freely translated: *Our Tempestuous Life Overseas*], ed. Tao Kangde (Shanghai: Yuzhoufeng, 1938), here: pp. 66–67. Translated by Heiner Frühauf. In Heriner Frühauf, "Deutschland in der chinesischen Reiseliteratur der zwanziger und dreißiger Jahre," in *Mein Bild in deinem Auge. Exotismus und Moderne: Deutschland–China im 20. Jahrhundert*, trans. Wolfgang Kubin (Darmstadt: Wissenschaftliche Buchgesellschaft, 1995), pp. 283–99, here: pp. 292–93. German translation © Heiner Frühauf.

WILLIAM SHIRER

(1904–93)
Berlin Diary: The Journal of a Foreign Correspondent, 1934–1941 (New York: Alfred A. Knopf, 1941), pp. 142–43 (entry of 27 September 1938); pp. 197–99 (entry of 1 September 1939). Reprinted by permission of Don Congdon Associates, Inc. *Berlin Diary* © 1941, renewed 1968 by William L. Shirer.

GEORGES SIMENON

(1903–89)
"Europe 33. La génération du désordre," in *Voilà* 3:109, 22 April 1933, pp. 10–11. "Europe '33," in *Mes apprentissages. Reportages 1931–1946*, ed. Francis Lacassin (Paris: Omnibus, 2001), pp. 762–805, here pp. 798–99, 799–800. © Georges Simenon Family Rights Ltd.

HOWARD K. SMITH

(1914–2002)
Last Train from Berlin (New York: Alfred A. Knopf, 1942), pp. 91–97; 81–91, 105–6, 106, 108, 109, 109–10, 111–12; 162–68. © 1942 by Howard K. Smith.

KONRAD WARNER

[Helmuth Grossmann]
Schicksalswende Europas? Ich sprach mit dem deutschen Volk . . . Ein Tatsachenbericht (Rheinfelden, Switzerland: Langacker, 1944), pp. 128–30; 145–48; 16, 29–30, 54–55, 60–61, 106–7, 126, 148, 149–51, 152–53, 153–55, 160, 174–75, 201–2.

THOMAS WOLFE
(1900–1938)
"I Have a Thing to Tell You (*Nun Will Ich Ihnen 'Was Sagen*)," in *New Republic* 90:1162 (10 March 1937), pp. 132–36; 90:1163 (17 March 1937), pp. 159–64; 90:1164 (24 March 1937), pp. 202–7; in *The Short Novels of Thomas Wolfe*, ed. C. Hugh Holman (New York: Charles Scribner's Sons, 1961), pp. 233–78. © 1961 Charles Scribner's Sons. Renewed 1989.

VIRGINIA WOOLF
(1882–1941)
Entries of 9 May and 12 May 1935 from *The Diary of Virginia Woolf, Volume IV: 1931–1935*, ed. Anne Olivier Bell with Andrew McNeillie (San Diego/New York/London: Harcourt Brace & Co., 1982), pp. 310–12. © 1982 by Quentin Bell and Angelica Garnett, reprinted by permission of Houghton Mifflin Harcourt Publishing Company. Also with permission of The Hogarth Press, London.

BIBLIOGRAPHY

SAMUEL BECKETT

Beckett, Edward (Samuel Beckett Estate), written communication, 25 September 2004.

Birkenhauer, Klaus, *Samuel Beckett*, pp. 63–64 (notes: p. 153). Reinbek: Rowohlt, 1971.

Dittrich, Lutz, Carola Veit, and Ernest Wichner, "Obergeschoss Still Closed." Samuel Beckett in Berlin 1936/37. Exhibition at the Literaturhaus Berlin. Berlin: Matthes & Seitz, 2006.

Fischer-Seidel, Therese, and Marion Fries, ed., *Der unbekannte Beckett. Samuel Beckett und die deutsche Kultur*. Frankfurt: Suhrkamp, 2005.

Garforth, Julian Alexander (Reading University Library), written communication, 24 March–13 June 2003.

Knowlson, James (University of Reading), written communication, 19 April–28 August 2003.

——. "Germany: The Unknown Diaries 1936–37," in *Damned to Fame: The Life of Samuel Beckett*, pp. 230–61 (notes: pp. 748–53). London: Bloomsbury, 1997.

Nixon, Mark (University of Reading), written communication, 20 May 2003–24 July 2006.

Quadflieg, Roswitha, *Beckett Was Here: Hamburg im Tagebuch: Samuel Becketts von 1936*, Hamburg: Hoffmann und Campe, 2006.

Tophoven, Erika, *Becketts Berlin*. Berlin: Nicolai, 2005.

KAREN BLIXEN

Arendt, Hannah, "Isak Dinesen, 1885–1962" (foreword), in Isak Dinesen, *Daguerreotypes and Other Essays*, translated by P. M. Mitchell and W. D. Paden, pp. vii–xxv. Chicago: University of Chicago Press, 1979.

Brennecke, Detlef, *Tania Blixen*, pp. 76–78 (notes: p. 136). Reinbek: Rowohlt, 1996.

Daub, Sigrid, "Vorwort," in Tania Blixen, *Mottos meines Lebens. Betrachtungen aus drei Jahrzehnten*, translated by Sigrid Daub, Walter Boehlich, Hanns Grössel, and Hans Hjort, pp. 6–14. Reinbek: Rowohlt, 1993.

Günter, Martin, "Karen Blixen i Hitlers Berlin," in *Cras* 42 (1985): pp. 57–72.

GÖSTA BLOCK

Block, Henning (Kungälv, Sweden), telephone interview, 21 and 22 September 2004.

Reichssicherheitshauptamt, report on Gösta Block's *Tyskland inifrån*, 18 June 1943: Bundesarchiv R 58/1091.

Sennerteg, Niclas (Borås, Swedish broadcasting; writer), telephone interview, 24 September 2004; written communication, 26 and 27 September 2005.

ALBERT CAMUS

Camus, Albert, *Carnets I. Mai 1935—Février 1942*, pp. 55–56. Paris: Gallimard, 1962.

———. *La mort heureuse (Cahiers Albert Camus I)*, edited by Jean Sarocchi, pp. 113–17. Paris: Gallimard, 1971.

Camus, Catherine (Lourmarin, France), written communication, 22 January 2004, 5 February 2004.

Ferrand, Philippe (Centre de documentation Albert Camus, Aix-en-Provence), written communication, 4 March 2004.

Lottman, Herbert R., "Death in the Soul," in *Albert Camus—A Biography*, pp. 106–19 (notes: p. 592). New York: Doubleday, 1979.

Lubrich, Oliver, "Über die Grenze der Bedeutung. Albert Camus in Nazi-Deutschland, 1936," in *Umwege. Ästhetik und Poetik exzentrischer Reisen*, edited by Bernd Blaschke, Florian Cramer, Rainer Falk, Dirck Linck, Oliver Lubrich, Volker Woltersdorff, and Friederike Wißmann, pp. 227–48. Bielefeld: Aisthesis, 2008.

Quilliot, Roger, "L'envers et l'endroit. Commentaires. Notes et variantes. Textes complémentaires," in Albert Camus, Bibliothèque de la Pléiade. Volume 2: *Essais*, edited by Roger Quilliot and Louis Faucon, pp. 1169–1219. Paris: Gallimard, 1990.

Todd, Olivier, "La lettre de Salzbourg," in *Albert Camus, une vie*, pp. 148–60 (notes: pp. 1069–70). Paris: Gallimard, 1996.

JACQUES CHARDONNE

Anonymous, "Avant-propos," in Jacques Chardonne, *Le Ciel de Nieflheim*, pp. 5–10. Bucarest: n.p., 1991.

Chardonne, Jacques, "Voir l'Allemagne," in *La Gerbe*, 13 November 1941, p. 1.

———. "Über die deutsch-französischen Beziehungen," in *Phönix oder Asche? Frankreichs geistiges Ringen nach dem Zusammenbruch*, edited by Bernhard Payr, pp. 382–84. Dortmund: Volkschaft-Verlag, 1942; revised second edition, 1943.

Dufay, François, *Le voyage d'automne. Octobre 1941, des écrivains français en Allemagne. Récit*. Paris: Plon, 2000.

Lagarde, André, and Laurent Michard, "Jacques Chardonne," in *XXe siècle. Les grands auteurs français. Anthologie et histoire littéraire*, pp. 500–502, Paris: Bordas, 1988.

MARTHA DODD

Anonymous, "Der neue amerikanische Botschafter in Berlin eingetroffen," in *Völkischer Beobachter*, 14 July 1933.

Bailey, Fred Arthur, *William Edward Dodd. The South's Yeoman Scholar*. Charlottesville: University of Virginia Press, 1997.

Beard, Charles A., "Introduction. Retrospect and Recollection," in William Edward Dodd, *Ambassador Dodd's Diary, 1933–1938*, edited by William E. Dodd, Jr., and Martha Dodd, pp. 7–16. London: Victor Gollancz, 1941.

Brysac, Shareen Blair, *Resisting Hitler. Mildred Harnack and the Red Orchestra. The Life and Death of an American Woman in Nazi Germany*, specifically: chapter 9, "Hostess," pp. 133–65 (notes: pp. 412–17); chapter 10, "Literary Figure," pp. 167–88 (notes: pp. 417–20); chapter 11, "Stranger," pp. 189–220 (notes: pp. 420–24); and "Postcript," pp. 395–98 (notes: p. 450). Oxford: Oxford University Press, 2000.

Dallek, Robert, *Democrat and Diplomat: The Life of William E. Dodd*, pp. 146, 166, 195, 373–74, 391. New York: Oxford University Press, 1968.

Dodd, Martha, "Death in Tiflis," in *Penguin Parade 6: New Stories, Poems, etc., by Contemporary Writers*, edited by Denys Kilham Roberts, pp. 196–211. Harmondsworth: Penguin, 1939.

———. *L'ambassade regarde*. Paris: Aubier, 1940.

———. *The searching light*. London: John Calder, 1956.

———. *Sowing the wind* [1944–45]. Berlin (GDR): Seven Seas Publishers, 1960.

———. "Porträt meines Vaters" [1961], in William Edward Dodd, *Diplomat auf heißem Boden. Tagebuch des USA-Botschafters William E. Dodd in Berlin 1933–1938*, edited by William E. Dodd, Jr., and Martha Dodd, translated by G. F. Alexan, pp. 15–25. Berlin (GDR): Verlag der Nation, 1964 (revised third edition).

Martha Dodd Papers. Washington, D.C.: Library of Congress.

"Martha Dodd. 1908–1990," in *Traces*, http://www.traces.org/marthadodd.html (June 2004).

Dodd, William Edward, *Ambassador Dodd's Diary, 1933–1938*, edited by William E. Dodd, Jr., and Martha Dodd. London: Victor Gollancz, 1941.

Fox, John F., Jr. (FBI), written communication, 26 and 28 October 2004, 25 January 2005, 8 February 2005.

———. *"In Passion and in Hope": The Pilgrimage of an American Radical, Martha Dodd Stern and Family, 1933–1990*. Ph.D. diss., University of New Hampshire, 2001.

Fromm, Bella, *Blood & Banquets: A Berlin Social Diary* [1943]. New York: Kensington, 2002.

Gellermann, Günther W. . . . *und lauschten für Hitler. Geheime Reichssache: Die Abhörzentralen des Dritten Reiches*, p. 88. Bonn: Bernard & Graefe, 1991.

Hitler, Adolf, *Monologe im Führerhauptquartier 1941–1944*, recorded by Heinrich Heims, edited by Werner Jochmann, pp. 117–18 (30 October 1941). Munich: Wilhelm Heyne, 1982.

Ledig-Rowohlt, Heinrich Maria, "Statt eines Vorworts. Thomas Wolfe in Berlin," in *Große Erzähler des 20. Jahrhunderts*, edited by Heinrich Maria Ledig-Rowohlt, pp. 7–28; here, pp. 10, 14–15, 25–26. Reinbek: Rowohlt, 1983.

Lubrich, Oliver, "Formen historischer Erfahrung: Die Metamorphosen der Martha Dodd," in *Oxford German Studies* 34:1 (2005): pp. 79–102.

———. "Umwege. Martha Dodd in Nazideutschland," in Martha Dodd, *Meine Jahre in Deutschland, 1933–1937*, translated by Ursula Locke-Gross and Sabine Hübner, pp. 404–39. Berlin: Eichborn Berlin, 2005.

Metcalfe, Philip, *1933*. Sag Harbor: Permanent Press, 1988.

Minnick, Wendell L., *Spies and Provocateurs: A Worldwide Encyclopedia of Persons Conducting Espionage and Covert Action, 1946–1991*, pp. 86, 216. Jefferson, NC: McFarland, 1992.

Morros, Boris, *My Ten Years as a Counterspy*. New York: Dell, 1959.

Morss Lovett, Robert, *All Our Years*, pp. 205–6. New York: Viking, 1948.

Muhlen, Norbert, "Das seltsame Leben der Martha Dodd. Eine Frau im Zeitalter des Verrats," in *Der Monat* 11:121 (October 1958): pp. 59–66.

Pritt, D. N., "Nachwort" [1961], in William Edward Dodd, *Diplomat auf heißem Boden. Tagebuch des USA-Botschafters William E. Dodd in Berlin 1933–1938*, edited by William E. Dodd, Jr., and Martha Dodd, translated by G. F. Alexan, pp. 499–505. Berlin (GDR): Verlag der Nation, 1964 (revised third edition).

Rokotow, T., "Wahrheitsgetreue Schilderung eines Augenzeugen," in Martha Dodd, *Aus dem Fenster der Botschaft* [abridged], edited by T. Rokotow, pp. 3–7. Berlin: Verlag der Sowjetischen Militärverwaltung in Deutschland, 1946.

Shirer, William L., *Berlin Diary: The Journal of a Foreign Correspondent, 1934–1941* [1941], edited by Gordon A. Craig, pp. 42, 66–67, 540. Baltimore/London: Johns Hopkins University Press, 2002.

Weinstein, Allen, and Alexander Vassiliev, "Love and Loyalties, I: The Case of Martha Dodd," in *The Haunted Wood. Soviet Espionage in America—the Stalin Era*, pp. 50–71 (notes: pp. 349–50). New York: Random House, 1999.

Wolfe, Thomas, letter to Martha Dodd from New York dated 10 July 1935, in *The Letters of Thomas Wolfe*, edited by Elizabeth Nowell, pp. 477–79. New York: Charles Scribner's Sons, 1956.

W. E. B. DUBOIS

Anonymous, "Farbiger bereist Nazi-Deutschland" [interview], in *N. Y. Staats-Zeitung und Herold*, 30 January 1937.

Bechhaus-Gerst, Marianne, "Schwarze Deutsche, Afrikanerinnen und Afrikaner im NS-Staat," in *AfrikanerInnen in Deutschland und schwarze Deutsche—Geschichte und Gegenwart*, edited by Marianne Bechhaus-Gerst and Reinhard Klein-Arendt, pp. 187–95. Münster: Lit, 2004.

Campt, Tina M., *Other Germans. Black Germans and the Politics of Race, Gender, and Memory in the Third Reich*. Ann Arbor: University of Michigan Press, 2004.

W. E. B. DuBois: A Reader, edited by David Levering Lewis, pp. 734–37. New York: Henry Holt, 1995.

Lewis, David Levering, *W. E. B. DuBois: The Fight for Equality and the American Century, 1919–1963*, pp. 388–421 (notes: pp. 645–52). New York: Henry Holt, 2000.

Lusane, Clarence, "Color and Fascism: W. E. B. DuBois and the Nazis," in *Hitler's Black Victims. The Historical Experiences of Afro-Germans, European Blacks, Africans, and African Americans in the Nazi Era*, pp. 124–28 (notes: p. 281). New York/London: Routledge, 2003.

Massaquoi, Hans J., *Destined to Witness: Growing up Black in Nazi Germany*. New York: Perennial, 2001.

Sollors, Werner, "DuBois' Aufenthalt im nationalsozialistischen Deutschland 1936," in "Deutschsprachige Texte/Amerikanische Literatur: Eine Herausforderung an die Amerikanistik?" in *Deutsch-amerikanische Begegnungen. Konflikt und Kooperation im 19. und 20. Jahrhundert*, edited by Frank Trommler and Elliott Shore, pp. 135–48; here, pp. 142–44. Stuttgart/Munich: DVA, 2001.

———. "W. E. B. DuBois in Nazi Germany, 1936," in *Amerikastudien* 44:2 (1999): pp. 207–22.

Zwischen Charleston und Stechschritt. Schwarze im Nationalsozialismus, edited by Peter Martin and Christine Alonzo. Hamburg/Munich: Dölling und Galitz, 2004.

GUNNAR EKELÖF

Ekelöf, Gunnar, *Brev 1916–1968*, edited by Carl Olov Sommar, pp. 47–53. Stockholm: Bonnier, 1989.

———. "Zoologische Gärten," in *Der ketzerische Orpheus. Essays, Skizzen, Briefe. Zur Autobiographie und Poetologie*, edited and translated by Klaus-Jürgen Liedtke, pp. 20–26. Münster: Kleinheinrich, 1999.

———. "Reiseeindrücke: Mitropa-Schlafwagen . . . ," ibidem, pp. 42–43.

———. "Berliner Elegien (1933)," translated by Richard Pietraß, in *Der Weg eines Außenseiters. Erzählungen und Essays*, edited by Sieglinde Mierau, pp. 40–42. Leipzig: Philipp Reclam, 1983.

———. "Ein Schicksal der dreißiger Jahre," translated by Thabita von Bonin, ibidem, pp. 43–53.

Liedtke, Klaus-Jürgen (Berlin), written communication, 15 September 2004.

———. "Zeittafel," in Gunnar Ekelöf, *Der ketzerische Orpheus. Essays, Skizzen, Briefe. Zur Autobiographie und Poetologie*, edited and translated by Klaus-Jürgen Liedtke, pp. 286–89. Münster: Kleinheinrich, 1999.

THEO FINDAHL

Bergh, Sverre, with Svein Sæter, *Spion i Hitlers rike. Student og agent: Sverre Berghs dramatiske dobbeltliv*. Oslo: N.W. Damm & Søn, 2006.

Findahl, Theo, *Lange skygger. Dagbok fra krigens Berlin 1939–1945*. Oslo: Dreyer, 1964.

Hegge, Per Egil (*Aftenposten*, Oslo), written communication, 19 October 2004, 29 and 31 August 2006, 5 and 7 September 2006.

Jager, Benedikt, "Die gepolsterte Nussschale des Bootes—Der Luftkrieg aus der Sicht skandinavischer Korrespondenten," in *Bombs Away! Representing the Air War over Europe and Japan*, edited by Wilfried Wilms and William Rasch, pp. 131–46. Amsterdam/New York: Rodopi, 2006.

———. "*Friendly Fire*: luftkrigen sett gjennom skandinaviske korrespondenters øyne," in *Nytt Norsk Tidsskrift* 4 (2007): pp. 421–29.

Meyer, Claus Heinrich, "Letzter Akt Berlin," in *Süddeutsche Zeitung*, 24 February 2003.

Norsk biografisk leksikon, editor: Jon Gunnar Arntzen, volume 3, pp. 98–99. Oslo: Kunnskapsforlaget, 2001.

Sebald, W. G., "Luftkrieg und Literatur. Züricher Vorlesungen," in *Luftkrieg und Literatur. Mit einem Essay zu Alfred Andersch*, pp. 9–110. Frankfurt: S. Fischer, 2001.

HARRY FLANNERY

Flannery, Harry W., and Gerhart H. Seger, *Which Way Germany?* New York: Hawthorn, 1968.

Harry W. Flannery Collection, Walter P. Reuther Library, Detroit.

Smith, Howard K., *Events Leading up to My Death: The Life of a Twentieth-Century Reporter*, pp. 104–5. New York: St. Martin's Press, 1996.

Yoder, Pat (Clinton Township, U.S.A.), written communication, 12 October 2004.

MAX FRISCH

Durth, Werner, *Deutsche Architekten. Biographische Verflechtungen 1900–1970* [1986], pp. 57–73, 137–53. Munich: dtv, 1992.

Frisch, Max, *Tagebuch 1966–1971*, in *Gesammelte Werke in zeitlicher Folge*, edited by Hans Mayer with Walter Schmitz, volume 6 (1968–75), part 1, pp. 5–404; here, p. 163 ("Reminiszenz"). Frankfurt: Suhrkamp, 1976.

———. *Montauk. Eine Erzählung* [1975], in *Gesammelte Werke in zeitlicher Folge*, edited by Hans Mayer with Walter Schmitz, volume 6 (1968–75), part 2, pp. 617–754; here, pp. 727–29 ("Die jüdische Braut aus Berlin [zur Hitler-Zeit]"). Frankfurt: Suhrkamp, 1976.

Hage, Volker, *Max Frisch*, pp. 24–27 (notes: pp. 137–38). Reinbek: Rowohlt, 1983.

"Lebensdaten," in *Jetzt: Max Frisch*, edited by Luis Bolliger, Walter Obschlager, and Julian Schütt, pp. 343–46. Frankfurt: Suhrkamp, 2001.

Lubrich, Oliver, "'wie fremdartige Geschöpfe aus einem Aquarium.' Berlin-Wahrnehmung nach 1933 durch ausländische Reisende," in *Europa. Stadt. Reisende. Blicke auf Reisetexte 1918–1945*, edited by Walter Fähnders, Wolfgang Klein, and Nils Plath, pp. 121–50. Bielefeld: Aisthesis, 2006.

JEAN GENET

Dichy, Albert, and Pascal Fouché, *Jean Genet, Essai de chronologie 1910–1944*, Paris: Bibliothèque de Littérature française contemporaine 1988, pp. 149–56, 283–84.

Lubrich, Oliver, *Das Schwinden der Differenz. Postkoloniale Poetiken*, Bielefeld: Aisthesis 2004, pp. 269–79.

———. "Enttäuschung in Berlin. Die Gegenräume des Jean Genet," in: *Zeitschrift für französische Sprache und Literatur* 114:3 (2004), pp. 252–66.

Moraly, Jean-Bernard, *Jean Genet. La vie écrite. Biographie*, pp. 51–67. Paris, 1988.

Sartre, Jean-Paul, *Saint Genet, comédien et martyr*. Paris: Gallimard, 1952.

White, Edmund, *Genet. A Biography*, pp. 124–27. New York: Vintage, 1994.

HEINRICH HAUSER

Bienert, Michael, "Heinrich Hausers Verwandlungen (1932/33)," in *Die eingebildete Metropole: Berlin im Feuilleton der Weimarer Republik*, pp. 180–96 (notes: pp. 241–44). Stuttgart: Metzler, 1992.

Delabar, Walter, "Zur Besinnung gekommen—Heinrich Hauser als Autor des Eugen Diederichs Verlags. Eine Fallstudie über einen Verlagswechsel samt Varianten," in *Romantik, Revolution und Reform. Der Eugen Diederichs Verlag im Epochenkontext 1900–1949*, edited by Justus H. Ulbricht and Meike G. Werner, pp. 248–70. Göttingen: Wallstein, 1999.

Graebner, Grith, "*Dem Leben unter die Haut kriechen . . .*" *Heinrich Hauser—Leben und Werk. Eine kritisch-biographische Werk-Bibliographie*. Aachen: Shaker, 2001.

Lubrich, Oliver, "Topographien des Terrors. Deutsche Großstädte in Berichten ausländischer Reisender, 1933–1945," in *Blickwechsel*, volume 2, edited by Ulrich J. Beil, Claudia S. Dornbusch, and Masa Nomura, pp. 381–86. São Paulo: EDUSP, 2004.

Streim, Gregor, "Als nationaler Pionier inner- und außerhalb des Dritten Reichs. Heinrich Hauser 1933–45," in *Spielräume des Einzelnen. Deutsche Literatur in der Weimarer Republik und im Dritten Reich*, edited by Walter Delabar, Horst Denkler, and Erhard Schütz, pp. 105–20. Berlin: Weidler, 1999.

———. "Flucht nach vorn zurück. Heinrich Hauser—Portrait eines Schriftstellers zwischen Neuer Sachlichkeit und 'reaktionärem Modernismus,'" in *Jahrbuch der Deutschen Schillergesellschaft* 43 (1999): pp. 377–402.

———. "Junge Völker und neue Technik. Zur Reisereportage im 'Dritten Reich,' am Beispiel von Friedrich Sieburg, Heinrich Hauser und Margret Boveri," in *Zeitschrift für Germanistik* 2 (1999): pp. 344–59.

Werner, Johannes, "Einer, der nirgends blieb. Über Heinrich Hauser," in *Aus dem Antiquariat* 168:34 (2001): pp. 209–15.

SVEN HEDIN

Brennecke, Detlef, "Ein Werbeträger der Nazis," in *Sven Hedin*, pp. 102–7 (notes: pp. 131–32). Reinbek: Rowohlt, 1986.

Hedin, Sven, *Tyskland och Världsfreden*. Stockholm: Medéns Förlags, 1937.

———. *Fünfzig Jahre Deutschland*. Leipzig: Brockhaus, 1938.

———. *Det kämpande Tyskland*. Malmö: Dagens Böcker, 1941.

RICHARD HILLARY

Faulks, Sebastian, "Introduction," in Richard Hillary, *The Last Enemy: The Memoir of a Spitfire Pilot*, edited by Sebastian Faulks, , pp. ix–xiv. Short Hills, New Jersey: Burford Books, 1998.

———. "Richard Hillary," in *The Fatal Englishman. Three Short Lives* [1996], pp. 109–208. New York: Vintage, 2002.

MEINRAD INGLIN

Büeler, Werner (Kantonsbibliothek Schwyz), written communication, 23 September 2002.

Hürlimann, Thomas, *Der Gesandte*, in *Das Lied der Heimat. Alle Stücke*, pp. 219–60. Frankfurt: S. Fischer, 1998.

Inglin, Meinrad, correspondence with W. Imhoof (Auslandschweizer-Werk of the Neue Helvetische Gesellschaft), 5 January 1940, 8 January 1940, 11 January 1940, 25 January 1940, 26 January 1940, 6 February 1940, 16 February 1940, 15 March 1940, 16 July 1940. Meinrad Inglin estate, Kantonsbibliothek Schwyz.

———. Typewritten letter [22 March 1940] to W. Imhoof. Meinrad Inglin estate, Kantonsbibliothek Schwyz.

———. "Missglückte Reise durch Deutschland. Februar/März 1940," typescript, 28 pages, date: "Sommer 1943." Meinrad Inglin estate, Kantonsbibliothek Schwyz.

———. "Missglückte Reise durch Deutschland," typescript, 22 pages, ca. 1961/62. Meinrad Inglin estate, Kantonsbibliothek Schwyz.

Lubrich, Oliver, "Meinrad Inglin (1940)," in "En el corazón de las tinieblas: Escritores viajeros en la Alemania nazi," in *Revista de Occidente* 266–67 (July/August 2003): pp. 158–85; here, pp. 174–78.

Matt, Beatrice von, *Meinrad Inglin. Eine Biographie*, pp. 200–205. Zurich: Atlantis, 1976.

Niederer, Ulrich (Zentral- und Hochschulbibliothek Luzern), written communication, 21 September 2002.

Schoeck, Georg (Brunnen, Switzerland), written communication, 24 September 2002.

VIRGINIA IRWIN

Caldwell Sorel, Nancy, *The Women Who Wrote the War*. New York: Perennial, 2000.

Correspondence between the headquarter of US-American troops in Europe and the People's Commissariat of Foreign Affairs in Moscow, 2 May 1945, 3 May 1945, 7 May 1945, *National Archives* II, College Park, Maryland.

Reporting World War II, Part II: *American Journalism 1944–1946*, p. 917. New York: Library of America, 1995.

"SHAEF announces disaccrediting of Irwin and Tully," in *St. Louis Post-Dispatch*, 10 May 1945, p. 3A.

Tully, Andrew, "Story Number 2," for *Boston Traveller*, Berlin, 27 April 1945, 7 pages, *National Archives* II, College Park, Maryland.

CHRISTOPHER ISHERWOOD

Blaicher, Günther, "Das Berlin der frühen dreißiger Jahre: Christopher Isherwood, *Mr. Norris Changes Trains* (1935) und *Goodbye to Berlin* (1939)," in *Das Deutschlandbild in der englischen Literatur*, pp. 217–26 (notes: p. 280). Darmstadt: Wissenschaftliche Buchgesellschaft, 1992.

Cushman, Jane C., "Cabaret—An Introduction," in Joe Masteroff, John Kander, and Fred Ebb, *Cabaret* [1966], pp. iii–vii. New York: Scholastic Book Services, 1973.

Druten, John van, *I Am a Camera* [1951]. New York: Dramatists Play Service, 1983.

———. "Note to Producers," ibidem, pp. 5–8.

Isherwood, Christopher, *Mr. Norris Changes Trains*. London: Hogarth Press, 1935.

———. *Sally Bowles*. London: Hogarth Press, 1937.

———. *Christopher and his Kind, 1929–1939*, pp. 94–106. London: Eyre Methuen, 1977.

———. *Lions and Shadows. An Education in the Twenties* [1947]. Minneapolis: University of Minnesota Press, 2000.

Lubrich, Oliver, "Kontrastaufnahmen. Berlin in den Berichten ausländischer Reisender 1933–1945," in *"Weltfabrik Berlin." Eine Metropole als Sujet der Literatur*, edited by Matthias Harder and Almut Hille, pp. 145–64. Würzburg: Königshausen & Neumann, 2006.

Masteroff, Joe, John Kander, and Fred Ebb, *Cabaret* [1966]. New York: Scholastic Book Services, 1973.

White, John J., "Sexual Mecca, Nazi Metropolis, City of Doom: The Pattern of English, Irish and American Reactions to the Berlin of the Inter-War Years," in *Berlin: Literary Images of a City. Eine Großstadt im Spiegel der Literatur*, edited by Derek Glass, Dietmar Rösler, and John J. White, pp. 124–45. Berlin: Erich Schmidt, 1989.

WIKING JERK

Hillblad, Thorolf, "Foreword" [2002], in *Twilight of the Gods: A Swedish Waffen-SS Volunteer's Experiences with the 11th SS Panzergrenadier Division Nordland, Eastern Front 1944–45*, edited by Thorolf Hillblad, translated by Jackie Logan with Thorolf Hillblad, pp. 5–6. Solihull (England): Helion & Company, 2004.

Lagerström, Anders, "Förord," in Wiking Jerk, *Ragnarök. En berättelse om slutstriden i Europa 1945*, pp. 9–11. Linköping: Nordiska förlaget, 2004.

Schön, Bosse, *Svenskarna som stred för Hitler*. Stockholm: Dagens Nyheter, 2000.

Sennerteg, Niclas (Borås, Swedish broadcasting; writer), telephone interview, 24 September 2004; written communication, 13 and 15 October 2004, 21 March 2005.

RENÉ JUVET

Anonymous, "Numa Tétaz gestorben," in *Neue Zürcher Zeitung*, 25 November 1986.

City Archive Munich, civil registration documents.

Juvet, René, *Die Deutschen im kommenden Europa*. Bern: Herbert Lang, 1945.

Moser, Marlys (Europa Verlag, Zurich), written communication, 23 March 2004.

Schneider-Tétaz, Alice (Cologne), telephone interview, 27 and 28 September 2004.

Schweizerisches Bundesarchiv, dossier on René Juvet, *Ich war dabei . . .* (censorship files, section press, and broadcasting).

Tétaz-Gramegna, Myriam (Lausanne), written communication, 21 September 2004.

Tétaz, Numa, autobiography, unpublished manuscript, 538 pages.

————. *Du darfst leben*. Zurich: Flamberg, 1970.

JOHN F. KENNEDY

Dallek, Robert, *An Unfinished Life: John F. Kennedy, 1917–1963*, pp. 49–66 (notes: p. 723–24). Boston: Little, Brown and Company, 2003.

Hamilton, Nigel, *JFK, Reckless Youth*, pp. 191–95 (notes: p. 826). New York: Random House, 1992.

Kennedy, John F., *Prelude to Leadership: The European Diary of John F. Kennedy. Summer 1945*, edited by Deirdre Henderson, introduction by Hugh Sidey, pp. 43–74, 102–18, 123–26. Washington: Regnery, 1995.

Leamer, Laurence, *The Kennedy Men. 1901–1963. The Laws of the Father*, pp. 112–35 (notes: pp. 760–63), especially: pp. 131–32 (notes: p. 762). New York: HarperCollins, 2001.

Leaming, Barbara, *Jack Kennedy: The Education of a Statesman*, pp. 35, 89 (notes: p. 452), pp. 198–99 (notes: p. 463). New York: Norton, 2006.

Mahoney, Richard D., *Sons & Brothers: The Days of Jack and Bobby Kennedy*, p. 6. New York: Arcade, 1999.

Reeves, Thomas C., *A Question of Character: A Life of John F. Kennedy*, pp. 46–47 (notes: p. 431). New York: Free Press, 1991.

Schild, Georg, *John F. Kennedy: Mensch und Mythos*, pp. 15–16. Göttingen/Zurich: Muster-Schmidt, 1997.

Sidey, Hugh, "Introduction," in *Prelude to Leadership: The European Diary of John F. Kennedy. Summer 1945*, edited by Deirdre Henderson, , pp. xv–xlv. Washington: Regnery, 1995.

JACOB KRONIKA

Friedrich, Jörg, *Der Brand. Deutschland im Bombenkrieg 1940–1945* [2002], p. 369. Berlin: List, 2004.

Jager, Benedikt, "Die gepolsterte Nussschale des Bootes—Der Luftkrieg aus der Sicht skandinavischer Korrespondenten," in *Bombs Away! Representing the Air War over Europe and Japan*, edited by Wilfried Wilms and William Rasch, pp. 131–46. Amsterdam/New York: Rodopi, 2006.

———. "*Friendly Fire*: luftkrigen sett gjennom skandinaviske korrespondenters øyne," in *Nytt Norsk Tidsskrift* 4 (2007): pp. 421–29.

Der Kampf um Berlin 1945 in Augenzeugenberichten, edited by Peter Gosztony. Munich: dtv, 1975.

Kronika, Jacob, *Lys i vinduet. Slesvigske Dagbogsblade fra Berlin 1933–1939*. Copenhagen: Det danske forlag, 1957.

———. *Midt i fjendens lejr. Slesvigske Dagbogsblade fra Hitler-krigens Berlin*. Copenhagen: Gyldendal, 1966.

———. *Kronika fortæller*, pp. 72–73. Flensburg: Skandia, 1968.

———. Personal papers, Studieafdelingen/Arkivet ved Dansk Centralbibliotek for Sydslesvig, Flensburg.

Rasmussen, René (Tønder), written communication, 23 October 2006, 16 November 2006; telephone interview, 31 October 2006.

———. *Front og bro. Flensborg Avis i spil mellem Danmark og Tyskland 1930–1945*, 2 volumes, especially: pp. 67–72, 110–16, 249–55, 255–59, 454–60, 557–66, 701–13, 763–66, 892–905. Flensburg: Dansk Centralbibliotek for Sydslesvig, 2005.

———. "Jacob Kronika in Berlin 1939–1945," in *Grenzfriedenshefte* 1 (March 2002): pp. 25–42.

Reichspressechef der NSDAP/Reichspressestelle: "Auslandspresse" (section: Denmark), index cards 101 and 273 on Jacob Kronika (notes, cited statements, photos, and a cut-out signature): Bundesarchiv, NS 42/48.

MARIA LEITNER

Fell, Karolina Dorothea, "Maria Leitner: Amerika, hast du es besser?" in *Kalkuliertes Abenteuer. Reiseberichte deutschsprachiger Frauen (1920–1945)*, pp. 114–30 (notes: pp. 296–301). Stuttgart/Weimar: J. B. Metzler, 1998.

Leitner, Maria, *Elisabeth, ein Hitlermädchen. Erzählende Prosa, Reportagen und Berichte*, edited by Helga W. Schwarz. Berlin/Weimar: Aufbau, 1985.

Schwarz, Helga W., "Nachwort," ibidem, pp. 469–88.

JÓZSEF NYÍRÖ

Burger, László-Attila (Budapest), written communication, 16 August 2004, 28 September 2004, 16 October 2004.

Hausmann, Frank-Rutger, "Dichte, Dichter, tage nicht!" *Die Europäische Schriftsteller-Vereinigung in Weimar 1941–1948*, pp. 316–20. Frankfurt: Klostermann, 2004.

DENIS DE ROUGEMONT

Altwegg, Jürg, "Denis de Rougemont—Philosophie der Freiheit, Politik der Person," in Denis de Rougemont, *Journal aus Deutschland 1935–1936*, translated by Tobias Scheffel, pp. 129–48. Vienna: Paul Zsolnay 1998.

Simon, Pierre-Henri, "Journal d'une époque (1926–1946), de Denis de Rougemont," in *Le Monde*, 22 May–5 June 1968.

JEAN-PAUL SARTRE

Cohen-Solal, Annie, *Sartre*, pp. 144–52 (notes: pp. 670–71). Paris: Gallimard, 1985.

Granjon, Marie-Christine, "L'Allemagne de Raymond Aron et de Jean-Paul Sartre," in *Entre Locarno et Vichy. Les relations culturelles franco-allemandes dans les années 1930*, edited by Manfred Bock, Reinhart Meyer-Kalkus, and Michel Trebitsch, volume 1, pp. 463–79. Paris: CNRS, 1993.

Sartre, Jean-Paul, *Les carnets de la drôle de guerre. Novembre 1939—Mars 1940*, pp. 224–26 (entry of 1 February 1940), pp. 338–39 (entry of 28 February 1940), p. 345 (entry of 29 February 1940). Paris: Gallimard, 1983.

RENÉ SCHINDLER

City Archive Munich, civil registration documents.

Duttli, Ariane (community administration of Binningen, Switzerland), written communication, 20 September 2004.

George, Stefan, "Geheimes Deutschland," in *Das neue Reich* [1928], *Sämtliche Werke*, volume 9, pp. 45–49. Stuttgart: Klett Cotta, 2001.

Hoffmann, Peter, "Das geheime Deutschland," in *Claus Schenk Graf von Stauffenberg und seine Brüder*, pp. 61–78 (notes: 488–94), p. 443 (note: 598–99). Stuttgart: Deutsche Verlags-Anstalt, 1992.

Keilson-Lauritz, Marita, "Hans von Prott und das 'Geheime Deutschland,'" in *Castrum Perigrini* 148/149 (1981): pp. 18–34.

Moser, Marlys (Europa Verlag, Zurich), written communication, 23 March 2004.

Rieppel, Franz Wolfgang, *Die Entschuldung der Schweizerischen Landwirtschaft nach dem Bundesgesetz über die Entschuldung landwirtschaftlicher Heimwesen vom 12. Dezember 1940*. Zurich: Kommerzdruck und Verlags AG, 1943.

———. *Jugend, Liebe und Tod. Ausgewählte Gedichte*. Basel: Buchverlag Basler Zeitung, 1995.

———. *Die Krone war an allem schuld. Ein Märchen für Erwachsene* (illustrated by Helga Zilcher). Basel: Buchverlag Basler Zeitung, 1996.

———. *Requiem. Für ein fremdes Mädchen. Für einen jungen Freund* (illustrated by Helga Zilcher). Basel: Buchverlag Basler Zeitung, 1997.

Schweizerische Bundesanwaltschaft, dossier on Wolfgang Rieppel (1942–44).

Schweizerisches Bundesarchiv, dossier on René Schindler, *Ein Schweizer erlebt das geheime Deutschland* (censorship files, section press, and broadcasting).

ANNEMARIE SCHWARZENBACH

Fleischmann, Uta (Oldenburg), written communication, 18 October 2004.

———. "Vorwort" (2001) and introductory remarks (1992), in Annemarie Schwarzenbach, *"Wir werden es schon zuwege bringen, das Leben." Annemarie Schwarzenbach an Erika und Klaus Mann, Briefe 1930–1942*, edited by Uta Fleischmann, pp. 11 and 12–13. Herbolzheim: Centaurus, 2001.

———. "Kurzbiographie Annemarie Schwarzenbach," ibidem, pp. 193–97.

Kroll, Fredric, "Der schutzlose Engel und ihr Unbehauster: Eine ungeschlossene Ehe," ibidem, pp. 207–14.

Lühe, Irmela von der, "'Welch störrischer Unglücksengel!'—Die Briefe Annemarie Schwarzenbachs aus der Sicht Erika Manns," ibidem, pp. 199–205.

Schwarzenbach, Annemarie, *"Wir werden es schon zuwege bringen, das Leben."* *Annemarie Schwarzenbach an Erika und Klaus Mann, Briefe 1930–1942*, edited by Uta Fleischmann, , pp. 83–85, 101–3. Herbolzheim: Centaurus, 2001.

Annemarie Schwarzenbach. Autorin—Reisende—Fotografin, edited by Elvira Willems, Herbolzheim: Centaurus, 2001 (second edition).

SHI MIN

Frühauf, Heiner (Portland, OR), written communication, 13 July 2003, 6 September 2004.

———. "Deutschland in der chinesischen Reiseliteratur der zwanziger und dreißiger Jahre," in *Mein Bild in deinem Auge. Exotismus und Moderne: Deutschland—China im 20. Jahrhundert*, edited by Wolfgang Kubin, pp. 283–99. Darmstadt: Wissenschaftliche Buchgesellschaft, 1995.

WILLIAM SHIRER

Craig, Gordon A., "Foreword to the Johns Hopkins Edition," in William Shirer, *Berlin Diary: The Journal of a Foreign Correspondent, 1934–1941*, edited by Gordon A. Craig, pp. ix–xiii. Baltimore/London: Johns Hopkins University Press, 2002.

Keegan, John, "Introduction," in William Shirer, *"This Is Berlin": Reporting from Nazi Germany, 1938–40*, pp. ix–xii. London: Arrow, 2000.

Lubrich, Oliver, "Keine Erdbeeren, kein Burgunder. Ausländische Autoren und der Luftkrieg," in *Berichte aus der Abwurfzone. Ausländer erleben den Bombenkrieg in Deutschland 1939 bis 1945*, edited by Oliver Lubrich, pp. 7–40. Frankfurt: Eichborn, 2007.

Schebera, Jürgen, "Nachbemerkung," in William Shirer, *Berliner Tagebuch. Aufzeichnungen eines Auslandskorrespondenten 1934–1941*, translated and edited by Jürgen Schebera, pp. 342–45. Leipzig: Reclam, 1995.

———. "Nachbemerkung," in William Shirer, *Berliner Tagebuch. Das Ende. 1944–45*, translated and edited by Jürgen Schebera, pp. 454–57. Leipzig: Gustav Kiepenheuer, 1994.

Shirer Dean, Inga, "Preface," in William Shirer, *"This Is Berlin": Reporting from Nazi Germany, 1938–40*, pp. 1–10. London: Arrow, 2000.

Shirer, William, *"This Is Berlin": Reporting from Nazi Germany, 1938–40*. London: Arrow, 2000.

———. *End of a Berlin Diary*. New York: Popular Library, 1947.

———. *The Rise and Fall of the Third Reich: A History of Nazi Germany* [1959]. New York: Touchstone, 1990.

———. *The Nightmare Years, 1930–1940: A Memoir of a Life and the Times*, pp. 444–616. Boston/Toronto: Little, Brown and Company, 1984.

Vollnhals, Clemens, "Einleitung," in William Shirer, *This Is Berlin. Rundfunkre-portagen aus Deutschland 1939–1940* [selection], translated by Stefan Welz and Thomas Irmer, edited by Clemens Vollnhals, pp. 7–29. Leipzig: Gustav Kiepenheuer, 1999.

Voss, Frederick S., "Broadcasting the War," in *Reporting the War: The Journalistic Coverage of World War II*, pp. 119–33 (notes: p. 214). Washington, D.C.: National Portrait Gallery/Smithsonian Institution, 1994.

GEORGES SIMENON

Du 734 (March 2003).

Geeraert, Nicole, *Georges Simenon*, p. 70 (notes: p. 117). Reinbek: Rowohlt, 1991.

Lacassin, Francis, "Note de l'éditeur pour la nouvelle édition," in Georges Simenon, *Mes apprentissages. Reportages 1931–1946*, edited by Francis Lacassin, pp. i–ii. Paris: Omnibus, 2001.

———. "Simenon journaliste," ibidem, pp. 9–25.

———. "Le reportage selon Simenon," ibidem, pp. 355–63.

———. "Entre les décombres du passé et les nuages de l'avenir," ibidem, pp. 697–99.

———. "Repères biographiques 1928–1946," ibidem, pp. 1033–40.

Lenk, Elisabeth, and Katherina Kaever, *Peter Kürten, genannt der Vampir von Düsseldorf*. Frankfurt: Eichborn, 1997.

Marnham, Patrick, *The Man Who Wasn't Maigret: A Portrait of Georges Simenon*, pp. 154–55. London: Bloomsbury, 1992.

HOWARD K. SMITH

Bernstein, Mark, and Alex Lubertozzi, *World War II on the Air: Edward R. Murrow and the War That Defined a Generation*, pp. 187–88. Naperville: Sourcebooks, 2003.

Kadritzke, Niels, "Anmerkungen des Übersetzers," in Howard Kingsbury Smith, *Feind schreibt mit. Ein amerikanischer Korrespondent erlebt Nazi-Deutschland*, translated by Niels Kadritzke. Berlin: Rotbuch, 1982, pp. 307–10; Frankfurt: S. Fischer, 1986, pp. 306–9.

Smith, Howard K., "Nachwort des Autors" (afterword to the 1982 German edition), in Howard Kingsbury Smith, *Feind schreibt mit. Ein amerikanischer Korrespondent erlebt Nazi-Deutschland*, translated by Niels Kadritzke. Berlin: Rotbuch, 1982, pp. 304–6; Frankfurt: S. Fischer, 1986, pp. 303–5.

———. *Events Leading up to My Death: The Life of a Twentieth-Century Reporter* ("1939–1941"), pp. 77–115. New York: St. Martin's Press, 1996.

KONRAD WARNER

Berlin im Zweiten Weltkrieg. Der Untergang der Reichshauptstadt in Augenzeugenberichten, edited by Hans Dieter Schäfer, p. 389. München: Piper, 1985.

Bleuler, Simone (Schweizerische Landesbibliothek, Bern), written communication, 16 September 2004.

Friedrich, Jörg, *Der Brand. Deutschland im Bombenkrieg 1940–1945* [2002], pp. 365, 370. Berlin: List, 2004.

Probst, Rudolf (Schweizerisches Literaturarchiv, Bern), written communication, 16 September 2004.

Schweizerisches Bundesarchiv, dossier on Konrad Warner, *Schicksalswende Europas* ... (censorship files, section press, and broadcasting).

Warner, Konrad, "Eine Weltstadt stirbt" (pre-publication in five parts), in *Die Weltwoche* 12:547 (5 May 1944), p. 3; 12:548 (12 May 1944), p. 3; 12:549 (19 May 1944), p. 9; 12:550 (26 May 1944), p. 9; 12:551 (2 June 1944), p. 9.

———. *Dans la Cité mourante ... Le vivant témoignage d'un Suisse qui a vu de ses yeux crouler Berlin sous les bombardements.* Lausanne: Éditions Spes, n.d.

THOMAS WOLFE

Beja, Morris, "The Escapes of Time and Memory," in *Modern Critical Views: Thomas Wolfe*, edited by Harold Bloom, pp. 29–58. New York/New Haven/Philadelphia: Chelsea House, 1987.

Clements, Clyde C., Jr., "Symbolic Patterns in *You Can't Go Home Again*," ibidem, pp. 9–18.

Donald, David Herbert, *Look Homeward: A Life of Thomas Wolfe*, pp. 319–26 and 384–421. Boston/Toronto: Little, Brown and Company, 1987.

Eisele, Susanne, "Thomas Wolfe: 'A great people ... desperately ill with some dread malady of the soul,'" in *Das Deutschlandbild in der amerikanischen Literatur des Zweiten Weltkrieges*, pp. 13–18. Ph.D. diss., Erlangen, 1959.

Evans, Elizabeth, *Thomas Wolfe*, pp. 22–23, 83, 131, 137 (notes: pp. 168, 172, 175). New York: Frederick Ungar, 1984.

Holman, C. Hugh, "Introduction," in *The Short Novels of Thomas Wolfe*, edited by C. Hugh Holman, pp. vii–xx. New York: Charles Scribner's Sons, 1961.

Idol, John L., Jr., "The Narrative Discourse of Thomas Wolfe's 'I Have a Thing to Tell You,'" in *Studies in Short Fiction* 30 (1993): pp. 45–52.

———. "Germany as Thomas Wolfe's Second Dark Helen: The *Angst* of *I Have a Thing to Tell You*," in *The Thomas Wolfe Review* 19:1 (Spring 1995): pp. 1–9.

Johnston, Carol Ingalls, "The Posthumous Novels," in *Of Time and the Artist: Thomas Wolfe, His Novels, and the Critics*, pp. 143–58. Columbia: Camden House, 1996.

———. "The Authority of the Text," ibidem, pp. 159–77.

Kennedy, Richard S., "A Political Awakening: *I Have a Thing to Tell You*," in *The Window of Memory: The Literary Career of Thomas Wolfe*, pp. 325–33. Chapel Hill: University of North Carolina Press, 1962.

Klimke, Wolfgang, "About the Author," in *I Have a Thing to Tell You* (from *You Can't Go Home Again*), edited by Wolfgang Klimke, pp. 4–6. Paderborn: Schöningh, n.d.

Ledig-Rowohlt, Heinrich Maria, "Statt eines Vorworts. Thomas Wolfe in Berlin," in *Große Erzähler des 20. Jahrhunderts*, edited by Heinrich Maria Ledig-Rowohlt, pp. 7–28. Reinbek: Rowohlt, 1983.

Lubrich, Oliver, "Thomas Wolfe (1936)," in "En el corazón de las tinieblas: Escritores viajeros en la Alemania nazi," in *Revista de Occidente* 266–67 (July/August 2003): pp. 158–85; here, pp. 168–73.

Nowell, Elizabeth, *Thomas Wolfe: A Biography*, pp. 269–78, 325–36. London/Melbourne/Toronto: Heinemann, 1961.

Raynolds, Robert, *Thomas Wolfe. Memoir of a Friendship*, pp. 143–45. Austin/London: University of Texas Press, 1965.

Ryssel, Fritz Heinrich, "Es führt kein Weg zurück," in *Thomas Wolfe*, pp. 66–83. Berlin: Colloquium, 1963.

Wilson, Frank, "Anticipation, Adulation, Separation, and Epiphany: Thomas Wolfe's German Experience," in *The Thomas Wolfe Review* 21:1 (Spring 1997): pp. 1–7.

Wolfe, Thomas, "Oktoberfest," in *Scribner's Magazine* 101 (6 June 1937): pp. 26–31.

———. *You Can't Go Home Again*, pp. 585–667. New York: HarperCollins/Perennial Classics, 1998.

———. *The Notebooks of Thomas Wolfe*, edited by Richard S. Kennedy and Paschal Reeves, volume 2, pp. 821–36. Chapel Hill: University of North Carolina Press, 1970.

———. *The Letters of Thomas Wolfe*, edited by Elizabeth Nowell, pp. 459–67, 470, 477–79, 540–42. New York: Charles Scribner's Sons, 1956.

Zacharasiewicz, Waldemar, "Deutschland als Gegenbild und Kontrastfolie bei Thomas Wolfe," in *Das Deutschlandbild in der amerikanischen Literatur*, pp. 184–94 (notes: pp. 332–35). Darmstadt: Wissenschaftliche Buchgesellschaft, 1998.

VIRGINIA WOOLF

Alexander, Peter F., *Leonard and Virginia Woolf: A Literary Partnership*, pp. 177–81 (notes: pp. 246). New York: Harvester Wheatsheaf, 1992.

Bell, Anne Olivier, "Editor's Preface," in *The Diary of Virginia Woolf. Volume Four: 1931–1935*, edited by Anne Olivier Bell with Andrew McNeillie, pp. vii–ix. San Diego/New York/London: Harcourt Brace & Company, 1982.

———. "Editorial Note" and "Acknowledgments," ibidem, pp. ix–xi and xi–xiii.

Bell, Quentin, *Virginia Woolf: A Biography*, volume 2, pp. 189–91 (notes: p. 279). New York: Harcourt Brace Jovanovich, 1972.

Cuddy-Keane, Melba, *Virginia Woolf, the Intellectual, and the Public Sphere*. Cambridge: Cambridge University Press, 2003.

Füger, Wilhelm, *Eine "Extravagante Engländerin." Untersuchungen zur deutschen Frührezeption von Virginia Woolf*, pp. 77–78. Heidelberg: Carl Winter, 1980.

Gruber, Ruth, *Virginia Woolf: A Study*. Bochum: Pöppinghaus, 1935.

Lee, Hermione, "Fascism," in *Virginia Woolf*, pp. 678–98 (notes: pp. 856–60). London: Vintage, 1997.

Marcus, Laura, *Virginia Woolf*, pp. 150–51. Plymouth: Northcote House, 1997.

Mepham, John, "Art and Politics," in *Virginia Woolf. A Literary Life*, pp. 159–72. Basingstoke/London: MacMillan, 1991.

Nicolson, Nigel, *Virginia Woolf*, pp. 102–5. London: Weidenfeld & Nicolson, 2000.

Nunez, Sigrid, *Mitz: The Marmoset of Bloomsbury*, pp. 51–58. New York: Harper-Collins, 1998.

Poole, Roger, "Führer, Duce, Tyrant," in *The Unknown Virginia Woolf*, pp. 216–31. Cambridge: Cambridge University Press, 1978.

Reichert, Klaus, "Vorbemerkung zu Band 4 der deutschen Ausgabe der Tage-bücher," in Virginia Woolf, *Tagebücher 4. 1931–1935*, translated by Maria Bosse-Sporleder, edited by Klaus Reichert, pp. 7–10. Frankfurt: S. Fischer, 2003.

Reid, Panthea, *Art and Affection: A Life of Virginia Woolf*, pp. 373–75 (notes: p. 522); pp. 461–64 (notes: pp. 530–31). Oxford/New York: Oxford University Press, 1996.

Schöneich, Christoph, *Virginia Woolf*, pp. 21–27. Darmstadt: Wissenschaftliche Buchgesellschaft, 1989.

Silver, Brenda R., *Virginia Woolf's Reading Notebooks*. Princeton: Princeton University Press, 1983.

Spater, George, and Ian Parsons, *A Marriage of True Minds: An Intimate Portrait of Leonard and Virginia Woolf*. London: Jonathan Cape/Hogarth Press, 1977.

Szasz, Thomas, *"My Madness Saved Me": The Madness and Marriage of Virginia Woolf*. New Brunswick/London: Transaction, 2006.

Waldmann, Werner, *Virginia Woolf*. Reinbek: Rowohlt, 1983.

Whitworth, Michael H., *Virginia Woolf*, p. 25 (notes: p. 229). Oxford/New York: Oxford University Press, 2005.

Wiggershaus, Renate, *Virginia Woolf*, pp. 145–47. München: dtv, 2006.

Woolf, Leonard, *Downhill all the Way: An Autobiography of the Years 1919–1939*, pp. 185–94. London: Readers Union/Hogarth Press, 1968.

Woolf, Virginia, *Three Guineas*. New York: Harcourt, Brace & Co., 1938.

———. "Thoughts on Peace in an Air Raid" [1940], in *The Death of the Moth and Other Essays*, pp. 243–48. New York: Harcourt, Brace & Co., 1942.

———. *The Letters of Virginia Woolf. Volume Five: 1932–1935*, edited by Nigel Nicolson and Joanne Trautmann, pp. 389–96. San Diego/New York/London: Harcourt Brace & Company, 1982.